# THE FATHERS OF CONFEDERATION AT QUEBEC CITY, 1864

1. HEWITT BERNARD
   (*Secretary of the Conference*)

2. W. H. STEEVES (N.B.)

3. E. WHELAN (P.E.I.)

4. CHARLES FISHER (N.B.)

5. W. A. HENRY (N.S.)

6. E. PALMER (P.E.I.)

7. J. H. GRAY (P.E.I.)

8 GEORGE COLES (P.E.I.)

9. S. LEONARD TILLEY (N.B.)

10. J. C. CHAPAIS (Can.)

11. F. B. T. CARTER (Nfld.)

12. AMBROSE SHEA (Nfld.)

13. E. B. CHANDLER (N.B.)

14. ALEXANDER CAMPBELL (Can.)

15. A. G. ARCHIBALD (N.S.)

16. HECTOR LANGEVIN (Can.)

17. JOHN A. MACDONALD (Can.)

18. GEO. E. CARTIER (Can.)

19. E. TACHÉ (Can.)

20. GEORGE BROWN (Can.)

21. T. H. HAVILAND (P.E.I.)

22. ALEXANDER T. GALT (Can.)

23. PETER MITCHELL (N.B.)

24. OLIVER MOWAT (Can.)

25. JAMES COCKBURN (Can.)

26. R. B. DICKEY (N.S.)

27. CHARLES TUPPER (N.S.)

28. J. H. GRAY (N.B.)

29. W. H. POPE (P.E.I.)

30. WILLIAM MCDOUGALL (Can.)

31. T. D'ARCY MCGEE (Can.)

32. A. A. MACDONALD (P.E.I.)

33. JONATHAN MCCULLY (N.S.)

34. J. M. JOHNSON (N.B.)

## THE CARIBOO ROAD - 1862

When gold was discovered on the upper reaches of the Fraser River in 1856, many prospectors swarmed into the interior to pan river and creek beds for gold. By 1858, thousands of people seeking gold had made their way up the Fraser River to Hope or to Yale, the terminus of the fur-brigade trail from the interior. Yale became the jumping-off point for mining sites farther upriver, particularly the gold-rich Cariboo region.

At the request of James Douglas, Governor of the colony of Vancouver Island, a detachment of 165 Royal Engineers was sent out from Britain as an aid in maintaining law and order. Picked to assist in the tasks of settlement as well, it included surveyors, engineers, architects, draughtsmen, carpenters, blacksmiths, sappers and miners, tailors, shoemakers, boatbuilders, and many other trades. They performed great service in surveying and laying out several town sites, guarding gold shipments, establishing a government printing office and, in particular, constructing two sections of a great wagon trail into the Cariboo region— The Cariboo Road.

Winding partly through the valley of the Fraser from Yale, the head of steamboat navigation, to Barkerville, the so-called capital of Cariboo, the Road was about 480 miles long and, where possible, 18 feet wide. Completed between 1862 and 1865, it was the greatest achievement in road-building ever accomplished in British North America.

In the painting, the Royal Engineers are shown at a particularly difficult point on the Road. A solid rock wall has been breached with gunpowder, and a cleft is being "cribbed" and filled as horses drag heavy logs on "goboy" skids or sleds. Sappers and Chinese labourers toil in the background.

Winding around mountain curves, clinging to the sides of cliffs, bored through solid rock, the Cariboo Road became the great commercial highway of the new Crown colony of British Columbia and carried a permanent population into the interior of the continent. The Road encouraged the beginnings of settlement and, eventually, such permanent industries in the Fraser valley as agriculture and lumbering. The Road also helped to bring law and order into the Cariboo country. However, the great importance of the Cariboo Road was that it altered the prospects of the colonies of British North America. Now, there were two British colonies on the Pacific. Now, there was a chance of a transcontinental, Canadian nation.

*One Dominion*

"*It shall be lawful for the Queen,
by and with the Advice of
Her Majesty's Most Honourable
Privy Council, to declare
by Proclamation that, on
and after a Day therein
appointed, not being more
than Six Months after the
passing of this Act,
the Provinces of Canada,
Nova Scotia, and
New Brunswick shall form and be*

*—from Clause 3 of* THE BRITISH NORTH AMERICA ACT, *29* MARCH, *1867*

*By*
# GEORGE E. TAIT
*Professor of Education, University of Toronto*


*Illustrated by*
# VERNON MOULD
*Head of the Art Department, Upper Canada College, Toronto*

*Second Edition*

# One Dominion *under the*
## *name of* CANADA "
The Story of Canada from 1800 to 1970

**McGRAW-HILL RYERSON LIMITED**
Toronto   Montreal   New York   London   Sydney
Mexico   Johannesburg   Panama   Düsseldorf   Singapore
São Paulo   Kuala Lumpur   New Delhi

ISBN 0-07-092974-2

4 5 6 7 8 9 10   THB73  10 9 8 7

## Acknowledgments

The author is indebted to a host of historians, living and dead, whose names are so numerous that they cannot be mentioned here. Among those who read the manuscript, Mr. H. J. P. Schaffter, Head of History and Geography, The Preparatory School, Upper Canada College, deserves special mention. His sympathetic criticisms and suggestions have been of the greatest help to me in writing this book. For careful guidance and assistance in the production of *One Dominion*, I offer much thanks to The Ryerson Press, particularly, Mr. James K. Smith, Assistant Editor, Mr. Garry Lovatt, Editorial Assistant and Mr. Arthur Steven, Art Director. I am again especially grateful to my friend, Vernon Mould. He has combined painstaking research and superb artistry to produce the illustrations that contribute so much to this book.

*Maps* on pages xi to 293 *by* **ROBERT KUNZ**

# TO THE TEACHER

*One Dominion* is a history of Canada in the nineteenth and twentieth centuries.

In order to make the book as attractive and useful as possible, every care and attention have been given to the illustrations, maps and diagrams. To assist readers in locating information, such aids as unit headings, unit summaries, marginal headings and an index of illustrations have been included.

A selection of biographical sketches, accompanied by portraits, has been included in the Appendix. Although these are very brief studies that supplement information already provided in the text, they are intended to stimulate the interest of readers in some of the personalities who have helped to shape Canadian history.

In the creation of *One Dominion*, the author and illustrator have made every effort to provide material that is interesting, informative and, above all, historically accurate. Mr. Mould has designed his illustrations to provide an attractive and authentic supplement to the text. The captions appearing below the illustrations are intended to provide a maximum of information.

The author and artist hope that *One Dominion* offers an enjoyable and rewarding study of Canadian history and that it will give readers a greater appreciation of their country's past.

G.E.T.

# MAPS

# DIAGRAMS

# CONTENTS

# INTRODUCTION

THE FIRST BRITISH EMPIRE was completely disrupted by the American Revolution (1775-1783). In a bitter conflict, the Thirteen Colonies rose against the mother country, declared their independence and formed the United States of America. It is true that British lands still remained in North America, but no one in Britain felt that these undeveloped areas could ever possibly take the place of the colonies that had been lost.

As the nineteenth century dawned, British North America consisted of vast territories stretching from the Atlantic Ocean to the Rocky Mountains, but only a few, tiny portions of this huge area were populated. In the east, there was an international boundary line running along the line of the St. Lawrence River and through the Great Lakes. However, in the west, where the Hudson's Bay Company and the North West Company traded for furs, no one knew exactly where British lands ended and American lands began. On the northern Pacific coast, too, there was no international boundary, and American, British and Russian traders vied with each other for furs.

In the east, settlement hugged the Atlantic coast, the river valleys, the broad reaches of the St. Lawrence and the shores of the lower Great Lakes. In the north and the north-west, there was no settlement — just a few trading posts in the forests and on the lonely prairies.

Newfoundland was still a fishing colony populated by a sturdy breed of men who fought the wind and the sea. Hundreds of tiny fishing villages, some clinging to the sides of steep hills, lay half-hidden in snug coves. Cape Breton Island, too, was a rocky, rolling countryside. Farming was almost impossible, and so these people also made fishing their way of life. On the third island lying off the coast, Prince

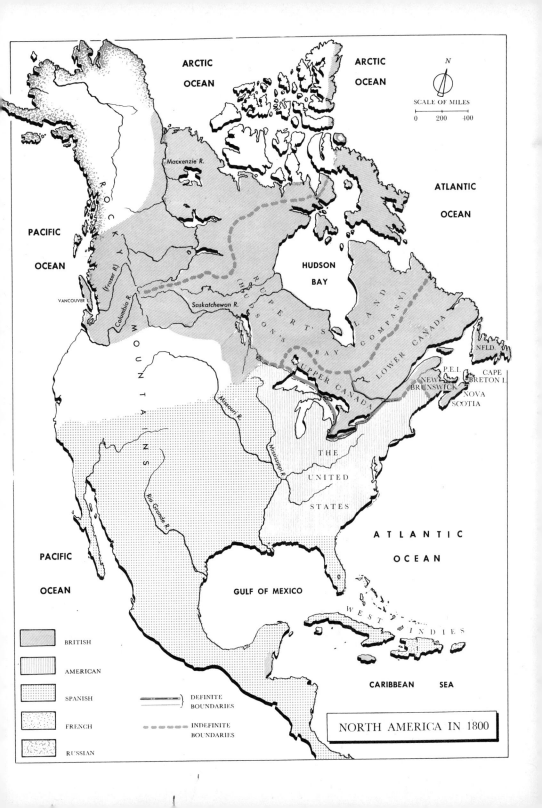

NORTH AMERICA IN 1800

Edward Island, conditions were somewhat different. Its rich, red soil made farming the chief activity of the inhabitants.

Settlement in Nova Scotia and in the young province of New Brunswick was concentrated along the coast and in such large river valleys as the St. John and the Miramichi. Farming was important in fertile regions, but hundreds of families looked to the sea for their main source of income.

The Maritime provinces were so widely separated from Lower and Upper Canada that an overland journey between the two regions was long and hazardous. It actually proved easier for New Brunswick and Nova Scotia to maintain economic and social contact with Britain and the West Indies than with their sister provinces to the west.

American immigrants were attracted to the southern parts of Lower Canada, particularly to the region below the St. Lawrence and to the east of Montreal, in the area known as the Eastern Townships. On the whole, these people became good citizens, establishing new farms and founding small businesses. Many an inn and many a tavern was owned and operated by an enterprising newcomer from the United States.

Lower Canada began to enjoy a prosperity unknown before. Farmers found markets for the products of their fields and pastures. Montreal and Quebec City became busy ports frequented by sailing ships from Great Britain and the other trading nations of the world. Lumber rafts made their way down the Ottawa river. At Quebec City, new centre of the timber trade, thousands of feet of sawn lumber were loaded on board ships bound for British ports.

In Upper Canada, the original United Empire Loyalists who had founded the province were soon joined by a steady stream of English, Irish, Scots, Dutch, Germans and others. These were by no means the only people to arrive as new settlers. Americans, too, flocked in. The governments of both Upper and Lower Canada extended invitations to Americans to settle in the provinces. Upon swearing an oath of allegiance to the Crown, an applicant could obtain two hundred acres of free land. As a result, large numbers of people crossed the border, became British subjects and secured the land they sought.

The settlers found the fertile soil of Upper Canada well suited to the production of vegetables, fruits and grains. They carried on a mixed type of farming (some crops and a few cattle) but wheat gradually became the most important single crop.

West of the Great Lakes lay the seemingly endless prairies and beyond them the mountains that eventually rolled down to the edge of the Pacific Ocean. All this was the domain of the two great rival fur companies, the North West Company and the Hudson's Bay Company. To people in eastern Canada, this vast area was little more than a land of myth and legend. Great stretches of the territory were known only to its Indian inhabitants and the small bands of traders who probed westward in search of more furs to satisfy the elegant tastes of fashionable society in Britain and Europe.

In 1800, the Canadian prairie was a far cry from the well-ordered civilization of Europe, and for that matter the same could be said of the whole of British North America. But the British North America of 1800 was also a far cry from the Dominion of Canada of 1900. Instead of canoe and boat, roads and a railway carried passengers and freight across a nation that stretched from the Atlantic to the Pacific. Indeed, where once the Hudson's Bay Company had ruled a vast commercial empire, new Canadian provinces were being established. In short, by 1900, a nation had been created where only a hundred years before a few scattered settlements had existed, separated from each other by seemingly unconquerable distances and controlled and governed by men in a country that lay on the opposite side of the Atlantic Ocean.

How did these isolated settlements manage to unite? How did these people, divided both by interest and by distance, find a common bond of union?

# THE WAR OF 1812

Britain and France at war ▪ The Louisiana Purchase, 1803 ▪ Blockade in Europe ▪ Search of American ships ▪ The *Leopard* and the *Chesapeake* ▪ The Embargo Act, 1807 ▪ The War Hawks ▪ Tecumseh and the Prophet ▪ The United States declares war, 1812 ▪ Disunity in the United States ▪ American troops invade Upper Canada ▪ The British capture Detroit ▪ Battle of Queenston Heights ▪ Death of General Brock ▪ The War at sea ▪ The sack of York, 1813 ▪ Stoney Creek and Beaver Dams ▪ American naval victory on Lake Erie ▪ British retreat from Amherstburg ▪ Battle at Moraviantown ▪ Death of Tecumseh ▪ Chateauguay and Crysler's Farm ▪ British blockade of the American coast, 1814 ▪ American raids on Lake Erie shore ▪ Fort Erie and Chippawa ▪ Lundy's Lane ▪ British raid the American coast ▪ The sack of Washington ▪ The Treaty of Ghent, 1814 ▪ The Battle of New Orleans, 1815 ▪ Effects of the War ▪ The Rush-Bagot Agreement, 1817.

# 1. The Way to War

THE YOUNG PROVINCES of Upper Canada, New Brunswick and Prince Edward Island had scarcely established themselves before there were signs of serious trouble in store for them. Events in continental Europe, the United States and Great Britain were following a course that was to breed conflict, a conflict in which the British colonies of North America were to become involved.

In Europe, France and Britain were at war between 1793 and War in Europe 1802. There were a few months of peace, and then, in 1803, the French dictator, Napoleon Bonaparte, again declared war. An ambitious person, Napoleon was anxious to re-create the mighty French empire of earlier days. One step in this direction was persuading Spain to return to France the North American territory of Louisiana granted to Spain in 1763.

The news that lands lying to the west of the Mississippi River had again become French proved disturbing to the Americans. There was the possibility, they believed, that if Britain should defeat France in Europe, Louisiana might fall into British hands. In either case, the people of the United States were not happy with the new development.

By 1803, Napoleon had become discouraged by the success of The Louisiana Purchase, 1803 British sea power. The chance of France's holding and developing Louisiana was growing so slim that Napoleon decided, rather hurriedly, to sell the territory to the United States. American statesmen, including President Thomas Jefferson, were stunned by the offer but soon recovered and happily agreed to the purchase. Here was a magnificent opportunity to acquire vast areas of land by means of a simple and friendly business arrangement.

1

On April 12, 1803, the *Louisiana Purchase Treaty* was signed by representatives of the French and American governments. Not since King Charles II of England had signed the Charter of the Hudson's Bay Company had such a huge territory changed hands in North America by peaceful means.

For the price of fifteen million dollars, the Americans bought a territory stretching from the Gulf of Mexico to Canada, from the Mississippi to the Rockies. Here was a land area, approximately one-third the size of the present United States, which in time was to be divided into new and vigorous states. In 1803, the purchase of the Louisiana Territory actually doubled the size of the United States.

Although peaceful conditions existed between the United States and Great Britain after the American Revolution (1775-1783), there were a number of Americans who still harboured ill will towards the former mother country. There were even some who believed that all of British North America properly belonged with the new nation. They felt that Canada should have been conquered during the Revolution and added to the United States.

**Blockade in Europe**

Many Americans were soon given added reason for ill feeling as a result of events taking place during the European conflict. After the Royal Navy, in 1805, had defeated the French in the sea battle of Trafalgar, Britain became "Mistress of the Seas" with no other nation strong enough to challenge her rule. In order to cripple the British, Napoleon Bonaparte issued decrees ordering Russia, Prussia and other European nations to cease trading with Britain. In reply, the British Navy blockaded European ports, preventing ships from delivering their cargoes to the continent.

**The effect on American trade**

This sudden stoppage of trade affected the United States as it affected other countries engaged in trading. Although considerable business was lost, many Americans, particularly those in the eastern states, accepted the situation because substantial trade was still being conducted with Great Britain. However, elsewhere in the United States, particularly in the south, groups of business men were greatly angered by the British blockade.

During the nineteenth century, navigation on the Great Lakes was greatly aided by lighthouses placed along the shores. One of the earliest lighthouses was the Gibraltar Point Lighthouse, built in 1809 on what is now Toronto Island at the entrance to York Harbour. Originally fifty-four feet in height from the ground to the floor of the lamp room, it was a solid structure built of Kingston limestone. A wooden balcony around the outside of the lamp house enabled the lighthouse-keeper to signal the approach of a vessel.

Another British war measure served to increase bitterness in the southern regions of the United States. This activity was the Royal Navy's practice of stopping American merchant ships at sea in order to search for deserters. When seamen suspected of being deserters were discovered, they were removed and pressed into British service. There is no doubt that British deserters were serving aboard American vessels where the pay was higher and working conditions were better. It was, therefore, a great temptation to many British sailors to escape from their own ships and seek work with the Americans. The British procedure of taking men by force was considered a high-handed and lawless act, an infringement of American liberty on the high seas. There is no doubt, too, that great injustice was often done when men who had never served in the Royal Navy were seized.

**The Leopard and the Chesapeake, 1807**

Anger regarding this matter reached a new peak in the United States when the British frigate *Leopard* fired upon an American warship, the *Chesapeake*. Having raked her decks with gunfire, killing three men and wounding eighteen others, the British went aboard the American vessel and removed five men who were suspected of being deserters. Later, it was discovered that only one of these men was actually a deserter.

**President Jefferson avoids war**

War might well have developed then and there between the United States and Great Britain had it not been for the coolness and clear thinking of President Thomas Jefferson. He knew that his nation's organized military power was not equal to a full-scale conflict. He believed, too, that Britain might eventually be weakened or even humbled by France in the European fighting. Therefore, instead of resisting with arms, Jefferson chose to protest in a different manner—using trade as a weapon. Accordingly, by the

**Embargo Act, 1807**

*Embargo Act* of 1807, the American government forbade any ship to leave American ports for any foreign destination. Jefferson and his government thought that as a result Britain would be seriously handicapped by the loss of food and supplies.

The Embargo Act, however, did not have any such effect. It is true that the loss of American goods was disturbing to Britain but it is equally true that the loss of British trade was a hard blow to merchants in the eastern United States. One American historian states:

> Farmers could no longer sell their produce; ships were left to rot at the wharves; shipyards and warehouses were deserted and empty. The value of American export trade dropped from $108,343,150 in 1807 to $22,430,960 in 1808.

However, it appears that a few daring American traders were Smuggling American goods willing to disobey the Embargo Act. One method was to load ships with goods that seemed to be destined for ports in the southern United States. Once out of sight of land, the ships sailed eastward to meet British vessels at pre-arranged points. There, the cargoes were transferred to British vessels, and sometimes both ships and cargoes were handed over to the British.

The results of the Embargo Act caused so much dissatisfaction Embargo Act repealed, 1809 in the United States that the Act was repealed by Congress in 1809.

James Madison became President in 1809, and after the election The "War Hawks" of 1810 a number of new men found their way into Congress, men who were determined to fight for American liberties at home and on the high seas. They believed in taking a stronger attitude toward Great Britain or any other country that threatened American rights. It was also natural that they should be attracted by British North America with its fertile soil and richly wooded areas, so desirable and apparently so defenceless. It was their belief that the whole continent, from ocean to ocean and from the Gulf of Mexico to the North Pole, should be under the Stars and Stripes—a dream that was a nightmare for their northern neighbours. Strong, proud men, they soon held such power in Congress that they became national leaders of importance. Among them were such persons as thirty-five-year-old Henry Clay of Kentucky and John C. Calhoun of South Carolina, then only twenty-nine years of age. These men and their supporters came to be known as the "War Hawks."

Americans who were pushing westward into the Ohio valley Conflicts with Indians and on toward the Mississippi found what they imagined to be still another cause of resentment toward Britain. They came into conflict with Indian tribes who considered the westward surge of settlers an invasion of their lands. There were quarrels, murders, scalpings and scattered raids.

Because some of the Indians were equipped with fire-arms, the frontiersmen complained loudly that the British in Canada were arming the Indians and inciting the tribesmen to fight the Americans. These charges were grossly exaggerated. It is true that Indians did acquire a few muskets through normal trade, as they had done for many years, but the British forces in North America were so poorly equipped that they had no surplus guns to give to American Indian tribes. Unfortunately, the noisy charges of the frontiersmen deceived a large number of American citizens.

**Chief Tecumseh**

The Indians themselves, fearful of the American advance, prepared to protect their lands. There rose to power among them

Early nineteenth-century artillery was generally of two, distinct kinds. First, there were stationary cannon—usually of large calibre—employed aboard ship and also used in the defence or siege of forts. Second, there were lighter field-cannon that could be moved about from place to place. (Some mortars and some howitzers—short-barrelled, high-trajectory guns—were also employed on occasion.) Stationary cannon, such as the twenty-four pounder shown here, differed from field-pieces in calibre and in the type of supporting carriages. (The term "pounder" refers to the weight of cast-iron shot fired.) This weapon had a heavy, massive, wooden carriage fitted with small, iron wheels and was therefore unsuited to movement over rough ground. Field-guns had large wheels and light carriages to allow of easy movement. Around 1800, firing cannon was still a very involved procedure. The barrel was loaded with a bag of powder, and then a cannon ball was rolled down on top of the powder. The actual firing was accomplished by igniting (with a lighted wick) a small charge of powder placed in the "touch hole" at the rear of the barrel. This action, in turn, ignited the main charge, which blasted the ball out of the barrel.

one of the greatest Indian leaders in North American history, a Shawnee chief, Tecumtha or Tecumseh. Seeing some hope of stemming the tide of American settlement, Tecumseh planned a great Indian confederacy that would be strong enough to resist the white men. He travelled the Mississippi valley as far south as Tennessee, arguing, pleading, encouraging and demanding assistance. In the meantime, his brother, a medicine man known **The Prophet** as the Prophet, exerted great influence, teaching that the tribesmen should return to their old ways and give up the evil habits and customs they had learned from the white men. The two brothers were a powerful force in uniting the western tribes against American settlers.

Serious trouble developed over a bitter disagreement regarding the American purchase of three million acres of land in Indian territory. Angered by the incident, Chief Tecumseh protested the arrangement and demanded the return of Indian land. In a fiery speech, he said:

> These lands are ours, and no one has the right to remove us, because we were the first owners; the Great Spirit above has appointed this place for us on which to light our fires, and here we will remain. As to the boundaries, the Great Spirit above knows no boundaries, nor will His red people know any . . . If my great father, the President of the Seventeen Fires, has anything more to say to me, he must send a man of note as his messenger . . .

Tecumseh used his powers of oratory to rally even more tribes to his cause, and an increasing number of warriors collected at the Prophet's town on the Tippecanoe River.

In 1811, disturbed by the hostility of the Indians and a number **The battle** of unpleasant incidents, Governor Harrison of the Indiana Terri- **at Tippecanoe,** tory sent for troops and called out his militiamen. Determined to **1811** take a firm grip on the situation, he marched with a thousand men in the direction of the Prophet's town on the Tippecanoe. Near the town, contact was made with the Indians and arrangements were completed for a council. Unwisely, the Prophet decided to attack the Americans while they lay sleeping that night in camp. In the battle that followed, the Indians were routed and the Indian town was put to the torch.

Tecumseh, who had been among tribes to the south, returned to find the town in ruins, his warriors scattered and his brother making weak excuses for the defeat. Tecumseh was so angry that he shook the Prophet by the hair of his head. Years of careful planning and organization had gone to waste.

**Tecumseh joins the British, 1812**

Early in June, 1812, Tecumseh, accompanied by a small group of his followers, left the Indiana territory and joined the British at Amherstburg, on the Canadian side of the Detroit River.

# 2. The Campaign of 1812

THE WAR HAWKS GAINED such power in the Congress of the United War Hawk confidence States that their words were listened to with growing attention. It became increasingly obvious that these aggressive men were bent on war with Great Britain. By the autumn of 1811, they were openly demanding an immediate invasion of British North America.

Despite opposition from other members of Congress and protests from various parts of the nation, Henry Clay and his supporters "beat the drums of war." Clay was so confident of an easy victory in a strike across the border that he said, "I trust I shall not be presumptuous when I state that I verily believe that the militia of Kentucky alone are competent to place Montreal and Upper Canada at your feet." He estimated that it would take American troops no more than four weeks to overrun and hold the important regions of British North America.

By February of 1812, Congress had ordered the creation of a volunteer army of 50,000 men. Four months later came a declaration of war against Great Britain.

However, the War Hawks had displayed much more energy in War is declared talking about war than in planning and preparing for war. At the beginning of hostilities there were but 7,000 men in the regular forces and these were commanded by senior officers who were old, incompetent or lacking in experience. Congress had voted for war, but seemed reluctant to spend the necessary funds upon equipment and supplies. A bill introduced into Congress with the purpose of increasing the size of the American Navy was turned down by the members. Volunteer soldiers were badly fed and disgracefully clothed. In winter, the unfortunate sentries who patrolled the Canadian-American border shivered and shook on duty because they lacked overcoats.

Lack of
unity in
war effort

To make matters even more embarrassing for the War Hawks, people in the New England states openly disapproved of the war. In Massachusetts, the New Englanders placed their Stars and Stripes at half-mast when war was declared. As the conflict progressed, they refused to volunteer for military service and they withheld financial support for the war effort. Some merchants actually kept on selling beef to British army authorities.

It soon became clear that great numbers of Americans were not at all united in approving the conflict with Great Britain. Many felt that it was a contest fought for purposes other than those which had been declared by the War Hawks. These feelings were put into eloquent words by the famous American orator and statesman, Daniel Webster, when he spoke in Congress:

> Whoever would discover the causes which have produced the present state of things, must look for them, not in the efforts of the opposition, but in the nature of the war in which we are engaged . . . Quite too small a portion of public opinion was in favor of war to justify it originally. A much smaller portion is in favor of the mode in which it has been conducted . . . Public opinion, strong and united, is not with you in your Canada project. . . The acquisition of the country is not an object generally desired by the people. . . You are you say, at war for maritime rights, and free trade. But they see you lock up your commerce and abandon the ocean. They see you invade an interior province of the enemy. They see you involve yourselves in a bloody war with the native savages; and they ask you if you have, in truth, a maritime controversy with the Western Indians, and are really contending for sailors' rights with the tribes of the Prophet.

Conditions
in British
North
America

If the American prospects of waging a successful war appeared disappointing, the British prospects of defence were even less promising. The British provinces lacked the population, the food supplies, the military equipment, the manufacturing resources and the troops available to the United States. Officials in all seriousness wondered if the French Canadians and the former Americans might not prove a danger during the tense days of warfare. It was sobering to consider the possibility of thousands

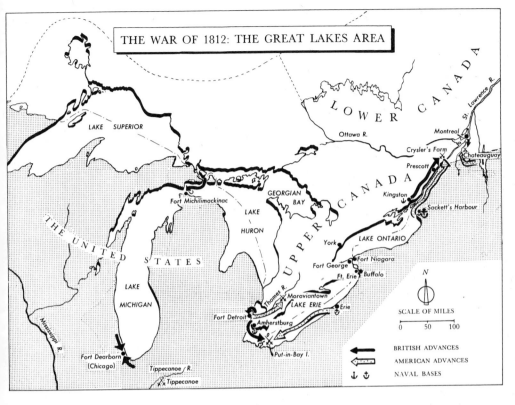

THE WAR OF 1812: THE GREAT LAKES AREA

of Canadian inhabitants welcoming the American invaders and taking up arms against the British government.

The British army in North America, a mere 4,450 men, was faced with the staggering problem of defending a border that stretched for a thousand miles to the south and west of Montreal. Fortunately, this hardy little force was commanded by General Isaac Brock, a daring, skilful officer. It was perhaps fortunate, too, that overland travel along the frontier was still a difficult procedure. The undeveloped nature of the land and the lack of proper roads were to prove a severe handicap to the invading Americans.

On July 11, 1812, 2,500 American troops under General Hull reached the Detroit River and camped at Fort Detroit. At Amherstburg on the Canadian side of the river were 100 British regulars, 300 militia and 150 Indians led by Tecumseh.

**Americans invade Upper Canada**

**General
Hull's
Proclamation**

Hull crossed the Detroit and made his headquarters in a **Cana-**dian farm house. He issued a proclamation which was printed for distribution among Canadians. It began:

INHABITANTS OF CANADA

After thirty years of peace and prosperity, the United States have been driven to arms. The injuries and aggressions, the insults and indignities of Great Britain have once more left them no alternative but manly resistance or unconditional submission. The army under my command has invaded your country. The standard of the Union now waves over the territory of Canada. To the peaceful unoffending inhabitants it brings neither danger nor difficulty. I come to find enemies, not to make them; I come to protect, not to injure you. . .

I have a force which will break down all opposition, and that force is but the vanguard of a much greater. If, contrary to your own interest, and the just expectations of my country, you should take part in the approaching contest, you will be considered and treated as enemies, and the horrors and calamities of war will stalk you. . .

**American
forts seized**

General Hull was so preoccupied with his attempts to terrify Canadians with printed words that he neglected to protect American forts on Lake Michigan. As a result, a small force of British and Indians captured Fort Michilimackinac, while other Indians seized Fort Dearborn (Chicago).

**Indians
rally for
war**

After these small but strategic victories, the Indians took such courage that small bands of them hurried northward from the Ohio and Mississippi Rivers to join Tecumseh on the Canadian frontier. Within a short time, the great Indian commander had more than six hundred braves ready and eager for battle.

**Americans
retreat to
Detroit**

Hull waited uneasily as Indians swarmed across the border and as Canadian militiamen rallied to the defence of their land. The general became increasingly nervous at the thought of facing an enemy force composed of British regulars, sharpshooting backwoodsmen and hundreds of angry Indians. His nervousness finally gave way to near panic. On August 11, he ordered his army to retreat across the river to Detroit.

Two days after the withdrawal of the Americans, General Isaac Brock arrived at Amherstburg, where he held an immediate

conference with his officers and with Tecumseh. A British officer
who was present has described Tecumseh's appearance:

Tecumseh was very prepossessing, his figure light and finely propor-
tioned, his age I imagined to be about five-and-thirty, his height five
feet nine or ten inches, his complexion light copper, his countenance
oval, with bright hazel eyes beaming cheerfulness, energy and decision.
Three small crowns or coronets were suspended from the lower
cartilage of his aquiline nose, and a large silver medallion of George
the Third, which I believe his ancestor had received from Lord
Dorchester when Governor-General of Canada, was attached to a mixed
coloured wampum string which hung around his neck. His dress
consisted of a plain, neat uniform, a tanned deer-skin jacket with long
trousers of the same material, the seams of both being covered with
neatly cut fringe, and he had on his feet leather moccasins much
ornamented with work made from the dyed quills of the porcupine.

After a brief consideration of the border situation, Brock
decided to cross the river and make a direct attack on Fort Detroit.
Pleased with this firm and courageous decision, Tecumseh pointed
at the British general and shouted, "Ho! Here is a man!"

On August 16, 1812, British regulars, Canadian militiamen and **British capture Detroit**
Indians advanced on Detroit as the guns of Amherstburg threw
sheils across the water. The sight of the advancing redcoats and the
sound of the shrill, wild Indian war whoops caused an uneasy stir
among the Americans. General Hull's own forces still outnumbered those of the approaching enemy, but he did not know
this. Feeling that the situation within the fort was hopeless, he ran
up a white flag and quickly agreed to surrender. In addition to an
easy victory, the daring invaders captured valuable goods, including thirty-three cannon, a large quantity of stores and equipment,
a number of horses and a newly built sailing ship. As a token of
appreciation of Tecumseh's part in the affair, Brock slipped off
his own red military sash and wrapped it about the chief's waist.
In quick response, Tecumseh removed his beaded sash and
handed it over to the General.

Fearing another threat to the Canadian border, Brock hurried **Brock returns to Niagara**
back to Fort George at Newark (Niagara-on-the-Lake). An Ameri-
can crossing at or near this point would be a serious matter since
it lay so close to York, the capital of Upper Canada. Brock's fears

were justified. The Americans had gathered 6,300 men on the Niagara River and had strengthened their naval forces on Lake Ontario.

**Battle of Queenston Heights**

Brock was certain the enemy would attempt a river crossing, but just where he did not know. The answer came on the morning of October 13, as American troops moved across the swift, dangerous waters and landed close to the Canadian village of Queenston. In the face of fire directed by the defenders of the village, the American boats shuttled back and forth, landing soldiers at the foot of Queenston Heights.

Meanwhile, the British garrison at Fort George was roused by the roar of guns in the distance. General Brock leaped to his saddle and galloped off in the direction of Queenston. As the morning sun rose in the east, he raced through the Niagara farm lands, shouting the alarm to those he passed along the way.

On Queenston Heights he stopped at a spot where a gun crew and troops were shooting at the Americans who clung to the Canadian shore at the river's edge. Believing the Heights could be held by a few gunners, Brock ordered most of the troops to join the forces below at Queenston village. This proved to be an error. Two hundred of the enemy, following a pathway through the trees, reached the crest of the Heights and took possession. Brock himself was almost caught in the sudden surge of invaders.

Determined to regain the lost ground before the enemy troops could consolidate in overwhelming numbers on the Heights, Brock took command of one hundred British regulars and Canadian militia. Facing the Heights, he ordered the charge, knowing full well that his hope of success was small. It was a gallant, reckless action, but one doomed to failure.

A volunteer in the action, George Jarvis, has described the event:

**Death of General Brock**

He [Brock] was loudly cheered as he cried, "Follow me, boys!" and led us at a smart trot toward the mountain. Checking his horse to a walk, he said, "Take your breath, boys, we shall want it in a few minutes." Another cheer was the hearty response from the regulars and militia. At that time the top of the mountain and a great portion of

This British infantryman wears a uniform of the period of the War of 1812. By this time, British army uniforms had undergone the most significant changes in over two centuries. Such changes included the discarding of knee breeches and stockings in favour of full-length trousers. The latter were similar to modern trousers, except for a slight split at the ankles. In addition, coats were now gathered behind and were somewhat shorter than those worn previously. Stiff hats or shakos replaced the earlier triangular or cocked hats, and wigs and pigtails had given way to close-cut hair, clipped to the shape of the head.

the side was thickly covered with trees, and was now occupied by American riflemen. On arriving at the foot of the mountain where the road diverges to St. David's, General Brock dismounted, and waving his sword, climbed over a high stone wall followed by his troops. Placing himself at the head of the light company of the 49th, he led the way up the mountain at double-quick time, in the very teeth of a sharp fire from the enemy's riflemen, and ere long he was singled out by one of them, who coming forward, took deliberate aim and fired. Several of the men noticed the action and fired, but too late, and our gallant General fell on his left side, within a few feet of where I stood. Running up to him, I enquired, "Are you much hurt, sir?" He placed his hand on his breast, but made no reply and sank down.

Taking their fallen commander with them, the troops retreated to the base of the Heights. A second charge was made, but it, too, was broken up and pushed back by American fire. By this time, enemy blue-coats were scampering up the Heights in groups to join their comrades on the top. The American position was becoming stronger by the minute.

The situation seemed gloomy to the Canadians on the scene. The Stars and Stripes flew from a gun on the Heights; more troops were crossing the river; enemy artillery was throwing a steady barrage from the opposite shore. So confident were the Americans of victory that they despatched messengers with the news of success at Queenston.

The combatants, however, did not know that the British guns at Fort George had silenced the opposing batteries at Fort Niagara directly across the river. The main body of the British garrison, under General Sheaffe, was marching toward the Heights, and Indian allies were gathering.

As British reinforcements began to arrive, the Americans on the Heights became nervous, feeling that their position was no longer secure. Indian war cries added to the tension among the invaders. Americans on the opposite shore became alarmed and refused to cross over and join their comrades on the Canadian side.

General Sheaffe judged that the river front could be held by units already stationed there, so he marched inland, circled about and came towards the Heights from the landward side where his approach was screened by forest.

**Defeat of Americans at Queenston Heights**

Sheaffe's men advanced slowly with Indians on either flank. His battle formation was an enveloping, curved line, tough as a fortress wall, and it closed in on the Americans on the Heights. The invaders stood firm, but the British fired and then charged with naked bayonets. With shrill, blood-curdling cries, the Indians leaped ahead. After firing a nervous volley, the American line

After the death of General Isaac Brock, American troops remained in control of Queenston Heights. In order to dislodge them, General Sheaffe advanced from the landward side of the American position and attacked the invaders from the rear. With their backs to the Niagara River and faced by about 1,000 British regulars and Canadian militia, the Americans fought on bravely but hopelessly. Confronted by Sheaffe's ever-tightening semi-circle of troops, some of the survivors scrambled down the Heights by the path they had ascended; some, clinging to shrubs and rocks, tried to hide; many were dashed to pieces and a number drowned. About 1,000 surrendered and 400 were lost by bullet, steel and flood. Ironically, on the very day Brock was killed, the guns of the Tower of London were proclaiming his victory at Detroit.

became limp, then collapsed entirely. In the mêlée, enemy troops were shot down and bayonetted. Some tumbled over the edge of the Heights. An American officer seized a handkerchief, tied it to his sword and raised it in token of surrender. On the other side of the river, dispirited American militia watched the plight of their countrymen but made no move to rescue them from the British and Canadians.

There were several other enemy attacks, small and scattered, on Canadian soil during the remainder of 1812, but they too were miserable failures. American militia, it seemed, had little desire to fight beyond the boundaries of their own nation.

**War at sea** Although enemy efforts on land were weak, it was a different story at sea. American seamen enjoyed a series of startling victories during which ships of the Royal Navy were captured and British merchant vessels seized. Such daring actions shocked the British and delighted the citizens of the United States.

One curious development of sea warfare was the appearance of numerous "privateers." These were privately owned ships, each armed with a few cannon, that preyed on enemy merchant shipping. British and American privateers prowled Atlantic waters attacking merchantmen at every opportunity. One armed schooner based in Nova Scotia, the *Liverpool Packet*, captured about thirty American vessels during the course of a very adventurous career.

The events of the campaign of 1812 gave the people of British North America good cause to be alarmed. Although the Americans appeared to be weak and ill-prepared, the Canadian defenders did not seem to be in much better shape. To make matters worse, the most competent British general, Brock, had been killed at Queenston. Thus, it is little wonder that the colonists looked to the future with apprehension.

# 3. The Campaign of 1813

DURING 1812, THE BRITISH provinces had been saved from invasion largely through the bungling of enemy leaders and the unpopularity of war in certain parts of the United States.   But, by the beginning of 1813, it appeared that the War Hawks, who still controlled Congress, were making a more serious attempt to launch a strong offensive.   From the Mississippi valley to the shores of the Atlantic there was a stir of military preparation, and on Lake Ontario and Lake Erie the Americans began building powerful naval squadrons.

However, north of the border, no attempt was being made to provide strong reinforcements for the meagre forces that existed. There were now about 7,000 regulars, a varying group of Indians under Tecumseh, whatever militia could be raised for short periods and a rather ineffective naval squadron on the Great Lakes. In the course of the year, Great Britain managed to send some regular troops, some seamen, gunners and marines but these seemed few in comparison with the numbers of men being mustered across the border in the United States. *Military forces in British North America*

At York, the military defences were weak and ineffective; the British squadron on Lake Ontario had been battered by the Americans in 1812. It is not surprising that in the spring of 1813 American authorities decided to attack the capital of Upper Canada.

Transported across the lake on ships, American forces landed a short distance west of York, in the area now known as Sunnyside Beach.  The British commander, General Sheaffe, hurried more troops to meet the invaders but was pushed back by American riflemen.   The retreating British regulars and militia pulled back *Attacks on York and Fort George*

The Martello tower was a form of defensive work much favoured by British military engineers in the early part of the nineteenth century. Such towers were constructed largely for coastal defence and, in British North America, were located along the St. Lawrence River and also in the Maritime provinces. Built of thick, solid masonry, the tower was used for rearguard or delaying actions against a numerous enemy. Normally, the tower was too small to sustain a full-scale attack by a determined invader. The top of the tower contained a platform that housed two or three pieces of artillery; just below this platform was a chamber reached by an inside or outside stairway. The chamber was designed to accommodate a small garrison of troops. A number of Martello towers still stand today in eastern Canada.

to the western battery, which was located on the present-day Canadian National Exhibition grounds. Just as they reached the battery, the ammunition store blew up, killing forty men and dismounting the cannon. Having lost 200 men during the skirmish and the explosion, General Sheaffe was fortunate in escaping along the road to Kingston with several hundred redcoats. The militia and a few Indians melted away in the direction of their homes.

Unfortunately, the American militia took over the town of York. These wild, undisciplined men entertained themselves by releasing prisoners from jail and by stealing from homes and shops. Some removed religious objects from St. James Church; others took armfuls of books from the town library. As a final indignity, they set fire to the parliament buildings of Upper Canada.

For some reason or other General Dearborn did not hold his strong position at York. Perhaps he felt he had completed his task. At any rate, he sailed off in the direction of Niagara, his ships loaded with loot. As a farewell gesture, he had ordered the barracks, the blockhouse and government storehouses to be burnt.

The next American strike was made at Fort George. The fort fell into enemy hands after a three-hour battle. Withdrawing from the scene, the British regulars and Canadian militia fell back in the direction of Beaver Dams and then proceeded to Burlington Heights.

In an effort to smash this force that had escaped, the Americans **Battle at Stoney Creek** sent out 2,000 men — infantry, artillery and cavalry. On June 6, 1813, having reached Stoney Creek (seven miles from the Canadian position), the Americans made camp. At two o'clock in the morning, the redcoats and militiamen struck hard, capturing two American generals and over one hundred prisoners.

Encouraged by the arrival of reinforcements in the form of the 104th (New Brunswick) Regiment, the Canadian defenders pushed on towards Niagara. A company or two of troops were sent to Beaver Dams to protect the British right flank.

Sensing a serious threat in these enemy movements, the Americans **Battle of Beaver Dams** hurried several hundred men in the direction of Beaver Dams. But this American action was noticed by Indians who prepared an ambush. When close to the British position, the Americans entered a narrow valley. There, they suddenly found themselves surrounded by Indians. After a grim, two-hour skirmish among the trees, the discouraged Americans were on the point of retreating, but their escape was cut off by Canadian militia and British redcoats. The American commander surrendered his whole force.

The successes at Stoney Creek and Beaver Dams put fresh fighting spirit into the Canadian defenders. Moving up to the Niagara at several points, they re-occupied some positions previously held by the Americans.

Conditions appeared much brighter to the Canadians on the Niagara frontier, but an unexpected move by the American squadron on Lake Ontario caught York by surprise. For the second time, the invaders had no difficulty in taking the town, looting shops, releasing prisoners and destroying buildings.

**Newark burned by the Americans**

As the year 1813 drew to a close, the American forces in the Niagara Peninsula found themselves in an alarming position. Many of the regular troops had been withdrawn to the region of Montreal, leaving numbers of undisciplined plunderers in the area held by American forces. Canadian farmers, angered by enemy raiding and pillaging, fought back as best they could, shooting and capturing small groups of stragglers. As a result, the Americans withdrew from Fort George at once. In leaving, the American commander committed the barbarous act of setting fire to the whole town of Newark. On December 12, 1813, men, women and children were given just two hours to gather together a few possessions and leave their homes—on a cold night in the midst of a snow storm.

Angered by the destruction of Newark, British forces crossed the Niagara River a week later and captured Fort Niagara. Twenty-seven cannon and a large quantity of stores fell into the hands of the attackers.

**Burning and looting**

During the days that followed, the British, Canadians and Indians burned homes along the whole course of the Niagara. So great was their fury that they captured the town of Buffalo and there destroyed several American ships.

The British redcoats, the Canadian militia and the Indians, in effect, behaved as badly as the Americans had at York and Newark. The war had turned into a savage, bitter affair, completely devoid of mercy—even for women and children.

**British defeat on Lake Erie**

In the late summer of 1813, the main scene of war shifted to the waters of Lake Erie. Both sides had been building additional ships and enlisting more seamen. The British, believing that Lake Ontario was the region that required the greatest protection, stationed their largest and best squadron there. Thus, British strength on Lake Erie became relatively weak. Meanwhile, American authorities had decided to establish a strong squadron on both lakes.

Captain Barclay, in command of the British Erie squadron, became alarmed after the Americans had succeeded in adding several new ships to their Erie force. In order to make the best of a threatening situation, he decided to attack the enemy before they were further reinforced. It was a desperate venture, for Barclay's squadron was outnumbered, outmanned and outgunned.

Leaving Amherstburg on September 9, he arrived the following morning off Put-in-Bay Island, the point at which the American squadron was located. Captain Perry, commander of the American force, was not slow to take up the challenge.

Perry's squadron closed in quickly, for the powerful, short range guns of the American fighting vessels were best at firing destructive broadsides. In the beginning, British gunners knocked out the American flagship and damaged other vessels but, as time went by, the fighting drew into extremely close range and the American guns took a heavy toll. Sharpshooting Kentucky riflemen on Perry's ships raked the British decks with a deadly fire. In the end, after three hours of fighting, the British squadron was shattered.

The destruction of British naval power on Lake Erie encouraged American land forces in the western region. The British posts at Detroit and Amherstburg were now much more vulnerable to attack, and General Harrison, the American commander in the west, felt that the time had come to strike. He was made even more eager when he received intelligence reports that there were less than 875 British regulars and 1,200 Indians defending the river border. The Canadian militiamen appeared to be back on their farms harvesting crops.

Americans threaten Detroit and Amherstburg

During the Battle of Lake Erie, a superior squadron of American ships under Commodore Perry decisively defeated a British squadron under Captain Barclay. In the course of the engagement, Perry's own ship was so badly damaged that he was forced to abandon it and make his way through a hail of bullets to another vessel. When victory became evident, Perry sent the message: *We have met the enemy and they are ours—two ships, two brigs, one schooner and one sloop.* This naval defeat was a most serious blow to the British because it left their land forces along the Detroit River without naval aid or protection.

**British retreat up the Thames valley**

By the end of September, the American commander had moved several thousand infantry and cavalry by ship into the Detroit area. The prospects for a British defence of that region seemed poor. Feeling that retreat was the only sensible action to take in view of the enemy's strength, General Proctor announced his intention of withdrawing up the Thames valley.

Tecumseh made an impassioned speech in which he urged Proctor to remain and fight the invaders:

Listen, Father! The Americans have not yet defeated us by land, neither are we sure that they have done so by water. We, therefore, wish to remain here and fight our enemy, should they make their appearance. If they defeat us, we will then retreat. . . Father, you have got the arms and the ammunition which our Great Father sent for his red children. If you have any idea of going away, give them to us, and you may go. . . Our lives are in the hands of the Great Spirit. We are determined to defend our lands, and, if it is His will, to leave our bones upon them.

General Proctor insisted on leading his British and Indian forces northeastward along the valley of the Thames River. He hoped that when the invaders had been drawn away from their main supply base, they could be dealt with more easily. The British retreat, however, developed into a dismal, heartbreaking action. American cavalrymen, in hit-and-run raids, captured guns, stores and men. Tecumseh's Indians became discouraged and large numbers of them drifted away.

Proctor finally made a stand against his pursuers near the village of Moraviantown. Taking shelter in a beech forest and a cedar swamp, the British and Indians, a small force of tired, hungry, ill-equipped men, waited for the enemy.

The Battle of the Thames was over in a few minutes. American horsemen thundered into the wood, throwing aside resistance with the speed and power of their charge. Having lost forty-eight men, the British surrendered. Turning next to the cedar swamp, the cavalry made short work of the Indians, although the gallant Tecumseh and a small group of his warriors put up a desperate fight in which the great Shawnee chief was killed. **The Battle of the Thames** **Death of Tecumseh**

The American commander was satisfied with his accomplishment. Instead of pushing on up the Thames valley, he returned to Detroit.

In the late fall of 1813, Lower Canada had its moments of dread as American forces, striving to gain control of that important British supply-route, the St. Lawrence, made a two-pronged attack on Montreal.

Chateauguay

One enemy thrust, coming from Lake Champlain, was stopped at Chateauguay on October 26. Through an incredible series of errors, some American troops were lost in a swamp, several companies fired at each other and their officers overestimated the strength of the Canadian defence. An actual battle never took place at Chateauguay; after only a few, brisk skirmishes, the Americans withdrew from Canadian soil.

To the French Canadians, Chateauguay was a real triumph. A

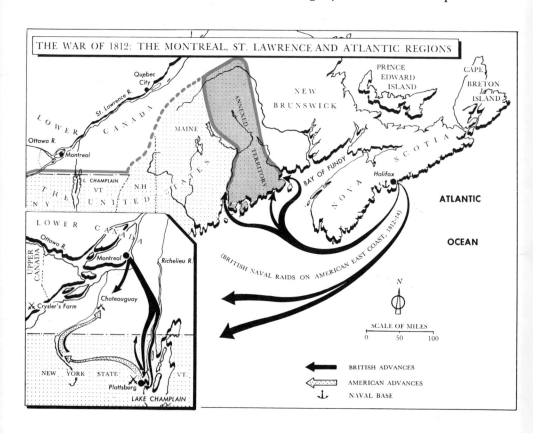

THE WAR OF 1812: THE MONTREAL, ST. LAWRENCE AND ATLANTIC REGIONS

(BRITISH NAVAL RAIDS ON AMERICAN EAST COAST, 1812-14)

ATLANTIC

OCEAN

N

SCALE OF MILES
0    50    100

BRITISH ADVANCES
AMERICAN ADVANCES
NAVAL BASE

French-Canadian historian has said: "Chateauguay was the affirmation of our undeniable loyalty and of our ardent patriotism."

Americans were shocked when they heard the details of the affair. Four thousand troops had retreated in the face of a tough little Canadian force of only one thousand men. It had, indeed, been a victory for French-Canadian militiamen and a few redcoats.

The second enemy thrust came from Sackett's Harbour on Lake Ontario. At first, it seemed as if Kingston would be attacked; however, the enemy began to move downstream toward Montreal. Seemingly undisturbed by the Chateauguay disaster, the American flotilla slowly descended the St. Lawrence. In the meantime, the British had set up headquarters at the farm house of a Mr. John Crysler. It was on November 11, at Crysler's Farm, that the decisive battle of the "grand invasion" of the St. Lawrence valley took place.

Again, the Americans suffered a defeat at the hands of a force one-quarter the size of their own—this time a force of British soldiers and militiamen from Upper Canada. **Americans defeated at Crysler's Farm**

The British success at Crysler's Farm was a deadly blow to the spirit of the American troops. At the same time, it stiffened the backs of the Canadians, who had so recently been badly disappointed by the disaster at Moraviantown.

During the early part of 1813, the British suffered a series of humiliating defeats in their attempts to blockade the Atlantic ports of the United States. Outgunned and outmanned by larger American ships, many British men-of-war were captured or destroyed. For a time, it seemed that the control of the seas was passing to the Americans. British dominance was restored by one engagement fought off Boston in full view of many of its citizens. The British frigate *Shannon,* manned mainly by Nova Scotians, defeated and captured the larger *Chesapeake,* one of the principal ships of the young American Navy, and towed her as a prize of war to Halifax. This victory boosted the morale of the Nova Scotians and destroyed the myth of American naval invincibility.

The campaign of 1813 was at an end. In the west, the British had been defeated, Detroit was lost, and Brock and Tecumseh were dead. But there had been encouraging successes on the Niagara frontier and in the Montreal region. Nevertheless, despite a brighter picture, there was no reason to feel satisfied or secure. British victories had been won because of the blunders of American commanders rather than through any military superiority, and it was not safe to count on the enemy repeating their mistakes in the future.

# 4. 1814, The Year of Peace

EARLY IN 1814 BRITAIN was still at war with France. No large Blockade of the American coast military forces could be released to protect the British provinces in North America, but squadrons of British ships maintained a tight blockade of the American coast. These vessels operated from bases in Halifax, Bermuda and Jamaica and were so successful in sealing off ports in the United States that goods moving from the northern to the southern states had to be transported in wagons.

The British strategy for 1814 was to maintain the blockade and American raids on the Erie shore attack various coastal towns and cities. The Americans, on the other hand, were again organizing their forces to make powerful thrusts across the border.

Early in 1814, American forces raided the north shore of Lake Erie. Mrs. Amelia Harris, who lived at Port Ryerse, has given the following description of the invaders:

On the following morning, the 15th of May, as my Mother and myself were at breakfast, the dogs made an unusual barking. I went to the door to discover the reason. When I looked up, I saw the hillside and the fields as far as the eye could see covered with American soldiers. They had landed at Patterson's Creek, burned the mills and the village of Port Dover and then marched to Port Ryerse. Two men stepped from the ranks, selected some large chips, came into the room where we were standing and took coals from the hearth without speaking. My Mother knew instinctively what they were going to do. She went and asked to see the commanding officer. A gentleman rode up to her and said that he was the person she asked for. She entreated him to spare her property and said she was a widow with a young family. He answered her civilly and respectfully and regretted that his orders were to burn, but that he would spare the house, which he did, and said in justification that the buildings were used as barracks and the mill furnished flour for British troops. Very soon we saw a column of smoke arise from every building and of what at early morn had been a prosperous homestead, at noon there remained only smouldering ruins.

Early in July, a serious threat to the Niagara Peninsula took shape as American troops crossed over from Buffalo. It was in this area that the main fighting centred. After the surrender of the British post at Fort Erie, the invaders pushed northward along the Niagara River.

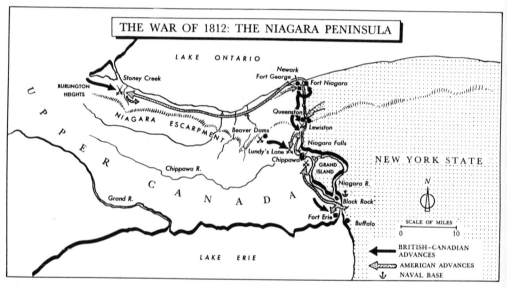

THE WAR OF 1812: THE NIAGARA PENINSULA

LAKE ONTARIO

Stoney Creek
BURLINGTON HEIGHTS
Newark
Fort George
Fort Niagara
NIAGARA ESCARPMENT
Queenston
Lewiston
Beaver Dams
Niagara Falls
Lundy's Lane
Chippawa
Chippawa R.
GRAND ISLAND
NEW YORK STATE
Grand R.
UPPER CANADA
Niagara R.
Black Rock
Fort Erie
Buffalo
N
SCALE OF MILES
0        10
LAKE ERIE

➤ BRITISH–CANADIAN ADVANCES
⇦ AMERICAN ADVANCES
↓ NAVAL BASE

**British defeat at Chippawa**  British forces were rushed to Chippawa to block this advance. From the position at Chippawa, British cavalry and Indians were sent out to meet the enemy. This daring, reckless thrust was so unexpected that Pennsylvania riflemen and allied Indians fell back in panic. However, when the main body of Americans attacked, the defenders were forced to retreat to Fort George at the north end of the Niagara River.

**Battle of Lundy's Lane**  It soon became apparent that the American thrust lacked real strength. Thus, British authorities felt safe in sending troops from York and Kingston to the Niagara Peninsula. The clash between defenders and invaders took place on July 25, near a farm lane on the property of a Mr. Thomas Lundy, not far from Niagara Falls.

The Battle of Lundy's Lane was a strange, confused encounter that began at sunset and continued into the night. At one point in the clash, British guns actually fired on Canadian militia as they arrived on the scene. The summer heat and the lack of water caused intense suffering among the men of both armies. In the end, neither side won this odd battle; both became so exhausted they stopped fighting.

A remarkable rôle in the battle was played by a young woman still in her early teens. She was Mrs. Catherine Lundy, wife of Thomas Lundy, whose home stood on the rim of the battlefield. Even before the beginning of the clash, she was handing out drinking water to thirsty redcoats and militia who had already walked fourteen miles on that hot day. While the battle raged, she tended wounded soldiers in her kitchen. The gallant young woman's contribution was considered so important that a senior British officer paid Mrs. Lundy a visit and presented her with his sword. **Mrs. Catherine Lundy**

Though neither side could rightly claim a victory at Lundy's Lane, the Americans retreated to Fort Erie, leaving the exhausted defenders on the field of battle.

By 1814, Napoleon Bonaparte had been defeated in Europe, making it possible for Britain to release troops for action in North America. In July and August of that year, some 12,000 veterans landed at Quebec City and moved on to the Montreal region. **Help from Britain**

The British commanders in North America now provided an example of feeble leadership. In a timid southward thrust at Plattsburg, British naval and land forces met disaster. A squadron of ships was beaten on Lake Champlain, while redcoats retreated without making an attack. So angered were many of the British veterans, that they deserted in the hundreds. A needless retreat was deep humiliation after many victories on the battlefields of Europe. **British defeat in Lake Champlain region**

In addition to the troops released for service in North America, more British ships were able to harass the eastern coast of the **British raid the American coast**

In comparison with today's electronic marvels, early nineteenth-century communication systems were simple and straightforward. Two land-based signalling systems were widely used to provide ships with weather warnings. The first, shown here, employed standardized combinations of flags, flown from a pole with two cross-arms. One serious disadvantage of this system was that seamen found it difficult to read the signals when the wind caused flags to fly directly toward or away from ships.

United States. As a consequence, Halifax became a busy centre for assembling and refitting fighting vessels. Raids from this port enabled the British to capture and annex most of the eastern part of Maine.

During the summer of 1814, the British attacked farther south along the coast. The city of Washington was occupied for about twenty-four hours while soldiers looted and burned a number of buildings. Among the buildings badly scorched by fire was the president's mansion, which had to be painted white to restore its beauty. It was due to this incident that the term "White House" came into use.

The attack on Washington was undoubtedly in retaliation for the looting and destruction of York by American troops in 1813. The chief purpose of naval action along the coast, however, was to keep American attention away from the British provinces.

The British government hoped that the great military hero of the Napoleonic Wars, the Duke of Wellington, would take command of British troops in North America and win his usual series of victories. After studying maps of North America, the Duke indicated that the defeat of United States forces could only be obtained at a tremendous cost in money and human lives. He strongly advised the British government to make peace on the best terms possible.

Americans, too, were thinking of peace, for many of them could see little profit in pursuing a war that seemed to settle nothing.

## 1814, The Year of Peace

A group of British and American representatives had already been at work in the Belgian town of Ghent, trying to discover some reasonable basis for an honourable settlement. They met time after time during the year of 1814 without coming to agreement. Finally, on Christmas Eve, they found agreeable terms of peace and signed the *Treaty of Ghent*.

Before the news of peace arrived in North America, one more grim battle took place, the Battle of New Orleans, during which 10,000 British veterans were whipped by a force of half as many frontiersmen. Taking up a position that was extremely difficult to assault, the Americans, under a future President, Andrew Jackson, calmly defended themselves as the British wore themselves down in futile attacks.

The Treaty of Ghent clearly indicated that neither side had won the war. All the territory occupied and held at the close of the war was to be returned to its former owner. Thus, boundaries remained as they had been in 1812. So anxious were both governments to reach agreement, that no mention was made of the problems that had originally caused friction between the two nations. The matter of British seamen searching American vessels was ignored, and Indian claims to land in the American west were not discussed.

In terms of men, money and materials, the cost of this tragic struggle cannot be calculated with any degree of accuracy. Official reports suggest that British losses were 8,600

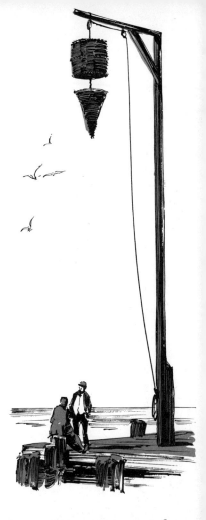

A communication system superior to flag messages was that using a barrel and cone— a large, wicker, basket-like device which was hoisted as shown in the illustration. The distinctive appearance of these objects against the sky made it possible to read signals from considerable distances, wind or no wind. The signal shown here warned: "probability of a heavy gale from an easterly direction." The cone placed above the barrel indicated: "probability of a heavy gale from a westerly direction." The cone alone, pointing downwards, meant: "probability of a gale from an easterly direction." The cone alone, pointing upwards, announced: "probability of a gale from a westerly direction."

killed, wounded and missing, while the Americans suffered a total of about 11,300 casualties. Undoubtedly, there were many more on both sides, since the records kept by many militia units were neither complete nor accurate. Deaths from disease among the regulars, militia and Indians also would add substantially to the above totals.

In Upper Canada, where the hand of war had struck most heavily, a bitter distrust of the United States persisted among the inhabitants for many years. This unfortunate legacy of suspicion proved a serious handicap in the development of goodwill between the two peoples.

**Effects of the war**

Oddly enough, the War of 1812 brought some lasting benefits to British North America; there was a new sense of pride among the people, a pride in having defended their lands with courage and skill. There was, too, a better understanding between French-speaking and English-speaking Canadians, for each race had fought a common foe.

Certain practical advantages resulted from the conflict. Large sums of British money spent in the British provinces on war supplies brought a degree of prosperity previously unknown. In Nova Scotia, additional funds had been gained from the sale to Britain of captured American ships and cargoes. In New Brunswick, merchants had profited by a brisk business in food and other supplies with the blockaded states of New England. In Lower Canada, such towns as Quebec City and Montreal had become prosperous centres of trade and transportation. In Upper Canada, the flow of British funds affected the economy of the province from one end to the other. York recovered rapidly from its misfortunes, and Kingston thrived on the work provided by its busy shipyards. Farmers located near military centres had no trouble in selling their produce at high prices.

It was not realized at the time, but the conflict with the United States was the first step toward the ultimate union of the provinces of British North America. The war had, in effect, forced the provinces to co-operate with one another in the urgent matter of defence. As the Canadian historian, Arthur Lower, says: "It therefore does not seem too far out to say the War of 1812 is one of the massive foundation stones of modern Canada."

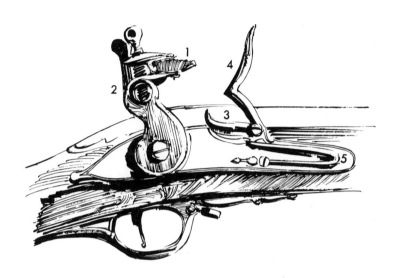

Shown here is the lock mechanism of a famous military weapon, the Brown Bess. At the time of the War of 1812, the Brown Bess was, 150 years after its first introduction, still the standard fire-arm of the British Army. The preparation and operation of the firing mechanism involved the following parts and movements. A flint (1) was held tightly in the clamps of the cocking mechanism (2). The pan (3) was a hollowed-out ledge attached to the musket and connected to the inner barrel by a hole drilled through the metal. The pan was filled with fine gunpowder, which spilled through the hole and came in contact with gunpowder already poured into the barrel during the loading operation. The pan was covered by an L-shaped device, (4), the frizzen, which was lowered over the pan and held tightly in place by a spring (5). When the trigger was pulled, the cock and flint, (2) and (1), snapped forward, striking the frizzen and creating a spark. The spark ignited the powder in the pan, which almost instantaneously ignited the powder in the barrel. The ensuing explosion shot the ball forcibly from the muzzle of the weapon.

During the four years following the War of 1812, the United States and Britain concluded several agreements that have had a lasting effect upon North American history. Since the boundary west of the Great Lakes had never been clearly defined, it was con-

*Settlement of western boundary*

sidered necessary to settle the matter. Both nations agreed that the 49th parallel of latitude was a suitable line of division from the Lake of the Woods to the Rocky Mountains. From there to the Pacific, however, there was cause for dispute. Americans wanted the boundary line to continue westward along the 49th parallel; British traders demanded that it follow the Columbia River southwestward to the ocean. After much discussion, it was eventually agreed that the Americans and the British would jointly occupy the fur country of the Oregon Territory. This arrangement was to last until 1846 when the boundary was shifted north to the 49th parallel, where it has since remained.

**Fishing rights**     Another delicate problem arose out of disputes concerning the fishing grounds of the Atlantic coast. Fishermen in the Maritime provinces claimed that Americans had forfeited their fishing rights because of the War of 1812. Americans, on the other hand, protested that they had been given definite legal rights at the close of the American Revolution. The problem was settled in 1818 by permitting Americans to fish along stretches of the Newfoundland and Labrador coasts. This was the first of a series of agreements that led to peaceful relationships in the fishing industry.

**Rush-Bagot Agreement, 1817**     A third important agreement was arranged in 1817 by the American Secretary of State, Richard Rush, and the British ambassador to Washington, Charles Bagot. This treaty, known as the *Rush-Bagot Agreement,* dealt with disarmament along the international border. The United States and Great Britain agreed that armed vessels should be limited to one apiece on Lakes Champlain and Ontario and a total of two vessels for each nation on all the remaining Lakes.

**Suspicion and ill feeling**     Despite these various agreements and treaties, distrust and suspicion continued to exist between Canadians and Americans. The provinces, fearing other invasions from the south, remained wary of the United States. In fact, this fear was still great enough in 1832 to prompt the British to build Fort Henry, at Kingston. Americans, on the other hand, felt that Great Britain had become a permanent and dangerous foe threatening freedom in North America. The War of 1812 left wounds that were not to heal for many years.

## SUMMARY — SECTION 1

Scarcely had the young provinces of Upper Canada, New Brunswick and Prince Edward Island been established, when British North America became involved with the United States in the War of 1812. The conflict was largely the outcome of ill-feeling between the United States and Great Britain.

In the course of her war with the French Emperor, Napoleon Bonaparte, Britain imposed a naval blockade on Europe. As a direct result, Americans were prevented from trading with European countries. Britain also made a practice of stopping American ships on the high seas and searching them for deserters from the British Navy. These actions angered many Americans, who considered them direct insults to their independence.

On the North American continent itself, American settlers moving into the mid-west came into conflict with Indians who deeply resented being forced off their ancestral lands. The noted chief, Tecumseh, rallied the tribes of the Mississippi valley to oppose the western surge of settlement. After the Americans had routed the Indians at Tippecanoe in 1811, Tecumseh allied his people with the British. The Americans misinterpreted this move as proof of their long-standing suspicion that the British were arming the Indians and encouraging them to harass American settlers.

A group of young American political leaders known as the "War Hawks" urged strong military action against Great Britain. They reasoned that by invading British North America the United States would drive the British from the continent and at the same time acquire vast and valuable new territories. By 1810, the "War Hawks" had gained considerable power in Congress. After only two years in office, their war campaign was successful. In June, 1812, though the nation was ill-prepared and divided, the United States government declared war on Great Britain.

During the first year of conflict, American troops made a brief invasion of Upper Canada in the Detroit region. Shortly afterward, British and Indian forces under General Isaac Brock and Chief Tecumseh captured Detroit. Brock then returned to the Niagara frontier where, in August, he engaged an invading American force at the Battle of Queenston Heights. Although the Americans were defeated, Brock was killed.

In the spring of 1813, an American force captured and looted York, the capital of Upper Canada. The Americans soon left York and made for the Niagara Peninsula, where they seized Fort George (at Newark). This success was followed by defeats at Stoney Creek and Beaver Dams. United States' forces then attacked York a second time and burned Newark itself. Angered by these actions, British and Canadian troops crossed the Niagara River and proceeded to burn and loot on American soil.

On Lake Erie, a British naval squadron was shattered by an American naval force under Captain Perry. This serious defeat left the British and Indian forces along the Detroit River in a dangerous position. As a result, they retreated eastward by way of the Thames River valley. The British and Indians were followed by the Americans and defeated in the Battle of the Thames (at Moraviantown) in which Chief Tecumseh was killed.

Further east, along the St. Lawrence, the Americans were repulsed at Chateauguay and Crysler's Farm. Although these two successes were not outstanding victories and were due, in part, to the blunders of American leaders, they did give considerable encouragement to Canadians.

Early in the third year of war, 1814, American forces raided settlements along the north shore of Lake Erie. Later, the British were defeated at Chippawa. Finally, after the bloody, indecisive Battle of Lundy's Lane, American forces retired to Fort Erie. In the meantime, British naval squadrons had been blockading the eastern coast of the United States. Such cities as Alexandria, Baltimore and Washington were attacked and looted.

On both sides of the Atlantic, people became weary of the useless, costly conflict. After weeks of discussion at Ghent, Belgium, representatives of the American and British governments signed the **Treaty of Ghent** on Christmas Eve, 1814, thus bringing the war to a close.

The War of 1812 brought suffering, bitterness and death, but it also left in its wake certain indirect benefits. The free flow of British money into the provinces for military purposes brought a greater degree of prosperity than had been previously known. The years of conflict also developed a new feeling of confidence among the Canadian people and a pride in their ability to assist in their own defence. These were probably the first, faint feelings of nationalism—a nationalism that was to bear fruit fifty years later in the federation of the British provinces.

# 2

## PIONEER LIFE AND PROGRESS

Isolation and loneliness ▪ Homes in the wilderness ▪ Homes in Lower Canada and the Maritimes ▪ Destruction of the forests ▪ Clearing the land ▪ Methods of agriculture ▪ Importance of wheat ▪ Wood ashes, lye and potash ▪ Maple syrup and maple sugar ▪ Timber rafts and shanty men ▪ Local sawmills ▪ Timber in the Maritimes ▪ Privileged place of the Church of England ▪ The Clergy Reserves ▪ The Methodist circuit riders ▪ Common schools and grammar schools ▪ Roads, stage-coaches, steamships and canals ▪ Early manufactures ▪ The Tories ▪ Democratic feelings among the people ▪ Relations with Great Britain ▪ British control of colonial government.

# 5. Pioneer Homes

EARLY IMMIGRANTS LEAVING Great Britain literally said good-bye Isolation forever to their relatives before crossing the Atlantic to make homes in the Canadian wilderness. Living in tiny clearings carved from the endless forests, they were so completely isolated that it was a fortunate family that could see the distant smoke of a neighbour's chimney. There were few roads, no regular system of transportation, no regular mail service, few newspapers and only the simple entertainments the settlers could devise for themselves. During the long winter months, the sense of loneliness was sharpest; at times, the dim yellow flicker from a cabin window was the only light in miles of black forest. When the temperature sank below zero, when cabin timbers cracked in the frost and wolves howled, the pioneer family must have thought longingly of brighter and happier days.

Even a man who settled only a few miles from York at the Dalziel property on Jane Street (now Pioneer Village, near Toronto) was actually a full day's journey from civilization. In the 1830's, it cost him one dollar to send a letter from York to England, and the letter often took six to ten weeks to reach its destination. Even in Upper Canada at that time it took three days for a letter to go from York to Newark. It was not until Empire penny postage was established in 1851 that a cheap mail service came into existence.

The first home of many a pioneer family was little more than First homes a log shanty twelve to fifteen feet square with a slanting roof and one small window fitted with a sheet of oiled paper to admit light. The chimney, which stood outside one end of the little building, was constructed of mud and sticks. These rough shanties were extremely uncomfortable; in winter, wind blew through the cracks and in wet weather rain leaked through the roof. One early resident of Bruce County said that she often went to bed with an umbrella to keep herself dry and warm.

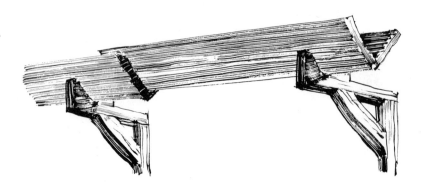

During part of the nineteenth century, even the very eavestroughs placed on roofs were made by the pioneer. The eavestrough was a V-shaped wooden channel, or perhaps a series of overlapping troughs as shown in the illustration. In early dwellings no downspouts were used and rain-water simply spilled to the ground from the ends of the eavestroughs. Shingles, too, were handmade. These were produced by splitting blocks of cedar, ash, pine or even oak. Shingles were very thick and sometimes as long as three feet, thus allowing them to be placed directly on the rafters rather than on a wooden sheathing as is done today. Later in the century, smaller shingles became popular and were widely used.

Inside, the cabin was dark, unfinished and devoid of the simplest comforts. The floor was of split logs, or perhaps bare earth trampled smooth by the feet of the pioneer family. Furniture was of the simplest and most practical design, consisting of homemade benches, perhaps a chair or stool, a rough table and bedsteads made of poles. One cabin, built in 1800, had a flat-topped stump in the centre of the floor that served as a table for the family. A few pioneer cabins boasted a loft or second storey, which was reached by means of a crude ladder. Children in the pioneer household were often required to sleep in the loft.

An important feature of any cabin was, of course, the fireplace, which actually served as furnace and kitchen stove and, in winter,

This illustration is based on a reconstructed log house now located at Upper Canada Village, near Morrisburg, Ontario. A solid building of the period 1830-1840, it was probably the second home a settler would construct. It has a kitchen, two bedrooms, a family room and a sleeping loft upstairs. When the settler became a little more prosperous and could afford a more substantial house, the log structure may have been used by his hired help, perhaps being furnished with articles the farmer no longer needed in his new and larger home. This is the type of house which employed the form of eaves-troughing illustrated on p. 90.

provided light for work and entertainment. A roaring log fire was one thing in the house that provided some definite comfort on winter evenings as members of the family crowded around the cheery hearth. These were perhaps the most pleasant and enjoyable hours that the early settlers spent, for their days were taken up with a heavy round of chores and duties.

**Second homes**   As families established themselves and made progress in land clearing, conditions changed to the point where they were able to erect sturdier and more attractive dwellings of stone, clapboard, stucco or brick. These second homes had a number of rooms, each fitted with glass windows, and containing large, solid fireplaces and better furniture. Chairs, tables, chests and cupboards created at this time are popular items in Canadian antique shops today and are frequently sold to collectors for high prices.

Mr. Michael Sherck of Newark, who wrote under the pen-name "Canuck," has left a fine description of the equipment that went with the fireplaces found in the homes of the more prosperous settlers:

The appurtenances of the well-equipped fireplace were the hand-bellows for blowing the embers into a flame, the tongs, the long-handled shovel, the poker, the spit for roasting fowl over the hot fire, the fire irons (sometimes called fire dogs) for placing the sticks of wood on, so they burned more easily and the fender in front of the fire-place. On the mantel over the fireplace were placed the brass candle-sticks and some of the family bric-à-brac. In the summer time the crickets got into the fireplace and broke the monotony of the evening by their chirping; sometimes they would venture out of their hiding-places on the hearth, when the playful kittens would gambol around and stealthily grab some of them up.

Some inhabitants of Upper Canada were content to have second homes that were no more than improved log cabins, but the majority were anxious to enjoy better accommodation. There was, of course, a great variety of shapes and sizes in the homes constructed in various parts of the province. The settler's country of origin often determined the design and comfort of the home he erected. People who had come from the United States preferred large, white, frame houses. People of Dutch descent took delight in having porches attached to their homes. Irish settlers tended to make their houses as small as the cottages they had left behind them in Ireland.

**Stone and brick**   Fine houses made of limestone were constructed at Kingston, at Bytown (Ottawa) and in other districts. In some areas a second house was actually made from stones removed from the fields. Brick buildings were considered a rarity in early days, although a few structures of this material existed in the province as early as 1790.

After kilns came into operation, brick homes became fairly common in villages and towns.  By the 1830's, brick homes, stores and other buildings were to be found at Port Talbot, in communities bordering the Detroit River, at Brockville, Cobourg, London and York.  However, it was not every town and village that was composed of fine, well-constructed homes.  A traveller of 1830 reports that in a trip along the western end of Lake Erie he found: "The dwelling-houses and farm offices are of the shabbiest kind, and only two brick houses were seen in a distance of twenty-seven miles, passing from Amherstburg round Lake Erie." Brick farm houses in the rural areas of Upper Canada did not become common for another twenty or thirty years.

Most of Upper Canada in the early nineteenth century was little more than a frontier region. While settlement there was just beginning to make important progress, there were other parts of British North America that, by comparison, were well-established. This contrast is shown clearly in the types of buildings and homes in these older areas.

**Homes in Lower Canada and the Maritimes**

In Lower Canada, the habitants lived in their one-storey timber or stone houses on the well-planned seigneuries, while in Montreal and Quebec City there were many substantial buildings and homes of brick or stone that had been built as early as the seventeenth century. A famous example of this type of home is the Château de Ramezay, built in 1705 in Montreal as a residence for the governor.  Today, it serves as a museum.

New Brunswickers and Nova Scotians had also built many attractive homes by this time. In these provinces the forests provided cheap lumber and so most houses were of frame construction, as they are to this day. Such centres as Fredericton, Halifax and Liverpool boasted many spacious, comfortable homes.

Newfoundland was probably closer to Upper Canada in its degree of settlement. Although the town of St. John's had been settled in the sixteenth century, it did not have real roads for more than two hundred years. Even in 1811, St. John's was described as a "tangle of buildings pressing down on the harbour." Along the coast of the colony tiny settlements devoted to sealing and fishing lay snuggled in small coves and inlets. They were completely isolated from each other and depended on ships for all contact with the outside world.

In the first quarter of the nineteenth century, Upper Canada was the new frontier of British North America. While Nova Scotia and Lower Canada had their well-developed towns, the capital of Upper Canada was still ridiculed with the nickname "Muddy York." Nevertheless, in time, hard work was to make areas of Upper Canada as comfortable and as civilized as older sections of British North America.

# 6. *Working the Land*

BUILDING ROADS AND cultivating farms inevitably led to the destruc- tion of valuable timber in British North America. Concerned only with making a home and planting crops, the pioneer viewed the virgin woodland simply as a handicap to be overcome. For most settlers there was neither time nor the means to transport and sell the timber which fell before their axes. Thus, thousands of valuable pine, cedar, oak, walnut and maple trees were cut down and burned.

The virgin forests of one hundred and fifty years ago were composed of seemingly endless expanses of very large trees. Nowhere in eastern Canada today are there stands of trees to give us a true picture of the forests of pioneer days. Only by examining some of the timbers and boards used in old barns, houses and in pieces of early furniture can we appreciate the amazing width and height of the trees. An immense amount of labour was involved in felling these giants and sawing such timber.

Clearing the land was a slow and painful process when the settler worked alone. He might fell all the trees on an acre of land in one week, but to destroy the trunks and branches took much longer. He felt very fortunate indeed if he could clear ten acres in a year.

The settler's first task on his small holding was to clear a small patch of land as quickly as possible and plant crops. But once established, he maintained a regular programme of further clearing. In the fall, he went through the area to be cleared, cutting underbrush, small trees and shrubs. This made it possible to move more easily when the serious business of felling began. During the winter months, the big trees were felled so that they dropped into piles or into long rows called "winrows." In late

47

During the course of the nineteenth century, great improvements were made in agricultural implements. In the earliest years, however, the crudest of ploughs were used, some being little more than pieces of bent oak sheathed in iron, or the natural crooks or roots of trees fitted with iron tips. As the century progressed, iron and then steel were used increasingly until steel eventually replaced wood entirely. Fall fairs, still very much a part of Canadian country life, were held as far back as the 1820's. Ploughing matches, horse-racing and exhibits of fruits, grains and vegetables were some of the interesting events on fall fair programmes.

spring or summer, the "burning" began as fire was put to the fallen trees, or "fallow" as the piles were called. The large pieces of timber that remained after the first burning were cut into lengths, piled up and set afire again. This operation was often accomplished with the help of neighbours in a "logging bee."

Another means of removing trees involved "girdling" or "ringing." By this method, a wide cut was made in the bark around the whole circumference of the trunk, causing the slow death of the tree.

Mrs. Anna Jameson, who in 1838 wrote *Winter Studies and Summer Rambles in Canada,* was saddened by the destruction of the forests. She wrote:

> . . . I cannot look on with indifference, far less the Canadian's exultation, when these huge oaks, these umbrageous elms and stately pines are lying prostrate, lopped of all their honours and piled in heaps with the brushwood, to be fired—or burned down to a charred and blackened fragment—or left standing leafless, sapless, seared, ghastly, having been "girdled" and left to perish.

Not all settlers cleared land through their own efforts or with the help of their neighbours. Those fortunate enough to possess financial means of their own were able to hire "choppers" who cleared land at a price ranging from ten to twenty dollars per acre.

Even when the land was cleared, huge stumps still sank their **Stump removal** thick roots deep into the soil. This condition, however, did not prevent the seeding and the harvesting of crops in the stump-strewn fields. In three to five years time hardwood stumps decayed to the point where they could be pulled out by oxen or burned out by setting fire to them. Pine stumps, however, created a much more difficult problem, for their rate of decay was much slower. They had to be removed by digging, blasting or by using a stumping machine.

Mr. Michael Sherck of Newark has described the manner in which one of these machines operated:

> It was the stumping machine that pulled out all sizes, by means of a screw fastened to a framework placed over the stump and attached to a chain placed around it. Above the machine was a long pole fastened to the screw. A horse hitched to the other end of the screw pole was driven round the machine and elevated the screw, stump and all.

Stumps removed from clearings were often placed in long straight rows to form fences. These stump fences can still be seen in various parts of eastern Canada.

The average settler in Upper Canada had to be satisfied with a modest way of life, for he could not produce surpluses of grain, meat, fruits and vegetables to sell at a profit. While it is true that some industrious farmers who lived near Kingston, York and like centres profited from the ready sale of produce at good prices, most settlers did not share this degree of abundance and prosperity. The average man, in fact, had to be content to provide a plain living for his family.

**Self-sufficiency**

The pioneer was a jack-of-all-trades, for he coped with a variety of tasks. He was farmer, veterinary, butcher, hunter, carpenter, toolmaker, mason and sometimes blacksmith, cabinet-maker and shoemaker. His wife was equally versatile, acting as housewife, nurse, candlemaker, soapmaker, spinner of yarn, weaver of homespun, dressmaker, milliner and tailor. These early families were amazingly self-sufficient, producing most of their daily needs.

**Farming methods**

The basic methods of pioneer agriculture were, by modern standards, unbelievably slow and laborious. Earth was turned over by crude, unwieldy ploughs and broken up by means of wooden harrows fitted with metal teeth. Seed was scattered by hand as the settler strode across his land, a bag of seed suspended by a strap from one shoulder. The first crops were often a field of wheat and peas, with a small patch of potatoes, corn and pumpkins.

Ripened grain was cut with a sickle or with the more efficient cradle. This latter tool was a scythe fitted with wooden ribs that laid the grain in winrows as it fell. A skilled "cradler" was capable of cutting a swath four to six feet in width as he advanced across the field. When the grain had been cut, it was bound by hand into sheaves and then taken away to be threshed.

The actual threshing took place on the barn floor, or on some other surface that was relatively smooth and level. With a flail in hand, the settler pounded the stalks of grain until all the kernels had been threshed from the heads. The flail itself was made of two smooth, straight pieces of hardwood joined together by a leather thong. After threshing, the kernels of grain were still mixed with

This illustration shows a pioneer farmer using a flail. (This was essentially the method of threshing used in Biblical times.) In the early years of the nineteenth century, much grain was also trodden out by horses or oxen, a method even less efficient than the flail. In addition to wheat, which was the principal crop, early settlers successfully grew buckwheat, rye and some oats. Indian corn, too, was widely cultivated in the western parts of Upper Canada. Potatoes and turnips were also grown. Squash proved to be an easily grown crop and was much used as cattle-fodder.

a quantity of chaff which had to be removed. This was accomplished by winnowing—pouring the grain from one container to another while standing outdoors on a windy day. The movement of the wind blew away the light chaff, leaving the kernels of grain in the containers.

Wheat

The soil and climate of Upper Canada proved particularly favourable to growing wheat. Indeed, as the number of farms increased, the production of wheat reached a point where export of the grain to Great Britain became possible. By 1830, Upper Canada had gained an international reputation for the quality of its wheat. In that year, a circular issued by Horatio Gates and Company of Liverpool, England, stated:

The Upper Canada wheat that has come here by the late ships is beautiful, and sales of it have been made as high as 10s. 6d. Sterling per 70 lbs. which is higher by much than any other description of wheat will bring in our market.

Having threshed and winnowed his grain, the Upper Canada settler had it ground into flour. Small hand-mills for this purpose had been supplied by the British government to the United Empire Loyalists, but these machines were slow and rather inefficient. Most men preferred to transport their wheat to the nearest grist-mill. Those who owned horses made the journey more easily than those who had no animals and were forced to carry heavy sacks of grain on their backs. Occasionally, when the settler and the nearest mill were located near navigable water, it was possible to transport grain and flour by canoe or rowboat.

Grist-mills

Different sources of power were used to rotate the huge millstones that did the actual grinding. Some mills, particularly along the Detroit River, were windmills; mills on rivers and streams were water-powered; still others were powered by the labours of horses or oxen. It was not until the middle of the nineteenth century that steam mills came into use.

Soap and Potash

Quite a different by-product of the soil was the light grey ash that remained after logs had been burned. Ashes of the hardwood timber were seldom left in the clearings or in the fireplaces, for they had a definite commercial use. Such ashes were carefully stored away in a dry place until required in the manufacture of soap and potash.

The first step in making soap was to allow water to seep through a bed of wood ashes, thus forming a solution known as "lye." The

Soap, one of the many items that had to be made by the pioneers, was produced outdoors over an open fire. The process involved boiling tallow and lye in large iron kettles. The thick mass that formed after prolonged boiling was poured out, allowed to cool and then cut into bars. The product was known as "soft soap" but "hard soap" could be made simply by adding salt during the boiling. The cleaning properties of these early soaps would compare unfavourably with the modern product.

lye was then heated along with tallow (made from meat fat) in a large kettle over an open fire.

If the pioneer family wanted to make potash, they boiled the lye until it thickened into a dense mass. After cooling, the potash thus formed was made into cakes.

There was a ready market for ashes and potash in most towns and cities in Upper Canada, since many centres had potash-works. Indeed, some families in the early years would have received little "cash money" if it had not been for the regular sale of these two products. As early as 1800, the following advertisement appeared in York:

Ashes wanted. Seven pence, Halifax currency, per bushel for house ashes will be given delivered at the Potash Works (opposite the jail) and five pence, same currency, if taken from the houses; also eight pence, New York currency, for field ashes delivered at the work. It is recommended to those persons who have ashes to be careful in keeping them dry, otherwise they will not be taken. Any quantity will be received at any time by W. Allen, York.

(Both British currency and New York currency were commonly used in Upper Canada at this time.)

Most of the potash produced in Upper Canada was taken by Durham boats, bateaux and timber rafts to Montreal and Quebec City, whence it was shipped to Great Britain for use in industry. The demand for potash in Great Britain became quite marked after an Englishman, John Mercer, discovered in 1844 that cotton material dipped in a potash solution acquired greater strength and an attractive sheen. The treatment of cotton fabrics in this manner later became known as "mercerization." Such mercerized fabrics as cotton broadcloths are still very important British products. Potash, of course, is now produced synthetically.

Maple sugar

Since imported cane sugar was scarce and expensive, the manufacture of maple sugar became a vital operation on the pioneer farm. The process (first learned from the Indians) was basically the same as that employed today, although the early equipment used was much cruder. Wooden tubes were driven into the maple trees and troughs or buckets were used to collect the sap. The sap was then boiled in huge iron kettles suspended over open fires. The process was long and hard, for it took twelve gallons of sap to make one gallon of rich maple syrup.

One Irish servant girl, after seeing the sugar-making operation for the first time, wrote home to a friend:

But what flogged all that I have ever seen, was making sugar out of a tree, Mary—not a word of a lie do I tell you; you take a big gimlet and make a hole in the tree (the *maypole* I think they call it), and out comes the sugar, like sweet water thick like, and you boil it, and you —but where's the use of my telling you anything about it, as you have no sugar trees at home.

It has been estimated that the average amount of maple sugar made in Upper Canada each year during the 1830's was about one hundred pounds per family, although some families produced as much as 1,000 pounds in the course of a season. The manufacture of maple sugar still represents an important activity in this country, because Canadians continue to produce millions of pounds of this product each year.

Although many of the early inhabitants of Upper Canada made their living by farming, there were others who were attracted to the vast forests where they were employed in the timber trade.

# 7. The Timber Trade

DURING THE FRENCH period in North America, the Richelieu River district had been the main lumbering area, but after the conquest of New France—particularly after the arrival of the United Empire Loyalists—lumbering activity shifted to the St. John River area of New Brunswick, the Ottawa River valley, the upper reaches of the St. Lawrence and the eastern end of Lake Ontario. The people of these areas found lumbering more profitable than farming because there was a steady demand in such ports as Halifax, Quebec City and Montreal for squared timber, ships' masts, planks and barrel-staves.

**Lumbering on the Ottawa**

Americans who settled with Philemon Wright on the Ottawa River took such an active interest in the timber trade that lumbering soon became the most important industry in the area. In 1807, their first timber raft was floated down the Ottawa to the St. Lawrence and on to Quebec City, a journey that took thirty-five days. Lumbering expanded so quickly on the Ottawa that sixteen years later there were more than 300 rafts making the journey annually to Quebec City.

Lumbering began in Upper Canada as a family affair, or a co-operative venture started by a few families living close together. However, as time went by, large-scale operations involving numbers of employees became quite common.

**The "shanty men"**

The rugged, agile men who worked in the early lumbering industry were French Canadians, Indians, half-breeds, Scottish Highlanders and a few Irish, English and Americans. They wore heavy grey trousers, flannel shirts, blanket-cloth coats, brightly coloured sashes, knitted wool caps and sturdy leather boots with metal spikes. During the cutting season they lived in large lumber-shanties (hence their name, "shanty men") equipped with bunks built in tiers along the walls. After the day's work, the men spent the evenings singing, card-playing, gambling or dancing to the music of fiddles.

During the winter months, they felled trees and with broad **Squared timber** axes cut the heavy logs into "squared timbers," an operation that required speed, skill and patience. Using only axes, these men transformed heavy round logs into straight, square timbers. It was a wasteful process, of course, because much good wood was chopped away and left to rot in the forest.

During the great nineteenth-century days of lumbering, a number of special log-handling tools were employed—hand-spikes, peavies, and the cant-hook illustrated here. The cant-hook, a metal claw fitted to a wooden handle, was used in rolling logs. It was particularly useful in stowing wet, slippery lumber in the great holds of timber ships. This tool could be adjusted by means of a bolt-and-hole arrangement to handle logs of varying sizes. The timber ships themselves were a special type of vessel with large bow and stern portholes for taking in cargoes of lumber.

Long teams of oxen drew timbers (and trees destined to become **Timber rafts** ships' masts) on massive sleighs to a river where they were tumbled onto its frozen surface. When the ice melted in the spring, the timbers were bound together into "cribs" or rafts, and the exciting journey to Quebec City began. During the warm days of spring, hundreds of these rafts, fitted with flags and sails, could be seen drifting down the Ottawa, moving slowly eastward toward the St. Lawrence.

John McTaggart, who in 1829 wrote *Three Years in Canada,* stated:

On these rafts they had a fire for cooking, burning on a sandy hearth; and places to sleep in, formed of broad strips of bark, resembling the half of a cylinder, the arch about four feet high and in length about eight feet. To these beds or "lairs," handles are attached, so that they can be moved from crib to crib, or from crib to shore as circumstances render it necessary. When they are passing a "breaking-up" rapid they live ashore in these lairs, until the raft is fixed on the still water below.

In later years, wide wooden chutes were constructed at the rapids on the Ottawa River so that rafts, with cookhouses and men aboard, rode smoothly above or alongside the rough waters.

**Rafts on the St. Lawrence** The St. Lawrence River timber rafts were of somewhat different construction from those built on the Ottawa. The St. Lawrence rafts, known as "drams," were tremendous affairs consisting of many layers of timber, so that some rafts drew as much as ten feet of water. Construction of the drams was so complicated and laborious that it sometimes took fifteen men a full month to complete the work. Nails, spikes or chains were not used in the early days to hold the timbers together, this being accomplished with birch or hazel "withes"—slender branches used as ropes. Shanty men travelling on the St. Lawrence were sheltered in wooden cabins rather than in the bark lairs provided on the Ottawa.

After months of winter work in the forests, the shanty men were ready to enjoy themselves on the long journey to Quebec City. They drank, sang and danced as the rafts slid along with the river's current. The behaviour of the shanty men on the long water journeys was often alarming to citizens who lived along the way. At such places as Bytown (Ottawa), the shanty men often stopped off for entertainment. Their favourite forms of pleasure, unfortunately, consisted of drinking, boasting and fighting. Along the rivers, however, there were Irishmen, Scotsmen and French Canadians who were only too happy to accept the freely offered challenges of the swaggering shanty men. These meetings invariably ended in furious brawls and bloody encounters marked by wild punching, butting, scratching, clawing, biting, gouging and kicking. Some of the roughest and toughest of the shanty men who won victories in these cruel fights became famous for their ability to swing fists and boots.

After the rafts reached Quebec City and the timber had been sold, the unmarried shanty men normally remained in town until they had spent their entire wages. Then they were off once again to the dark, silent woods along the Ottawa and the St. Lawrence.

Most timber that arrived in Quebec was put on board ships bound for Great Britain. Often, the ship and its cargo were sold together. Hundreds of ships collected in the busy port solely for the purpose of picking up timber cargoes. Breaking up the log rafts and stowing away the timber aboard the ships required men of skill and experience. F. W. Wallace, author of *Wooden Ships and Iron Men,* writes:

**Timber for Britain**

> Engaged in this work were expert gangs of timber-stowers, mostly Irish, and rough, powerful men who could work like horses throughout the heat of a Canadian summer, and drink and fight with equal ability. These men were variously classed as timber-swingers, hookers-on, holders, porters and winchers.

The timber trade encouraged the establishment of more small sawmills in Upper Canada. As settlement increased, the number of sawmills multiplied at an astonishing rate. So fast was this expansion that, before 1850, Upper Canada alone had almost two thousand sawmills. The owners of these small mills charged settlers a fee for sawing their logs into lumber, or sometimes accepted lumber in payment of their services.

**Sawmills**

There were also in Upper Canada a number of large sawmills that did much more than cut a few logs for local residents. For example, at Hawkesbury on the Ottawa River there was, in 1816, a sawmill employing no less than eighty men. This establishment was manufacturing large quantities of high quality lumber.

Since timber at this time was becoming scarce in the northeastern parts of the United States, there soon arose a demand for Canadian lumber. Export from New Brunswick mills to the

**Maritime timber and shipbuilding**

United States was rather slow in the beginning, but as time went on the trade grew and prospered.

Indeed, in the Maritime provinces timber was just as important as in the two Canadas. Growing shipbuilding industries drew on the vast supplies of timber in the forests of New Brunswick, particularly the famous white pines. Moreover, the Royal Navy bought vast supplies of Maritime timber for use in its shipyards.

Before 1812, most of the ships built in Nova Scotia had been small vessels used for fishing or trading along the coast. However, after the War of 1812, the merchants of the colony became more active in trade with the West Indies, Great Britain and the Mediterranean. For these long distance voyages more and larger ships were needed. Soon, many of the coastal towns of Nova

In the frontier community, early efforts were made to build a mill for the use of the district. At first, a good grist-mill could serve one or two townships until considerable land was under cultivation. Since the majority of mills of the time were water-powered, it was necessary to construct a dam in order to maintain a constant head of water to drive the mill machinery. One method of dam construction is illustrated here. Elm and pine logs were placed in the stream facing into the flow of the water and then other logs, fastened crosswise, were positioned to form a sturdy framework or cribbing. Filled with heavy stones, the cribbing provided the dam with greater weight and solidity. On the right of the illustration, note the timber frame of the "flume," which carried water to the mill-wheel.

Scotia were occupied in building ships and trading on the seas. In fact, shipping was so important to Nova Scotia that the colony's merchant fleet became one of the largest in the world.

# 8. Religion and Education

WHILE THE FRENCH-SPEAKING people of Lower Canada could call on the services of their Roman Catholic parish priests, the English-speaking people of Upper Canada at first had few clergymen to perform religious duties. In 1791, there were only two Protestant clergymen in the entire province, an Anglican and a Presbyterian, both of whom were United Empire Loyalists.

**Privileged position of the Church of England**

While the Church of England was not legally the established or official Church in Upper Canada, it actually enjoyed the privileges that accompanied such status. In England, the monarch was officially head of the Church, and all important posts in government were held by members of the Church of England. In Upper Canada, the situation was very similar. To the Protestant denominations—Presbyterian, Congregational, Baptist and Methodist—the privileged position of the Church of England seemed to be unjustified, particularly since the Anglicans were actually a minority group in the province.

**The Clergy Reserves**

The Constitutional Act of 1791 had provided that one-seventh of the land in each township would be reserved "for the support and maintenance of a Protestant clergy." Lands set aside for this purpose came to be known as the *Clergy Reserves.* (These blocks of unoccupied, unworked lands were to be kept for sale or rental at a time when the improvement of surrounding lands had increased the value of the Clergy Reserves.) It was unfortunate that the wording of the Act was not more definite, for in later years the term "Protestant clergy" was to be interpreted in several ways.

Such prominent Anglican leaders as the Reverend John Strachan stoutly maintained that the Clergy Reserves were intended for the Church of England alone. In 1822, the Presby-

62

terians of Upper Canada demanded a share of the income from the Reserves on the ground that the Church of Scotland (Presbyterian) had been recognized as an established Church in the Act of Union of 1707 between England and Scotland. The other Protestant denominations later claimed a share, arguing that the Clergy Reserves had been intended for the benefit of all Protestant denominations.

By 1825, there were no less than two million acres of land in Upper Canada that had been withheld from settlement and marked on maps as being part of the Clergy Reserves. This situation caused increasing dissatisfaction and even bitterness among the religious bodies of the province.

**The Methodists**

Despite the fact that the Church of England enjoyed revenues from the Reserves and other special privileges (such as the sole right to perform marriage ceremonies), it showed little growth in comparison with some Protestant denominations. Government officials, military officers and well-to-do citizens tended to be Anglicans, while many humble settlers, particularly those from the United States, were Methodists. Many settlers from Scotland were Presbyterians and many from Ireland were Roman Catholics.

**Lay preachers and circuit riders**

Among the Americans there was a large group of Methodists, a number of whom were eager, aggressive preachers. These Methodist clergymen did not wait for churches to be established before beginning their religious duties. Like the Jesuit priests of former years, they travelled widely, visiting homes and holding religious services wherever they could. Some of them, known as "circuit riders," travelled on horseback on a more or less regular route among the small settlements. In addition to these clergymen, the Methodist Church used "lay preachers"—persons who delivered sermons and performed some of the duties ordinarily conducted by ministers. Some of the lay preachers were rough, uneducated men, but they gave religious leadership and comfort to the pioneers.

Hundreds of settlers in the backwoods actually had no contact with religious life other than that provided by the circuit riders

The Methodist circuit rider often travelled as many as forty or fifty miles between appointments, enduring hardships that now seem incredible. Travelling in all manner of weather through forests and fording streams and rivers, these riders frequently carried their few worldly possessions in saddle-bags. When they finally arrived at a community, the place of worship was often a house, a barn, a school or a tavern—and in rare cases, a church. Many a circuit rider was responsible for the religious welfare of communities scattered throughout hundreds of square miles of territory.

and the lay preachers. Indeed, a large number of inhabitants lacked any religious guidance in their lives; children were denied the blessing of baptism and the dead were buried without receiving funeral rites.

It was probably the simple language, the fiery sermons and the devout behaviour of the Methodist preachers that won the respect of the settlers. One well-to-do citizen, who was himself a member of the Church of England, wrote in a letter:

The Methodist dissenters have obtained an ascendency over our infant population. Their habits of home visitation, their acquaintance with the tastes and peculiarities of the Canadians, their readiness to take long fatiguing rides in the discharge of their self-imposed labours, render them formidable rivals to our own more easy-going clergy.

The same writer went on to state that many residents of Upper Canada, accustomed to the free-and-easy life of pioneering society, were impatient with the more elaborate form of worship of the Church of England. A few were opposed to the Anglican ceremony of marriage. According to the writer, one young woman of Upper Canada walked out in the middle of a wedding because she refused to promise that she would "obey" her husband-to-be.

Many of the Methodist lay preachers were greatly admired and loved by those among whom they worked. For example, a witty Irishman, "Uncle Joe" Little, who for many years served as a lay preacher in Lambton County, travelled about on a sturdy little Indian pony called Toby. This intelligent animal understood his master's habits, especially his custom of stopping to talk with everyone he met along the road. On meeting a person, Toby would stop automatically and Uncle Joe would say, "See that! Toby knows every sinner he meets!" This expression became well-known throughout the county and caused much amusement among the people.

While it is true that the number of clergymen of all denominations in Upper Canada increased with the passing of years, progress was slow. (By 1820, there were still less than one hundred Protestant clergymen.)

It was fortunate for Upper Canada that the Loyalists and later **Education** immigrants from the United States brought with them a concern for education. This concern, however, was not the same vital interest that people today display in education. There was no compulsory school attendance, no means of training teachers, no supplies of textbooks and no property taxation to support schools.

At this time in Great Britain and in European countries, there **Education in** was little serious thought given to the idea that the government **Britain** was responsible for the provision of education. The Church and the home, it was believed, held full responsibility in this regard. Children from wealthy families were taught at home by tutors or attended private schools. The children of poor people attended church schools, Sunday Schools or charity schools supported by various organizations. Many children actually had no educational opportunities of any kind.

Before the manufacture of cheap paper and copy-books, the most common writing surface was slate (still used for school blackboards today). Cut into small rectangles and mounted within wooden frames, two slates hinged together formed the "book" shown here. School pupils employed slender pencils of slate with which to write on the smooth, black surface.

**Common schools**

At the beginning of the nineteenth century, conditions in Upper Canada were somewhat similar. The only local elementary schools or common schools that existed had been established through the efforts of the people themselves, who erected the building, hired the teacher and paid "rates" to provide his salary. All of this was accomplished without any aid from the government of the province.

Leaders of the Church of England in Upper Canada hoped to transplant the authority of the Church in education to the provinces and, in the beginning, they enjoyed considerable success. The influential, wealthy or aristocratic people who rose to power in government were members of the Church of England. These Anglican leaders in Upper Canada took an early interest in the

Some of the earliest schools were simply a room or a section of the local school-master's home, equipped with a few supplies—maps, books, copy-books, slates, benches and perhaps a globe. When a school was built, it was often a plain, small building, such as the one illustrated here. In small communities, these buildings were constructed as cheaply as possible—often of logs—with small windows cut in the walls as shown above. As the century progressed, frame, brick and even stone structures became common, frequently reflecting the building method favoured in the community.

development of schools and universities. However, members of the ruling class were concerned solely with the provision of education for boys of wealthy and influential families—boys going into the professions, business or government service. It is not surprising then that an act, passed in 1807 in Upper Canada, set the stage for the creation of district grammar schools (high schools) that were **Grammar schools** to be assisted by government grants. Such schools were of value only to the well-to-do families; the poor could not afford to pay the fees which were charged, nor could they pay the expenses of children living away from home.

It was not until nine years had passed that another act provided government aid to local common schools. This act did not make the provision of such schools a compulsory matter, nor did it give much real financial help to local communities.

These first common schools were pathetic little buildings—dark, crowded, cold and uncomfortable. School attendance was irregular, for children were kept on the farm whenever their help was required. In winter, when farm work was less pressing, older boys and girls, eighteen to twenty years of age, swelled the enrolment of the tiny schools.

In the early years of the nineteenth century, school benches and desks were of local design and construction. They were solid, sturdy and functional, but gave very little consideration to the comfort of pupils. Many of the desks were designed to seat more than one pupil, as in the case of the one shown here. Later in the century, single desks became common and these were produced by manufacturers of school equipment. Such desks had cast-iron legs and supports. Most schools were heated by an iron stove of some sort, and somewhere in the classroom there was usually a convenient pile of firewood. Mr. Canniff Haight, a nineteenth-century writer, who as a boy attended a small school in the 1830's, states in his memoirs: *We were closely packed together and were either shivering with the cold or being cooked by the red-hot stove.*

Teachers, for the most part, were poorly educated people who had received no professional training; few of them possessed any natural ability to teach. Some were crippled soldiers, some were drunkards, some were men in poor health and some were mere wanderers. Only a very few communities were fortunate enough to secure able, devoted teachers who worked miracles under difficult conditions.

Perhaps the most noted of the early teachers was the Reverend John Strachan, who has already been mentioned in connection with Glengarry and with the Clergy Reserves. Strachan began his career in Upper Canada by establishing a grammar school at Cornwall. After moving to York, this brilliant teacher and clergyman became the first Anglican Bishop of Toronto and for years played a vital rôle in the religious and educational life of the province. *The Reverend John Strachan*

Strachan shared the same view on education that was held by the upper and ruling classes of the province—that the Church of England should be in complete control of education. To this end, Strachan supported the Anglican claim to the Clergy Reserves, the maintenance and expansion of the grammar school system and the establishment of a college of higher learning, King's College (later, the University of Toronto). Being a Bishop of the Church of England and an influential member of the provincial government, Strachan became a very powerful and important figure. Until nearly 1840, he dominated the educational policies of the provincial government.

The attitude of the majority of settlers in Upper Canada was directly opposed to the aims of education advocated by Bishop Strachan. Popular sentiment would not accept grammar schools created for the privileged few and would not accept a form of education controlled by the Church of England. The inhabitants of the province continued to criticize a government that at times was willing to spend nine times as much money on grammar schools as it did on common schools. However, the real fight for equality of education lay some years ahead. *Popular opposition to privileged education*

# 9. Stage-coach, Steamship and Canal

**Roads**

THE ROADS THAT had been built under the direction of Governor Simcoe, Colonel Talbot and the Canada Company gradually acquired additions and side branches leading to newer settlements. In 1816, Montreal and Kingston were finally connected by road; the following year, this link was extended to York. Of course, such a road was vastly different from the highway now joining the above-mentioned cities. Those early roads were little more than forest tracks, with surfaces far worse than even that of a present-day gravel road. In particularly bad stretches the pioneer roads were "paved" with logs laid side by side across the road in a fashion known as "corduroy." Crude paving of this type may have increased the solidity of the surface, but it did very little toward making travel more comfortable.

**Stage-coaches**

Other road-building developments east of Upper Canada were progressing so well that, by 1827, it was possible (if the passenger could endure it) to travel all the way from Halifax, Nova Scotia, to Amherstburg on the Detroit River. Indeed, by 1837, even greater improvement had taken place in Nova Scotia itself, and Joseph Howe, the famous Nova Scotia newspaperman and politician, was able to write with pride of the changes made in ten years:

> Had any one told them, ten years ago, when Hamilton used to carry the mail on horseback, from Halifax to Annapolis, and sometimes in a little cart, with a solitary passenger beside him, who looked as if he was going to the end of the world, and expected to pay accordingly, that they should have lived to see a Stage Coach, drawen by four horses, running three times a week on the same road . . . would they have believed?

When travelling outside the larger centres, people were dependent upon the services of small country or wayside inns and taverns. Accommodation in these hostelries varied from excellent to indescribably bad, the average being rather poor. John Howison, a celebrated traveller of the 1820's, wrote: *Most of the taverns in Upper Canada are a burlesque — a tolerable meal can scarcely be procured at any one of them; nay, I have visited several which were not even provided with bread. It is immaterial what meal the traveller calls for, as the same will be set before him morning, noon and night.* However, they were all fairly inexpensive. For example, in 1832, the best hotel in Cobourg, Upper Canada, charged $2.50 per week for accommodation, which included three meals a day.

Travel in Upper Canada was marked by hardship and sometimes by danger, for occasionally passengers were injured or killed when wagons, sleighs or coaches overturned. Winter travel was actually swifter and more pleasant than that of other seasons, because it was only in cold weather that the roads were relatively smooth. In summer, people preferred to travel by water if possible.

Although stage-coaches were operating in the Niagara region in the 1790's, it was some years before they became common on the roads of Upper Canada. By 1808, some coaches were moving over limited sections of the road between Kingston and Montreal. The first Kingston to York stages operated in 1817. During the next ten to fifteen years, scheduled stage routes were created between York and London, York and Detroit, York and Newark and a few other centres.

Until about 1830, the so-called stage-coaches were little more than crude wagons or sleighs with a light covering to protect passengers from rain, wind and snow. A British army officer who travelled in one of these vehicles declared it was "one of the roughest conveyances on either side of the Atlantic." During the 1830's and 1840's, more elaborate, graceful and comfortable coaches made their appearance on the roads. One description of such a coach states:

> It was strongly built, the carriage part of it adapted to go through rough roads if necessary. The body was closed at the front and back and covered with a stout roof. The sides were open, but protected by curtains that could be let down if rain came on; there was a door at each side fitted with a sliding window that could be lowered or raised as the weather was fine or stormy. There were three seats inside. . . . Outside there was the driver's seat and another immediately behind it on the roof; each of these would hold three persons. . . . The coach body, including the baggage-rack, was suspended on strong leather straps, which were stretched on the elaborate framework of the carriage. The whole affair was gaudily painted, and, with its team of four fine horses, looked very attractive and was by no means an unpleasant mode of travelling when the roads were good and the weather fine.

**Steamships**　　Progress was being made, too, in water travel. An American citizen, Robert Fulton, developed the first successful steamship in North America, the famous *Clermont,* which operated on the Hudson River in 1807. Two years later, the second steamboat on this continent was built by the Honourable John Molson of **The Accommodation, 1809** Montreal. This Canadian craft, known as the *Accommodation,* was a paddle-wheeler, seventy-two feet in length. On her maiden voyage, she left Montreal on a Wednesday afternoon and arrived at Quebec City on the Saturday morning. She chugged along at a rate of about four and a half miles an hour and tied up at night, for she was not equipped with navigation lights. The return journey, however, took better than a week since the six-horsepower engine had considerable difficulty with the river's current. At one point, teams of oxen had to be employed to drag the *Accommodation* through a particularly rough stretch of water.

Molson then realized that, to be effective on the St. Lawrence, steamships had to be larger and equipped with more powerful engines. By 1818, his company had no less than six craft in operation, chiefly between Quebec City and Montreal. These vessels were most useful in transporting large numbers of immigrants who arrived at Quebec City bound for Upper Canada.

In the meantime, the first steamship to sail the Great Lakes, the *Frontenac,* was constructed on the Bay of Quinte and put into operation on Lake Ontario. This vessel was equipped with sail as well as two steam-driven paddle wheels. A Scotsman, John Howison, who in 1818 travelled on the *Frontenac* from Kingston to York, was very pleased with the journey:

**The Frontenac, 1818**

> I could not but invoke a thousand blessings on the inventors and improvers of the steamboat for the delightful mode of conveyance with which their labours have been the means of furnishing mankind. It required some recollections to perceive that I was not in the Kingston hotel.

Under such conditions as those described by Mr. Howison, it is not surprising that travellers preferred to journey by water instead of bouncing about in a stage-coach.

In 1823, the steam tug *Hercules* was built to tow ocean-going sailing ships from Quebec City to Montreal. This daring venture proved so successful that, in following years, more and more ocean vessels dropped anchor at Montreal.

**The Hercules, 1823**

Other steamships were constructed and put into operation, but it was not until the 1830's that the age of steam was in full swing. Small steam vessels made their appearance on the Detroit River, Lake St. Clair and the St. Clair River, some of them making regular runs between Detroit and Sarnia.

Early steamships used wood as fuel and, since wood burned rapidly, they had to make frequent stops to replenish their supply of fuel. Wood was cut by local farmers during the winter and piled at convenient places along the lakes and rivers. Mr. Victor Lauriston, in *Lambton's Hundred Years,* writes:

> In the great days of wood-burning steamboats, both banks of the St. Clair were dotted with wood-docks. Practically every concession line had its dock. The farmers had to clear the land; they needed the money; the steamboats needed fuel.
>
> Steamboats in 1836 were estimated to have burned 150,000 cords of wood valued at $250,000, and this was only the beginning of a traffic that steadily increased to a peak in 1870.
>
> Mostly, the general stores located on the river at the ends of the roads. Merchandise was brought in by boat; the storekeepers took wood from the farmers at $1 to $1.50 a cord in payment for supplies; and in turn sold to the steamers at $3 against the freight on goods brought in. With tugs or through steamers, the wood sales were for cash.

**The Royal William, 1833**

Canadians played no small part in the development of steam travel. In 1833, a Canadian ship built at Quebec City, the *Royal William,* was the first vessel to cross the Atlantic Ocean using only steam-power. A description of the famous vessel reads:

> The *Royal William* is rigged like a three-masted schooner with three square sails on her foremast, besides large fore-and-aft sails. Her masts are as lofty as those of a vessel of three hundred tons. Her upper deck is fitted with upwards of fifty ample berths and a large parlour. In a round house on deck is a spacious dining-room. The whole . . . is fitted with an elegance and taste of the best style.

One of the owners of the *Royal William,* Samuel Cunard, of Halifax, secured contracts in 1839 to carry mail by steam vessels from Great Britain to Halifax and Boston. Thus was born a famous British company, the Cunard White Star Line, which has become one of the leading steamship companies of the world.

Sailing vessels, of course, did not disappear with the first coming of steam craft. They actually continued in service, in diminishing numbers, for about one hundred years. (It is interest-

Travelling on the deck of an early, wood-burning steamship was often a dirty, unpleasant experience. The furnace belched great clouds of thick, black smoke, which often enveloped the deck below. Although the steamship *Accommodation* shown here could carry twenty passengers, only ten persons were bold enough to undergo her first passage to Quebec City. They each paid a fare of $8.00. The return fare to Montreal was $9.00, a small difference considering the additional days needed for the return trip against the strong currents of the St. Lawrence River.

ing to note that two sailing ships were carrying grain from Australia to Europe as late as 1949.)

Inland navigation was seriously handicapped by rapids in the St. Lawrence River, and, of course, by the great falls of the Niagara River. Early in the nineteenth century, it became obvious **Canals** that if canals were built to bypass these obstacles, it would be possible to sail freely from the Atlantic Ocean to the southern reaches of Lake Michigan.

**The Lachine Canal, 1825**

A good start was made between the years 1818 and 1825, when a canal eight and a half miles long was constructed around the Lachine Rapids just west of Montreal. By modern standards, it was a small canal, one designed to accommodate vessels of no more than four and a half feet draught.

**The Welland Canal, 1829**

By 1829, a second waterway project, the Welland Canal, was completed, making it possible for ships to travel around Niagara Falls. This canal linked Port Dalhousie on Lake Ontario with the village of Port Robinson (near the present-day city of Welland), at which place the waterway joined the Welland River flowing into the Niagara and thence to Lake Erie. A newspaper in St. Catharines commented:

> Saturday was a proud day for St. Catharines; and indeed for Upper Canada. A scene was witnessed within its borders, that will long be held in remembrance by the active friends and steady supporters of the splendid plans of internal improvement now in progress in this section of the colony—the free and uninterrupted passage of the first loaded vessel that ever floated on the waters of the Welland Canal, from this village to Lake Ontario, a distance of five miles of artificial steam boat navigation . . . It was a matter of sincere regret that the projector of this great work, William Hamilton Merrit, was not present —being now in London endeavouring to procure the necessary means for its completion to Lake Erie; and there can be little doubt but his efforts will be crowned with success.

**The Rideau Canal, 1832**

Mr. Merrit was successful. In the 1830's, the Welland Canal was extended all the way to Lake Erie.

The third important waterway project of this period was the Rideau Canal, which made possible a water route from Kingston to Bytown on the Ottawa River. The cost of this endeavour, completed in 1832, was borne by the British government. The Rideau Canal provided an alternate route between Upper and Lower Canada, a route that would be less exposed to attack in wartime than the St. Lawrence River.

It is interesting to note that Colonel John By, a Royal Engineer, Bytown was in charge of the construction of the Rideau Canal. The place where his workers set up headquarters in 1826 was named Bytown. The town was literally an enormous work camp filled with more than 2,000 workers. Bytown soon became the most important lumbering centre on the Ottawa River, a wild, crude, colourful place with muddy streets and noisy taverns. No one at the time suspected that this unlikely spot would eventually become the capital of a nation.

Early Canadian canal development was an astonishing achievement for provinces so thinly populated and so poor financially. In terms of money and labour alone, the successful completion of canals was a remarkable feat. It was unfortunate that Canadians of the time could not know that, within a relatively short time, railways were to replace canals as the major means of transportation.

It should be noted that during this period the American people Canal-building in the United States also became keenly interested in water transport. Between 1820 and 1837, thousands of miles of canals were built. The most famous of the new artificial waterways was the Erie Canal, completed in 1825, joining Lake Erie and the Hudson River. By using the Great Lakes, the Erie Canal and the Hudson River, it was possible for ships of a certain draught to travel all the way from Chicago to New York City.

In addition to the important achievements that had been made Early manufactures in travel and transportation, progress was also being made in manufacturing. Although lumber, potash and whisky were being produced, items of a more complicated nature were making an appearance. In the early 1830's, paper was being manufactured at Belleville. At York, the York Foundry and Steam Engine Manufactory was turning out tin goods, ploughs, wheels and steamship engines. This company employed eighty men and utilized about one ton of iron per day. According to the Montreal *Gazette,* there was no better industrial establishment anywhere in the provinces of British North America. By 1834, the firm of Evans, Mills and Millar was making "as substantial and beautiful carriages as can

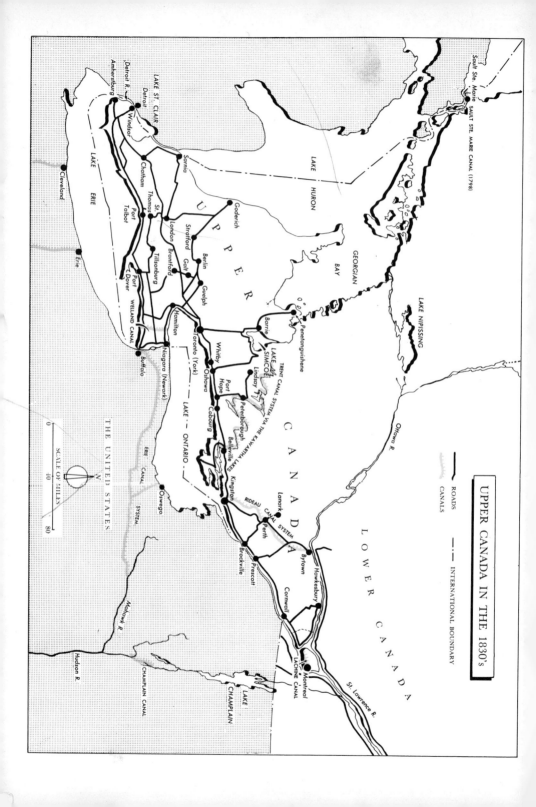

UPPER CANADA IN THE 1830's

ROADS ————————
CANALS —·—·—·—
INTERNATIONAL BOUNDARY

SCALE OF MILES
0    40    80

THE UNITED STATES

UPPER CANADA

LOWER CANADA

Sault Ste. Marie
SAULT STE. MARIE CANAL (1798)

LAKE HURON

GEORGIAN BAY

LAKE NIPISSING

Ottawa R.

Cleveland
Erie
LAKE ERIE
ERIE CANAL SYSTEM
Oswego
Mohawk R.
Hudson R.

LAKE ST. CLAIR
Detroit R.
Amherstburg
Detroit
Windsor
Chatham
Thomas
Port Talbot
St. Thomas
London
Sarnia
Goderich
Stratford
Galt
Berlin
Guelph
Brantford
Tillsonburg
Port Dover
WELLAND CANAL
Hamilton
Niagara (Newark)
Buffalo

Toronto (York)
Whitby
Oshawa
Port Hope
Cobourg
Barrie
LAKE SIMCOE
Lindsay
Peterborough
Penetanguishene
TRENT CANAL SYSTEM VIA THE KAWARTHA LAKES
Belleville
Kingston
LAKE ONTARIO

Lanark
Perth
RIDEAU CANAL SYSTEM
Bytown
Hawkesbury
Brockville
Prescott
Cornwall
Montreal
LACHINE CANAL
St. Lawrence R.
LAKE CHAMPLAIN
CHAMPLAIN CANAL

N

be manufactured anywhere." The carriages must have won approval; in 1835, one of them was ordered for the use of the Anglican Bishop of Quebec.

Promising though manufacturing may have been in Upper Canada, it was not as far advanced as in Lower Canada, where paper, leather, glass, wool, rope, stoves and steam-engines were being produced. Upper Canada, by contrast, was still an undeveloped province.

# 10. Government and People

PEOPLE IN THE British provinces of North America had mixed feelings about the United States. Their attitude was a peculiar blend of antagonism, suspicion, envy and admiration.

People of Loyalist stock still retained bitter memories that went all the way back to the American Revolution—memories of insults, injuries, ruined homes and lost fortunes. Of course, there were more recent and vivid memories from the War of 1812—the pillage of York and the raids along the Erie shore. The loss of lives, the destruction of property and the terrible cost of war, all remained fixed in Canadian memories—particularly among many people who lived in Upper Canada.

Canadians felt a pride in the successful defence of their lands, and this pride encouraged a new sense of unity, a stirring of Canadianism that, in time, was to become a strong force. A fresh sense of confidence, however, did not lessen the suspicion of the United States. There was a very real dread that a second armed conflict might again flare up. Although this feeling of uneasiness persisted, there was no actual hatred of Americans.

**The Tories**  Unfortunately, there was one group of Canadians, the Tories, as they were called, who found it useful to stir up anti-American feeling. The Tories were devoted to British traditions—an aristocratic society, the establishment of the Church of England as the official Church and firm government control. They believed that a governor and the advisers he appointed (the Executive Council) should play a prime rôle in the management of provincial affairs. There was no reason, in their opinion, for granting authority to the assemblies elected by the people of the provinces. British traditions, according to the Tories, could only be maintained by placing government firmly in the hands of a few, educated, aristocratic gentlemen.

80

As more and more land was cleared and settled, property boundaries became a definite problem. The original surveys rarely marked anything more than the frontal limits of a property—often on the road allowance—and left other boundaries to be marked by the settler himself. As settled regions became more populous, disputes inevitably arose over boundaries between neighbouring farms. Disagreements over the proper location of fences sometimes lasted for years. So many disputes of this kind occurred in Upper Canada that, in 1834, an act was passed establishing the official position of "fence viewer." According to the act, these officials were "fit and discreet persons" appointed to investigate boundary disputes and to determine how and where fences should be built. They often also decided the quality and the type of fence to be used and even the date by which it had to be erected. Fence viewers also possessed authority to determine the positioning and construction of drains. They were usually paid two dollars a day, which, considering the power and the responsibility they held, was a small sum even for those days.

Since the Tories were so much concerned with the rule of the chosen few in government, they feared American democracy in which the people elected representatives with power to govern. For these reasons, any demand by Canadians for reform was condemned as being dangerous American thought, a form of dis-

Tory suspicions of the United States

loyalty to the British crown. By raising this constant cry of disloyalty, the Tories frightened many inhabitants into accepting the situation as it was. Indeed, so vigorously did the Tories seek out and condemn American influences that bitterness against the United States lasted long after it should have waned.

**Democratic feelings among Canadians**

It is true that some demands for change in government were prompted by a knowledge of conditions in the United States, but Canadians who wanted improvements were not necessarily disloyal. Those persons who had emigrated from the United States to find new homes in the British provinces found it difficult to accept some of the British practices. They had grown accustomed to certain freedoms, rights and responsibilities. Many of them had come from districts where the people enjoyed a definite say in government. Frequently, they—through their elected representatives—had created laws for good roads, transportation facilities and schools for their children. In British North America, they found good land and opportunities for success, but they could not help feeling that this was far from everything they should have.

Those who came from the United States were by no means the only persons who desired changes in the Canadian way of life. There were also Scots, Irish, English and French Canadians who believed that too much power in government was being wielded by the privileged few.

**Relations with Great Britain**

The inhabitants of the British provinces found themselves in a colonial society that was largely dependent upon Great Britain. This close connection did offer both advantages and disadvantages.

Without Britain, the provinces were neither large enough nor strong enough to defend themselves against a powerful enemy. It was very comforting to know that the British Army and the Royal Navy were prepared to protect Canadians.

In addition to the advantage of military protection, Great Britain provided the provinces with trade opportunities. Canadian wheat, timber, flour, potash and furs found a ready British market, while British manufactured goods were welcomed in the provinces. Without this steady, dependable trade, British North America might have developed at a very much slower pace.

In government, the provinces were almost wholly dependent upon Great Britain, for it was the British Colonial Office that made decisions on provincial matters. British governors represented the reigning monarch in the provinces and carried out the decisions of the Colonial Office. British control of colonial government

Due to the bitter lesson of the American Revolution, Great Britain considered it very necessary to rule her colonies with a firmness she had not used in former years. It was now considered a mistake to allow colonies to develop on their own and to create governments to solve their own particular problems. There was a definite British fear that, unless colonies were well supervised, they would soon demand independence and break away from the British Empire—just as the United States had done.

There is no doubt that the form of government imposed upon the provinces offered the advantages of stability and continuity. Canadians could count upon receiving the guidance of men, some of whom had already proven themselves as skilful leaders. There was little danger of sudden upsets in government or of dictators rising to power.

Unfortunately, the system of government in the provinces proved to be too rigid for the desires of many Canadians. This was by no means the fault of the British authorities only; some of the blame can be placed upon ambitious Canadian Tories who rose to high office in provincial governments. However, British officials could not see, or refused to recognize, the growing tide of popular anger. In time, there was to be a bitter struggle for responsible government, government in which the people could play some part as law-makers.

## SUMMARY — SECTION 2

The first settlers in Upper Canada lived a lonely, isolated life, often separated from their nearest neighbours by considerable distances. They enjoyed none of the modern means of communication, and what roads existed were little more than tracks worn by horses and carts.

The first pioneer homes were, in most cases, small log cabins fitted with the crudest of furniture. After families had established themselves, they erected more comfortable, substantial structures of clapboard, stone, stucco or brick.

For some years, a major portion of the pioneer's time and energy was absorbed in the task of clearing land in order to plant crops. Pioneer agriculture was a laborious, tiring occupation carried out with the simplest of tools. Nevertheless, Upper Canada proved to be such a fine wheat-producing region that, by 1830, the province's wheat was earning a high reputation in European markets.

Most settlers had neither time nor opportunity to sell the timber they cut while clearing their lands, but in those districts close to large rivers or lakes lumbering became an imporant industry. In the early years of the nineteenth century, this was particularly true of districts along the Ottawa River, the upper St. Lawrence and the eastern end of Lake Ontario. Each spring, great timber rafts, guided by shanty men, could be seen floating down to Quebec City. At that busy port, hundreds of sailing ships gathered to load cargoes of timber for Great Britain.

Gradually, transportation and communication were improved. Pioneer roads were extended and new sections constructed. By 1827, it was possible to travel from Halifax, Nova Scotia, to Amherstburg in Upper Canada. On these roads appeared an increasing number of stage-coaches, which provided a rough and ready method of travel. By the 1830's, sailing ships on the St. Lawrence River and the Great Lakes were facing competition from wood-burning steamships. Indeed, it was a Canadian ship, the **Royal William,** that in 1831 was the first vessel to cross the Atlantic using only steam-power.

Another remarkable improvement in transportation was achieved by the construction of canals, usually built to by-pass rapids, falls and stretches of shallow water. Between 1818 and 1825, the Lachine Canal was built to circumnavigate the Lachine Rapids of the St. Lawrence River. By 1830, the construction of the Welland Canal made it possible for ships to travel around Niagara Falls. A third canal, the Rideau, completed in 1832, linked Kingston with Bytown (Ottawa).

The development of manufacturing was rather slow in Upper Canada, but by the mid-1830's some progress was evident; paper was being made at Belleville, and several firms at York were turning out tin goods, ironware, ploughs, wheels, carriages and engines for steamships. In the older colony of Lower Canada, a wider variety of manu-factured goods was being produced.

Education in all the provinces progressed rather slowly. The pro-vision of schools and schooling was usually left to the Church of England, with the result that it was often only children belonging to wealthy or influential families who received the benefits of a full education. The people were forced to establish their own common schools, aided by small grants of money from provincial treasuries. It was not until the 1840's and the 1850's that serious attempts were made to create public education systems. In addition, since many people were not Anglicans, there was considerable opposition to the privileged position of the Church of England in the provinces.

After the War of 1812, the people of the provinces remained sus-picious of the United States. However, there was no real hatred of the American people, and, indeed, there was a certain admiration for the democratic trend in American government and the economic prosperity of the neighbour to the south. Those in particular who had emigrated from the United States felt that the provinces might well copy some American practices. The people of the British provinces in North America felt a strong attachment to Great Britain, but they were not altogether satisfied with the form of colonial government imposed by the mother country. Many persons thought that the governors and their Tory advisers wielded too much power. They felt that the inhabitants of British North America, even with their legislative assemblies, had little real voice in the operation of government. Canadian Tories, on the other hand, were opposed to any movement not British in origin and condemned as disloyal any suggestion of support for the "radical" and "democratic" ideas of the American people. Nonetheless, the signs of failure were already present in colonial government. Before long, the Tories were to be rudely shocked by a bitter struggle for improved government.

# 3

## THE NORTH-WEST, 1800-1860

Lord Selkirk's purchase of Assiniboia ▪ The Métis ▪ Establishment of the Selkirk Settlement in the Red River valley, 1812 ▪ The "Pemmican Proclamation" ▪ Attack on Fort Douglas ▪ Destruction of Fort Gibraltar ▪ Massacre at Seven Oaks, 1816 ▪ Seizure of Fort William by Lord Selkirk ▪ Rebuilding the Selkirk Settlement ▪ Death of Selkirk, 1820 ▪ Rivalry in the fur trade ▪ Union of the North West Company and the Hudson's Bay Company, 1821 ▪ Governor George Simpson.

# 11. The Selkirk Settlement

THE FIRST IMPORTANT attempt to establish a settlement in what Lord Selkirk is now western Canada was made by a Scottish nobleman, Thomas Douglas, fifth Earl of Selkirk. This wealthy, well-educated, young man became absorbed by the plight of the hundreds of poor Scottish crofters who had been evicted from their small holdings by greedy landowners who were converting their estates into profitable sheep ranges. The situation of many persons in the Scottish cities was little better, for the growth of large factories was causing unemployment among those who had been operating small businesses. To the youthful earl, the suffering he saw in his native land was so disturbing that he determined to seek some means of assisting his less fortunate countrymen.

Selkirk had read with pleasure and excitement the journals of First attempts at settlement Alexander Mackenzie describing the explorer's travels in the North-West. It struck him that the western prairies might very well be the place to found a Scottish colony. In 1802, he tried to interest the British government in a scheme of settlement in what is now southern Manitoba, but the area was considered too remote for the purpose. In consequence, between 1803 and 1809, Selkirk promoted colonizing ventures in Prince Edward Island and in an area near Lake St. Clair in Upper Canada. For various reasons, his attempts met with failure.

In 1810, Lord Selkirk returned to his original idea of settling Selkirk buys H.B.C. lands Scots on land in the Red River valley, land which was then under the control of the Hudson's Bay Company. In order to secure Company approval, he quietly purchased one-third of the Company's stock during a period of trade depression; as part of the purchase deal, Selkirk was also able to secure thousands of square miles of land stretching from Lake Winnipeg south to the headwaters of the Mississippi and from the Lake of the Woods to the junction of the Red and the Assiniboine rivers. This little empire, which came to be known as Assiniboia, was actually the fur region opened up eighty years before by the La Vérendrye family.

In addition to assisting poor Scottish families, Selkirk hoped that his proposed settlement would be of practical value to the Hudson's Bay Company. There was the possibility that the products of the farms would provide additional food for fur traders, and that the sons of settlers might in time become Company employees.

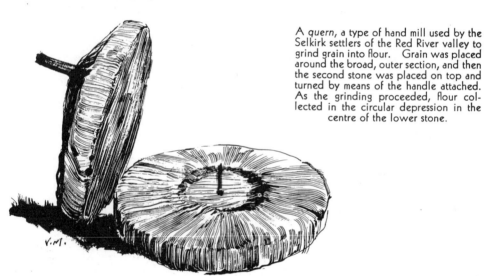

A *quern*, a type of hand mill used by the Selkirk settlers of the Red River valley to grind grain into flour. Grain was placed around the broad, outer section, and then the second stone was placed on top and turned by means of the handle attached. As the grinding proceeded, flour collected in the circular depression in the centre of the lower stone.

**The pemmican trade**    Both the Hudson's Bay Company and the North West Company traded and hunted in the Assiniboia region. They were both dependent upon the area for their annual supplies of pemmican. (Pemmican was a highly concentrated, nourishing food made by pounding dried buffalo meat into powder and then mixing it with melted buffalo fat and wild berries. It was packaged in ninety-pound units encased in buffalo hide. Pemmican was a staple food used by traders and explorers.) This product was made and sold by a half-breed people who lived in Assiniboia, the *Métis*, descendants of French fur traders who had taken Indian women as their wives.

It soon became obvious that settlement in Assiniboia could cause trouble. The spread of farming would inevitably interfere with buffalo hunting and the pemmican trade. The coming of white settlers was almost certain to anger the Métis, who considered the Assiniboia region their own. The prospect was considered so serious that Nor'Westers (men of the North West Company) began writing letters to Scottish newspapers warning readers not to emigrate.

Lord Selkirk either ignored, or was ignorant of, the feelings of the inhabitants of Assiniboia; he went ahead with his plans. A small advance party under a Glengarry Highlander, Miles Macdonnell, the new Governor of Assiniboia, reached the Red River in August, 1812. It had been a long, arduous journey by way of Hudson Bay, the Hayes River and Lake Winnipeg. Close to the junction of the Red and Assiniboine rivers, Macdonnell chose a site, Fort Douglas, that was to serve as headquarters for the colonists. **Red River Settlement**

Each year, more settlers arrived, but the colony grew slowly. Families were given long, narrow plots of land which ran down to the muddy banks of the Red and the Assiniboine. This was, curiously enough, the same pattern of land holding that had existed on the St. Lawrence in the days of New France.

In 1814, friction arose between the colonists and the Nor' Westers. Governor Macdonnell, fearing that food supplies for his colony were running short, decreed that no food supplies were to be sent out or taken out of Assiniboia: While this "Pemmican Proclamation" might have been beneficial from the standpoint of the colony, it cut off supplies to the trading companies and interfered with the livelihood of the Métis. **The "Pemmican Proclamation"**

Macdonnell went even further. He seized a quantity of pemmican belonging to the North West Company. So confident had the governor become that he boasted he had enough strength to "crush all the Nor'Westers on this river, should they be so hardy as to resist my authority."

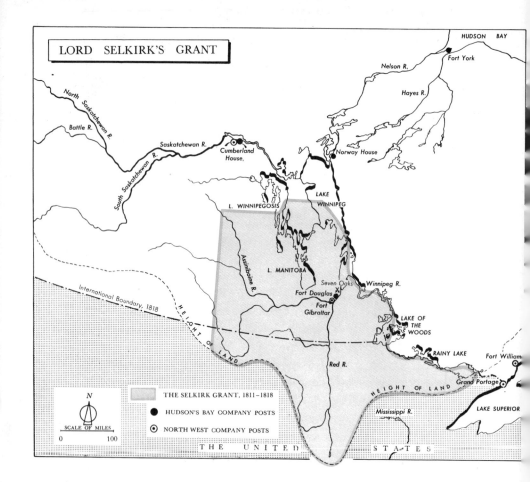

LORD SELKIRK'S GRANT

HUDSON BAY
Fort York
Nelson R.
Hayes R.
North Saskatchewan R.
Battle R.
South Saskatchewan R.
Saskatchewan R.
Cumberland House,
Norway House
L. WINNIPEGOSIS
LAKE WINNIPEG
Assiniboine R.
L. MANITOBA
Seven Oaks
Fort Douglas    Winnipeg R.
Fort Gibraltar
International Boundary, 1818
HEIGHT OF LAND
LAKE OF THE WOODS
RAINY LAKE
Fort William
Red R.
HEIGHT OF LAND
Grand Portage
Mississippi R.
LAKE SUPERIOR

N
SCALE OF MILES
0      100

THE SELKIRK GRANT, 1811–1818
● HUDSON'S BAY COMPANY POSTS
◉ NORTH WEST COMPANY POSTS

THE    UNITED    STATES

**Fort Douglas attacked**    The result was open warfare, complete with raids and property destruction. Macdonnell was seized and sent off to Montreal; Fort Douglas was attacked and some buildings burned. Alarmed by the turmoil and bitterness of the conflict, the Selkirk settlers began to scatter. Some travelled down river to Lake Winnipeg; some took employment with the North West Company; some accepted transportation on canoes heading east for Montreal. (A number of these latter families settled in Upper Canada near Lake Simcoe.)

The settlers' cabins were destroyed, and Fort Douglas was burned to the ground.

Just when it seemed that the Selkirk Settlement would disappear entirely, a fresh party of eighty settlers arrived under Robert Semple, who pompously announced that he was the new Governor-in-chief of Rupert's Land (the lands of the Hudson's Bay Company). Semple soon proved that he, too, understood little of conditions in the North-West; his first action was to destroy Fort Gibraltar, a North West Company fur post. This was all that was necessary to arouse the wrath of the traders and the Métis, who immediately thought that men who dared to destroy Fort Gibraltar might easily turn next to the destruction of Métis homes.

*Semple destroys Fort Gibraltar*

On June 19, 1816, a party of Métis, Indians, voyageurs and traders under a Nor'Wester, a nineteen-year-old half-breed, Cuthbert Grant, was travelling in the area of Fort Douglas. Governor Semple, seeing the approaching party, left his fort with some men. The two groups made contact in a grove called Seven Oaks. At first neither party intended to take hostile action; however, a bitter argument soon developed. In violent anger, Semple snatched a gun from the hands of a man in the opposing group. This was enough to set rifles barking. Eleven more colonists hastened from the fort to rescue their comrades. They too were killed. When the "Massacre of Seven Oaks" was over, Grant counted twenty settlers and one of his own men dead.

*"Massacre of Seven Oaks"*

Meanwhile, Lord Selkirk was journeying towards the Red River accompanied by one hundred Swiss soldiers. When the tragic news reached him, he abruptly changed his plans and advanced on Fort William, the western headquarters of the North West Company (located near the former fur trading centre of Grand Portage on Lake Superior).

*Selkirk seizes Fort William*

Acting without consideration of consequences and without any legal authority, the angry Selkirk seized Fort William, arrested a number of Nor'Westers and sent them east as prisoners. His prisoners included such famous personages as Simon Fraser, the explorer, and William McGillivray, the rich, Montreal fur trader.

The clash between Governor Semple's men and the Nor'Westers commenced when Semple tried to grab a gun away from a half-breed clerk employed by the North West Company. Within seconds, there was a blaze of gunfire and Semple fell to the ground, having taken one of the first shots in the thigh. His opponents numbered about seventy in all and many of the Métis, dressed in the buckskin and feathered headpieces of their Indian companions, were heavily armed with guns, spears and bows and arrows. The wounded Semple was promised safe conveyance back to his fort by Cuthbert Grant, the leader of the Nor'Westers, but before he could arrange this an Indian ran up and shot Semple to death. The dead were stripped of their clothing and left lying on the prairie, some to be buried later by friendly Indians.

So crowded were the canoes that during a storm some capsized, causing the death of nine men. When word of Selkirk's actions reached the Canadas, there were expressions of utter disbelief and of violent anger.

Encouraged by his success at Fort William, Selkirk dispatched a number of soldiers westward to the Red River valley. They quickly recaptured Fort Douglas. In May, 1817, Selkirk himself saw the site of the colony he had established and busied himself with plans for the construction of houses, a church, a school, a mill and a number of bridges. Selkirk rebuilds his colony

Leaving his colony in the belief that it was well on the road to recovery, Selkirk returned to Upper Canada to face what he knew would be a difficult situation. In the stormy months that followed, the British Colonial Office, the Hudson's Bay Company, the North West Company and Selkirk were all involved in a bewildering web of charges and counter-charges which found their way into the law courts of Upper Canada. These cases dragged on month after month with little concrete result. In the end, one conviction was made against an employee of the North West Company and two fines amounting to £2,000 were imposed upon Selkirk. Charges and counter-charges

Already suffering from ill-health, the founder of the Red River settlement returned in the autumn of 1818 to England where he died two years later. Death of Selkirk

Lord Selkirk still remains a controversial figure in Canadian history. To some historians, he was a gallant, noble figure, fighting for the welfare of his poorer brethren in Assiniboia against the selfish interest of fur traders. To others, he was a stiff-necked, blundering autocrat, who foolishly persisted in maintaining a personal empire without regard for the interests of others.

Whatever his motives may have been, the Red River Settlement persisted, growing slowly and steadily with the years. More settlers arrived including French-speaking people from Lower Canada; farms increased in number; missionaries arrived; the Métis gradually lost some of their distrust and fear of the hard-working colonists. The Settlement succeeds

# 12. The Fur Trade

AFTER THE BITTER Red River lawsuits had been settled, the North West Company reoccupied Fort William and continued its trade rivalry with the Hudson's Bay Company. For their part, the employees working out of Hudson Bay were determined to show that they could be as tough, aggressive and shrewd as any of the "Pedlars from Quebec."

**Difficulties of the North West Company**

At this time, the North West Company was feeling the sharp pinch of fierce competition. Beaver skins were becoming scarce except in the most distant regions; each year it was becoming more and more expensive to haul trade goods almost four thousand miles from Montreal up into the north-west reaches of the continent; some of the partners were seriously alarmed by diminishing profit margins, and the Company finances were falling into disorder. Despite the amazing efficiency of the canoe brigades, the Nor'Westers, using the long route from Montreal, simply could not compete with the much cheaper and much more direct sea route used by the Hudson's Bay Company.

**Union of the companies, 1821**

A union of the two companies had been proposed at various times in earlier years but, until 1820, men on both sides opposed any such suggestion. However, in the end, the evils of costly competion and the threat of financial ruin led officials of both organizations to realize that only in union did there lie any chance of future gain.

Thus, in 1821, an agreement was reached whereby the two rivals united under the name of the Hudson's Bay Company. To the veteran Nor'Westers who heard the news at Fort William, it was a bitter pill to swallow. They found it very hard to realize that the fur trade. was now controlled from London and not from Montreal, that the bustling activity at Fort William was now transferred to York Factory on Hudson Bay and that the historic canoe routes had been abandoned. The songs of the voyageurs would no longer echo across the Great Lakes. Grass and shrubs would gradually cover the age-old pathways of the many portages between Lachine and Lake Winnipeg. The stirring days of the big fur brigades were over.

Thus, the movement of furs, trade goods and fur pelts was channelled through Hudson Bay. The desertion of the old canoe routes cut the former connection between east and west. It was not until the latter part of the century, when roads and a railway probed westward, that effective communication was once again restored.

After 1821, the operation of the Hudson's Bay Company was reorganized. The direction of the Company's Canadian affairs was entrusted to a thirty-two-year-old man of tremendous energy and foresight called George Simpson. **Governor George Simpson**

Governor Simpson was, for almost forty years, the ruler of a western fur empire, recognizing only the superior authority of his Queen and that of senior Company officials in England. A vigorous man with a barrel-shaped chest and a round, florid face, Simpson travelled fantastic distances in the execution of his duties. He took the greatest delight in pomp and display, travelling in the largest canoes at headlong speed, accompanied by servants and kilted Highland pipers. His most remarkable trip was one made in 1828, when he travelled all the way from York Factory to the Rockies, down the Fraser River and on to Fort Vancouver on the lower reaches of the Columbia River. This was no mean feat; he travelled 3,000 miles in eighty-four days—nearly forty miles a day —much of it under trying conditions.

With Simpson in charge, the Company affairs displayed an astounding growth. Taking a sharp interest in the smallest details, he promoted new policies under which the trade in liquor was vastly reduced, Indians were offered reasonable values at the fur posts and conservation in trapping was encouraged.

Simpson also introduced improvements and economies in transportation. Since the canoes traditionally employed in the North-West carried relatively small cargoes, he initiated the use of **York boats**

York boats. These sturdy craft, equipped with square sails and twenty-foot oars, were able to withstand the roughest water and could be hauled over portages by means of rollers. The chief advantage of the York boat was that, with a small crew, it could transport a much heavier cargo than any freight canoe. The smaller crew and the increase in carrying capacity reduced transportation costs and boosted company profits.

**Tripmen**

Instead of voyageurs, the York boats carried tripmen, most of whom were Métis. These wiry, hard-working men proved to be as rough in their ways as were the raftsmen of the Ottawa River. Nicknames applied to the various groups of tripmen referred to the regions from which they came and to the foods it was thought they ate. In consequence, there were the *poissons blanc*, the "whitefish," the *taureaux*, the "buffalo bulls" and the *blaireaux*, the "badgers."

This illustration shows the crew of a York boat struggling to manhandle their craft over a shallow stretch of water. Built of the finest spruce wood, these boats had bows and sterns that slanted upward at an angle of forty-five degrees. Their length varied from twenty-eight to forty feet and the largest ones could carry over four tons of freight. The cargo was stowed under canvas during bad weather. When rowing with twenty-foot oars, the crew rose to their feet on the dip and pull of the oars and crouched down while completing the stroke. In the distance are two York boats under sail.

A new type of transportation developed with the wide use of **Red River carts** a remarkable vehicle known as the Red River cart. This two-wheeled vehicle, made entirely of wood, could carry loads of up to half a ton in weight. Gradually, a number of Métis made it their occupation to move goods by means of the Red River carts. Long wagon trains, squeaking and swaying over rough trails, moved southeastward to St. Paul, Minnesota, unloaded buffalo hides and furs and then loaded up with American manufactured goods. In time, goods were actually moved by cart the entire distance from the upper reaches of the Mississippi River to the Saskatchewan River country.

At first, there was no need for Simpson to use Red River carts in the movement of Company cargo because his established system of water transportation suited his purpose. Shortly after mid-century, however, the Hudson's Bay Company found it useful to

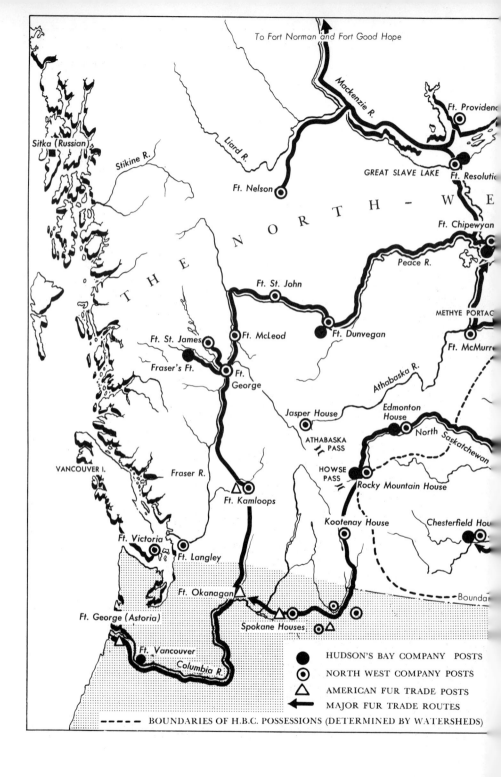

To Fort Norman and Fort Good Hope

Mackenzie R.

Ft. Providenc

Liard R.

GREAT SLAVE LAKE   Ft. Resolutio

Sitka (Russian)

Stikine R.

THE NORTH - WE

Ft. Nelson

Ft. Chipewyan

Peace R.

Ft. St. John

METHYE PORTAC

Ft. McLeod   Ft. Dunvegan

Ft. St. James

Ft. McMurr

Fraser's Ft.   Ft. George

Athabaska R.

Jasper House

Edmonton House

North Saskatchewan

ATHABASKA PASS

VANCOUVER I.   Fraser R.

HOWSE PASS

Rocky Mountain House

Ft. Kamloops

Kootenay House

Chesterfield Hou

Ft. Victoria

Ft. Langley

Ft. Okanagan

Boundar

Ft. George (Astoria)

Spokane Houses

Ft. Vancouver

Columbia R.

● HUDSON'S BAY COMPANY POSTS
⊙ NORTH WEST COMPANY POSTS
△ AMERICAN FUR TRADE POSTS
← MAJOR FUR TRADE ROUTES
--- BOUNDARIES OF H.B.C. POSSESSIONS (DETERMINED BY WATERSHEDS)

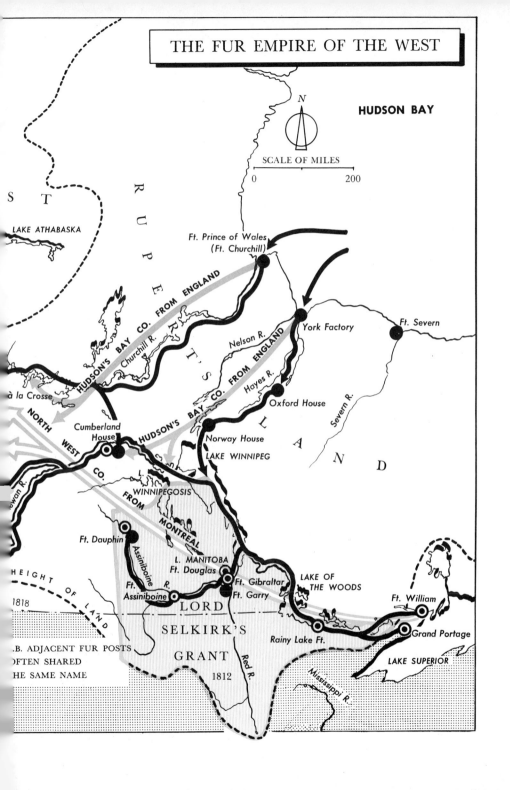

# THE FUR EMPIRE OF THE WEST

**HUDSON BAY**

N

SCALE OF MILES

0          200

S   T

LAKE ATHABASKA

R   U   P   E   R   T  '  S

Ft. Prince of Wales
(Ft. Churchill)

HUDSON'S BAY CO. FROM ENGLAND

Churchill R.

à la Crosse

Nelson R.

York Factory

Ft. Severn

HUDSON'S BAY CO. FROM ENGLAND

Hayes R.

NORTH

Cumberland
House

HUDSON'S BAY

Oxford House

Severn R.

L

Norway House

CO.

WEST

LAKE WINNIPEG

A

N

D

wan R.

L.
WINNIPEGOSIS

CO.

FROM

Ft. Dauphin

MONTREAL

Assiniboine

L. MANITOBA
Ft. Douglas

Ft.
Assiniboine

R.

Ft. Gibraltar
Ft. Garry

LAKE OF
THE WOODS

Ft. William

HEIGHT

OF

LAND

LORD

1818

SELKIRK'S

Rainy Lake Ft.

Grand Portage

.B. ADJACENT FUR POSTS
OFTEN SHARED
HE SAME NAME

GRANT

Red R.

1812

LAKE SUPERIOR

Mississippi R.

import some goods by way of St. Paul, as well as by Hudson Bay. Thus, it was York boats and Red River carts that bore the heavy burden of transportation in the North-West until freight trains and steamboats became available.

**Sir George Simpson**

Simpson was successful in gradually eliminating the old bitterness that once existed between the men of the rival companies. His tactful, friendly and shrewd leadership brought the employees of the Hudson's Bay Company and the old North West Company together to form a smoothly operating and vastly profitable organization. Queen Victoria honoured his achievement with a knighthood, and an historian has said of this remarkable man:

The Governor knew how to attach people to himself, and he gathered around him in the course of his career of forty years a large number of men most devoted to the interests of the Company. His visits to Fort Garry on the Red River were always notable. He was approachable to the humblest, and listened to many a complaint and grievance with apparent sympathy and patience. He had many of the arts of the courtier along with his indomitable will.

## SUMMARY — SECTION 3

In 1810, a Scots nobleman, Lork Selkirk, acquired 116,000 square miles of land from the Hudson's Bay Company in what is now Manitoba, North Dakota and Minnesota. His intention was to provide a place of settlement for impoverished Scottish families. The first group of settlers from Scotland reached Assiniboia in 1812 by way of Hudson Bay, the Hayes River and Lake Winnipeg. They built Fort Douglas and occupied land at the junction of the Red and Assiniboine Rivers. Their settlement came to be known as the Red River Colony.

The new settlement in Assiniboia was most disturbing to the Métis, who hunted buffalo and made pemmican in the region, and to the Nor'Westers who traded for furs. The rivalry existing between the Hudson's Bay Company—with which Selkirk was associated—and the North West Company added further tension.

In 1814, after the "Pemmican Proclamation" was issued, violence broke out in Assiniboia. The Nor'Westers seized Fort Douglas, captured Governor Macdonnell and sent him off to Montreal. The settlers began to leave. A new governor, Robert Semple, arrived. Acting with little thought, Semple attacked and destroyed Fort Gibraltar, a North West

Company fur post. Then a party of Métis, led by a Nor'Wester, killed twenty settlers in a tragic encounter now known as the "Massacre of Seven Oaks."

In the meantime, Lord Selkirk was travelling westward with a group of soldiers. When the shocking news of Seven Oaks reached him, Selkirk promptly captured Fort William, western headquarters of the North West Company, seized a number of officials and sent them east as prisoners.

Lord Selkirk restored the fortunes of his shattered colony, but his high-handed actions at Fort William caused a storm of protest and, eventually, long months of dispute in the law courts of Upper Canada. Eventually, an employee of the North West Company was convicted and Lord Selkirk was fined. Selkirk died shortly afterward in England, but his colony on the Red River struggled on, growing slowly but steadily.

The Red River conflict did not lessen the bitter trade rivalry between the North West Company and the Hudson's Bay Company. Yet, the Nor'Westers were finding it increasingly difficult to compete with their shrewd rivals. Each year, the canoe routes from Montreal into the North-West were becoming longer and more expensive to maintain. For years, there had been talk of uniting the two companies, but this was not considered seriously until about 1820. By that date, extreme financial difficulties were forcing the Nor'Westers to change their viewpoint. In 1821, a union took place, and the two companies merged under the name of the Hudson's Bay Company. The expensive canoe routes to and from Montreal were abandoned; the transportation of most supplies and furs was routed through Hudson Bay; Montreal lost its importance as a fur trade centre and London became the headquarters of the Company.

Between 1820 and 1860, the Canadian affairs of the Hudson's Bay Company were administered by the remarkable George Simpson. A vigorous person, Simpson travelled widely and kept a watchful eye on all operations of the Company. He improved and expanded Company trade through new business policies and the introduction of the York boat, a watercraft that was a great cargo-carrier and sturdier than the birch-bark canoe. Simpson knew how to manage men and was successful in ultimately removing the bitterness that existed between the former employees of the North West Company and the Hudson's Bay Company after the amalgamation of 1821.

# THE FIGHT FOR RESPONSIBLE GOVERNMENT

Colonial government  ▪  The Family Compact in Nova Scotia  ▪  Joseph Howe  ▪  The Family Compact in Upper Canada  ▪  John Strachan and John Beverley Robinson  ▪  The Clergy Reserves  ▪  The Reform party  ▪  William Lyon Mackenzie  ▪  Rebellion in Upper Canada, 1837  ▪  Louis Joseph Papineau  ▪  Rebellion in Lower Canada, 1837  ▪  Lord Durham's *Report,* 1839  ▪  The Union of Upper and Lower Canada, 1841  ▪  Governors Sydenham and Metcalfe  ▪  Lord Elgin  ▪  The Rebellion Losses Bill  ▪  The grant of responsible government.

# INTRODUCTION: The Failure of Colonial Government

AFTER THE SUCCESS of the American Revolution, Great Britain found it necessary to reorganize her Empire. The result has often been called the Second British Empire. Unfortunately, few real changes were made, and it was not long before signs of another British failure began to appear in North America.

Some Loyalists who found refuge in the northern colonies were determined to create a society that was an exact replica of society in Great Britain. In fact, they were so bent on this policy that it has sometimes been said of them that they were more English than the English themselves. There quickly developed in each colony a small group of wealthy Loyalists, who, in addition to being called Tories, were commonly given the unflattering name of the "Family Compact," since they tended to promote the political and financial welfare of close relatives and friends.

The Family Compact was so powerful that it controlled appointments to political offices, grants of land and the supervision of education and banking. In defence of this group of privileged persons, it should be noted that they did not think of themselves as ruling just in their own best interests. They considered themselves loyal supporters of British political and religious traditions. They believed that government, the process of law-making, should quite naturally be attended to by "responsible and educated persons" and not be left to "the ignorant masses." Members of the Family Compact, whether laymen or senior Church of England officials, were serious-minded, conservative men who had not yet grasped the idea of democratic government. Moreover, they were not alone in their belief, for many British political leaders still thought in exactly the same way.

103

The government of a colony or province was composed of four elements. At the top was the *Governor* (always an Englishman), who was responsible for his actions to the British Colonial Office. To assist him and to give him advice, the Governor had an *Executive Council,* which he himself appointed. Its members were, of course, members of the Family Compact. Though the Governor was not bound to accept the advice of his Council, he frequently did so because he was often personally unfamiliar with conditions in the colony. Thus, it is easy to see how the Governor could be influenced by the Family Compact.

The Family Compact also controlled the *Legislative Council.* This senior, law-making body was intended to be a model of the British House of Lords, with its members appointed for life.

The only persons elected by the people of the colony were the members of the *Legislative Assembly.* But even here the members of the Compact were able to maintain their power by using their wealth and prestige to influence the results of elections and also to determine many of the laws proposed in the Assembly.

The colonists were not satisfied with this organization of government; it was not producing the results they desired. Their dissatisfaction produced reform movements in each colony. The Reformers were strongly influenced in their thinking by several factors. In the first place, many of them had come from the United States where democratic ideas had been put into practice.' Although these former Americans did not want British North America to become a part of the United States, they could see the benefits to be gained from a popular form of government, as could other colonists, whatever their origin. Reformers and colonists alike could also see that events in the mother country were leading to the introduction of a greater degree of democratic government. In Britain, the Reform Act of 1832 gave many people the right to elect their representatives to Parliament. These representatives were *responsible* to the electors for their actions in Parliament.

One obvious result of the manner in which colonial government was organized was the irresponsible behaviour of both Tories and Reformers.  Since the Tories held office without popular approval, they did not have to justify their law-making to anyone except the Governor. On the other hand, the Reformers did not have to carry out their promises because they were never in a position to act upon them.  Indeed, the Reformers might hold all the seats in the Legislative Assembly, but the Tories in the Executive Council were still the only persons permitted by the Colonial Office to authorize laws.

Because colonial government operated in this way, people frequently found that the affairs of their province—the granting of land, the provision of schools, and so on—were not being managed to their satisfaction.  It is not surprising, therefore, to find that the Reformers sought to accomplish two aims—to introduce improved government and to effect the laws most desired by the people of the colony.

The period from about 1820 to 1849 is the story of the main Reform struggle to accomplish these aims—the struggle for government that would be *responsible to the people* for its actions.

# 13. Protest in Nova Scotia

IN THE MARITIME provinces, there were perhaps fewer abuses in government than in Upper and Lower Canada. Nevertheless, the inhabitants were not at all pleased with certain actions taken by the lieutenant-governors and their advisers. The strongest protests against colonial government took place in Nova Scotia.

Nova Scotia possessed a legislative assembly that dated back to 1758, but the Assembly, in spite of its age, exercised little real authority. Halifax, being an important naval base and a provincial capital, had an upper class society of wealthy merchants, military officers, naval officers and politicians. These were the type of people who, for various and sometimes selfish reasons, had little interest in promoting democratic government.

**Thomas Chandler Haliburton**

A brilliant supporter of the ruling class in Nova Scotia was the handsome, dignified Thomas Chandler Haliburton, who during the course of his life was a lawyer, author, Assembly member and judge. Today, we remember him best, not for his political or legal activities, but for his writings —in particular for his creation of that shrewd, fast-talking Yankee pedlar, Sam Slick, whose adventures were first related in Haliburton's famous book, *The Clockmaker.*

Judge Haliburton had little patience with the idea of responsible government, or with the democratic ideas accepted in the United States. "Responsible government," he said, "is responsible nonsense." Even in his humorous writings Haliburton expressed the opinion that government should be left to the educated upper classes. In one story, for example, he writes, "Let the people attend to business, build their railways, develop their water-power, their farms and their forests, secure under the fostering care of the select few."

Skating was a very popular winter recreation during the nineteenth century. Long, severe winters and the availability of lakes and rivers combined to provide plenty of ice for the sport. Note the long, loose winter garment worn by the woman and the narrow trousers and tight-waisted coat of the gentleman. These costumes were common in the 1830's and 1840's. It is interesting to note that, although skating was popular with both men and women throughout the entire century, it was not until about 1880 that the upper-class group in a community regarded skating as a socially acceptable winter recreation for women.

If the ruling group in Nova Scotia had a champion in Judge **Joseph Howe** Haliburton, it also had an enemy in the person of a hot-tempered, courageous newspaperman named Joseph Howe. This intelligent, aggressive man, born of Loyalist stock, established a Halifax newspaper, the *Novascotian*. When still in his twenties, Joseph Howe was making use of his newspaper columns to lash out at the provincial government. His bold, witty language delighted the people of Nova Scotia but drew the anger of the ruling class. So effective were Howe's attacks that members of the Family Compact looked about for some means of squelching their tormentor.

They were heartened, therefore, in 1835, when the *Novascotian* contained an attack on the magistrates of Halifax. Magistrates at that time were appointed by the Crown and held important responsibilities in the government of Halifax and the other towns of the province. Thus, it caused a sensation in the colony when Howe accused these dignified officials in print of being guilty of neglect, mismanagement and corruption.

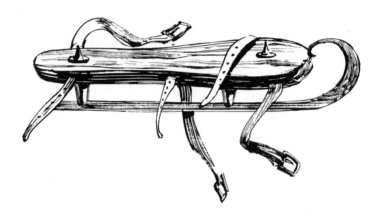

This skate of about 1835 consists of a metal runner fastened to a wooden sole, which, in turn, was strapped to the skater's boot. The cleats at either end of the wooden sole fitted into corresponding holes in the skater's boots, thus securing skate and boot more firmly. Although designs for these early skates were often elaborate, the skates themselves were difficult to keep sharp. Later in the century, the single boot and skate unit that we know today became popular.

**Howe defends himself in court**

Here was the opportunity for the Family Compact to strike back at Howe. The outspoken newspaperman could now be brought to court on a charge of libel. The magistrates laid charges against their enemy. Howe consulted several local lawyers regarding his chances of being acquitted and was informed that they were very poor indeed. Nonetheless, Howe decided to defend himself against the libel charge.

News of the coming court case spread quickly, causing intense excitement throughout the province. Popular sympathy was with Howe. When the day of the trial arrived, the court-house was packed to overflowing. Most of those present had only good wishes for Joseph Howe, but they feared that he would be found guilty and sent to prison.

Howe had spoken in public before, but only to small groups and never on such an important occasion as this. Even he began to wonder if he had been wise in attempting his own defence. There was much more than the trial of a man at stake. It was, in effect, the trial of the whole system of government by the Family Compact. The question in everyone's mind was, "Can one courageous man stand up in a court of law and defend himself successfully against such a powerful group?"

When the time came for Howe to take the stand, he appeared **Howe's** calm and firm. All eyes were upon him as he began the remarkable **famous** address of defence that has become famous in Canadian history. **defence** As he spoke, Howe's voice took on sincerity and authority—qualities that caught and held his audience spellbound.

Hour after hour his eloquent voice rolled across the courtroom, bringing smiles and nods from the people and scowls of anger from the magistrates. So powerful was Howe's appeal that it became evident long before he ceased talking—six hours later—that he had won a victory. The following day, the jury rendered a verdict of "Not guilty!" Halifax citizens, wild with joy, lifted Howe to their shoulders and marched triumphantly from the courtroom.

Overnight, the young newspaperman had become the hero of Nova Scotians. Not only had he been acquitted, but the magistrates and the Family Compact as a whole had suffered a humiliating, public defeat.

Early the following year, 1836, Howe was elected as a **Reform** member of the Legislative Assembly. The great respect in which he was held is indicated by the fact he very soon was recognized as the leader of his party in Nova Scotia.

The fight for responsible government in Nova Scotia had barely begun, for the form of government desired by the people could not be achieved until Great Britain changed the whole system of colonial rule. In the meantime, startling events occurred in Upper and Lower Canada.

# 14. Unrest in Upper Canada

IN UPPER CANADA, examples of abuses in government and popular discontent were even greater than in Nova Scotia.

**Clergy Reserves**

To the settlers of Upper Canada, the Clergy Reserves, the lands set aside as belonging to the Church of England, were a particular source of annoyance. Not only did they represent the privileged position of the Church of England, but they were also a handicap to the expansion of settlement. As a result of the policy of the Reserves, large blocks of land remained vacant, and no taxes for local use were paid upon them. These undeveloped, forested areas only served to increase the difficulties of road-building. It is perhaps important, too, that they provided shelter for the wolves that killed settlers' sheep and poultry. When settlers' children grew up, their parents could not afford to buy adjoining land in the Reserves and thus their sons and daughters were forced to move some distance away from their parents. For these reasons, the Clergy Reserves greatly angered many people in the province.

Other annoying features of life in Upper Canada were the lack of adequate roads, the practice of granting land to land companies at the expense of individuals, the lack of popular education and the prestige and power enjoyed by only one church, the Church of England. It was always the Family Compact which appeared to tolerate and even encourage these inequalities and abuses.

**The Family Compact**

Among the most prominent members of the Family Compact in Upper Canada was the Reverend John Strachan. Strachan was a member of the Executive Council, chairman of the General Board of Education for the province and, of course, a priest of the Church of England. His determination to maintain the Church of England as the official church and to have schools placed under the control of the Church won him many enemies among the people—particularly among the Methodists. Strachan,

110

# PATTERN OF TOWNSHIP IN UPPER CANADA IN
## THE EARLY NINETEENTH CENTURY

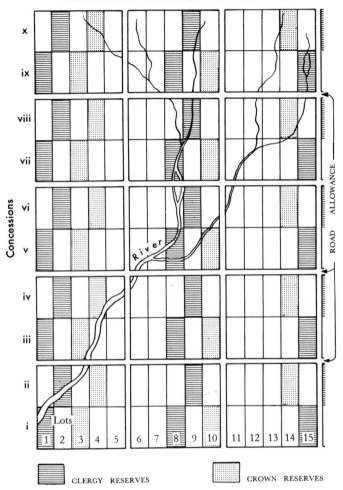

CLERGY RESERVES      CROWN RESERVES

The basic unit of settlement in Upper Canada was the township, a tract of land usually ten miles square. (The above diagram shows *part* of such a township.) Of this area, a seventh was set aside as clergy reserves and another seventh as crown reserves. By 1825, the crown reserves of Upper Canada had been sold to private land companies. Similar arrangements were made in 1834 in Lower Canada. In 1827, the gradual sale of the clergy reserves of Upper Canada was authorized, and those remaining unsold in 1854 became government property.

(It should be noted that in Lower Canada the system of seigneurial tenure, which had been the basis of settlement since the days of New France, was abolished in 1854 and replaced by the township system.)

on his part, was very outspoken in his condemnation of Methodist clergymen, at times accusing them of being disloyal to the Crown.

Another important member of the Family Compact was the handsome, distinguished John Beverley Robinson (a former pupil of Strachan's grammar school at Cornwall). A clever young man, Robinson became a lawyer, was elected to the Legislative Assembly, became a member of the Legislative Council and, at the early age of thirty-eight, was appointed Chief Justice of Upper Canada.

**Robert Gourlay** In 1817, an incident that involved a Scotsman, Robert Gourlay, who was employed at Kingston as a land agent, focused attention upon misrule in the province.

In the course of his work, Gourlay became greatly interested in promoting immigration from Great Britain. In order to provide information about Upper Canada, he began to collect data on schools, churches, roads, wages and working conditions. He soon began to suspect that the government was not doing all it might to improve conditions in the settled regions and he also became suspicious that certain prominent men were making fortunes in land speculation. In the course of his investigations, Gourlay, without proper authority, sent out circular letters asking for answers to specific questions. One question asked, "What in your opinion retards the improvement of your township in particular, or the province in general . . .?"

Angered by these enquiries, John Strachan and John Beverley Robinson charged that Robert Gourlay was deliberately attempting to stir up discontent among the people of Upper Canada. Gourlay, in turn, lashed out at the Family Compact and called a convention of citizens at York in 1818, with the purpose of discussing grievances against the government. To the hundreds of discontented people who came to hear him, Robert Gourlay became a hero.

Alarmed by these events, the government of Upper Canada had Gourlay arrested, held in prison and then brought to trial—a trial that made an absolute mockery of justice by banishing the unfortunate Gourlay from the province. The Gourlay incident clearly revealed two things: first, there was a mounting dissatisfaction among the people of Upper Canada, and second, the Family Compact was quite prepared to take extreme measures to protect itself from criticism. Surprising though it may seem, the government of Upper Canada failed to learn a lesson from the Gourlay affair. It was still unable to appreciate the growing force of popular discontent.

In 1826, John Strachan, now Archdeacon Strachan, preached a **Egerton** sermon in which he made a particularly bitter attack on the **Ryerson** Methodist clergymen of the province. In the course of his remarks, he stated that such preachers were lazy, ignorant and tainted by ideas from the United States. These statements were resented by the Methodists as a whole, for many of them were United Empire Loyalists. To them, a slur on their patriotism was the deepest of insults. The reply to Strachan's attack came in a letter written by a little-known circuit rider named Egerton Ryerson. So effective was his reply that the young Methodist clergyman became widely known throughout Upper Canada. Ryerson's bold stand against John Strachan was hailed with delight by the many inhabitants opposed to the Family Compact. In time, the young circuit rider was to become famous as the editor of the *Christian Guardian* newspaper and as an educator who played a leading role in the establishment of Ontario's educational system.

The Reform party slowly gained strength in the Legislative Assembly. By 1828, it actually held a majority of seats. Among the leading reformers of that time were Dr. John Rolph, founder of medical education in Upper Canada, Marshal Spring Bidwell, an astute lawyer, and Dr. William Warren Baldwin, father of Robert Baldwin.

One of the most important members of the Reform party was **Robert** Robert Baldwin, a man noted for his strict honesty and common **Baldwin** sense. He was first elected to the Legislative Assembly of Upper Canada in 1829, but was defeated in the following year. Although he was out of office for the next ten years, except for a brief month in 1836, Baldwin was the leader of the moderate Reformers and became a champion of responsible government.

The Parliament Buildings at Toronto as they appeared in 1835. This was the third group of buildings to serve as the headquarters of government in the early days of Upper Canada. Erected in 1832 at the corner of Simcoe and Front Streets, they overlooked the harbour, the docks and a favourite, public bathing-spot, Ree's Wharf, where, it has been recorded: *on a fine summer's morning many of the leading merchants and clerks might be seen indulging in this healthy exercise.* The Parliament Buildings were simple and unpretentious structures, designed as an adaptation of the Georgian style of architecture. It was here in July, 1838, that a crowd of several thousand people gathered to receive Lord and Lady Durham, "the steps being carpeted and a crimson chair of state awaiting his reception."

**William Lyon Mackenzie**

However, the most colourful — and dangerous — of all the Reformers was a tiny, hot-tempered, hard-eyed Scotsman who wore a flaming red wig over his bald head. He was William Lyon Mackenzie—owner and editor of a weekly newspaper, the *Colonial Advocate*. Mackenzie was already well-known in Upper Canada for his biting attacks on the Family Compact. A courageous, stubborn and outspoken man, Mackenzie had dared to make very frank criticisms of the conduct, private and public, of prominent persons in Upper Canada. On one occasion he described the Legislative Council as being:

The most extraordinary collection of sturdy beggars, parsons, priests, pensioners, army people, place-men, bank directors, and stock and land jobbers ever established to act as a paltry screen to a rotten government. They cost the country about £40,000 a year, and the good laws by which it might benefit, they tomahawk. They don't like to be called a *nuisance*.

Two years before entering the Assembly, Mackenzie had attacked the Family Compact so viciously in the columns of the *Colonial Advocate* that a number of young gentlemen decided to teach the little Scot a lesson. One evening in June, 1826, sixteen of them marched to Mackenzie's printing shop on Front Street, York. They broke down the door, smashed the press and dumped quantities of type into the harbour. Mackenzie was away at the time and no one interfered with this bold act of destruction. *Raid on Mackenzie's press*

Mackenzie seems to have taken the destruction of his property with relative calmness, but he did bring suit against the culprits. The invasion and destruction of his business quarters had been so daring and so open that the court could scarcely do less than bring in a verdict of guilty. Mackenzie was awarded damages. The whole episode, in fact, did more good than harm to the stubborn little newspaperman, for it brought him added sympathy and popularity among the people. In addition, Mackenzie had been on the point of bankruptcy, but now, with the damages awarded by court, he was able to pay his debts, buy new printing equipment and bring the *Colonial Advocate* back into circulation.

Mackenzie continued to fight for reform both in his newspaper and in the Assembly. He became a member of several committees and took an active part in government proceedings. In 1830, however, the entire legislature was dissolved on the death of King George IV, as required by law. In the following election, the Reformers suffered a defeat when the Tory party won a majority of seats in the Assembly. Determined to get rid of the troublesome Mackenzie, Tory members had him expelled from the Assembly on the basis of statements made in the *Colonial Advocate*. Mac- *Mackenzie expelled from Assembly* kenzie's supporters in York County promptly re-elected him, but once again he was expelled. Between the years 1830 and 1835, Mackenzie was elected five times and expelled five times.

**Reformers appeal to Britain**

In the belief that the new British monarch, King William IV, was a liberal-minded man, the Reformers decided to appeal to him directly. In 1832, Mackenzie left for England, taking with him petitions signed by more than 25,000 citizens. The petitions begged His Majesty and the British government to investigate conditions in Upper Canada and to make changes in the rule of the province.

Mackenzie was well received in England and had the opportunity of talking with senior officials in the British government. While some of them sympathized with the visitor, and, indeed, would have liked to have helped him, they could do little for him. Disappointed, Mackenzie returned home.

His popularity among the people had not faded during his absence. In 1834, when the town of York became the city of Toronto, he was elected its first mayor.

**The Seventh Report on Grievances**

A year later, the Reformers were once again in the majority in the Assembly, and Mackenzie was able to resume his seat without further expulsion. As chairman of a committee he brought in *The Seventh Report on Grievances,* which listed the demands of the Reform party. One important demand was that the Legislative Council should be elected by the people of the province.

**Sir Francis Bond Head**

The rising importance of the Reform party, however, was checked in 1836 when Sir Francis Bond Head was appointed Lieutenant-Governor of Upper Canada. Without experience in high office and with no interest in reform, the new governor was soon at odds with the Assembly. Conditions became serious when the Assembly refused to vote the monies required by the government. Shocked by such stubbornness, Sir Francis dissolved the Assembly and then ordered a new election, in which—to everyone's utter amazement—he himself played an active part. Always speaking sternly, he warned many inhabitants of the province that if the Reformers were not defeated, Great Britain might decide to break its ties with the province. This threat was more than enough to

In June, 1826, a band of young gentlemen boldly raided William Lyon Mackenzie's printing shop on Front Street in York. In a vain attempt to intervene, two of Mackenzie's apprentices rushed forward but were driven back by the raiders. Meanwhile, this outrage was being witnessed from the street by many citizens of York, among whom were two prominent officials. All of them stood idly by, watching this lawless incident with amused interest.

return the Tory party to power, all the leading Reformers, except Dr. Rolph, being defeated.

This totally unexpected turn of events so embittered and angered Mackenzie that he began to think of more dangerous means of securing reform in Upper Canada.

# 15.  1837–Rebellion in Upper Canada

Mackenzie
renews
attacks
on Family
Compact

UNREST THROUGHOUT THE PROVINCE increased during 1837, because economic conditions were extremely bad and, in addition, many people were moving south into the United States. The prosperity of the previous years disappeared. Almost every inhabitant of Upper Canada was affected by a sudden decline in business, industry and farming. The government of Upper Canada, which had lost money in a banking venture in Britain, was nearly bankrupt.

After the first shock of defeat in the 1836 election, Mackenzie returned to his newspaper career, this time with another paper he founded, *The Constitution.* His attacks on the Family Compact and on all those who had voted for the Tories were much more stinging than anything he had written before. He was by this time obsessed by his belief that government was a sacred trust to be administered on behalf of the people.

Mackenzie was in contact with Reformers in Lower Canada who were equally restive under their government. Information from Lower Canada seemed to indicate that many French Canadians were ready to take stern measures to gain reforms. There was some hope, Mackenzie believed, that, if the two Canadas stood together, there might be some chance of mutual success.

Mackenzie
plans
rebellion

By the early summer of 1837, Mackenzie had reached the point where he was actually planning an armed rebellion. Moving about from place to place in the vicinity of Toronto, he addressed groups of farmers and villagers and organized "vigilance committees." In addressing one such meeting, he made the following bold statement:

> When government is engaged in systematically oppressing a great people, it commits the same species of wrong to them that warrants an appeal to force against a foreign army . . . The glorious revolutions

of 1688 [in Great Britain] and of 1776 [in the United States] may serve to remind those rulers that they are placing themselves in a state of hostility against the governed.

In order to prevent any interference from Tories or others at meetings, farmers armed themselves with clubs, hickory sticks, pikes, muskets and shotguns. Tory newspapers threatened Mackenzie with death if he did not cease stirring up the people, but this only resulted in an increase in the number of armed men who accompanied Mackenzie on his rounds.

Mackenzie's vigilance committees soon began to collect fire-arms and practise marksmanship. (Their target practice sessions in many cases were made to appear innocent forms of recreation—shooting at turkeys and wild pigeons.) Bullets were cast; metal pike heads were forged in blacksmith shops. Men held secret sessions at night. Some of the would-be soldiers who had no fire-arms solemnly drilled with canes and umbrellas. A few mounted "lancers" took part in these drills, and those who did not have proper lances employed carving knives tied to the ends of fishing poles. Altogether, such military preparations could scarcely be considered efficient, but they were indications of approaching trouble. **Vigilance committees**

The Lieutenant-Governor, Sir Francis Bond Head, was aware of Mackenzie's activities, but he did not take them seriously. After all, the election had indicated that the people of the province were loyal to the government. Why not let Mackenzie rave, rant and fume? It could do no harm. So confident was the governor, that he allowed troops from York and Kingston to be sent to Lower Canada to cope with the violence that threatened. This foolish gesture gave Mackenzie the opportunity for which he had been waiting. **Bond Head ignores Mackenzie**

In October, 1837, Mackenzie had received word from Lower Canada that the *Patriotes* (Reformers) there were ready to launch a "brave stroke for liberty." They urged him to make a strike at the same time. In November, Mackenzie called the Reformers **Mackenzie calls for action** into conference in a Toronto brewery and begged for immediate action:

... seize Sir Francis ... carry him to the City Hall ... seize the ammunition there ... rouse our innumerable friends in town and country ... proclaim a provisional government and either induce Sir Francis to give the country an Executive Council responsible to a new and fairly chosen Assembly, or if he refuses to comply, go at once for Independence, and take proper steps to obtain it.

Since most of the Reformers present were unwilling to commit themselves to immediate action, Mackenzie had to be satisfied with a postponement. He realized the rebellion would have a better chance of success if a few of the moderate and highly respected Reformers committed themselves to action. Eventually, he persuaded Dr. John Rolph that the revolt could be managed with very little risk.

Mackenzie then proceeded energetically with the final preparations for the date set for rebellion—December 7, 1837. Plans called for the assembly of 5,000 men at Montgomery's Tavern, four miles north of Toronto on Yonge Street. (This tavern stood near the present-day intersection of Eglinton Avenue and Yonge Street.)

**Rebellion in Lower Canada**

Toward the end of November, the government at Toronto was startled to learn that rebellion had indeed broken out in Lower Canada and that British troops had fought a hard engagement with the *Patriotes* at St. Denis in the valley of the Richelieu River. Colonel James Fitzgibbon, a veteran officer of the War of 1812, alarmed by reports of impending rebellion in Upper Canada, tried to persuade Sir Francis Bond Head and John Beverley Robinson that the militia should be called out to meet the emergency. The governor refused permission. Robinson said stiffly, "I am sorry to see you alarming the people in this way."

However, so many reports of rebel activity reached Toronto that the governor agreed to mobilize two regiments of militia and to issue a warrant for the arrest of William Lyon Mackenzie. On hearing of this development, Dr. Rolph dispatched a letter to Mackenzie, urging him to strike earlier than December 7. Any further delay, Rolph feared, would end in disaster.

The doctor's letter only succeeded in causing confusion, for

Mackenzie could not be found, and other rebel leaders changed the date of rebellion to December 4.

Small groups of men bearing a weird assortment of arms and banners demanding "LIBERTY OR DEATH" began moving southward on Yonge Street.

In the meantime, learning of Rolph's message, Mackenzie sent out orders that the original date was to be maintained. However, it was then too late to recall the rebels moving toward Toronto. Mackenzie had no choice but to hurry to Montgomery's Tavern.

Rebels straggled in to the point of assembly—cold, tired and hungry. There was confusion everywhere. The new owner of the Tavern was unfriendly toward Mackenzie . . . arms and ammunition which had been expected did not arrive . . . news of the uprising in Lower Canada was disheartening . . . some of the men deserted and struck out immediately for home.

Mackenzie urged the attack on Toronto, demanding that the rebels capture the government. The rebels preferred to wait until the next day. It was a costly delay, for news of the rebel assembly at Montgomery's Tavern had reached the city. Mackenzie, discouraged by the turn of events, behaved as if he had lost his reason. He screamed at the men and insulted some of his most faithful followers.

On the morning of December 5, the actual march on Toronto began. Mackenzie pulled on several bulky overcoats, mounted a white farm horse and placed himself at the head of the motley column of men. It was a pathetic little army of a few hundred cold, bewildered and hungry men that straggled down Yonge Street, bearing their muskets, pikes, spears, clubs, pitchforks and knives. A long halt was made while rations were handed out.

In the meantime, the citizens of Toronto waited fearfully for what they thought was an invading army of 5,000 rebels. About 300 men of the Family Compact, the Tory party and other loyal groups seized their muskets and assembled hastily in the marketplace. A picket of thirty volunteers, led by Sheriff Jarvis, stood guard by a barricade on the northern outskirts of the city.

Rebel march on Toronto

The most modern equipment of its day, this Toronto fire-engine of 1837 had to be pulled to the scene of action by volunteer firemen. It was little more than a large, wooden tank and pump mounted on wheels. Long, wooden pumping handles or "brakes," one on each side, extended lengthwise along the engine. When in operation, the handles were worked up and down by the firemen, twelve or fifteen to a side. Their vigorous pumping actions forced water out of the tank and through the leather hose. In order to maintain the flow of water, it was necessary to refill the tank by carrying water from the nearest source of supply—a well, cistern, lake or river. This particular machine was called out in 1837 when Mackenzie's rebels set fire to a bridge over the Don River. The rebels heard the rumble of the fire-engine and ran away, thinking that a cannon was being brought into action against them. Fortunately, the firemen arrived in time to save the bridge.

**The skirmish on Yonge Street**

In the gathering twilight, Mackenzie's force finally reached a point in the vicinity of the present-day Maple Leaf Gardens. There, the thirty-man picket opened fire and then flung away their arms and fled.

Riflemen in the front ranks of Mackenzie's force returned the fire and then dropped to the ground to reload. The sudden fall of the riflemen, however, made it appear that they had been mown down by musket fire. This was all that was required to make the rebels turn and run in blind panic. For all they knew, thousands of loyal troops were lying in wait along the borders of Yonge Street. Not even Mackenzie's wildest screams of rage could stop the mad retreat that swept him, still on his horse, back toward Montgomery's Tavern.

No one realized that thirty frightened men had broken the back of Mackenzie's rebellion.

Mackenzie and his chastened forces gathered once more at Montgomery's Tavern, while loyal militia poured into the city to support the government. Two days after the twilight encounter, the militia marched northward along Yonge Street with Colonel Fitzgibbon, Sir Francis Bond Head and John Strachan riding at the head of the main body. With them went two light cannon. **The end of the rebellion**

Mackenzie hurried 150 of his men southward to a wooded knoll half a mile or so south of the Tavern. It was there that the clash occurred, a brief encounter punctuated by the sharp crack of fire-arms and the low boom of cannon. For a brief time, the rebels stood firm, but as a group of Fitzgibbon's men made a curving flank attack, the rebels broke cover and took to their heels. Advancing steadily, the militia moved their guns and, when within range of rebel headquarters, continued fire. Mackenzie and other leaders of the rebellion fled. The uprising was over.

After an adventurous journey, during which he narrowly missed capture, Mackenzie managed to cross the Niagara River and reach the safety of the American side.

Mackenzie won enough support among American radicals and British residents in the United States to establish what he called a provisional government on Navy Island, three miles above Niagara Falls. Money, arms, supplies and food were dispatched to the little rebel from various parts of the northern states. By the end of December, Mackenzie had a volunteer army of about 200 men, and a number of "invasions of Canada" took place, but they accomplished nothing. Then, a party of Tory supporters from Upper Canada attacked the little American steamer, the *Caroline*, Mackenzie's link with supplies on the American mainland. Set on **The provisional government**

fire and cut loose from her moorings, the steamer went over Niagara Falls. Eventually, the rebels were forced to withdraw to the American mainland.

United States authorities, alarmed by Mackenzie's war-mongering activities, arrested him on a charge of endangering the peace between the United States and the Canadas. After a year in prison at Rochester, he went to New York City and remained there until 1849, when he was allowed to return to Upper Canada.

Many of Mackenzie's followers were less fortunate. After the rebellion, several of his lieutenants were hanged for treason and almost one hundred others were sent into exile.

The Rebellion of 1837 was an utterly farcical affair, badly organized and doomed to failure almost from the start. However,

The battle near Montgomery's Tavern, December 7, 1837, was all over in half an hour. The retreat saw arms abandoned in the fields. Following the brief bombardment of the Tavern itself, in the words of an eyewitness: *A crowd of men rushed from the doors and scattered wildly in a northerly direction. Those on the hill wavered, receded under the shelter of the undulating land and then fled like their fellows.* Sir Francis Bond Head then ordered that the Tavern should be burned to the ground to mark the end of "that perfidious enemy, 'responsible government.'" Today, a modern post office occupies the site.

it is historically important because it did focus British attention upon the turmoil and unrest in Upper Canada. As a startling protest against colonial misgovernment, it set in motion a series of events that ultimately was to have an important effect on the future form of government in the provinces.

# 16. 1837—Rebellion in Lower Canada

IN COMPARISON WITH the fight for reform in Upper Canada, Lower Canada witnessed a struggle that was, in part, a clash between French-speaking and English-speaking politicians and peoples.

**The Château Clique**

An English-speaking group of wealthy businessmen constituted the Family Compact, or, as it was usually called, the Château Clique. (This expression resulted from the close association of the Clique with the Château St. Louis, the one-time Quebec residence of the governors of New France.) Members of the Château Clique controlled the English-speaking Executive and Legislative Councils, while French-speaking members held a majority of seats in the Legislative Assembly. Thus, although an assembly was again at odds with two councils, there was an additional friction caused by differences of race and custom.

**French and British**

The French and the British had lived together in fairly peaceful fashion from 1763 until about 1820. In 1821, however, the Hudson's Bay Company and the North West Company had combined to form one trading organization. As a result of this union, Lower Canada lost the great wealth created by the fur trade and the Montreal merchants invested their time and money in the export of timber and grain. These English-speaking businessmen had urged the construction of canals on the St. Lawrence River to lower the transportation costs of grain and, at the same time, increase the flow of British immigrants. Neither of these aims was welcomed by the French; they disliked being taxed for transportation projects that brought them little direct benefit and they feared a great influx of British people into their province.

At about the same time, the Family Compact of Upper Canada and the Château Clique of Lower Canada almost succeeded in persuading the British government to unite the two Canadas into

126

one province. Under this arrangement, French-speaking members were convinced that they would lose their control of the proposed joint assembly. In consequence, the Assembly decided to resist the growing ambitions of the Château Clique.

During the nineteenth century, settlers often found it necessary or economical to manufacture their own sugar. Vast maple stands provided a ready source of sap, which was collected in pails or troughs in the early spring and boiled slowly in great iron or copper kettles. The thin syrup thus obtained was cleared of impurities by a special process and then heated again for quite some time to "boil down" into maple sugar. When the sugar was of the right consistency, it was poured off into pans or moulds and allowed to set. Many of the sugar moulds were ornamented—as can be seen in this mould used on the Isle of Orleans in Lower Canada, about 1837. Some estimates of the amount of sugar obtained during a good season in Lower Canada run as high as five and one-quarter pounds per tree. However, average yields were probably below this figure. When cane sugar could be purchased easily and cheaply (after mid-century), many families ceased making maple sugar.

The French-speaking majority in the Assembly possessed a leader in the person of Louis Joseph Papineau, the son of a distinguished provincial parliamentarian. Like his father, Papineau was an eloquent, emotional speaker and a politician of unusual skill. His ability to revive bitter memories of the Conquest of 1763 and his burning desire to win political rights for his race made him a dangerous opponent.

*Louis Joseph Papineau*

Hostility between the Assembly and the Legislative Council became so severe that it led to a deadlock in government. The Council blocked bills that the Assembly desired to pass, while the Assembly, in turn, refused to vote the monies required by the Council.

*Deadlock in government*

By 1832, the situation was so acute and tempers so hot that rioting broke out during an election in Montreal. The incident was serious enough that troops had to be called out. In the clash that followed, stones and bullets were exchanged, and several French Canadians were killed.

**The Ninety-two Resolutions, 1834**

Two years later, Papineau and a number of his followers produced a list of grievances called *The Ninety-Two Resolutions*. Some of the complaints included were valid, but many were quite ridiculous, and the language of the document was both bitter and intemperate. It was evident that Papineau was moving away from his former attitude of moderation. So radical was his new viewpoint that he lost the sympathy of some of his followers as well as leaders of the Roman Catholic Church. The majority of French Canadians were anxious for reform but they had no desire for impulsive action or open rebellion.

By 1837, government in Lower Canada had ground to a virtual standstill as a result of the stubborn attitudes of the Assembly and the Council. Yet, even in the spring of that year, Papineau was not at all sure that rebellion was the proper course of action. In an address, he said:

> I have some acquaintance with my country, having studied its history and having for thirty years been thrown by circumstances most actively into the maelstrom of public life . . . The democratic flood has poured irresistibly down the slope of time and, growing faster and faster, will topple the unavailing barriers which may be erected against it. In these circumstances, must we take to slaughter, or might we not better wear down a bad government through the constitutional opposition which may, and which must, be shown in Parliament?

**The Ten Resolutions, 1837**

Deciding that some action had to be taken to get the machinery of government into action once again, the British government passed *The Ten Resolutions*. These, in effect, renewed a previous offer, which stated that the Assembly might control all government funds—if it agreed to pay permanent salaries to the governor and other officials. The Ten Resolutions, however, now added that if the Assembly did not agree to this arrangement, the governor would be empowered to pay out funds without the consent of the Assembly.

This development caused consternation among Papineau and

his followers, the *Patriotes*. In the session of 1837, the French members of the Assembly refused to surrender their old privilege of voting funds. In August, the Assembly was adjourned for an indefinite period of time. To the *Patriotes* it seemed that armed rebellion was the only course left to them.

Both sides began to prepare for hostilities. The government sought increased military support and the *Patriotes* collected arms and attended secret drill sessions. In imitation of the "Sons of Liberty" of the American Revolution, the radicals spoke of themselves as *"Fils de la Liberté."* During their rallies they shouted such slogans as *"La Nation Canadienne"* and *"Papineau et l'indépendance."* **Preparations for rebellion**

In Montreal, in November, 1837, the rebellion in Lower Canada began, almost accidentally, in a street brawl between members of the English-speaking Doric Club and some *Patriotes*. Next, Papineau was advised that perhaps he should leave the city so that his presence would not lead to further turmoil. Papineau accepted **Violence in Montreal**

During the seventeenth and eighteenth centuries, craftsmen in New France created beautiful furniture that was influenced by various European designs. After the fall of Quebec in 1759, French-Canadian designers were increasingly cut off from continental styles and more strongly affected by furniture brought to British North America by the United Empire Loyalists and by British army officers stationed in garrison towns. The birch vestry-desk illustrated here is a harmonious blend of the English Regency style with some earlier French styles. French-Canadian craftsmanship in furniture still lives on, for even today there is a vigorous group of furniture designers in the province of Quebec.

this advice. Then British authorities began to fear that he did so in order to be able to move about surrounding districts and incite rebellion. Warrants were immediately issued for the arrest of Papineau and his more important *Patriote* followers. When word of this action reached the *Patriotes,* they determined to protect their leaders.

Numbers of the aroused radicals collected in the valley of the Richelieu River (south and east of Montreal) for it was there that Papineau had gone after leaving the city. On learning that the Richelieu region had become the danger spot, the government dispatched troops to take prisoners and disperse any armed *Patriote* groups.

**British defeat at St. Denis**

On November 22, 1837, a small force of British troops marched through rain, mud and darkness toward the village of St. Denis on the Richelieu River. The following day, they fought a five-hour engagement with a large body of half-armed, untrained *Patriotes,* who put up such a strong resistance that the regulars retreated, leaving six dead.

**Rebel defeat at St. Charles**

Two days later, a second clash occurred at another Richelieu valley town, St. Charles, but this time the rebels were soundly defeated. The *Patriotes,* were, in fact, badly disciplined and armed only with some rusty cannon and a queer collection of hand guns, including ancient flintlocks tied together with wire.

After the defeat at St. Charles, Papineau escaped to the United States, leaving his hapless followers to face the consequences.

**Rebel defeat at St. Eustache**

In spite of Papineau's loss to the *Patriote* cause, the rebellion was not yet over. Several engagements took place, but the major one was the battle at St. Eustache, a village about eighteen miles to the north and west of Montreal and the only important centre of revolt left.

On a wintry, December day, troops closing in on the village opened fire with cannon on the church that sheltered a hard core of determined *Patriotes.* Then, as the scene was obscured by the smoke from a burning house, the troops hurled themselves forward. An officer who was present described the action:

The assembly was sounded and an order given to fix bayonets and advance at the double, a manoeuvre so promptly executed ... that our troops were under the walls and effected an entrance almost as soon as the besieged became acquainted with the movement. The rebels were found stationed in the gallery, still defending themselves, and their having cut away the staircase, every effort to dislodge them for a while proved utterly fruitless, but on a sudden the church was in flames and on the part of the rebels all was lost. The unfortunate and misguided people were then to be seen dispersing in every direction, few escaping. One hundred and twenty were taken prisoner, but the estimated loss in killed and wounded was great.

This flag was used in 1837 by the rebels in Lower Canada, the *Patriotes*, in the Battle of St. Eustache and also at St. Benoit, one of the minor skirmishes. The flag was originally designed to be used in celebrations following the adoption by the Assembly of Papineau's *Ninety-Two Resolutions*. The original flag is preserved today in Quebec City.

The rebellion had actually been confined to a region lying close
to Montreal. In such other centres as Three Rivers and Quebec
City the populace remained quiet. Only a small group of French
Canadians had participated in an uprising which, as a military
adventure, had been doomed to failure from the beginning. The
*Patriotes* had been poorly trained and organized, and the supply
of arms had been pathetically small for a serious operation. No
doubt it is also true to say that the opposition of the Church contributed to the cool, detached attitude of most of Lower Canada.
This was yet another serious blow to rebel strength.

Papineau himself remained for some time in the United States
and then crossed the Atlantic to France where he took up temporary residence. In 1845, he was allowed to return and resume
political life, but never again did he enjoy the prominence he
had once held in public affairs.

Although both rebellions were viewed with alarm in Great
Britain, the one in Lower Canada was by far the more serious of
the two, since it produced much bloodshed. It also filled jails
with political prisoners, disrupted the trade of the St. Lawrence
and caused many inhabitants to emigrate to the United States.
The total effect was to demonstrate to the government in London
that the provincial reform movements had to be taken much
more seriously.

# 17. Lord Durham

PROFOUNDLY DISTURBED by the rebellions in Upper and Lower Canada, the British government felt it necessary to appoint a forceful and intelligent governor-general to the North American provinces.

The man selected to deal with this difficult, uneasy situation overseas was John George Lambton, first Earl of Durham. He was a proud, aristocratic young man, gifted with remarkable powers of oratory and a keen interest in political affairs. Liberal in outlook, he could be counted upon to sympathize with the problems of the common people. Indeed, some British leaders feared he might be too sympathetic, for his reputation in England had gained him the nickname "Radical Jack." By nature, Lord Durham was also a moody individual possessed of a violent, and sometimes uncontrollable temper. These characteristics made it difficult for him to work smoothly with his associates.

**Lord Durham**

He left Britain with instructions to investigate the causes of the recent disturbances, to win the support of discontented people in the provinces, to improve relations with the United States and to make recommendations for the improvement of colonial government.

**Durham's duties**

The conditions he encountered in the British provinces were anything but encouraging to Lord Durham. Legislative assemblies in the two Canadas had been dissolved and groups of rebels were still held in prison awaiting trial.

One of Durham's touchiest problems was the question of the rebels still in confinement. It was a most difficult situation, for a lenient policy toward the rebels might be interpreted as a sign of weakness. On the other hand, the imposition of severe sentences could arouse the anger of liberal-minded people throughout the Canadas.

**Imprisoned rebels**

Until the introduction of kerosene (a by-product of petroleum) in 1858, the common source of household light was the tallow candle or lamp. In fact, even after the introduction of kerosene lamps, many older people continued to use candles because they liked their mellow flicker. One of the commonest types of candle-stands was the sconce (1), a simple holder fitted with a tin reflector. Sconces varied widely in shape and design. Sometimes a candelabrum (2) was used to give light or to provide decorative lighting in dining-rooms. In a draughty room, a candle-holder with a glass chimney (3) proved useful and helped to reflect more light. The slender, cone-shaped object beside it is a candle-snuffer, of sufficient length to reach down the chimney to the flame. (4) and (5) are lamps of the same period. They had wicks of rush or tow and burned tallow, fish-oil or whale-oil.

Durham decided that trial by jury might lead to a miscarriage of justice. Consequently, he arranged for the imprisoned rebels to plead guilty and ask for mercy. In due course, Papineau and the others who had escaped to the United States were declared banished; eight others were banished to Bermuda and the rest were set free.

These merciful decisions were greeted with considerable support in North America. Durham's treatment of the rebels pleased many French-speaking and English-speaking Canadians and won frank admiration in the United States. As for the rebels themselves, they were only too pleased to escape the gallows.

Lord Durham seems to have been the one person who suffered as a result of his action. In fact, not even a governor-general had the legal right to banish prisoners without trial and conviction. It would, however, have been simple for the British goverment to ratify Durham's sensible solution to a difficult problem. An act of Parliament could have legalized the banishment of the Canadian rebels. Unfortunately this was not done. Members of the opposition party attacked Durham viciously in the British House of Commons, while members of his own Whig party stood weakly by, offering little defence of the absent Durham. **Durham criticized in Britain**

Angered by what he considered shabby treatment in the British Parliament, Lord Durham submitted his resignation and left for England on November 1, 1838. He had been in North America only five months. **Resignation of Durham, 1838**

In spite of the discredit which had fallen upon him in Britain, Durham left a host of friends and admirers behind. The Americans were keenly disappointed when he departed in such haste, for he had planned to pass through the northern states and board a ship at New York City. His secretary, Buller, later wrote:

> On our return to England he [Durham] was informed by Mr. Stevenson, the American Minister, that at Washington he was to have remained with the President at the White House as a national guest—an honour never before conferred on anyone but Lafayette.

Many men in Lord Durham's position would have washed their hands of the whole Canadian business and turned to some other matter. Durham was not of that type. His conscience and his pride would not permit him to drop the responsibility in hand until he had made out a report on conditions in the Provinces. On his return to England, he threw himself energetically into the completion of his task, and in two months time produced one of the most

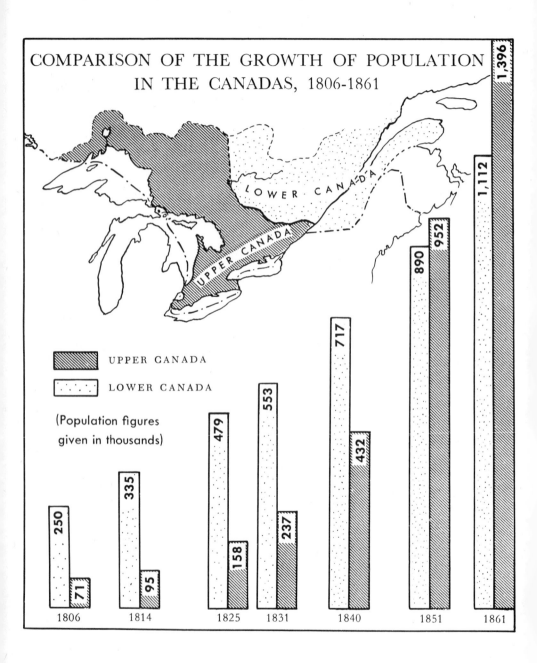

COMPARISON OF THE GROWTH OF POPULATION
IN THE CANADAS, 1806-1861

LOWER CANADA

UPPER CANADA

UPPER CANADA

LOWER CANADA

(Population figures
given in thousands)

| 1806 | 1814 | 1825 | 1831 | 1840 | 1851 | 1861 |

250 · 71 · 335 · 95 · 479 · 158 · 553 · 237 · 717 · 432 · 890 · 952 · 1,112 · 1,396

remarkable documents in British imperial history. Its official title is the *Report on the Affairs of British North America,* more frequently called "The Durham Report."

While Durham's document made reference to all the provinces, it was concerned chiefly with the troublesome areas of Upper and Lower Canada. His most important recommendation undoubtedly was the suggestion that these two provinces should be re-united into one. He suggested that the political boundary lying between the two had caused friction in the past and had handicapped the development of trade and transportation.

THE DURHAM REPORT, 1839

Re-union of the Canadas, he thought, might serve to break the deadlock that existed in the government of Lower Canada. In a new assembly elected at large, the French Canadians would be in a minority and therefore could not block the wishes of the English-speaking population. Durham felt that in the past there had been mismanagement by the governing group, but that the French, too, had been stubborn and narrow-minded in the conduct of Assembly affairs. The best hope for the future, Durham wrote, was to create a situation in which French Canadians would be exposed to British political techniques and practices. As he wrote in his *Report*:

> If the population of Upper Canada is rightly estimated at 400,000, the English inhabitants of Lower Canada at 150,000, and the French at 450,000, the union of the two provinces would not only give a clear English majority, but one which would be increased every year by the influence of English emigration; and I have little doubt that the French, when once placed, by the legitimate course of events and the working of natural causes, in a minority, would abandon their vain hopes of nationality.

Despite his usual astuteness, Durham believed that French Canadians would abandon their traditions, their practices and their language when placed in a minority. He, of course, sadly underestimated the vigour and the vitality of the citizens of Lower Canada. Canadian history has proved him wrong.

Convinced that the people of the Provinces had to be given a greater voice and authority in their own government, Durham outlined very liberal proposals. He suggested that the British govern-

Lord Durham completes his famous *Report*, a document that has been described as "one of the greatest state papers in the English language." (Durham was assisted in preparing the *Report* by his secretary, Buller, and by Edward Gibbon Wakefield, an English colonial statesman. Their assistance gave rise to the malicious comment made by Durham's political enemies that his only contribution to the entire work was his signature.) The *Report* was prepared, printed and submitted to the British Parliament in the remarkably brief period of two months. Durham's death a few months later robbed British politics of one of the greatest figures of that time. It is interesting to note that, while Lord Durham had a somewhat touchy nature, he also possessed and displayed a distinct charm. He made such a deep impression upon the American president, Van Buren, and his party in the course of a reception held at Niagara Falls that Buller, Durham's secretary, noted: *a million of money would have been a cheap price for a glass of wine which Lord Durham drank to the health of the American President.*

ment should retain control of foreign relations, commerce, the right to frame constitutions for colonial governments and the disposal of public lands. All other powers and duties would be handed over to provincial governments. He recommended, too, that all revenues (except revenue from the sale of public lands) should be placed at the disposal of provincial assemblies. Assemblies, in turn, would guarantee the payment of salaries to the governors and civil servants.

One vital recommendation he made was designed to give more power to the people. By his plan the old Executive Council was to be made *responsible* to the Legislative Assembly rather than to the Governor. Members of the new-type Council or *Cabinet* were to be chosen from the party that held a majority in the Assembly. Members of the Cabinet (ministers) were each to be given charge of a department of the government. This method of creating a Cabinet would prevent situations in which the Council and the Assembly would be at odds with each other and would also give elected representatives of the people effective control. Cabinet system proposed

It is worth noting that the original idea of responsible government for the Canadian provinces had been suggested by Robert Baldwin, the moderate Reformer of Upper Canada. Baldwin had persuaded Lord Durham that such a plan could be made to work successfully. Durham's great contribution was that he included the proposal in his *Report* and so brought it forceably to the attention of the British government.

Durham's shrewd analysis of the conditions he found amounted to a sweeping condemnation of government as it existed in Upper and Lower Canada. His words implied that many of the complaints of the rebel leaders were just. In his *Report,* Durham spoke critically of blunders made by the British Colonial Office, of greed on the part of the Family Compact, of dishonesty in the handling of public lands, of the sad condition of education and of the lack of government at the community level.

Durham's recommendations were received with enthusiasm by many Canadian Reformers, but other groups were loud in their protests against the *Report.* Tories in Upper Canada were alarmed by the thought of union with Lower Canada and shocked at the thought of responsible government. Members of the Family Compact ridiculed the *Report,* pointing out that Lord Durham had been in Upper Canada for only eleven days during his five-months in office. French Canadians were angered by the charges Support and condemnation for Durham's Report brought against them and feared the proposed plan of union. The British government was itself divided in opinion concerning Durham's proposals. Much confusion was caused because people could not understand how a colonial government could control its own affairs and still remain loyal to the British crown and Empire.

**Durham's importance**    The passage of time has thrown a kinder light upon Lord Durham and his remarkable *Report*. Today we recognize that his important recommendations pointed the way to self-government, to improved management of local affairs, to better educational conditions and to eventual federation of the Canadian provinces. Durham was one of the political architects of the Canadian nation.

Durham's health deteriorated rapidly after his return to England.  It is quite possible that his strenuous activities in the Canadas and the stress and strain of his resignation contributed to this condition.  He died in June, 1840.  It was evident that Canadian affairs were very much on his mind during his last days of life when he said, "Canada will one day do justice to my memory."

# 18. The Union of the Canadas, 1841

DURHAM'S REPORT was approved by the British government, but responsible government did not become a reality in the provinces for some years. It proved difficult to work out an arrangement by which authority could be divided agreeably between the Governor and the elected representatives of the people.

In the autumn of 1839, the new Governor-General, Charles Poulett Thomson, later Lord Sydenham, arrived at Quebec. The new Governor was both a man of business and an experienced politician. Filled with enthusiasm and good humour, he set about his task with tireless energy. **Lord Sydenham arrives, 1839**

After a quick survey of the situation, Thomson decided his first duty was to gain support for the union of Upper and Lower Canada. He secured approval for union in Lower Canada by working with a friendly Council and in Upper Canada by promising financial aid. Upper Canada was seriously in debt over the construction of canals and other projects, and the prospect of help was most welcome.

The British government, pleased with Thomson's skilful work, passed the *Act of Union,* which came into effect in February, 1841. **THE ACT OF UNION, 1841** Under the Act, Upper and Lower Canada were united to form the *Province of Canada.* There was to be one legislature composed of a Legislative Assembly or Lower House, a Legislative Council or Upper House and an Executive Council. Instead of following Durham's proposal of electing members on a population basis (which, at that time could have meant that the French-Canadian members would dominate the Assembly), the Act gave each former province an equal number of representatives. The Legislative Assembly was to have 84 members elected by the people. The

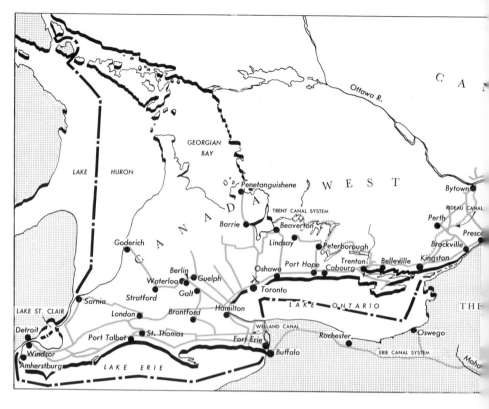

Legislative Council would consist of 20 members appointed by the Governor for life and would *still be responsible to the Governor*. In addition, the Executive Council was *still to be appointed by the Governor*. Members of the Executive Council were no longer to hold office for life but were to be heads of government departments, retaining office only as long as the Governor himself decided was necessary. However, they were required to appear before the representatives of the people in the Legislative Assembly to sponsor and defend government business.

The British government decided to take no chances on disloyal members finding their way into the parliament of the Province of Canada. By the Act of Union, all those taking a place in the Legislative Council or Legislative Assembly were required to swear an oath of allegiance in which they promised:

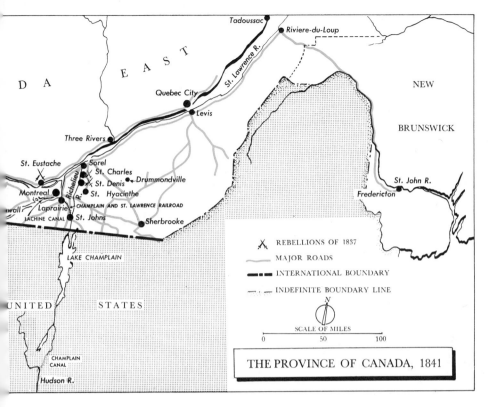

THE PROVINCE OF CANADA, 1841

Map legend:
- REBELLIONS OF 1837
- MAJOR ROADS
- INTERNATIONAL BOUNDARY
- INDEFINITE BOUNDARY LINE

SCALE OF MILES
0    50    100

Places shown: Tadoussac, Riviere-du-Loup, Quebec City, Levis, Three Rivers, St. Eustache, Sorel, St. Charles, St. Denis, Drummondville, Montreal, St. Hyacinthe, Laprairie, St. Johns, Sherbrooke, LACHINE CANAL, CHAMPLAIN AND ST. LAWRENCE RAILROAD, LAKE CHAMPLAIN, UNITED STATES, CHAMPLAIN CANAL, Hudson R., NEW BRUNSWICK, Fredericton, St. John R.

I . . . do sincerely promise and swear that I will be faithful and **Oath of allegiance** bear true allegiance to her Majesty, Queen Victoria, as lawful Sovereign of the United Kingdom of Great Britain and Ireland and of this Province of Canada, dependent on and belonging to the said United Kingdom; and I will defend her to the utmost of my power against all traitorous conspiracies and attempts whatever, which shall be made against her person, crown and dignity; and that I will do my utmost endeavour to disclose and make known to her Majesty, her heirs and successors, all treasons and traitorous conspiracies and attempts which I shall know to be against her or any of them; and all this I do swear without any equivocation, mental evasion, or secret reservation, and renouncing all pardons and dispensations from any person or persons whatever to the contrary, SO HELP ME GOD.

French Canadians were not pleased with two points in the new **Dissatisfaction in Canada East** arrangement of government. First, they felt that *Canada East* (formerly Lower Canada) should have the larger number of members in the Assembly because its population was greater than *Canada West* (formerly Upper Canada).   Second, the French Canadians did not relish the thought of helping to pay old debts incurred in former years by Canada West.

The Act of Union was by no means the complete solution to problems in the Canadas. In fact, it was in itself rather vague. Much depended on the way in which is was to be put into practice.

**First Union Parliament, 1841**

After an election, the first Union Parliament met in the new capital, Kingston, in June, 1841. The session opened with all the pomp and ceremony that could be arranged—including artillery salutes and a speech from the Throne, read by Lord Sydenham. It was, indeed, an important event in Canadian history; it saw French Canadians and British Canadians meeting on a new footing, and it saw the beginning of effective parties in Canadian politics.

**Sydenham's idea of government**

The new Governor was not prepared to follow all the recommendations made by Lord Durham. For example, Sydenham could not accept the proposal that a governor should hand over any part of his responsibility to others, and, in consequence, his advisers were treated as members of an executive council rather than a cabinet, that is, a group of elected representatives responsible for their actions to the Assembly.  He would listen, he said, to the advice of his Executive Council, but he did not consider himself bound to follow its suggestions.  However, Sydenham did choose a Council he hoped would retain the confidence and support of the Assembly.

**Opposition to Sydenham**

Sydenham's supporters claimed that this arrangement provided responsible government; the Reformers protested that it did not. Leaders in the Reform party pointed out that under true responsible government the cabinet was chosen by a prime minister who was elected by the people and who was leader of the party that held a majority. It was not democratic, they said, for a governor to act as the Queen's representative and at the same time perform the duties of a prime minister.

Lord Sydenham persisted in fighting off all attempts to lessen his own authority in government. He sincerely believed that the good of the Province and the mother country could best be served through skilful management on the part of the Governor and he was determined to strengthen the position of the Governor. The British Empire would surely disappear, he maintained, if more control were passed over to colonial assemblies elected by the people.

It is true that Sydenham was most skilful in the management of affairs and that he accomplished much in a short time. Had he been permitted to remain in power, however, it is probable that he would have encountered solid opposition from the Reformers. This contest was not to take place, for he died in September, 1841. His death was due to his poor health and to a leg injury suffered when he was thrown from a horse.

Lord Sydenham was succeeded by Sir Charles Bagot, a man who possessed long experience in diplomacy. He quickly decided that, in the interests of harmony, he must take French-speaking members into his Executive Council.

*Sydenham succeeded by Charles Bagot, 1841*

The Reform group in the Legislative Assembly had gained power through an alliance of French and English members. The French Reformers were led by a former follower of Papineau— Louis Lafontaine—who had become a moderate and able statesman. The English were led by the highly respected Robert Baldwin. These two men and their supporters formed such a strong combination that they made their desires felt in the government of the Province of Canada.

By 1842, the Reformers held a clear and undisputed majority in the Assembly. Recognizing and accepting this fact, Sir Charles Bagot appointed his Executive Council wholly from the Reform party members under the leadership of Baldwin and Lafontaine. For the first time, the Executive Council took the form of a cabinet. This was a long step toward responsible government.

*Reformers come to power*

It is important to realize that Sir Charles Bagot, unlike Sydenham, was prepared to adopt the cabinet system and was willing to give French-Canadian Reformers a trial at responsibility. This was a brave stand for Bagot to make, because he knew that it would not be a popular one in many quarters.

*Bagot's Reform*

Tory
opposition
to Bagot
Protests were not long in coming. Members of the Tory party, in particular, raised a storm of abuse in which they called Sir Charles such unflattering names as "old woman," "radical" and "puppet." French Canadians, on the other hand, were encouraged by the new development. Bagot's stand undoubtedly made them feel more sympathetic toward the union form of government. It was most unfortunate that, in 1843, fate should interfere with the progress towards responsible government. Sir Charles Bagot, suffering from a serious heart condition, was forced to resign. Two months later he was dead.

Bagot
succeeded
by Metcalfe,
1843
Sir Charles Metcalfe, Bagot's successor, had been Governor of Jamaica, but his service there did not prepare him for conditions in his new post. He was, by nature, opposed to any form of government that tended to weaken the authority of governors. He did not share Bagot's sympathy for the development of democratic government in the British colonies. It was impossible for Metcalfe to believe that a governor could look after the interests of his Queen and at the same time throw away control of government.

Reformers
opposed
to Metcalfe
It is not surprising, therefore, to find that Metcalfe and the Reformers in the Province of Canada were soon engaged in sharp disputes. The Governor at times ignored his ministers and, on occasion, appointed officials without consulting his cabinet.

This furniture of the period 1825-1850 was largely Ontario-made and of the simple, domestic type built by local craftsmen. High beds were often furnished with a canopy called a *tester*. The side curtains on the bed were originally designed to keep out draughts, but by this time they had largely become a mode of decoration. Modern bed springs were unknown, but a network of rope, stretching from front to back and side to side, served a similar purpose. On top of the rope network was placed a large, thick mattress filled with feathers. Above the bed can be seen a warming-pan of copper or brass. This metal utensil, filled with glowing embers from the fireplace, was moved about quickly between the sheets in order to warm the bed. Some of these nineteenth-century beds were so high that small steps were needed to enable people to climb into them. On the small bed-table are a china wash-bowl and jug made in one of the many potteries operating during the period. The chest of drawers is of simple design but beautifully constructed, with dovetailing at all joints. Taller chests, known as high-boys, were also common at this time. The chair is of a type called arrow-back because of the arrow-shaped rungs which formed the back of the chair. The thick seat and slightly splayed legs are typical of the period. Most of this furniture was made of pine or maple, often used in combination with lesser quantities of such woods as ash, hickory, elm and basswood. Although furniture was sometimes waxed or varnished, it was frequently painted terra-cotta red or dark green, grey or black or perhaps a soft grey-blue. The paints employed were often made in the home, some of them using buttermilk as a solvent.

V. MOULD

Conditions finally reached such a serious state that Baldwin and Lafontaine resigned.

Tories
returned
to power,
1844

During a bitter, violent election in 1844, the Reformers lost their majority and the Tories came into power. (One of the new Tory members was a bright young lawyer, John A. Macdonald, who represented Kingston. Not even the Tories themselves realized that in this young member they had acquired a future leader of great ability.) Metcalfe remained unyielding in his stand to retain power, for he felt as one author writes, "that he was fighting for his sovereign against a rebellious people." There would be no true responsible government so long as he was in power. Metcalfe resigned toward the end of the year 1845 and returned to England.

The struggle for responsible government was not yet over.

# 19. Responsible Government

IN 1847, JAMES BRUCE, eighth Earl of Elgin, became Governor-General. It was a most favourable appointment, for Lord Elgin possessed the necessary personality, experience and liberal outlook to deal with the restless situation in the Province of Canada.

With four years experience as Governor of Jamaica, Lord Elgin was no beginner in governmental affairs. His new connection with Canada was of great personal interest, because he was married to the daughter of Lord Durham, that remarkable man who had given such short, but distinguished service in this country. Elgin was well acquainted with his father-in-law's accomplishments and with his ideas for the improvement of colonial government. Indeed, the new Governor-General arrived in the Province of Canada determined to promote the recommendations included in Durham's *Report*. In short, Lord Elgin believed in responsible government.

Elgin's interest in responsible government

Unlike most governors who had preceded him, Lord Elgin made it known that he had no intention of taking part in election campaigns and that he would try to work agreeably with any government elected by the people. He showed, too, an early interest in French-speaking citizens and urged the home government to adopt a liberal policy toward them. He wrote that he was "deeply convinced of the impolicy of all attempts to denationalize the French."

The Tory party still held control in the Province of Canada, but its position had become insecure. It was so weak that in the election of 1849 the Reformers triumphed both in Canada East and Canada West. True to his promise, Lord Elgin took no part in the election campaign, and after the Reform victory he requested Robert Baldwin and Louis Lafontaine to form a new ministry. The two Reform leaders did so, and then proceeded to introduce in the legislature a long series of acts dealing with education, railway construction and government at the local level. Most of these acts were approved without serious opposition, but one called the *Act of Indemnification* brought hot debates, bitterness and violence.

Pioneer homes contained pieces of furniture that were unique in design and have no counterpart today. One of these pieces of furniture is seen here, a distinctly Canadian invention known as a *banc lit*, a pine bench that could be folded down to form a double bed. This was a particularly useful item of furniture in the pioneer home where space was usually limited and where there was often need for extra accommodation. This particular *banc lit* can be seen in the Schoolmaster's House in Upper Canada Village.

**"REBELLION LOSSES BILL," 1849**  This Bill, which came to be known as "The Rebellion Losses Bill," was created to compensate citizens in Canada East whose property had been destroyed or damaged during the Rebellion of 1837. In the various disturbances and battles, people had suffered loss of homes, barns, fences, domestic animals, tools, wagons and other personal property. Payment for similar damages had already been made in Canada West, but no settlement had been reached in Canada East.

The Rebellion Losses Bill proposed to compensate all those who had suffered "just losses" — except those few who had been convicted of treason for their parts in the rebellion. It was apparent, then, that rebels who had not been arrested could receive payment for damages suffered.

Introduction of the Bill caused a storm of protest which gave birth to angry discussion and even riots throughout the Province of Canada. The Rebellion Losses Bill was declared to be a ridiculous measure which rewarded rebels who had been guilty of disloyalty and treason. The Baldwin-Lafontaine government was termed a "rebel ministry." So hot were debates in parliament that, at times, it appeared the members might settle the matter with fists instead of words and votes. **Opposition to the Bill**

In spite of the strong opposition, the Rebellion Losses Bill was approved by the Assembly and Council. The next step was to have it given royal assent through the signature of the Governor-General. Lord Elgin, of course, was then placed in a difficult situation, for whatever action he took would be unpopular with a portion of the population.

Tories and others opposed to the Bill strongly urged Elgin to withhold approval or to delay action by referring the question to the British government. Lord Elgin, however, refused to be swayed by such urgent requests. Believing as he did in responsible government, he saw it as his duty to approve bills passed by both houses in the parliament. He realized that in this particular case he ran some personal risk, and that approval might lead to violence, but this did not deter him from carrying out his duty.

On April 25, 1849, Lord Elgin drove to the Parliament Buildings in Montreal. When word of this move spread through the city, a crowd collected in an effort to discover what the Governor-General proposed to do. Gathering in the streets outside the Parliament Buildings, they waited tensely. Then, when it was learned the Rebellion Losses Bill had been signed, the crowd buzzed in anger and eventually burst into violence when Lord Elgin reappeared.

Shouting and screaming, the enraged mob began to hurl anything upon which it could lay hands. Stones battered the side of Lord Elgin's carriage and a window was smashed. Fortunately, **Riots in Montreal** the coachman had the presence of mind to whip the frightened horses into a gallop and wheel the carriage swiftly from the scene of danger.

**Burning of the Parliament Buildings**

Riotous activity for the day was not yet over. That evening, a mob gathered again at the Parliament Buildings, where they smashed windows with stones and drove the members of the Assembly into the street. A witness, writing to a friend, has described the scene:

> Soon the doors were broken open and a stout fellow sprang into the Speaker's chair with the exclamation "I dissolve Parliament!" This was the Signal—and immediately in the face of the members, and an immense multitude of spectators the Gas Pipes were fired in a dozen places, and the building wrapped in flames—the "Golden Mace," sacred emblem of Royalty, was seized by the infuriated mob and borne into the street amid shouts of derision and scorn. The Members barely escaped with their lives, and that splendid Building with its rare paintings, all the records of the Provinces from the first settlement, all the acts of Parliament, that library, worth alone £100,000, all, all, are destroyed. That splendid portrait of the Queen, which you may remember, was dropped into the street, and torn into a thousand pieces. All was lost, nothing saved, and the structure now is but a heap of smoking ruins. The loss to the city cannot be less than £300,000. The fire engines were not allowed to play upon the fire at all; and it was only on the arrival of General Gore with a body of soldiers that the engines were allowed to approach for the protection of other property.

**British Parliament supports Lord Elgin**

Rioting went on for about three days, and order was not restored until soldiers and a large body of constables took stern action against unruly groups.

During the months that followed, Canadian Tories urged the British government to withdraw Lord Elgin from the Province and to disallow the Rebellion Losses Bill. The problem was debated in the British Parliament with prominent men voting either for or against Lord Elgin's policies. In the end, however, the courageous Governor-General was given the support he so richly deserved, and the Colonial Secretary refused to accept Lord Elgin's resignation.

This sensible and far-sighted action on the part of the British Parliament had a beneficial effect upon Canadian affairs. It indicated that the home government was not going to interfere with decisions made by provincial governments. It indicated that Canadian Tories could no longer gain support in Britain for their fight against responsible government. Lord Elgin's behaviour and the attitude of the British Parliament also had the effect of winning support among the French-speaking citizens of the Province of Canada.

Responsible government for the Province of Canada, 1849

While the Reformers in Canada were working for responsible government, progress toward that goal in Nova Scotia under the leadership of Joseph Howe had been even faster. Howe has been described by the distinguished Canadian historian A. R. M. Lower as the "most attractive, most vital personality of the period." He quickly grasped Baldwin's idea of responsible government and became its most outstanding supporter. In his "Open Letters" of 1839 to the British Colonial Secretary, Lord John Russell, he gave a brilliant explanation of the meaning and purpose of responsible government.

Responsible government in Nova Scotia, 1848

In 1840, the Governor of Nova Scotia was Sir Colin Campbell, a conservative, military man, who thought that only "the proper people" should take part in government. Campbell's attitude was vigorously attacked by Howe and, as a result, the Governor was called home. The new Governor, Lork Falkland, was little better and attempted to govern with a Council composed of members of all parties. Howe, by this time the central figure of the Reform party, complained bitterly that this system was not responsible government. He claimed, and correctly, that responsible government existed only when the members of the Council had confidence in each other and when they were dependent on the Assembly, rather than the Governor, for their authority. Howe insisted that Falkland's Council was nothing more than a group of department heads who gave advice to the Governor, advice which the Governor could accept or reject as he alone saw fit. As a result of Howe's protests, Falkland, too, was recalled and his successor, Sir John Harvey, was given instructions by the new

A disgraceful scene took place in Montreal in 1849 when Lord Elgin, after signing the Rebellion Losses Bill, was attacked by a mob in the street. Writing later, he remarked: *When I left the House of Parliament, I was received with mingled cheers and hootings. A small knot of individuals consisting, it has since been ascertained, of persons of a respectable class in society, pelted the carriage with missiles which they must have brought along for the purpose.* Fortunately, Lord Elgin was not injured during the incident.

Colonial Secretary, Earl Grey, to allow the creation of a responsible ministry. The Reform party won the election in 1847, and Howe and J. B. Uniacke formed a new ministry in January, 1848, the first responsible ministry in British North America.

**Responsible government in New Brunswick, 1854** Progress toward responsible government in New Brunswick was at first handicapped by the fact that revenue from crown lands was great enough to pay the salaries of government officials. Thus, the governor and others were not so dependent upon money voted by the Legislative Assembly. Working closely together, the governor and his Tory supporters fought off most attempts to reduce their own powers.

Slowly, however, steps were taken in the direction of responsible government as the privileged position of the Church of England was reduced and the Legislative Assembly gained control of the revenues from customs duties and crown lands. An election won by the Reformers in 1848 was the one vital event that hastened the change desired by so many citizens. But even with a Reform victory and the sympathy of the British government, the final stage in responsible government was not reached until 1854.

Development in Prince Edward Island differed from that of other Maritime provinces because most of the land on the Island had been granted to wealthy landlords who lived elsewhere. These men had agreed to place settlers on their holdings and to make certain improvements, but in actual practice they did very little.

Responsible government in Prince Edward Island, 1862

The struggle in Prince Edward Island, therefore, tended to be one between tenants and a group of wealthy landowners who had little real interest in the province. By 1850, the Legislative Assembly had gained control of revenues. Actual responsible government was only achieved on the island when, in 1862, members of the Legislative Council were elected by the people.

With the gradual introduction of responsible government in domestic affairs, the provinces of British North America had reached a new stage in their political development. The important voice they had gained in the management of their own affairs would, in the near future, lead to the creation of a new nation

## SUMMARY — SECTION 4

In the provinces of British North America, the form of government imposed by the British Parliament did not satisfy the people. Indeed, they deeply resented the control exercised by the Family Compacts and the support they received from the British government. As a result, reform movements developed in each of the provinces. The leaders of these movements challenged the theory and practice of colonial government and demanded responsible government.

In Nova Scotia, there was a Family Compact, but it ruled with somewhat more liberality than those of Upper and Lower Canada. This ruling group had a strong supporter in the noted lawyer and writer, Judge Thomas Chandler Haliburton, but gained a powerful enemy in the newspaperman, Joseph Howe. Howe frequently criticized colonial government in his newspaper, the **Novascotian**, and on one occasion was charged with libel but won his own acquittal. After entering the legislature as a Reform member, Howe took an active part in the struggle for political change in Nova Scotia.

In Upper Canada, leaders of the Family Compact included John Strachan and his former pupil, John Beverley Robinson. In opposition to them were such Reformers as Dr. John Rolph, Marshall Spring Bidwell, Dr. William Warren Baldwin and his son, Robert Baldwin. However, the most colourful and aggressive of all the Reformers was William Lyon Mackenzie, who continually attacked the Family Compact in the columns of his newspaper, the **Colonial Advocate.**

In 1835, the Reform party in Upper Canada gained a majority of seats in the Assembly but was defeated in the election of 1836, largely through the political interference of the Lieutenant-Governor, Sir Francis Bond Head. William Lyon Mackenzie was so embittered that he planned armed revolt.

The Rebellion of 1837 in Upper Canada lasted three days. After several skirmishes north of Toronto on Yonge Street, the rebels were scattered and Mackenzie fled to the United States.

The Rebellion of 1837 in Lower Canada, led by Louis Joseph Papineau, was also a Reform movement directed against a powerful ruling group, the "Château Clique." The fighting in Lower Canada was much more extensive than that in Upper Canada, but it ended in the same manner—the defeat of the rebels and the hasty flight of their leader to the United States.

Shocked by the rebellions, the British government sent Lord Durham to examine political conditions in British North America and to make recommendations for improvement. As a result, Durham produced the famous document known as "Durham's Report," or more officially, the **Report on the Affairs of British North America.** Among the important recommendations made by Durham were the union of

Upper and Lower Canada and the granting of responsible government.

By the **Act of Union,** 1841, Upper and Lower Canada were joined together, and a single legislature composed of a Legislative Assembly, a Legislative Council and an Executive Council was established. Responsible government, however, did not come automatically with the Act of Union. The Governor still appointed members of the Legislative Council and the Executive Council. Thus, he still was able to control the making of laws.

Lord Sydenham (Governor from 1839 to 1841) fought against Reform attempts to lessen his authority. His successor, Sir Charles Bagot (1841 to 1843), permitted the formation of **cabinet** government, but his liberal action brought protests from Canadian Tories and caused uneasiness in Great Britain. The next governor, Sir Charles Metcalfe (1843 to 1845), had little sympathy with democratic government and was soon quarrelling bitterly with the Reformers.

Conditions improved in 1847 with the arrival of Lord Elgin, who was genuinely interested in the promotion of responsible government. Lord Elgin demonstrated this in 1849, when he signed the Rebellion Losses Bill, an act passed by the Reform ministry of Baldwin and Lafontaine. This measure was extremely unpopular with the Tories and others not in favour of paying the losses of rebels in Lower Canada. The day the Bill was signed and made law, Lord Elgin was attacked by a mob and the Parliament Buildings in Montreal were burned. However, in signing legislation **proposed by representatives of the people,** Lord Elgin had, in effect, given official approval to the practice of responsible government in the Province of Canada.

Protests about Lord Elgin were sent by Canadian Tories to Great Britain, but the home government supported the governor's action. This was an important decision, because it indicated that Great Britain had at last decided not to interfere in provincial affairs.

Meanwhile, in Nova Scotia, Joseph Howe and the Reformers had continued the struggle and had triumphed over their political foes. In February, 1848, Howe and his colleagues formed the first responsible ministry in the British Empire.

Similar successes occurred in New Brunswick in 1854, and in Prince Edward Island by 1862.

# 5

## TRADE AND TRANSPORT

Conditions in Canada East and Canada West ▪ Prices and wages ▪ Canadian Corn Bill of 1843 ▪ British free trade, 1846 ▪ The Annexation Manifesto ▪ Reciprocity Treaty, 1854 ▪ Reciprocity ends, 1866 ▪ First railways in North America ▪ Early portage railways in British North America ▪ The St. Lawrence and Atlantic Railway ▪ The Great Western Railway ▪ The Northern Railway ▪ Organization of the Grand Trunk Railway Company, 1853 ▪ Howe's dream of an intercolonial railway ▪ Railway construction in Nova Scotia and New Brunswick.

# 20. Trade and Commerce

ALTHOUGH THE BRITISH provinces in North America had made considerable progress by 1840, the number and the variety of exports was small. About five-sixths of the people were still engaged in agriculture or lumbering, although there was a large fishing industry on the Atlantic coast.

In Canada East—formerly Lower Canada—the descendants of the *habitants* still laboured on their long narrow holdings, cultivating their fields as their forefathers had done. Only in Montreal, with a population of 40,000, and in Quebec City, with a population of 50,000, were there signs of change and commercial activity. Canada East

In Canada West—formerly Upper Canada—the spread of settlement had brought remarkable advances in the production of wheat and other crops. Since wheat was easily grown and often brought good prices, it received the most attention. It is amazing to realize that, in 1841, Canada West alone was able to produce thousands of bushels of wheat on land that a few decades before had been covered by virgin forest. Urban centres in Canada West were much smaller than the two big centres on the St. Lawrence, but they were showing steady growth. "Muddy York," which had become Toronto in 1834, was now a busy city of 15,000 people. Kingston, the capital of the Province of Canada, had 6,000 people and Hamilton, a growing community, had reached a population of 3,000. Canada West

By modern standards the wages and prices of the 1840's appear extremely low. Housewives were able to buy meat at eight cents a pound, milk at five cents a quart and butter at fifteen cents a pound. Those who could afford servants were able to hire maids, cooks or housekeepers at $8.00 per month, and farmers could employ the services of labourers at $12.00 per month. Carpen- Prices and wages

159

ters, masons and other tradesmen were available at $1.50 to $2.00, per day. It would seem that people with reasonable incomes could live very well indeed.

Canadian Corn Bill, 1843

The chief exports were still wheat and timber. In 1843, the British government passed the *Canadian Corn Bill* (corn is the British term for grain), which gave Canadian wheat growers a privileged position on the British grain market. This Act placed lower import duties on Canadian wheat and flour than those placed on foreign wheat or flour. The Act was part of an old British policy which encouraged trade within the British Empire at the expense of foreign commerce.

One curious result of the passage of the Canadian Corn Bill was that wheat was brought into the Province of Canada from the

One of the major, nineteenth-century industries in the Maritime provinces was shipbuilding. During what has been called the "Golden Age of Sail," vessels built in the Maritimes plied the sea lanes of the world and ranked with the finest vessels afloat. In the period 1786-1920, almost four thousand sailing ships of more than 500 tons were built in eastern Canada. Saint John, New Brunswick, and Liverpool, Nova Scotia, were the major shipbuilding centres. This illustration shows a ship on stocks nearly ready for launching at Saint John. This was a large vessel in the 1,200-ton category, a type widely used in the Canadian, Australian and New Zealand cargo trade.

United States, ground into flour and shipped off to Britain as Canadian flour. Business was so good for a time that the milling industry enjoyed rapid expansion, particularly in Montreal and Toronto.

This happy situation, however, came to an abrupt end in 1846 **British free trade, 1846** when Britain adopted a *free trade* policy. It had been decided that perhaps the old system of high duties on foreign products was not after all in the best interests of the nation and Empire. Duties on foreign grain and flour were gradually reduced and finally eliminated. This policy placed the Canadian provinces in direct competition with other grain growing countries and it encouraged the Americans to mill their own wheat and ship it directly to Britain. Canadian milling men who had dreamed of handling an increasing volume of grain from the United States were bitterly disappointed by this turn of events.

To make matters even worse, wheat and flour were not the only Canadian exports affected by the free trade policy. Import duties on timber were also reduced, placing Canadian timber in direct competition with that of northern Europe. Another measure that had an adverse effect upon business was the repeal of the old Navigation Acts. These Acts, designed to protect British trade, had required all goods reaching Empire markets to be carried in British-built ships owned by British subjects. With the repeal of the Navigation Acts, ships of foreign countries were now able to carry goods to Britain and the colonies. One immediate result was that Canadian shipowners lost their former privileged trade position in the West Indies.

**Results of free trade**

British free trade, therefore, caused falling prices, reduced trade, and brought unemployment and financial failure to many people in the Province of Canada. Those most directly concerned were not only alarmed by the situation but very angry with Britain. Even some long-time Tories, who for years had supported British policies and traditions, had harsh words for the new trade practices.

**Annexation Manifesto, 1849**

The English-speaking, Tory merchants of Montreal, frustrated by the British refusal to tamper with the Rebellion Losses Bill and faced with a destructive decline in business, were sure that Great Britain had purposely deserted them. Since American economic conditions appeared to be very good, it occurred to them that uniting with the United States would offer greater commercial advantages than remaining a British colony. With this in mind, they issued a document known as the *Annexation Manifesto,* which proposed: ". . . a friendly and peaceful separation from the British connection and a union upon equitable terms with the great North American Confederacy of Sovereign States."

The Montreal Annexation Manifesto encountered stiff opposition and sharp criticism throughout the Province of Canada. In Canada West, it had practically no support, and in Canada East the French-speaking citizens wanted nothing to do with it. In the

United States, particularly in the northern part, there was some support for the idea, but on the whole the question was not considered important. Americans, after all, had a problem of their own—a bitter problem arising out of slavery.

To Lord Elgin and other thoughtful men, the real answer to trade difficulties lay not in union, but in closer trade relations with the United States. This was not a new thought, on either side of the·border, but up until this time nothing had been done about it. Some people in the provinces and in Britain feared that increased trade with the United States might lead Canadians at some future time to break ties with Great Britain. Lord Elgin was not one of these, for he said, "Canada will remain attached to Britain though tied to her neither by the golden links of protection, nor by the meshes of old fashioned colonial office jobbing and chicanery." *Lord Elgin and Reciprocity*

Lord Elgin travelled to Washington and carried on discussions with the American government concerning closer trade relations. At first, there was some coolness to the plan, but Elgin's personal charm won him friends even among those who had been opposed to his ideas. Negotiations were conducted at a leisurely pace and punctuated by numerous dinners, dances and supper parties. Elgin's guests often departed "pleased with the monarchical form of government in England; pleased with the republican form of government in the United States; pleased with each other, themselves, and the rest of mankind." Some of Elgin's enemies later stated that his final arrangement with the United States "was floated on champagne."

Agreement was finally reached in the *Reciprocity Treaty* of 1854, which was accepted by the American government and by all the British provinces. *Reciprocity Treaty, 1854*

This vital treaty made provision for an exchange of fishing rights in British and American waters, an exchange of navigation rights on the St. Lawrence River, on canals and on Lake Michigan; the treaty also settled which products were to be admitted into each country free of duty. This list included such items as grain, fish, furs, timber and many foods.

**Prosperity in British North America**

The British provinces gained much from the Reciprocity Treaty, and the following ten years were prosperous ones. The coming of Canadian railways and a wartime market in Europe (from 1854 to 1856 Great Britain and France were engaged in the Crimean War against Russia) undoubtedly had some effect upon trade and business progress, but the newly won arrangement with the United States was of great assistance. This is indicated by the fact that between 1862 and 1866 exports to the United States were twice the value of imports.

**End of Reciprocity, 1866**

The Reciprocity Treaty unfortunately came to an end in 1866 when the United States refused to renew the arrangement. By that time, Americans were feeling less friendly towards Britain and some felt that industry and agriculture in the United States should be protected from a free trade policy.

# 21. The Railway Age

THE FIRST RAILWAYS in North America were simply roads composed of wooden rails over which loads were drawn by horses and wagons. In order to prevent excessive wear, the rails were sometimes covered with strips of thin metal. The first short lines were privately owned and were used chiefly in the transportation of such bulky products as coal, granite and limestone. First railways in North America

Railways of a similar nature, known as "portage railways," were constructed in some places to link waterways. These lines served as useful shortcuts between important natural waterways in much the same way as did canals. Railways, however, could be constructed more rapidly and more cheaply than canals, so that in time the railways began to compete with the man-made waterways.

Railway transportation changed radically with the appearance of the steam locomotive. Steam railway history actually began in Great Britain in 1825, when George Stephenson's engine, *Locomotion*, drew the first public passenger train over the Stockton and Darlington Railway. This successful experiment and others persuaded American groups that steam transportation would be useful on this side of the Atlantic.

In 1828, Mr. Charles Carroll, the only surviving signer of the Declaration of Independence, took a shovel and broke ground during a ceremony that marked the beginning of a railway designed to join Baltimore, Maryland, with the Ohio River. He said, "I consider this among the most important acts of my life, second only to that of signing the Declaration of Independence, if second to that." Mr. Carroll's statement was prophetic, for the beginning of the steam railway age in North America was indeed a significant event.

A steam locomotive was brought to the United States from England in 1829 but it did not work satisfactorily. The following First steam locomotive

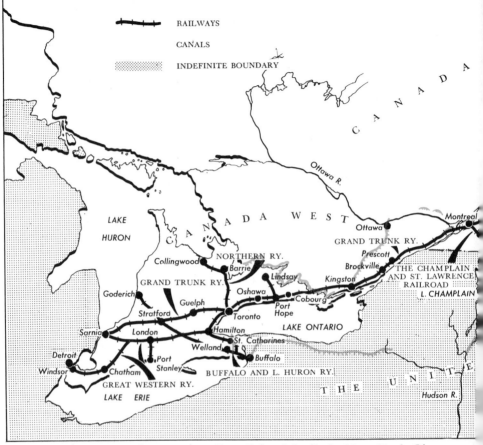

## EARLY RAILWAYS IN BRITISH NORTH AMERICA

RAILWAYS

CANALS

INDEFINITE BOUNDARY

year, however, a locomotive, *Best Friend,* built in New York City, was tested successfully on a six-mile stretch of line completed by the South Carolina Railroad. This was soon followed by other engines. The era of the steam railway had begun.

Travel by train in the beginning was very uncomfortable and sometimes dangerous. An English author, Miss Harriet Martineau, wrote in 1835:

One great inconvenience of the American rail-roads is that, from wood being used for fuel, there is an incessant shower of large sparks, destructive to dress and comfort, unless all the windows are shut; which is impossible in warm weather. Some serious accidents from

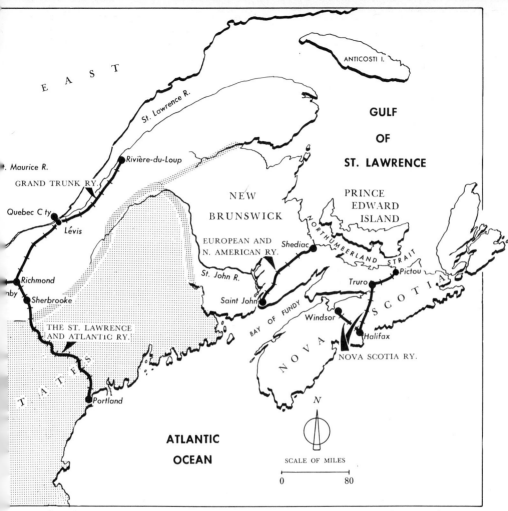

fire have happened in this way; and during my last trip on the Columbia and Philadelphia rail-road a lady in the car had a shawl burned to destruction on her shoulders; and I found that my own gown had thirteen holes in it; and my veil, with which I saved my eyes, more than could be counted.

Having once proved successful, railroads expanded at an astounding rate. By 1835, there were no less than twenty-two short lines operating in the eastern states—all less than 140 miles in length. By 1840, there were 2,799 miles of line and by 1850 there were 8,683 miles of line. (Railroads did not penetrate beyond the Mississippi until after 1850.)

Expansion of railroads in the United States

With the passing of years, railroads improved to the point where they handled most of the inland transportation. They moved passengers and freight swiftly and operated at all seasons of the year. Frozen rivers, lakes and canals stopped steamboats and sailing ships, but cold weather had much less effect upon trains.

**Value of railroad construction**

The coming of railroads made it possible for the United States to develop more rapidly and more extensively than the nation might otherwise have done. Trains moved settlers into the west, carried grain and cattle to the eastern states, moved coal and iron to the manufacturing centres and transferred manufactured goods to thriving communities in the mid-west. Railroads also served to create an increasing feeling of unity among the widely scattered regions of a country which sprawled across the entire breadth of a continent.

There was an early interest in railways in the British provinces of North America, but lack of funds, brought about by the recent boom in canal building, delayed construction until after successful lines had been established in Britain, the United States and Europe. In the meantime, Canadians were preparing a great many ambitious plans on paper.

**First railway on Canadian soil, 1836**

The first railway put into operation, the *Champlain and St. Lawrence Railroad,* was a short line, fifteen and one half miles in length, joining La Prairie (opposite Montreal) with St. Johns on the Richelieu River. This "portage railroad" was established to facilitate transportation between Montreal and New York City. Canadian railway history began on this little line on July 21, 1836, when a small train, drawn by a tiny, tall-stacked locomotive, the *Dorchester,* drew a train of cars carrying the Governor-General and more than 200 guests at a rate of about twenty miles an hour. It was a gala occasion with toasts in champagne at St. Johns. Only the grounding of the ferry in the St. Lawrence, on the return journey, marred the day.

**Expansion of railways in the British provinces**

Further railway construction, however, was slow, for even by 1850 there were no more than sixty miles of track in all the British provinces of North America. During the next ten years railways were beginning to come into their own as 2,000 miles of track were laid. This was encouraging progress, but it should be remembered that by this time there were over 8,000 miles of track in various parts of the United States.

By 1855, there were three significant railways in operation. The first of these was the *St. Lawrence and Atlantic,* which connected Montreal with an all-season port on the Atlantic—Portland, Maine. This railway, financed with some difficulty by Americans and Canadians, was unique in history, for it is said to have been the first international railway in the world. The second line was the *Great Western,* linking the Niagara River with Hamilton and with Windsor on the Detroit River. The third line was the *Northern,* running from Toronto to Collingwood on Georgian Bay. It not only acted as a valuable portage line between the Great Lakes but speeded the development and settlement of the land lying north and west of Toronto.

Meanwhile, in 1853, the *Grand Trunk Railway Company* was formed. Its purpose was to buy, rent or absorb existing railway lines and construct others so that there might be a continuous line of rail from Lake Huron to the Atlantic Ocean. An optimistic and exaggerated statement issued by the Company stated:

**Founding of the Grand Trunk Railway Company, 1853**

> The Grand Trunk Railway of Canada . . . pours . . . traffic in one unbroken line through the entire length of Canada into the St. Lawrence at Montreal and Quebec, on which it rests at the north, while on the south it reaches the magnificent harbours of Portland and Saint John on the open ocean. The whole future traffic between the western regions and the east, including Lower Canada, parts of the States of Vermont and New Hampshire, and the Provinces of New Brunswick, Nova Scotia, Prince Edward Island, and Newfoundland must, therefore, pass over the Grand Trunk Railway.

The actual accomplishments of the Grand Trunk Railway fell somewhat short of this glowing prophecy.

The eastern portion of the new trunk line was acquired by leasing the St. Lawrence and Atlantic- (Montreal to Portland) for a period of 999 years. A central section from Montreal to Toronto was constructed and opened for traffic in 1856. West of Toronto, the Company absorbed the partly finished Toronto and Guelph Railway and completed, in 1859, a line running through Stratford

The locomotive, *Dorchester*, steams through the Quebec countryside on July 21, 1836, making the fifteen-mile trip between La Prairie and St. Johns in fifty-nine minutes. Two small passenger cars carried the Governor-General and special guests, and several flatcars fitted with benches carried other "respectable persons." Two other cars, pulled by horses, set out with the party but were soon left far behind. The *Dorchester*, a late model British locomotive, was built at Newcastle, England. Railway tracks at this time were simply wooden rails covered with thin, protective strips of iron. These early tracks, known as "snake rails," proved unsatisfactory and even dangerous because they tended to warp and curl during hot weather. Later, iron rails and then steel rails replaced them.

to Sarnia. More construction on the eastern portion took the Grand Trunk Railway from Montreal to Quebec City and on to Rivière du Loup, where it stopped. Thus, while the Province of Canada gained a railway connection with New England and the Atlantic, it still had no railway link with the eastern provinces.

In Nova Scotia, Joseph Howe had dreamed of an "intercolonial" railway linking all the British provinces — a government-owned railway paid for by the provinces and Great Britain. He worked hard to achieve this aim, and for a time it appeared that he might be successful. However, differences of opinion concerning the route and financing of the proposed railway caused negotiations to collapse.

Howe's dream of an intercolonial railway

Nevertheless, Joseph Howe did become one of the railway commissioners for his province and under his leadership a government-controlled line was built in the period 1854 to 1858 from Halifax to Truro with a branch to Windsor, N.S. By 1867, the line was extended to Pictou, giving Nova Scotia about 145 miles of track.

Railway construction in Nova Scotia

In New Brunswick, two lines were completed, one stretching from St. Andrews to Woodstock and the other from Saint John to Shediac on the Northumberland Strait. Both of these lines had been intended as portions of major railway projects linking New Brunswick with Quebec City and Portland, Maine.

Railway construction in New Brunswick

The railways in the eastern provinces were not large, but they did serve a useful purpose. The lines in Nova Scotia linked the Gulf of St. Lawrence and the Bay of Fundy with the Atlantic Ocean. In New Brunswick, the Bay of Fundy was linked with the Gulf of St. Lawrence. These arrangements had one disadvantage, however, in that they took business away from local shipping companies that had built up a brisk coastal trade.

On the whole, throughout the British provinces, the first railways proved to be disappointing. It is true that goods and mail were moved more rapidly than ever before, that settlement was expanded and that co-operation among the provinces was increased, but the railways did not accomplish all that had been expected of them. Too many short lines were constructed by eager local groups who hoped railway transportation would bring sudden wealth and prosperity. As an example, there was an ambitious plan in Canada West to construct a line from Cobourg to Peterborough. This project involved the construction of three miles of wooden trestles across Rice Lake. Cobourg dreamed of

Disappointment in railways

Portable bath tubs of the type illustrated (dated about 1840) were not uncommon by mid-century. Made of painted metal, they were from three to four feet in width. The bather perched, perhaps uneasily, on the small seat on top and bathed as best he could from this position. A wide, sloping "collar" that fitted around the edge of the tub acted as a spillboard and drained splashed water back into the tub. A spout beneath the seat was used to empty the tub when bathing was completed. Hot water used in bathing had to be heated in a fireplace or over a wood stove.

carloads of flour, grain and lumber being shipped down from the north and then on to the United States. The expected flood of products never came, and today only remnants of the old trestles remain sunk in the bottom of Rice Lake.

The cost of railway construction was underestimated and the amount of profit overestimated, with the result that railway companies and governments found themselves faced with a never-ending series of financial troubles. Some bulk goods, such as wheat, were still carried by ships on rivers, lakes and canals. The expected rush of products from the western part of the United States through the Province of Canada to the eastern states did not materialize.

The future was to show that the fault lay not in the method of railway transportation itself, but in over-enthusiasm, poor planning and in the construction of unnecessary lines. Railways had yet to prove what they could do in British North America.

## SUMMARY — SECTION 5

In 1843, the British government passed the **Canadian Corn Bill,** giving Canadian wheat and flour a preferred position on the British market. For three years, this trade increased remarkably. However, in 1846, Britain adopted a free trade policy which badly affected the provinces of British North America. In the Province of Canada, in particular, free trade caused a reduction in exports and serious unemployment.

To the Tory merchants of Montreal, poor business conditions, coupled with their frustrations over the **Rebellion Losses Bill,** suggested that it could be to their advantage if the Province of Canada were united with the prosperous United States. Therefore, they issued a document called the **Annexation Manifesto.** Their plan received so little support in Canada West and among the French of Canada East that it was soon forgotten.

The Governor-General, Lord Elgin, believed that economic conditions in the British provinces might well be improved by arranging closer trade relations with the United States. His skilful negotiations in Washington led to the **Reciprocity Treaty** of 1854. Under this Treaty, a long list of Canadian products passed duty-free across the international boundary. Prosperity and progress gradually returned to British North America. The Reciprocity Treaty remained in force until 1866.

The steam railway era began in Britain in 1825 and in North America around 1830. The rapidity of railroad expansion in the United States was astonishing. Taking over from the canals, the railroads assumed a major rôle in transportation, thus enabling the nation to expand and develop with greatly increased speed.

There was an early interest in railways throughout British North America, but the boom in canal-building had consumed so much money that there was little left to spend on the "iron-horse." The first railway in the provinces was the Champlain and St. Lawrence Railroad, about fifteen miles in length and stretching from La Prairie (near Montreal) to St. Johns (on the Richelieu River). It first operated in July, 1836. Three important lines were in operation by 1855—the St. Lawrence and Atlantic (Montreal to Portland, Maine), the Great Western (Niagara to Windsor) and the Northern (Toronto to Collingwood).

In 1853, the Grand Trunk Railway Company sought to construct a continuous line of steel from Lake Huron to the Atlantic Ocean. By 1860, the Company's lines stretched from Sarnia to Rivière du Loup, but failed to provide a link with the Atlantic coast. There were several short lines in Nova Scotia and New Brunswick, but these found only local use.

Canadians discovered that the costs of railway construction and maintenance were high and the income to be gained very much lower than anticipated.

# 6

## CONFEDERATION

Growing feeling of unity among the British provinces of North America ▪ Growth and progress ▪ Gold rush to the Fraser Valley, 1858 ▪ Creation of the Colonies of Vancouver Island and British Columbia ▪ The Cariboo Road ▪ Union of Vancouver Island and British Columbia, 1866 ▪ Effects of the American Civil War on the British provinces ▪ Fenian Raids, 1866 ▪ Deadlock in the government of the Province of Canada ▪ Coalition government formed by Macdonald, Brown and Cartier, 1864 ▪ The Charlottetown Conference, 1864 ▪ The Quebec Conference, 1864 ▪ The Seventy-Two Resolutions ▪ Opposition to Confederation in the Maritime provinces and Newfoundland ▪ Changed feelings in Nova Scotia and New Brunswick ▪ The London Conference, 1866 ▪ **The British North America Act** ▪ The Intercolonial Railway ▪ The Dominion of Canada is born, July 1, 1867 ▪ Prime Minister John A. Macdonald ▪ Dissatisfaction in Nova Scotia ▪ The Hudson's Bay Company gives up Rupert's Land to the Dominion, 1869 ▪ British Columbia and Prince Edward Island join Confederation, 1871 and 1873 ▪ The Pacific Scandal, 1873 ▪ Liberals under Alexander Mackenzie win election of 1874.

# 22. The Eve of Confederation

AT THE BEGINNING of the nineteenth century, there had been little feeling of unity among the British provinces of North America. In 1800, each province was too fully occupied by its own pressing problems to give much thought to the others. Not even a system of trade linked them together, for what commerce existed was directed toward Great Britain and the West Indies.

It was in the War of 1812 that the British provinces began to realize that they faced common problems and common dangers. Since Great Britain had not been able to spare large military forces to fight the Americans, Canadian fighting men had played an important rôle in defending the border. It is true that the provinces had been blessed with extraordinarily good luck during the War, but the people still had every right to feel proud of their accomplishments. This feeling of satisfaction brought the provinces closer together in spirit and helped to promote a sense of nationalism.

*Continued suspicion of the United States*

The feeling of unity in the face of danger remained after the War, because many feared that the Americans had never forgotten their old desire to invade and conquer Canadian lands. From Lake Huron to the Atlantic shore, people in the provinces watched their southern neighbours with suspicion.

From time to time, there had been a few important people who felt that the British provinces should be joined by something more substantial than a feeling of kinship and co-operation. They believed that it was foolish for the colonies to remain separate, each with its own government. As early as 1789, the Governor-General, Lord Dorchester, had written:

*Union suggested by Lord Dorchester*

> I have to submit to the wisdom of His Majesty's councils, whether it may not be advisable to establish a general government for His Majesty's dominions upon this continent, as well as a governor general, whereby the united exertions of His Majesty's North American Provinces may more effectively be directed to the general interest and to the preservation of the unity of the Empire.

175

1

Domestic architecture in British North America about the middle of the nineteenth century. (1), a stone house of about 1840, is characteristic of the fine structures built by Loyalists along the St. Lawrence in the Glengarry region. These classical proportions and the Georgian style doorway can still be seen in certain Glengarry County homes. (This particular house is preserved today at Upper Canada Village.) Warmth was provided by a number of stoves at various points throughout the building, the heat circulating through large holes cut in the walls between rooms. Since the cooking and baking normally done in the kitchen would have overheated the house in summer weather, a summer kitchen adjoining the house was used during the hot months. A settler's first (or perhaps second) home can be seen in the background. (2) is a mid-century house of much different design, a design common throughout much of Canada West. Built of clapboard, it placed an emphasis upon vertical lines and sharp angles. It was, in fact, a deliberate adaptation of the Gothic style developed in Europe during the Middle Ages. (Victorians, being great imitators, evolved styles that borrowed heavily from architectural

3

2

forms of the past, notably Romanesque, Norman and Gothic.)   (3) is a Canada East house of about 1845.   The proportions of this structure reveal a British influence, although the sloped roof and overhanging eaves are traditionally French.   The lower floor was used for business (or as a workshop) and the upper floor contained the living quarters.   There was no inside staircase connecting the two levels.   This type of architecture began the "layer cake" type of construction that can still be seen in the blocks of apartment buildings in the province of Quebec that have only outside stairways.   The New Brunswick house (4) of about 1850 was solid and square-shaped.   It undoubtedly was influenced by the type of home built in the New England states.   The small, windowed tower set on the roof was popularly known as a "widow's walk," the theory being that the wives of seafaring men would go to this tower to watch and wait for the return of their husbands. However, it is quite likely that the widow's walk was added simply to make these homes appear more impressive.   Behind the house is an eighteenth-century Nova Scotian home. It is very similar to the "salt box" design that was popular in the New England states.

4

**Mackenzie supports union**

In the 1820's, there had been considerable discussion of a possible political union of the provinces, and among those in favour was the fiery little man who became the rebel leader in Upper Canada—William Lyon Mackenzie. In 1824, Mackenzie had said:

> . . . a union of all the colonies, with a government suitably poised and modelled, so as to have under its eyes the resources of our whole territory . . . would require few boons from Britain, and would advance her interests much more . . . than the bare right of possession of a barren, uncultivated wilderness of lake and forest, with some three or four inhabitants to the square mile . . .

**Durham's thoughts on union**

It is perfectly clear that, in 1839, Lord Durham had considered the possible advantages of a complete union of all the British provinces in North America. It may even be that he preferred such an arrangement but recognized that the time was not yet ripe. In his famous *Report* he wrote:

> But while I convince myself that such desirable ends would be secured by the legislative union of the two provinces, I am inclined to go further, and inquire whether all these objects would not more surely be attained by extending this legislative union over all the British Provinces in North America; and whether the advantages which I anticipate for two of them might not, and should not, in justice be extended over all. Such a union would at once decisively settle the question of races; it would enable all the provinces to co-operate for all common purposes; and, above all, it would form a great and powerful people, possessing the means of securing goods and responsible government for itself, and which, under the protection of the British Empire, might in some measure counterbalance the preponderant and increasing influence of the United States on the American continent. I do not anticipate that a colonial legislature thus strong and thus self-governing would desire to abandon the connexion with Great Britain.

Events that had taken place in the United States before, during and after Durham's time had made Canadians distrustful of American motives, for it was then that the United States had gained control of Florida, Texas, California and other wide territories in the south-west, all at the expense of Mexico. There had also been boundary disputes about the borders of Maine and the Oregon Territory. Indeed, some Canadians felt that the British provinces would be next on the list for annexation.

By the 1850's, astonishing progress had been made in transporta- tion, communication and settlement. Roads were more numerous and in better condition than ever before; railways stretched from Sarnia, Ontario, to Portland, Maine; steamboats sailed the St. Lawrence and the Great Lakes; canals were in operation; settlement was expanding and had almost completely filled the good farming land of Canada West; common schools and grammar schools were in operation; responsible government had been achieved in three of the provinces. Although this progress was welcome, it brought with it new problems that were to have an important effect on the colonies.

British North America had always depended for its livelihood on primary industries—fish, furs, timber and agriculture. With the coming of the age of steam and iron, the provinces continued to produce these staples but new energy was added to the older economy. Steam and iron also made it possible for new industries to begin operations. Most of these industries were in the Province of Canada. Clothing, shoes, furniture, farm implements and tools were the major products. Industry prospered until 1857, when progress finally began to slow down. The manufacturers began to have difficulty in competing with imported goods, and the government found itself unable to pay for all the railways that had been built during the prosperous years. To solve both problems, the government of the Province of Canada decided, in 1858, to place a tariff on a variety of imports. The tariff proved a successful measure, but it became an unnatural barrier between the provinces of British North America.

With the growth of settlement in Canada West it was becoming obvious that most good farming land would soon be occupied. Indeed, by 1850, there were already people moving from Canada West to the American west in search of new land. It was natural, therefore, that Canadians should become more interested in Rupert's Land and the North-West Territories. In this vast region beyond the Great Lakes were untouched thousands of square miles of potential farm land. American settlers were already moving into this region, and Canadians were afraid that it might be lost to the United States unless it were claimed for British North America. Some politicians in Canada West were particularly anxious to claim the North-West for Canada and, in 1857, they made this official party policy. However, there seemed little possibility that the Province of Canada alone could claim the North-West. On the other hand, a united British North America would be able to justify such a claim.

**"The Little Englanders"**    In addition to factors within the British provinces drawing them together, outside influences were also forcing them to consider union. Chief among these was a growing body of opinion in England that sought to get rid of the British Empire. These people, who were called "Little Englanders," complained of the expense and trouble of the Empire. As early as 1825, the Edinburgh *Review* had commented:

We defy any one to point out a single benefit, of any sort whatever, derived by us from the possession of Canada, and our other colonies in North America.

Although the "Little Englanders" were only a small group, they were a very vocal one and added their cries to those of other politicians and people demanding free trade. By 1846, the British government had instituted free trade.

Free trade was a shattering blow to the economy of the British provinces in North America. Although the provinces were able to recover by means of the Reciprocity Treaty with the United States, this Treaty came to an end in 1866. Once again, the economy of the provinces was upset. Thus, it seemed that one way to safeguard trade and commerce would be to unite. If the colonies joined together, they could assist each other and at the same time share common trade policies.

During the period between 1850 and 1867, there was a procession of events and movements that brought an answer to the long-standing question of political unity. Among these events and movements were new settlements on the prairies, a gold rush to the Fraser River valley, uneasy relations with the United States and attacks upon Canadian soil by Fenian raiders.

# 23. Beginnings in British Columbia

IT WILL BE REMEMBERED that, when David Thompson reached the mouth of the Columbia River in 1811, he found that the Pacific Fur Company of New York had already established a post named Fort Astoria. At the time, this was a keen disappointment to Thompson, but during the War of 1812, the North West Company was able to purchase the post from the Pacific Fur Company. When the Nor'Westers took over the post, they renamed it Fort George.

Nor'Westers acquire Fort Astoria

Following the union of the North West Company and the Hudson's Bay Company in 1821, Fort George became headquarters for activities in what the Hudson's Bay Company called its Columbia Department. However, the boundary of the Oregon Territory had not yet been settled, and Company officials began to wonder if their western headquarters was in a suitable position, standing as it did on the south shore of the Columbia River. They realized that final settlement of the boundary dispute could place Fort George in American hands.

Therefore, in 1825, a new headquarters, Fort Vancouver, was constructed eighty miles inland on the north bank of the Columbia. The Company felt safe in locating at that spot, since it was thought likely that the boundary settlement would name the Columbia River as the border between American and British land.

Construction of Fort Vancouver

Fort Vancouver was much larger and more elaborate than most posts of the time. Enclosed within a high wooden stockade were storehouses, trading rooms, a kitchen, a dining hall and two residences for senior officials. Outside the walls were homes for employees, a flour mill, a sawmill, a blacksmith shop, stables and an extensive farm area.

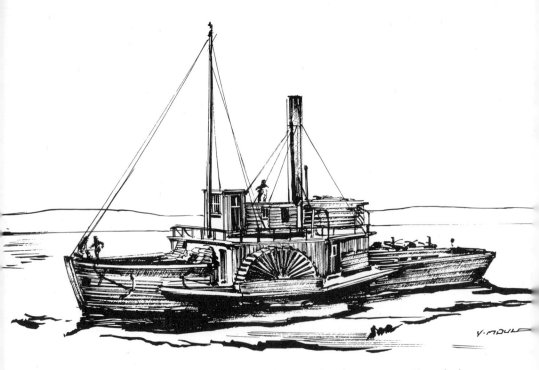

The *Beaver*, the first steamship on the Pacific coast, played an important rôle in the history of Vancouver Island and British Columbia. This sturdy, little vessel, built in England in 1835, was brought out to British Columbia in order to give the Hudson's Bay Company a trading advantage over American rivals. Carrying supplies to the outposts and bringing back furs, the *Beaver* was powered by two wood-fired steam-engines of thirty-five horsepower. It required four stokers and thirteen woodcutters to keep the engines going. (When sailing on a twenty-four-hour schedule, the Beaver consumed as many as forty cords of wood per day.) It was this ship that carried James Douglas' workmen to the site of Fort Victoria on Vancouver Island in March, 1843. During the construction of the fort, the *Beaver* continued to transport supplies, horses and cattle to the builders. This gallant little vessel, after fifty-three years of service, was wrecked while entering Vancouver Harbour.

Within a very short time, Fort Vancouver became a busy centre for the trade of the Hudson's Bay Company. Ships from Britain brought cargoes of supplies used in trading—beads, hatchets, rifles, kettles, blankets, tobacco and brightly coloured materials; the same ships returned homeward laden with furs.

**Trans-portation from Fort Vancouver**

Trade goods from Fort Vancouver were sent north to other posts of the Hudson's Bay Company in the region the traders called New Caledonia (New Scotland). These supplies were moved by canoes to the upper reaches of the Columbia. They were then transported by horses to the Thompson River (a branch of the Fraser River). Finally, they were taken by canoes to posts along the upper reaches of the Fraser River.

As time went by, it became obvious that the Columbia River was not going to form the international boundary line and that Fort Vancouver would eventually be on American soil after all. As a result, James Douglas, Chief Factor at Fort Vancouver, was sent northward in 1842 to select a location for a new headquarters. With six men he crossed to the island of Vancouver and after some exploration chose the "Port of Camosack," the site on which now stands the city of Victoria, British Columbia. To Douglas, it appeared to be an admirable place, for it possessed a good harbour, fertile soil, ample fresh water and splendid timber that could be used in the construction of a fur post.

Having received Company approval of his plan, Douglas made a second trip to the island the following year and immediately began construction of the new headquarters. In 1845, the post was given the name Fort Victoria, in honour of the Queen. An employee of the Hudson's Bay Company has described the post: **Fort Victoria, 1845**

> The fort itself is a square enclosure, stockaded with poles about twenty feet high and eight or ten inches in diameter, placed close together, and secured with a crosspiece of nearly equal size. At the corners of the square there are strong octagonal towers, mounted with four nine-pounder guns, flanking each side so that an attack by savages would be out of the question, and if defended with spirit, a disciplined force without artillery would find considerable difficulty in forcing the defences. The square is about 120 yards, but an increase which will nearly double its length to the south is contemplated. The interior is occupied by the officers' houses, or apartments, as they should be called, stores, and a trading house, in which smaller bargains are concluded, and tools, agricultural implements, blankets, shawls, beads and all the multifarious products of Sheffield, Birmingham, Manchester and Leeds, are offered at very high prices.

In 1846, the Oregon Treaty was signed by Great Britain and the United States, placing the international boundary line along the 49th parallel of latitude. At first, the Hudson's Bay Company

James Douglas of the Hudson's Bay Company selects a site for Fort Victoria on the southern tip of Vancouver Island. Later, he wrote: *The place itself appears a perfect "Eden" in the midst of a dreary wilderness of the North-West coast — and so different is its general aspect from the wooded, rugged region around, that one might be pardoned for supposing it had dropped from the clouds into its present position.* The construction of Fort Victoria was begun in March, 1843, and completed before the end of the year.

carried on its activities as before but, in 1849, it transferred Pacific coast headquarters from Fort Vancouver to Fort Victoria.

The new post rapidly became the western centre of trading and transportation. A sawmill and a grist-mill were erected, farms appeared and a little school was opened. Occasionally, visitors appeared—Russian traders from Alaska and gold miners from California.

**Crown Colony of Vancouver Island, 1849**
In 1849, the British Parliament created the Crown Colony of Vancouver Island and appointed Richard Blanshard as Governor. When Blanshard arrived at Fort Victoria the following March, he received a rather cool reception. Men of the Hudson's Bay

Company were accustomed to controlling the lands in which they traded and so they resented authority being given to an outsider. The new governor was extremely disappointed with conditions as he found them on Vancouver Island. In particular, he was disturbed by the fact that there were only nine residents of the colony who were not employees of the Company. Blanshard considered the situation so bad that, after staying only a year and a half, he submitted his resignation and returned to England.

It was obvious to the British Colonial Office that the next **Governor** governor would have to be a man who was acceptable to the Hud- **James Douglas** son's Bay Company and its employees. Accordingly, in 1851, James Douglas, then Chief Factor at Fort Victoria, was named Blanshard's successor. Douglas, who remained an employee of the Company, ruled the little colony with the help of a miniature Legislative Council. However, he was requested by the Colonial Office to establish a Legislative Assembly. This he did, and when the body met for the first time in the summer of 1856, it contained only six members.

In 1858, an event took place that was to bring swift and far-reaching changes to both Vancouver Island and the mainland. The event has been described by James Douglas in these words:

> Gold was first found on the Thompson River by an Indian a **Discovery** quarter of a mile below Nicomen. The Indian was taking a drink out **of gold** of the river; having no vessel, he was quaffing from the stream when he perceived a shining pebble which he picked up, and it proved to be gold. The whole tribe forthwith began to collect the glittering metal.

Quantities of this gold eventually were brought to Fort Victoria, where it was exchanged by the Indians for trade goods. Quite naturally the sudden arrival of precious metal caused excitement among the men of the Hudson's Bay Company. Even more excitement arose among the miners of California when the news reached them.

There was probably no one on Vancouver Island who even dreamed of the wild tumultuous scramble for gold that was to develop in the next few years—a scramble that would almost overwhelm the tiny backwoods settlements of the Crown Colony.

# 24. Gold in the Fraser Valley

IN THE SPRING OF 1858, the peaceful atmosphere of Fort Victoria was rudely disturbed by the arrival of prospectors from San Francisco. They were sturdy, grim-faced men in hobnailed boots. with packs on their backs and pistols at their hips. Hundreds upon hundreds of them disembarked—all anxious to secure supplies and to proceed to the mainland coast.

**Beginning of the gold rush** They stood in lines at the Hudson's Bay Company post to buy tobacco, rice, flour, bacon, salt, beans and mining equipment—picks, shovels, ladles and wire screens. The stockade of the little settlement at Fort Victoria was soon surrounded by a teeming tent city populated by thousands of miners. Shops and places of entertainment sprang up, and a newspaper, the *Gazette,* made its appearance.

During a four-month period in 1858, sixty-seven ships brought men from California, perhaps as many as 20,000 altogether. In the beginning, the gold-seekers made their way from Vancouver Island to the mainland in a wide variety of water-craft—canoes, rafts and hastily built boats of assorted sizes and shapes. Later, however, as the traffic increased, a number of American steamships shuttled back and forth between Fort Victoria and Fort Hope on the Fraser River. Two Hudson's Bay Company ships also operated between Fort Victoria and the company post at Fort Langley, a short distance up the Fraser.

**Douglas assumes control** Governor James Douglas realized that unless strong measures were taken immediately, lawlessness and chaotic conditions would become common. Although Douglas had no official authority outside Vancouver Island, he took control of the mainland mining fields. By imposing licence fees and enforcing British laws, the Governor made certain that the miners, many of whom had come

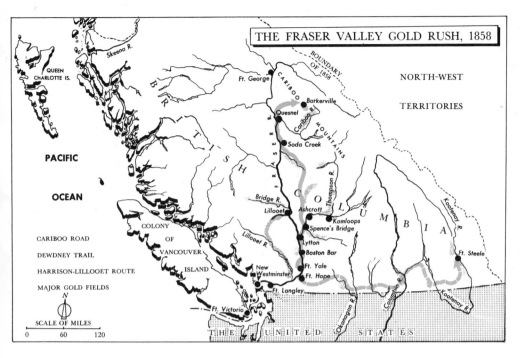

QUEEN CHARLOTTE IS.

Skeena R.

Ft. George

NORTH-WEST

Barkerville

Quesnel

TERRITORIES

Soda Creek

PACIFIC

OCEAN

Bridge R.

Lillooet

Ashcroft

Kamloops

Spence's Bridge

COLONY

OF

Lillooet R.

CARIBOO ROAD

Lytton

DEWDNEY TRAIL

VANCOUVER

Boston Bar

Ft. Steele

HARRISON-LILLOOET ROUTE

ISLAND

New
Westminster

Ft. Yale

MAJOR GOLD FIELDS

Ft. Hope

N

Ft. Langley

SCALE OF MILES

Ft. Victoria

0          60          120

THE    UNITED    STATES

from the United States, realized they were on British and not American soil.

Douglas also realized that proper government must be estab- **Creation of the Colony of British Columbia, 1858** lished on the mainland as soon as possible. At his suggestion, the British government created a new colony in the region the fur traders called New Caledonia. In November, 1858, James Douglas, in a ceremony at Fort Langley, was sworn in as the Governor of the Crown Colony of British Columbia, a name suggested by Queen Victoria herself. The granting of official authority on the mainland gave Douglas a much stronger hand in dealing with the many problems created by the gold rush.

The first men to arrive on the Fraser began working on the gold- **Mining on the Fraser** bearing sand bars at the lower end of the river. To these spots the men gave such fanciful names as China Bar, Mosquito, Boston Bar and Yankee Doodle. Some of the late-comers, finding the river crowded, turned back to the coast in disappointment, but

Most men who took part in the gold rush to British Columbia reached the colony by sea. Some adventurous (or foolhardy) spirits from Scotland, England, Canada West and Canada East actually journeyed across the whole continent. They travelled by railway to St. Paul, Minnesota, moved northward in Red River carts to Fort Garry, and made their way westward across the prairies in carts or on horseback. Their journey across the Rocky Mountains and down the wild waters of the Fraser River canyons on rafts was incredibly daring. Friendly Indians who helped them build their rafts tried to dissuade them from entering the hazardous waters. When the first of these rafts, laden with all their personal belongings, started downstream, the Indians are said to have observed: *Poor, poor, white men. No more see white men.*

others pushed on upriver, determined to stake claims in less crowded areas. Like mushrooms, little settlements sprang up, complete with boarding-houses, saloons and shops. A bustling, boisterous town developed at Fort Yale (a Hudson's Bay Company fur post) and became the centre of mining activity on the lower Fraser. When riots broke out at Fort Yale, Governor Douglas promptly despatched a small force of Royal Engineers. His quick action in this case—and in others—helped to maintain law and order. Governor Douglas had often heard of the violence and lawlessness that had existed in the California gold-fields and he made quite sure that there was no chance for such conditions to develop in his colony.

When autumn came, all the sand-bars on the lower Fraser had been claimed and were being worked. A few fortunate men were able to collect as much as $800 worth of dust and nuggets in a single day; some made modest but steady incomes; others did not find enough gold to pay expenses. Thousands of men were keenly disappointed. Between June and December, 1858, it is probable that miners secured a total of about half a million dollars of the precious metal along the lower river.

When gold was first discovered in the Fraser River, it was usually in small grains, mixed with the gravel and sand of the river bottom. It was obvious, however, that there must be a "mother lode" upstream from which the gold was being washed away. Many of the miners were aware of this fact and as they moved upstream they were constantly looking for the source of gold. **New strike in the Cariboo**

During 1859, the mining areas that had been worked the previous year began to yield less and the miners abandoned them to move further up the river. The men travelled upstream in canoes or by horse and mule along rough trails. They pushed farther and farther into the interior. At times, the journey was dangerous and some of the men disappeared, perhaps lost in swift streams or crushed under landslides. The advance guard of the miners reached Cariboo Lake on the upper reaches of the Fraser and there they found gold in abundance. The Cariboo strike was in fact the "mother lode," the actual gold-bearing rock. When word of the new strike in the Cariboo country reached the outside world, a second and greater rush began, this time from all over the world.

When, during the Fraser gold rush, Governor James Douglas requested troops for service in British Columbia, the British government sent out a picked company of Royal Engineers instead of infantry. British officials felt that the Engineers, with their knowledge of civil and military engineering, would prove most useful to the young colony. Shown here is a captain of the Royal Engineers in a dress uniform of the period. As a result of the Crimean War in Europe (1854-1856), many changes in military clothing appeared at this time. The private in the background wears a tunic instead of the tight coat of 1812. His uniform has fewer restricting straps across the chest than those of an earlier period. For generations, soldiers had complained that such straps interfered with their breathing and with their freedom of movement.

K. MOULD

**Harrison-Lillooet Road**

  One of the most remarkable features of development during the days of the gold rush was the construction of roads through the mountains. The first year of the rush, 1858, Governor Douglas organized parties of miners to widen and improve sections of an old Indian trail that joined a series of small lakes. The improved route, known as the Harrison-Lillooet Road, made it possible for travellers to avoid over one hundred miles of rough water on the Fraser.

It soon became clear that if the rich gold fields of the Cariboo region were to be developed properly, a good road had to be built between the Fraser River and the mining camps. Governor Douglas saw the need for a road and, in 1861, he ordered the construction of the Cariboo Road. When completed in 1865, this route was eighteen feet wide and 480 miles long. It wound across wooden bridges and over deep canyons and clung dizzily to the sides of sheer rock walls that fell hundreds of feet to the foaming waters below.

**Cariboo Road**

The completion of the Road made it possible for stage-coaches to operate all the way from the lower Fraser to the Cariboo region. The coaches were drawn by six horses which were changed at posts spaced about thirteen miles apart. So effective was this means of transportation that, in the year 1865, 1,500 passengers and gold shipments valued at four and a half million dollars were carried over the Road.

**Improved transportation**

Mule trains were usually used to transport supplies and equipment to settlements and mining camps. These trains consisted of from sixteen to forty-eight animals, each loaded with a pack weighing between 150 and 200 pounds. Since they moved at about fifteen miles per day, they could often make three round trips into the Cariboo region each season. With the introduction of mule trains, shipping charges on freight dropped sharply.

At one time it was thought that camels might be useful for freight transportation since they were capable of carrying loads up to a ton in weight. But when twenty-one camels were actually brought in, they proved a failure. Their feet could not stand the harsh condition of the rock trails, and their odour frightened passing horses and mules. They were soon removed from the Cariboo Road, and freight transportation was left to the mule trains.

After the easily obtained surface gold had been picked up by the miners, heavy machinery was needed to extract the gold from the rock. As a result, the gold rush lost its appeal, and thousands left the mining fields. However, close to ten thousand miners remained in the Colony to become permanent settlers.

**Union of Vancouver Island and British Columbia, 1866**

Despite Governor Douglas' valuable efforts, he was often considered too dictatorial in manner, and many people disliked his close connection with the Hudson's Bay Company.  In addition, many people thought that there was no need for two Crown colonies on the Pacific coast and, therefore, that they should be united.  This opinion seemed reasonable to the British government. In 1866, an *Act of Union* was passed uniting Vancouver Island and British Columbia to form the Crown Colony of British Columbia. A new governor was appointed and a legislative council established.

Even under these circumstances, the new colony was not entirely happy.  It was separated from the British provinces in the east and was even a long way from the closest western settlement—the Red River Colony.  Relations with the United States were close and convenient, particularly trade and mail service with San Francisco.  In 1867, when Russia sold Alaska to the United States, British Columbians found themselves between two areas of American soil, and some of them began to think that their colony should throw in its lot with the Americans.

However, by this time, the British provinces in the east were taking active steps to create a new nation out of the British North American territories.  This promising development proved to be of greater interest to many British Columbians than the prospect of becoming a state within the American union.

# 25. Canadian-American Relations

ALTHOUGH VARIOUS FACTORS relating to trade, communication and common defence tended to promote a spirit of unity among the British provinces of North America, before 1850 few people seemed interested in the question of political unity. The individual provinces were too absorbed in their own special problems and were quite content to remain as small, relatively unimportant units of the British Empire. Events in the 1860's, however, began to influence thoughts on provincial union. Among these events was the American Civil War. Although the conflict had no direct connection with the provinces, it ultimately had an important effect upon their future.

In the beginning, sympathies in British North America were with the North's stand against slavery. In fact, this feeling was one reason why 40,000 Canadians enlisted in the Union armies. However, the Canadian attitude gradually changed to one of irritation, alarm and even fear. The change was due, in part, to the strained relations that developed between Great Britain and the Northern states during the course of the war, and events that affected the mother country were bound to affect her colonies.

As it began to become obvious that the North would win the war, some politicians and newspapers in the Northern states suggested that instead of allowing their armies to break up and return home, they should invade the British provinces. One New York City newspaper promoting such action made the comment: "The Canadians have long been panting for more freedom than they can enjoy under British rule." This attitude only served to arouse anger and fear in the British provinces.

*Changed feelings in British North America*

Alarmed by the new attitude in the United States, Great Britain sent additional troops to British North America, increasing garrisons to a total of about 18,000 men.

Further tension along the border was caused by Union agents who sought to recruit Canadians for the Northern armies and by groups of Confederate refugees in the Province of Canada who plotted small-scale raids against the Union. Throughout all this, the British provinces tried to maintain a neutral position, favouring neither the North nor the South. Provincial governments refused to supply arms to the Northern states and reported the activities of Confederate agents to Washington.

**The Alabama Affair**

One of the unsettled disputes between the United States and Great Britain at the close of the War involved the Confederate warships that had been built in Britain. A number of these ships, particularly the *Alabama* and the *Florida,* had caused a great deal of damage to Northern shipping during the War. The United States claimed that Great Britain was legally responsible and must therefore pay a heavy bill of damages. During the dispute over this matter, an official of the American government suggested that the United States should seize the British provinces in order to balance the account. For a time, "the *Alabama* claims" remained a very dangerous question, but eventually they were settled when Britain agreed to pay damages of fifteen and a half million dollars.

**Fenian raids, 1866**

One other factor causing uneasiness in both British North America and in Great Britain also arose indirectly from the American Civil War. In the United States there was a society of Irish-Americans known as the Fenian Brotherhood. This society was a branch of one that existed in Ireland and was dedicated to the same aim as the parent society—the release of Ireland from English rule. In Ireland, British troops had just crushed a revolt, and the American Fenians were in a mood to avenge the defeat of their brethren in the homeland. The Fenians thought that this could be accomplished by invading British North America. An invasion, they reasoned, would be a blow to Great Britain and, if successful, would provide them with a base from which they could launch a military expedition to free Ireland itself. The plan

Compared to the previous century, male costume of the 1800's underwent few sweeping changes. By 1800, the use of knee breeches, the standard form of trouser for many generations, was declining as long pants (1) gained favour. These were slim, neat trousers not unlike today's "Ivy League" style. They were often held snugly in place by means of straps that ran under the insteps of the wearer's shoes. The coat was often cut away at the front below the waist, allowing sides and back to fall to the level of the knees. The hat illustrated here, a direct forerunner of the modern top hat, is marked by a suggestion of slimness and elegance. By 1867, the massive drabness so beloved by the Victorians was being reflected in men's clothing. The tight, slim trousers had become slack and loose fitting (2) and the frock coat was so full that it was almost voluminous. Grey and black were common colours, although some brown and navy blue were worn. Short ankle boots were often worn instead of shoes. By the end of the century, these styles were giving way to others fairly closely resembling those of today.

may sound foolish now, but the Fenians felt confident of success. Many of their members were experienced soldiers, fresh from the battlefields of the Civil War. On the other hand, they expected that the American government, already hostile towards Britain, would not interfere and would, perhaps, even give them assistance, Finally, they hoped that Canadians themselves would rise in revolt against Britain.

In the spring of 1866, after a period of planning and preparation, Fenian groups assembled at points along the border from Michigan to Vermont. Realizing what was taking place, the British provinces mustered 10,000 militia men and prepared for the coming invasion. In May, a body of about 1,500 Fenians crossed the border at Buffalo and advanced to Ridgeway. They met little opposition, but for some unexplained reason they quickly turned about and fled back across the border.

There were other Fenian raids at various points along the border, but none was successful. However, they did cause considerable expense and anxiety in the British provinces and made Canadians think more seriously about matters of defence. The important question was, were the separate provinces properly prepared to protect themselves if a really serious emergency arose?

# 26. Deadlock and Coalition

THE UNION OF Upper and Lower Canada into the Province of Political deadlock
Canada (1841) had not proved to be the success that Lord
Durham and others had hoped it would be. The old problems of
race and religion still remained as stumbling blocks to understanding and good government. By the time of the American
Civil War (1861 - 1865), conditions had become so serious that
there was literally a deadlock in the government of the province.

The two political parties, the Liberal-Conservatives (Tories)
and the Reformers (*Clear Grits* in Canada West, *Parti-Rouge* in
Canada East), were so evenly balanced in the Assembly that
neither could govern firmly or effectively. Each party contained
English-speaking and French-speaking members from Canada
West and Canada East, but they were not balanced in this regard.
The Conservative party, led by John A. Macdonald and Georges
Étienne Cartier, had a small number of members from Canada
West and a large number from Canada East, while the Reform
party, led by George Brown and A. A. Dorion, was composed
mainly of English-speaking members.

The three political leaders—Macdonald, Cartier and Brown—
were all men of outstanding ability. Although they held differing
views and ideals, they were eventually to work together in a vital
cause—the unification of the British provinces.

John A. Macdonald was born in Glasgow, Scotland. When he John A. Macdonald
was five years of age, his family moved to Upper Canada and
settled at Kingston. After attending the local grammar school, he
began the study of law, serving as a clerk in a Kingston law office.
He led a busy, active life—copying legal documents and reading
law. There was so little time for sport and recreation that in later
life Macdonald remarked rather sadly, "I had no boyhood."

In 1836, when he was twenty-one years of age, he became a fully qualified lawyer and began practising law on his own. Because of his good humour and his ability to get things done, he soon established himself as a popular and successful lawyer. During his first case in court, he was so carried away by the excitement of debate that he became involved in a fist-fight with another lawyer. It is said that a court official, who helped restore order in the courtroom, whispered, "Hit him, John. Hit him!"

Many a kitchen in the period 1825-1875 had a shelf such as this, supporting a few knick-knacks and most importantly, a clock. The clocks in most Canadian homes of this time were imported from Connecticut, the clock-building centre of North America, and were often purchased from salesmen or pedlars. In 1792, American craftsmen devised a means of mass-producing time mechanisms, first using wooden parts and later brass. The exterior designs of nineteenth-century timepieces were all very similar. Shown here is a simple box-like design of selected and polished mahogany about twenty-six inches high. Another common model was the steeple-clock, so named because it had a sharply pointed top and side pillars resembling church steeples in New England.

Macdonald was interested in politics and became a member of the Assembly for Kingston in 1844. At the beginning of his public life he was content to listen and learn, but as time went by, he became very vocal in the affairs of government. He always made it clear that he stood for strong ties with Great Britain and would support no movement leading to political union with the United States.

Macdonald rose rapidly in political life, holding such posts as Receiver-General and Attorney-General, and winning a leading position in the Conservative party. He possessed a genius for leadership that enabled him, as one writer said, to inspire "not merely his followers with a devotion almost without parallel in the political annals, but to draw to his side first one and then another of his opponents." This tall, gangling man with a shock of dark, curly hair and a pair of humorous eyes was destined to lead the British provinces into a great union. It was the genial wit, the political shrewdness and the infinite patience of John A. Macdonald that did so much to bring about Confederation.

By 1857, Macdonald and his good friend from Canada East, Georges Étienne Cartier, were joint leaders of the Conservative party of the Province of Canada.

Georges Étienne Cartier was a descendant of the explorer, Jacques Cartier, who played such a vital part in the early history **Georges** of New France. Another ancestor of Cartier's, an officer in the **Étienne** noted Carignan-Salières Regiment, settled on a seigneury in the **Cartier** Richelieu River district in 1672. On that seigneury, amid wealthy surroundings, Georges Étienne Cartier was born and raised. Unlike John A. Macdonald, he enjoyed a carefree boyhood, undisturbed by financial worries. Influenced by the gay social life of the community, young Cartier became a singer of folk songs and a writer of verses. He developed into an unusual person, a man of action as well as a dreamer, an idealist and a poet.

Like Macdonald, he became a lawyer. In Montreal, perhaps because of his idealistic nature, he was attracted to the fiery reformer, Louis Joseph Papineau. So strong was this attachment that Cartier carried arms in the Rebellion of 1837 in Lower Canada. When the revolt was crushed by military force, he escaped to the United States and remained there as an exile until pardoned.

Returning to Montreal, Cartier resumed his legal practice and became a member of the Provincial Assembly. His association with John A. Macdonald was to be of great, political importance.

George Brown, the political rival of Macdonald and Cartier, **George** was born in Scotland but was brought to the United States while **Brown** still a boy. After a stay of some years in New York City, his family moved to Toronto. There, in 1844, Brown and his father established a newspaper, the *Globe*, which became an important, influential publication. (The *Globe* and another Toronto newspaper, the *Mail and Empire*, amalgamated in 1936 to form today's *Globe and Mail*.)

In the course of his duties as publisher, George Brown travelled through Canada West and gained a wide knowledge of the region and its people. He was a tall, handsome, very dignified man, with a definite air of leadership. Even before he entered public life, he had gained a reputation as a speaker of unusual ability. Since Brown was keenly interested in reform movements, his speeches and his newspaper editorials strongly supported the activities and the programmes of the Reform party in the Province of Canada. He did not hesitate, however, to criticize anyone whom he thought was neglecting his political duty or maintaining weak policies.

In 1851, George Brown entered the Assembly as a Reform member and by 1857 he was leader of his party. His energies were spent in efforts to obtain the expansion of railways, the abolition of clergy reserves, the establishment of a free school system and the granting of the vote to more citizens. He also became the champion of the rights of Canada West against those of Canada East.

By 1864, both parties in the Legislature were so well-balanced in power and influence that government was at a standstill.

**Representation by population** Brown's Clear Grits were convinced that the French-speaking members held too much power. The French-speaking members, on the other hand, were resentful of the attitude taken by Brown and his followers. However, the one problem that above all others caused dissension between French and English was the Clear Grit demand for representation by population ("Rep by Pop") in the parliament of the province. By the Act of Union, 1841, Canada West and Canada East had been granted equal representation in the Assembly—even though Canada East had a larger population. By 1864, however, the situation had changed and Canada West had the greater number of inhabitants. This caused George Brown and his followers to demand representation by population. Any change in the Act of Union was, of course, strongly opposed by the French-speaking members because they had no desire to be outnumbered in parliament.

The stalemate in government became desperate. During the three years leading up to 1864 there had been two elections and three cabinets formed. It became increasingly clear that strong measures had to be taken immediately to prevent the stalemate from being prolonged.

Despite the bitterness that had grown up between the party **Coalition** leaders over many years, George Brown, John A. Macdonald and Georges Étienne Cartier agreed to join forces to form a unified or *coalition* government. George Brown took the first step towards coalition—a courageous step that was not supported by some of his friends. Macdonald and Cartier, in agreeing to coalition, also met with criticism from their party members. All three men were taking political risks, but in so doing they acted unselfishly, placing the good of the Province ahead of personal or party advantage.

When the coalition was announced in the Assembly in June, 1864, George Brown made a moving address. In the course of his remarks, he said:

> I do frankly confess, Mr. Speaker, that if I never have any other parliamentary success than that which I have achieved this day in having brought about the formation of a Government more powerful than any Canadian Government that ever existed before, pledged to settle, and settle forever, the alarming sectional difficulties of my country, I would have desired no greater honour for my children to keep years hence in their remembrance than that I had a hand, however humble, in the accomplishment of that great work . . .

While the politicians were trying to solve the problems of **A new** political deadlock, Great Britain solved another problem. Ever **capital** since the Parliament Buildings in Montreal had been burned in 1849 at the time of the riots over the Rebellion Losses Bill, there had not been a permanent meeting-place for the Parliament of the Province of Canada. Because politicians were unable to decide where the capital should be located, Parliament had shuttled laboriously back and forth between Kingston and Quebec City.

Gothic architecture was widely employed in church construction in the British provinces during the course of the nineteenth century. Gothic, the style of medieval Europe, was so much in demand that designers often travelled to England or Europe to study old buildings before constructing new ones in British North America. Some of the more eager designers even copied European buildings in full and exact detail. The narrow, arched windows and perpendicular lines so typical of the Gothic style are clearly seen in this illustration of the impressive Christ Church Cathedral, Fredericton, New Brunswick. Built between 1845 and 1853, it is said to have been influenced by the design of a parish church in Norfolk, England. See if you can find similarities between the Gothic style of Christ Church Cathedral and that of the Gothic-type house shown on page 292.

Finally, it was decided that the Queen should choose a location. When, in 1857, Queen Victoria announced that the capital would be located at Ottawa, Canadians were astonished. "Why," they asked themselves, "should our new capital be placed in such a wild, rowdy place as Ottawa?" American reporters in Canada treated the idea as a joke and wrote home amusing articles for their newspapers. However, the Queen had made the choice and it would have been an insult to have rejected it. Reluctantly, Canadians accepted the decision.

In 1860, the Prince of Wales—later King Edward VII—arrived at Ottawa to lay the corner-stone of the new Parliament Buildings. Workmen and others who stood in the Ottawa mud that day had no idea that they were witnessing the birth, not of a provincial capital, but of a national capital.

# 27. *The Charlottetown Conference*

**Idea of federal union**

BEFORE AGREEING to form a coalition, Macdonald, Cartier and Brown had agreed to promote a new type of government—*federal union*. Under this plan, each province would have a government to manage its own affairs but, in addition, a federal or central government would control such matters of common importance as defence, immigration and customs duties. (This proposal bore some resemblance to the form of government established in the United States after the American Revolution.)

The three leaders had discussed two types of federal union: the first was the union of Canada West and Canada East, with the later addition of other British provinces; the second proposed the immediate union of all the British provinces.

**Talk of union in the eastern provinces**

After some debate, it was agreed that the second plan should be supported. This decision may well have resulted from the fact that Macdonald, Cartier and Brown realized that the Maritime provinces were also considering union. Nova Scotia, New Brunswick and Prince Edward Island had, in fact, gone so far as to arrange a conference to discuss federation among themselves.

Interest in a Maritime union was not due to a deadlock in government, but to the realization that certain problems might be solved if the provinces shared a single government. There was a serious need for more railways, more inter-provincial trade and a unified system of defence in case of war. Desire for change in government, however, was not shared by all people along the Atlantic shore. It seems that political leaders in the Maritimes were more enthusiastic about the discussions to be held at Charlottetown, Prince Edward Island, than many of their followers.

The British government was also interested in promoting a union of the North American provinces. In particular, the cost

204

and difficulties involved in keeping troops in far-off colonies was a burden that Great Britain was trying to reduce. In any case, a unified British North America might be better able to defend itself with less aid from the mother country.

Realizing that the Maritime conference to be held at Charlottetown, September 1, 1864, offered a fine opportunity for discussion, Macdonald requested that a delegation from the Province of Canada be permitted to attend. This request caused some surprise in the east, but it was agreed, politely and stiffly, that representatives from Canada might be present at the meeting—provided they considered themselves as visitors.

In August, 1864, Macdonald travelled by steamship from Quebec City to Charlottetown in company with seven cabinet ministers, Georges Étienne Cartier, George Brown, Alexander Tilloch Galt, William McDougall, Thomas D'Arcy McGee, Alexander Campbell and Hector Louis Langevin. They were concerned about the reception they would receive on arrival, for their invitation had certainly been lacking in warmth. When their ship, the *Queen Victoria,* docked, they could see that the streets were filled with a gay throng. To their great disappointment, they soon discovered that the welcome was not for them, but for a circus, the first one on the island in twenty-one years. In addition, accommodation proved to be so scarce that some of the Canadian delegates were forced to sleep on board the *Queen Victoria.* **Delegates from the Province of Canada**

After this very discouraging beginning, conditions improved so rapidly that the Canadians were embarrassed by their first reactions. With heartwarming graciousness, the eastern delegates agreed that the Canadian representatives might speak to the Conference before discussion of Maritime union began. **Canadians invited to speak**

The Conference opened on September 1, and Georges Étienne Cartier made the first statement of the Canadian viewpoint, emphasizing the advantages of a federation of all the British provinces. He was followed the next day by John A. Macdonald. Thanks to his broad knowledge, his grasp of history and his ready wit, Macdonald made a deep impression upon the thirty-three

1

2

The years between 1800 and 1900 saw remarkable changes in the style of clothing worn by women. The century began with the "Empire" fashion (1), a mode that favoured simple dresses resembling the *tunica*, a garment widely worn by the women of ancient Rome. (It is really not surprising that women's clothing in 1800 imitated Roman dress, considering that Roman influences were being reflected in Western literature, art and architecture.) By about 1820, there was a swing away from "too simple" fashions. Women were beginning to look for costumes that flattered their waistlines. As a result, "hour-glass" dresses (2) became popular. In order to give the waist a neat, slim appearance, skirts were made unusually wide, as were the shoulders and puffed sleeves of the costume. The long skirts were made to flare at the bottom by wearing several petticoats. The weight of so many petticoats eventually became too much for women to tolerate. By 1850, a device known as the *crinoline* had been invented, a light framework made of hoops of metal, bamboo or whalebone and hung from the waist on tapes. The hoops were arranged in a series, increasing in circumference toward the bottom of the crinoline. With this device at their service, dress designers were able to produce skirts as wide as they wished. Thus began a period of enormous skirts that seemed to vie with each other in size and complexity. In this dress of 1865 (3) frills, flounces and ruffles were employed extravagantly throughout. During the last decade of the century, the wheel of fashion moved once more. Again, the slim, hour-glass figure became the mode. High collars were worn on dresses, except for evening gowns, such as the one seen here (4). The cone or bell-shaped skirt was sewn in panels that flared toward the hemline.

3

4

delegates at the Conference. George Brown and Alexander Galt also spoke, offering interesting information about the financial and economic advantages that could be expected from a larger federation.

It soon became apparent that the subject of Maritime union was receiving less attention as the delegates were caught up in the excitement of a greater vision.

When it was decided to move the location of the Conference to Halifax, the Canadians suggested that all the delegates should travel there aboard the *Queen Victoria*. The invitation was gladly accepted, and the delegates hastily packed their bags and hurried to the harbour.

**Conference moves to Halifax**

On September 10, the conference met in Halifax. Eastern delegates made another unsuccessful attempt to come to some agreement on Maritime union. Then, they agreed with delegates from the Province of Canada that a second conference should be held the following month, October 1864, this time at Quebec City. The purpose of the proposed meeting was to talk further of a federation of all British provinces.

Having reached this vital decision, the conference despatched a telegram to Newfoundland, inviting its government to send delegates to the October meeting at Quebec City.

At a final dinner held in Halifax, John A. Macdonald gave a stirring address in response to the toast of "Colonial Union" proposed by Charles Tupper, Premier of Nova Scotia. Macdonald told his listeners that they held the power in their own hands to create a new nation on the continent of North America ". . . a great British Monarchy, in connection with the British Empire, and under the British Queen."

After a short tour of the eastern provinces, the delegates from the Province of Canada hurried home to make preparations for the all-important meeting at Quebec City.

# 28. *The Quebec Conference*

PREPARATIONS FOR THE Quebec Conference progressed rapidly, and the *Queen Victoria* was sent east to pick up the Maritime delegates. By Sunday, October 9, 1864, thirty-three representatives, two of whom were from Newfoundland, had gathered together in the historic city that looks down on the St. Lawrence River.

The next morning, October 10, the Conference opened in the legislative building (which had originally been constructed as a post-office). It was not a grand structure but was none the less a pleasant, dignified place with its own grace and charm. It stood near the edge of the famous cliff at Quebec and commanded a magnificent view. From the windows of the Conference room the delegates could gaze down on the flat, broad waters of the St. Lawrence, the River of Canada, moving slowly past the rock of Quebec. To the north-east they could see the Ile d'Orléans where Cartier and his men had landed in 1535 to gather wild fruit. To the south-west they could see the remains of the old castle of St. Louis from which New France had been governed. Directly across the river was the dark line of the heights of Levis from which Wolfe's gunners had pounded Quebec in the fateful summer of 1759. Quebec had witnessed the beginning and the end of New France. It was now to witness the genesis of the Dominion of Canada.

John A. Macdonald became the vital, moving spirit of the Quebec Conference. If a greater share of credit for success can be accorded to one person, it must be granted to him. His sense of humour, his ability to work continuously and his willingness to make compromises enabled the Conference to overcome awkward and disturbing situations. In a brilliant address delivered on the second day of the Conference, Macdonald made such a deep impression that before the session was over a motion was passed in favour of federal union.

*Macdonald's leadership*

Delegates to the Quebec Conference of October, 1864, gather in the building used by the legislature of the Province of Canada until the completion of the Parliament Buildings in Ottawa. In the foreground are Leonard Tilley of New Brunswick and John A. Macdonald of Canada. The building in which the Conference convened was a gracious structure, marked by high windows with rounded tops. The long discussions and the dull, rainy weather proved a bit tedious to some of the Fathers of Confederation, but this feeling was lessened by a series of receptions, lunches, dinners and balls. It was during the Quebec Conference that the leading statesmen of the British provinces decided to seek confederation.

This was an encouraging development, but the really difficult work lay ahead. There were dozens of problems to be solved —the type of federal government to be established, the duties and powers of the federal government and the methods by which the provinces would be represented in the central government.

**Problem of representation** One question that threatened to end the Conference was the delicate matter of representation in the federal parliament.

At Charlottetown, it had been generally agreed that the central Parliament would be composed of an Upper and a Lower House. While the Maritime delegates at Quebec were agreeable to representation by population in the Lower House, they insisted on being given stronger representation in the Upper House. After several days of very heated debate—in which Macdonald was a great conciliating influence—the Conference agreed that the composition of the Upper House would be on a regional basis (that is, equal representation for each of the two Canadas and the three Maritime Provinces as a group). This compromise was not happily received by all eastern delegates, particularly those from Prince Edward Island.

The proposals of federal union agreed to at Quebec City are **THE SEVENTY-TWO RESOLUTIONS** contained in what are now known as *The Seventy-Two Resolutions,* sometimes referred to as the Quebec Resolutions.

The importance of the Resolutions is that they underlined two fundamental principles of future government. First, the details of federation were based on the practical political experience of Great Britain and the British provinces rather than on those of the United States. Indeed, the Fathers of Confederation were deeply suspicious of the numerous rights and privileges given to the individual states by the Constitution of the United States. The delegates at Quebec considered that the American states had been made so much more powerful than the federal or central government that argument and dissension had inevitably led to secession and civil war. Thus, whereas American federalism was based on a constitution that granted much power and privilege to the individual states, the members of the Conference insisted that Canadian federalism be made dependent upon a *strong* central government. The division of power was based on the principle that matters of national interest would be legislated by the central government and those of a particular or local interest by provincial governments. Second, the Fathers of Confederation insisted that the practice of responsible or cabinet government be continued. Again, they were extremely suspicious of the value of the American system of government whereby powers, privileges and responsibilities were divided among the president, his advisers and Congress.

On October 27, 1864, after seventeen days of deliberation, the Quebec Conference came to a close. Although the discussions were over, delegates went on a tour of cities including Montreal, Ottawa, Kingston, Belleville and Toronto. At Ottawa, they examined the Parliament Buildings, still in the process of construction.

The new nation did not automatically come into being as a result of the Quebec Conference. It was necessary for the legislatures of the various provinces to approve the plan for federation. Then, the plan would have to be submitted to the Parliament in London for approval and authorization.

**The Province of Canada debates Confederation**

In the Province of Canada, the discussion of the Seventy-Two Resolutions was long and heated. Various groups feared the idea of federation. Some English-speaking people in Canada East were afraid that they would be swamped by the French-speaking majority in the future province of Quebec. French-speaking people of Canada East, on the other hand, were afraid they might lose their old rights and privileges. Still other persons feared that federation might lead to a complete break with Great Britain. There was a deep suspicion that a central government might acquire too much power at the expense of the provinces. In addition, federation might lead to higher taxes in order to pay for railways and defence measures.

The debates in the Assembly over the issue of federation went on day after day for several weeks. Macdonald, Cartier and others delivered thoughtful, moving addresses urging the necessity of approving the Quebec Resolutions.

Macdonald kept pointing out the advantage to be gained by a strong union of all the British provinces:

> We find ourselves with a population approaching four million souls. Such a population in Europe would make a second, or at least, a third-rate power ... And when by means of rapid increase, we have become a nation of eight or nine million of inhabitants, our alliance will be worthy of being sought by the great nations of the earth.

In these debates, Cartier was the man who persuaded his fellow French Canadians that their future would be secure only in a federation of the British provinces. Enjoying the confidence of his people, he and he alone was capable of reducing their suspicions of Confederation and he convinced their representatives that they should support the Quebec Resolutions.

Eventually, the Quebec Resolutions were approved in the Parliament of the Province of Canada by a vote of ninety-one to thirty-three in the Legislative Assembly and forty-five to fifteen in the Legislative Council.

**The Province of Canada supports Confederation**

In the Maritime provinces and in Newfoundland, the struggle for approval produced a different decision.

Charles Tupper's support of Confederation at the Quebec Conference met with considerable opposition in his own province of Nova Scotia. It was natural that a number of persons in that region should have little interest in a wide political union of the provinces. Nova Scotians were geographically separated from Canada; they looked to the sea for fish and commerce; they had a close trade connection with Great Britain. Even the problem of defence did not seem important, for Nova Scotians considered that the Royal Navy was quite capable of protecting their shores and those of their provincial neighbours.

**Nova Scotia opposes Confederation**

Charles Tupper's attempts to interest the people of his province in Confederation were strongly attacked by that popular newspaperman, Joseph Howe, who himself had at one time favoured provincial union. However, he now took the position that the plan of Confederation drafted at Quebec was unprofitable to the Maritime provinces and should therefore be firmly rejected. Howe was easily able to arouse violent feelings against Confederation in Nova Scotia (and the other Maritime provinces).

In New Brunswick, the opposition to Confederation was even stronger than in Nova Scotia. The extent of this feeling may be judged by the fact that in the election of 1865 all the federalist cabinet ministers, including the premier, Leonard Tilley, were defeated. Candidates who opposed Confederation were swept into office.

**New Brunswick votes against Confederation**

**Prince Edward Island rejects Confederation**

In the Prince Edward Island legislature, Confederation was promptly rejected. It is surprising how little support the idea of union received in that province. Not a single member of the Council and only five members of the Assembly voted in favour of the Quebec Resolutions.

**Newfoundland rejects Confederation**

In Newfoundland, the people made it clear that they did not favour union with the other provinces. Newfoundland traded with many countries but hardly at all with the mainland. She felt that she had much stronger ties with Great Britain. In 1870, a newly formed anti-Confederation party gained office.

Even though Canadians in the nineteenth century lacked electricity, they nevertheless displayed great resourcefulness in many of their inventions. Shown above is a steam-iron of the period 1860-1870. It was charcoal-fired and worked on the same principle as today's steam-iron. Thus, this useful household appliance is not the modern invention many people believe it to be.

Thus, in not one of the three Maritime provinces nor in Newfoundland did the electors support the Quebec Resolutions. It appeared as if Confederation had been defeated.

**Canadian delegation in Britain**

During 1865, however, Macdonald, Brown, Galt and Cartier went to Great Britain to seek the support of the London government for the cause of provincial union. Their mission was highly successful. The British government decided that Confederation was indeed necessary to ensure the future safety and well-being of the provinces.

In spite of this development, Confederation still seemed far away at the close of the year 1865. During the spring months of 1866, however, certain events, touched off by Fenian raids into British North America, forced New Brunswick and Nova Scotia to reconsider Confederation. These invasions from the United States caused anger and alarm throughout the provinces. The problem of defence quickly became a real and pressing issue.

In New Brunswick, which had felt the Fenian threat, there was suddenly a new attitude toward Confederation. An editorial appearing in one of the newspapers commented:

> If there is one argument in favour of Union stronger than another it is the necessity that exists for a good and efficient system of mutual defence. We have sometimes regarded this as one of the weaker points in favour of Union; invasion or trouble seemed to be at so great a distance, but now when we see how soon sudden danger can threaten us, and how our enemies may concentrate within a gunshot of our very door, the man must be blind, infatuated or prejudiced who can fail to recognize its force.

So great was the change of feeling in New Brunswick that in an election held in the spring of 1866, Leonard Tilley was returned to power with a large majority. It is probable that the voters were influenced not only by the Fenian raids but by the knowledge that the British government now desired Confederation. With Tilley and his supporters back in office, the New Brunswick legislature agreed to proceed toward union with other provinces.

In Nova Scotia, under the leadership of Charles Tupper, the government agreed to support Confederation.

By 1866, three provinces—Canada, New Brunswick and Nova Scotia—were prepared to take the next step toward the establishment of a new nation.

*[margin notes: Fenian raids; Changed feelings in New Brunswick and Nova Scotia]*

# 29. *The British North America Act*

IN DECEMBER, 1866, sixteen delegates from three British provinces met in London with representatives of the British government in what was called the Westminster Palace Hotel Conference. Their task was to prepare a bill for the British Parliament enacting the confederation of the provinces of Canada, New Brunswick and Nova Scotia.

Sessions lasted for nearly two months as the members of the Conference carefully weighed each clause of the document under preparation. The delegates were anxious to ensure that their own provinces were properly treated. This caution is revealed in a letter written from London by Alexander T. Galt, the son of the founder of the Canada Company:

> We still continue occupied every day with meetings of our Conference, in which we are making satisfactory progress, but with a good deal of delay, as our friends from the Maritime Provinces are very fond of talking, and very naturally wish to have some changes made in their interest.

It is possible that the delegates from the Maritimes considered that their colleagues from Canada were also fond of talking and acting in their own interests.

John A. Macdonald, who played a vital rôle at the Conference, was most disappointed that the new nation was not to be called the "Kingdom of Canada." Lord Derby (the British Foreign Secretary) insisted that the three provinces should be united under the name *Dominion of Canada*. Derby suspected that the democratic feelings of Americans would be less disturbed by the word "Dominion" than by the term "Kingdom." Macdonald could never accept this viewpoint and for years afterward regretted the loss of the title "Kingdom."

On March 29, 1867, the Parliament of the mother country passed the legislation known as the *British North America Act*.

Among children's toys of the nineteenth century was a variety of tops. The wooden and plaster top shown here (dated about 1860) was painted in a gay, attractive design and had a clever device that caused it to spin rapidly. Popular with children, too, were cast-iron, mechanical savings banks. These were often amusing in operation, the idea being that when a coin was put in a slot, the bank put on a performance—to encourage saving. Different models offered different amusements. The one shown here (dated about 1865) was called "Always Did Despise a Mule." In operation, the mule threw its rider when a coin was inserted in the bank. Cast iron was employed widely in the manufacture of toy trains, stoves, steam-engines, fire-engines and so on.

The Act was a most unusual one in that its creation and preparation was almost entirely due to a small group of delegates from three colonial possessions. There had never been anything in British history to compare with it.

In accordance with the terms of the British North America Act, the new nation, the Dominion of Canada, consisted of the four provinces of Ontario (formerly Canada West), Quebec (formerly Canada East), New Brunswick and Nova Scotia.

The Parliament of the Dominion of Canada was composed of three elements. The head of government was the monarch (represented by a governor-general). The legislature consisted of two

A federal government

houses, an Upper House corresponding to the old legislative council and a Lower House corresponding to the old legislative assembly. The Upper House was to be called the *Senate,* its members being *appointed* for life in accordance with the following *regional* representation: Ontario 24, Quebec 24 and Nova Scotia and New Brunswick 24. The Lower House was to be called the *House of Commons,* its 181 members being *elected in proportion to provincial populations.* However, Quebec was to be given a total permanent representation of 65 members.

**Federal powers**

One important section of the British North America Act dealt with the powers of the federal government. Among the twenty-nine items subject to federal law and supervision were:

| | |
|---|---|
| trade and commerce | banking |
| raising money by taxation | weights and measures |
| postal service | patents and copyrights |
| the census | Indians and lands reserved for |
| defence measures | Indians |
| salaries of civil and other officers | marriage and divorce |
| navigation and shipping | criminal law |
| fisheries | penitentiaries |
| issue of money | |

**Provincial powers**

The provinces, on the other hand, were permitted to make laws affecting the following matters:

direct taxation within the province
appointment and payment of provincial officers
management and sale of public lands belonging to the province
establishment and operation of prisons for the province
establishment and operation of hospitals and asylums
issuance of licences to shops, saloons, taverns, etc.
development of railways, canals, telegraph, roads, steamship lines, etc.
administration of justice within the province
education.

**Education**

The subject of education had played a most important part in discussions leading up to the British North America Act. Naturally, the provinces were exceedingly anxious to protect the educational systems they had developed over the years. Various Roman Catholic and Protestant groups were concerned about maintaining the schools they had created to meet their own needs.

The British North America Act, therefore, was definite in its statement that education was a matter concerning the provinces *only*. It also stated that the educational rights enjoyed by various religious denominations before Confederation were to be maintained.

Since the expansion of railway communication was considered necessary to the growth of the new nation, the British North America Act made provision for the construction of an *Intercolonial Railway*. The Act stated that: **The Intercolonial Railway**

> . . . it shall be the Duty of the Government and Parliament of Canada to provide for the Commencement within Six Months after the Union, of a Railway connecting the River St. Lawrence with the City of Halifax in Nova Scotia, and for the Construction thereof without Intermission, and the Completion thereof with all practical speed.

(This task occupied nine years, and in 1876 the whole line was in service. Over 700 miles in length, the Intercolonial Railway joined six Atlantic ports with central Canada. Freight rates were kept low in order to promote trade between the Maritime and the central provinces and also to encourage the movement of freight through Canadian ports. Unfortunately, not even the *Intercolonial* could change the fortunate situation of Montreal on the commercial highway of the St. Lawrence, and thus Halifax and Saint John only received the occasional overflow of Montreal commerce.)

The Fathers of Confederation believed that the Dominion of Canada would expand beyond the three original provinces and they made careful provision for the entrance of new provinces: **Admission of other provinces**

> It shall be lawful for the Queen, by and with the Advice of Her Majesty's Most Honourable Privy Council, on Addresses from the Houses of the Parliament of Canada, and from the Houses of the respective Legislatures of the Colonies or Provinces of Newfoundland, Prince Edward Island, and British Columbia, to admit those Colonies or Provinces, or any of them, into the Union, and on Address from the Houses of the Parliament of Canada to admit Rupert's Land and the North-western Territory, or either of them, into the Union, on such Terms and Conditions in each Case as are in the Addresses expressed and as the Queen thinks fit to approve, subject to the Provisions of this Act; and the provisions of any Order in Council in that Behalf shall have the effect as if they had been enacted by the Parliament of the United Kingdom of Great Britain and Ireland.

**Canada not completely independent**

The British North America Act did not give complete independence to the youthful nation. The British government retained a certain amount of control. Among other things, the mother country still possessed the power to disallow measures passed by the Dominion Parliament, to manage foreign affairs, to control immigration, to command Canadian armed forces through British officers and to amend the British North America Act.

**Canada's Birthday, July 1, 1867**

On July 1, 1867, the Dominion of Canada officially became a nation. It must have been a day of deep satisfaction to those men who had worked with such devotion to convert the dream of Confederation into a reality.

The state ceremony performed at Ottawa on that pleasant summer day in 1867 was not an elaborate affair. It was perhaps

July 1, 1867, the birthday of the new nation of Canada, was a brilliant, summer day. Church bells rang and cannon boomed out twenty-one-gun salutes. Lively parades, military reviews and varied celebrations were held throughout the Dominion. Flags and long strips of red, white and blue bunting hung from the fronts of stores, business offices and public buildings. In many centres the highlight of the day was the reading of Queen Victoria's official proclamation declaring the birth of the Dominion of Canada. As night descended, the darkness glowed with Chinese lanterns, fireworks and special illuminations. Here, citizens of one of Canada's fledgling cities watch a military parade led by a Highland regiment in full dress.

a bit too simple for the liking of John A. Macdonald and others who would have preferred more pomp and ceremony.

Sir Charles Monck, in plain street clothes, arrived at the new Parliament Buildings, accompanied only by his secretary. After Monck had been sworn in as Governor-General of the Dominion of Canada, he took his seat in the chair of state and proceeded to announce a series of honours that had been conferred by Queen Victoria on certain leading Canadian politicians. However, one Canadian, due to his outstanding contribution to Confederation, was to receive a particularly high honour. This person was John Alexander Macdonald, now *Sir* John Alexander Macdonald, created a member of a famous British order of knighthood as a mark of his sovereign's esteem and favour.

221

# 30. *The Dominion of Canada*

Elections to the Dominion Parliament, 1867

IT WAS NECESSARY to hold immediate elections to choose members for the new House of Commons. These elections, held in the summer of 1867, brought forth several surprising results. The first was the defeat of the noted Father of Confederation, Macdonald's old political enemy, George Brown. The second was the vote in Nova Scotia that turned against those who had supported Confederation. So strong was this movement that Sir Charles Tupper was the only important supporter of Confederation to win a seat in the Commons.

Difficulty in forming a cabinet

Sir John A. Macdonald, who had been requested by the Governor-General to form a federal government, had difficulty in creating a cabinet. He realized that to be effective his cabinet must have the support of Liberals (formerly known as Reformers) and Conservatives, Roman Catholics and Protestants, French-speaking people and English-speaking people, easterners and westerners. The difficulties of choice were so great that a solution appeared impossible. Eventually, however, when Thomas D'Arcy McGee and Sir Charles Tupper sacrificed their own claims to be ministers, a cabinet was formed. Both of these Fathers of Confederation, richly deserving membership in the cabinet, showed admirable patriotism in their unselfish actions.

Sir John A. Macdonald, as might be expected, became the first Prime Minister of the new Dominion.

There were so many difficulties and handicaps to be overcome that it is nothing less than a miracle the young Dominion survived its first few years of life. That it managed to do so, was very largely due to the political genius and infinite patience of Sir John A. Macdonald. There was probably no other Canadian of the time who could have accomplished the task of holding the nation together.

It is true that Macdonald had his weaknesses. His habit of turning to liquor in times of stress was a constant source of worry to his family and friends. His tendency to postpone difficult decisions in the hope that they would resolve themselves earned him the nickname, "Old Tomorrow." However, he possessed one magnificent talent. He knew how to handle men, and this one great, personal asset is the real measure of his statemanship.

One thorny problem facing the new government was the cool *Dissatisfaction in Nova Scotia* attitude of Nova Scotia. Under the leadership of Joseph Howe, Nova Scotians were expressing considerable dissatisfaction with Confederation. Howe visited England with the purpose of securing Nova Scotia's release from provincial union. The British government, however, refused to approve this request, and Howe returned home without achieving his goal.

Fortunately, a new and friendly relationship developed between Joseph Howe and Sir John A., removing the threat of Nova Scotia's withdrawal and enabling Howe to take a place in the federal cabinet.

In 1869, just two years after Confederation, the nation received *The Dominion gains Rupert's Land and the North-West* additional territory when Rupert's Land was transferred from the Hudson's Bay Company to the Dominion. To complete this vital, historic land transaction, the British Parliament passed an act by which the Canadian government was required to pay about a million and a half dollars to the Hudson's Bay Company in exchange for this territory. The Company was to retain trading rights in the West and was to hold two sections of land in each township, together with the land lying close to its posts (about 50,000 acres). In addition, the British government agreed to transfer the North-West Territories to Canada.

In 1871, British Columbia entered the Dominion as a new *B.C. and P.E.I. enter Confederation 1871 and 1873* province. At the same time, opinion in Prince Edward Island was beginning to favour Confederation. Finally, in 1873, that province also became a member of the Dominion.

When British Columbia joined the Dominion (in 1871), the new province was promised a railway linking Ontario with the Pacific coast—a project to be completed within ten years. The need for such a railway was obvious, but the difficulties involved were frightening. Between eastern Canada and the Pacific lay the rocky, forested regions of the Canadian Shield, the broad prairies of the central West and then the greatest obstacle of all—the mountain ranges of the far West. The estimated cost of such a railway disturbed even the normally optimistic Sir John A. Macdonald. To make matters worse, there were those who prophesied that a railway to the Pacific would never receive enough income to pay its own costs.

**A railway to the Pacific**

Finally, it was agreed that a private company would construct a railway between Ontario and the Pacific with the assistance of the federal government. The government announced that the company chosen to undertake the project would be granted some fifty million acres of land along the right-of-way and a cash subsidy of thirty million dollars. Several groups of business men were eager to sign a contract under those conditions. One such group was led by Hugh Allan of Montreal, who was closely linked with leading financiers in the United States. Eventually, the federal government decided that Allan and his Canadian associates would be granted the contract—if they broke their connection with the Americans.

**The Pacific Scandal, 1873**

This agreement, unfortunately, led to the "Pacific Scandal," an affair that caused Sir John A. Macdonald embarrassment and political defeat. The storm broke in 1873 when a Liberal member of Parliament accused Macdonald and the Conservative party of receiving considerable funds for the election campaign of 1872 from Hugh Allan and his friends. The Liberal member claimed that Allan and his associates had bribed Macdonald and his party in order to secure the railway contract.

The accusations caused tremendous excitement, not only in the federal Parliament but throughout the provinces. Additional evidence later revealed that the Conservatives had indeed received thousands of dollars from Allan and his company. One particularly injurious piece of evidence was the copy of a telegram sent by Macdonald to Allan:

During the second half of the nineteenth century, many of the rivers in Ontario, Quebec and the Maritime provinces were crossed by means of covered bridges. Since the life of an ordinary bridge was little more than fifteen or twenty years when its floor and supporting beams were exposed to the destructive effects of the weather, in many localities the main structure was provided with a protective covering. This measure prolonged the life of the bridge indefinitely—as many century-old covered bridges testify today. These bridges were built on a truss system, which enabled them to span very wide gaps with short timbers. Some of the bridges were actually more than 1,000 feet in length. Due to the methods of bracing and counterbalancing employed, the bridges were incredibly strong. Indeed, there are records of covered bridges, forced off their foundations during floods, floating intact downstream and later being recovered and returned almost undamaged to their original positions. A remarkable number of covered bridges are still in use in eastern Canada. New Brunswick, with over 200 of them, probably contains the greatest number.

Immediate, private. I must have another ten thousand—will be the last time of calling. Do not fail me. Answer to-day.

Sir John A. Macdonald attempted to defend his party by stating that the money was merely a "campaign contribution" and not

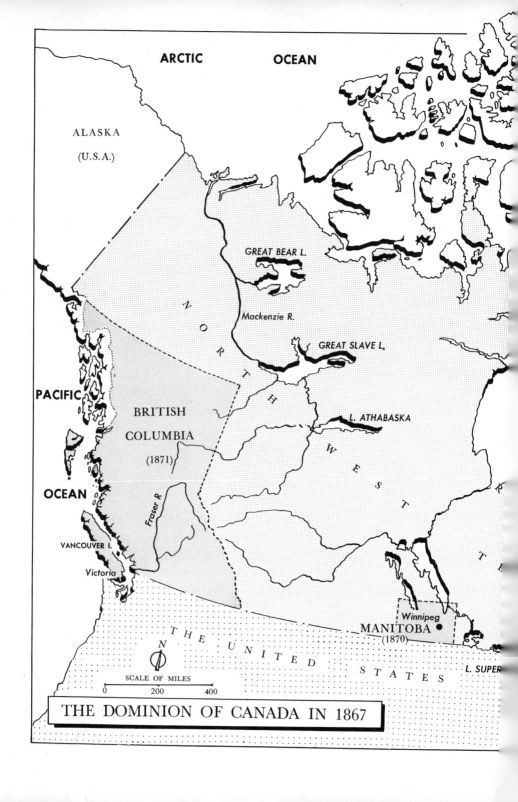

ARCTIC OCEAN

ALASKA
(U.S.A.)

GREAT BEAR L.

Mackenzie R.

GREAT SLAVE L.

PACIFIC

N O R T H

BRITISH
COLUMBIA

(1871)

L. ATHABASKA

W E S T

OCEAN

Fraser R.

VANCOUVER I.

Victoria

T E

Winnipeg

MANITOBA
(1870)

T H E    U N I T E D    S T A T E S

L. SUPER

N

SCALE OF MILES

0        200        400

THE DOMINION OF CANADA IN 1867

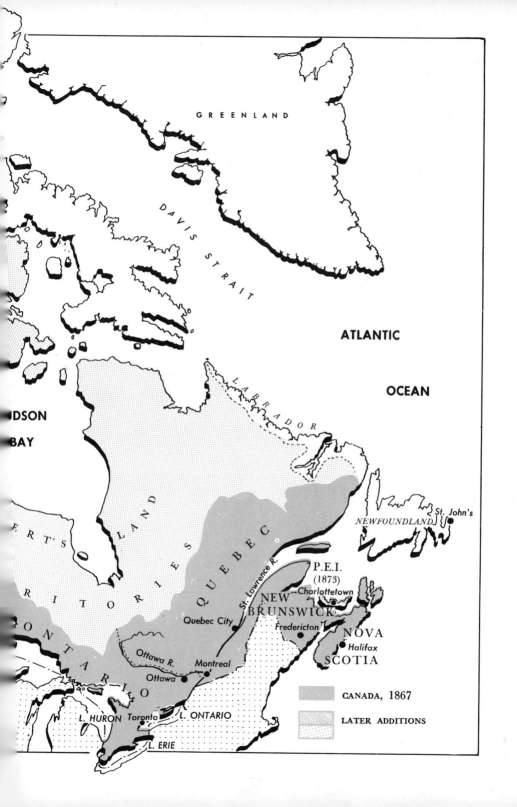

GREENLAND

DAVIS STRAIT

ATLANTIC

OCEAN

HUDSON

BAY

LABRADOR

RUPERT'S

TERRITORIES

QUEBEC

ONTARIO

St. Lawrence R.

NEWFOUNDLAND

St. John's

P.E.I.
(1873)

Charlottetown

NEW
BRUNSWICK

Quebec City

Fredericton

NOVA

Halifax

SCOTIA

Ottawa R.

Montreal

Ottawa

L. HURON    Toronto    L. ONTARIO

L. ERIE

CANADA, 1867

LATER ADDITIONS

a "bribe" to insure a railway contract. Skilful though he was in political matters, he was not able to withstand the waves of protest.   Criticism became so serious and the debates so bitter that Macdonald and his cabinet were obliged to resign.

Alexander Mackenzie, the Liberal party leader, was asked to form a new cabinet and take charge of the government.  In 1874, the Liberals won an overwhelming victory at the polls.

For the time being, at least, Macdonald was forced to be content with leading the opposition party in Parliament.

## SUMMARY — SECTION 6

Although for many years individuals had pointed to the advantages of a union of the provinces of British North America, the proposal did not gain any measure of acceptance until after the middle of the nineteenth century.  By that time, several events were contributing toward a growing feeling of unity among the peoples of the provinces. These events were the opening of Rupert's Land and the North-West to settlement, the establishment of British Columbia as a colony, the gold rush in the Fraser Valley and the American Civil War.

In addition, political deadlock in the Province of Canada had inspired an interest in provincial union.   John A. Macdonald, Georges Étienne Cartier and George Brown, the leading politicians in the Province, were far-sighted enough to realize that their coalition government of 1864 was only a temporary solution to the whole problem of government.

As it happened, the provinces of New Brunswick, Nova Scotia and Prince Edward Island were considering a Maritime union and in 1864 had arranged a conference at Charlottetown, Prince Edward Island. Sensing an opportunity in this development, John A. Macdonald succeeded in having representatives from the Province of Canada invited to attend the meeting.

The Charlottetown Conference opened on September 1, 1864.  By the time it finished, the delegates were so excited by the larger vision of federal union that they agreed to meet again the following month at Quebec City.  On October 9, 1864, delegates from all the provinces and also from Newfoundland began the first of seventeen days of long, difficult discussions. The fruit of their labours was **The Seventy-Two Resolutions**, which outlined proposals for a federation of the British North American provinces and the establishment of a strong, central government.

In the Province of Canada, the Resolutions were accepted. In Newfoundland and Prince Edward Island they were rejected. In New Brunswick and Nova Scotia, the provincial premiers were unable to overcome strong popular protest against federation. However, by a strange trick of fate, the Fenian raids of 1866 focused attention on the problem of defence and caused radical changes of view in New Brunswick and Nova Scotia.

In December, 1866, delegates from Canada, New Brunswick and Nova Scotia travelled to Great Britain where they worked out the details of **The British North America Act**. The Act, passed by the British Parliament in March, 1867, united the provinces of Canada, New Brunswick and Nova Scotia to form the Dominion of Canada. The Act also formed the new provinces of Ontario and Quebec out of the Province of Canada. In addition, the British North America Act listed the individual powers of Dominion and provincial governments.

The Dominion of Canada officially came into being on July 1, 1867, with Sir John A. Macdonald as Prime Minister.

The new nation expanded quickly. By 1870, Rupert's Land and the North-West Territories had been added to the Dominion and by 1873 British Columbia and Prince Edward Island had entered Confederation. At the same time, efforts were made to improve transportation. One of these projects, the Canadian Pacific Railway, involved the Macdonald government in 1873 in an unpleasant political affair known as the "Pacific Scandal." In the election of 1874, Macdonald's explanations were rejected by the voters, and his party suffered a crushing defeat at the hands of Alexander Mackenzie and his Liberal party.

## 7

# THE NORTH-WEST, 1869-1880

Conditions in the North-West ▪ Land transfers in the North-West ▪ Métis fears ▪ Surveyors on the prairies ▪ Louis Riel, leader of the Métis ▪ Governor McDougall barred at the border by rebels, 1869 ▪ Seizure of Fort Garry by Louis Riel and his followers ▪ Execution of Thomas Scott ▪ Flight of Louis Riel to the United States ▪ Arrival of troops under Colonel Garnet Wolseley, 1870 ▪ Province of Manitoba created, 1870 ▪ Establishment of The North-West Mounted Police, 1873.

# 31. The Métis

FOLLOWING THE UNION of the Hudson's Bay Company and the North West Company in 1821, trading had been reorganized in order to reduce expenses. Since there was no longer competition in the fur trade, it was unnecessary to have two or more posts serving a single trading district. For this reason, some posts had been closed and the number of fur brigades reduced. This reorganization had led to some unemployment among Métis who for years had been working in the fur trade. The Hudson's Bay Company had attempted to assist these men by encouraging them to engage in farming in what is now southern Manitoba. A few families did take to agriculture, but most of the Métis found it difficult to face what they considered to be a monotonous and difficult way of life. To them, the excitement and the adventure of the buffalo hunt held more appeal than farming. Hundreds of Métis were content to earn a living by hunting buffalo, making pemmican or finding employment as freight drivers. The extent of their activities may be judged by the fact that, in 1840, well over a thousand Red River carts were gathered together for the big, spring buffalo hunt. Well-organized operations of this size slowly reduced the size of the herds in what is now southern Manitoba, and the hunters were forced to push farther and farther west into what is now the Province of Saskatchewan.

At the same time, there was a renewed interest in Britain and Canada in the possibility of placing more settlers in the North-West. This interest was prompted to some extent by the fear that large numbers of restless American settlers might be tempted (as they had in Mexico) to occupy and to take over empty territory.

Rupert's Land and the North-West Territories transferred to Canada, 1869

After Confederation, the Macdonald government was concerned about the future of the North-West. This concern became even greater when the United States purchased Alaska from the Russians. American territory now lay to the north and to the south of the territory controlled by the Hudson's Bay Company. Would the Americans be tempted to link their two domains by occupying the land in between? This was a question that caused much nervousness in Canadian and British minds and prompted the Dominion in 1869 to purchase Rupert's Land from the Hudson's Bay Company. In addition, the North-West Territories in which the Company had held a trade monopoly were to be transferred by Great Britain to the Dominion.

The North-West

The vast area of land added to the Dominion of Canada by the purchase of Rupert's Land in 1869 brought serious problems as well as advantages to the nation.

A monumental task faced the federal government. Two and a half million square miles of territory had to be organized. In all that broad land there was little in the way of established industry or settled population to help share the cost of government. In the so-called North-West, lying between Ontario and the Rocky Mountains, there was a scanty population of 10,000 to 12,000 settlers — employees of the Hudson's Bay Company, descendants of the Selkirk settlers, French-speaking Métis, English-speaking Métis and various newcomers from the United States and the eastern provinces.

Métis alarmed by transfers

Unfortunately, the residents of Assiniboia were not consulted during the discussions that led up to the purchase, and even after the transfers were completed, no attempt was made to explain the government's plans. As a natural result, much misunderstanding arose.

The Métis, in particular, were alarmed. They feared for their religion, their language, their lands and their old, free way of life. They had known for some time that Canada was busy constructing a colonists' highway from Lake Superior to the Red River. (This route was known as the "Dawson Route," named after Simon Dawson of the Public Works Department in Ottawa.)

The many Métis who could not adjust to an agricultural way of life led a nomadic existence, ever in pursuit of the receding herds of buffalo upon which they were so dependent. Poorly clad, living in tents, cooking over open fires or small iron stoves, they led rough, difficult lives.   Nearly every Métis family owned a Red River cart similar to the one shown here.   Built entirely of wood, with no iron fastenings of any kind, the cart was remarkably strong and capable of carrying a half-ton load.   The Red River cart was balanced on two large wheels, each about five feet in diameter.   These wheels were made unusually wide to lessen the chance of the cart sinking into prairie mud.   Instead of using iron rims for protection against wear, the wheels were often bound with long strips of roughly tanned hide.   The body of the cart was held together by means of wooden pegs and wedges and also with pieces of rough hide called "shagganappé."   This crude leather was also employed in harness making.   No grease was placed on the wooden axles of the carts because grease would have absorbed prairie dust, which in time would have worn away the axles.   When a group of Red River carts was in motion, the loud, shrill creaking of their wheels could be heard over great distances.

Obviously, the Canadian government intended it to be used by the settlers it was encouraging to migrate to the North-West. What would happen to the buffalo hunt and the few Métis farms when thousands of farmers established themselves on the broad prairie lands of Assiniboia and beyond? The Canadian government said nothing of the future of *La Nation Métisse.*

The situation became tense when surveyors were sent into the North-West. The Dominion government expected a heavy flow of settlers, and it was considered a wise move to have the surveying well under way before settlement began in earnest. It was decided to use a system of land survey similar to that used in the western part of the United States. Townships were to be divided into thirty-six *sections,* each containing one square mile or 640 acres. The sections were then to be divided into *quarter-sections* containing 160 acres each. At that time, the quarter-section was thought to be enough land for each family settling in the North-West. (An interesting aspect of the survey system was the plan of setting aside two sections in each township for the future

An invention that had a vital influence on western grain farming was the all-steel "singing plough." In 1837, John Deere, an Illinois blacksmith, discovered that a polished steel ploughshare and mould-board could cut cleanly through the rich prairie soil that so quickly fouled the clumsy wooden or cast-iron ploughs then in use. The new plough, of course, gave prairie farmers an implement that lightened the task of cultivating their immense acreages. Although the steel plough was a notable invention, it was still a hand plough that required the labour of one or more horses or oxen.

support of education. The idea was to sell these sections at a later date and use the money for the construction of schools.)

When the survey began, friction occurred in those areas where the French-speaking Métis had settled along the rivers, occupying long narrow strips in the manner common in New France. Attempts were made by the surveyors to avoid disturbing the pattern, but in some cases the survey lines crossed the narrow holdings, leading the Métis to believe that their lands were being taken from them.

The alarmed Métis found a natural leader among their own people—Louis Riel, a dark-bearded, handsome young man, the son of the leader of a minor Métis revolt in 1849 against the Hudson's Bay Company. Born in the Red River region in 1844, Riel had been chosen as a possible candidate for the priesthood and had studied at the Jesuit Collège de Montréal. However, he failed to complete his religious studies and returned to the Red River in 1868, looking for employment. His powers of eloquence and his hot-tempered nature soon made him an outspoken defender of Métis grievances.

**Louis Riel, leader of the Métis**

# 32. The Red River Rebellion

Riel's
"Provisional
Government,"
1869

DETERMINED TO RESIST the rule of a government forced upon his people without consultation and without their agreement, Louis Riel took the daring step of establishing a "Provisional Government" for the Red River settlement. In time, an appointed council and an elected assembly were set up. In the beginning, Riel acted as secretary of the rebel organization but later became president. He expressed his loyalty to Great Britain and the Queen, but made it clear that he and his people were not to be treated as inferior citizens. They wished to come to a definite agreement with the Macdonald government before accepting any form of Canadian rule. The agreement would have to guarantee the rights of the Métis, specifically, written assurances that their language and customs would remain untouched and unchanged by the transfer of the North-West to the Dominion of Canada.

In 1869, when the newly appointed Lieutenant-Governor of the North-West, William McDougall, travelled westward through the United States to take up his official post, he found to his amazement that armed guards refused to allow him to cross the international boundary. In stopping the Governor at the border, Riel and the Métis sought to delay the date of transfer of the North-West until they could make terms of their own with Canada.

**Seizure of Fort Garry**

Having defied the Lieutenant-Governor, Louis Riel and his followers seized Fort Garry (where Winnipeg now stands) and made it their headquarters. During the winter of 1869-1870, they lived comfortably on food stores belonging to the Hudson's Bay Company.

Riel's rebellion created a most difficult situation for the Dominion government. Macdonald quickly realized that his government and the Hudson's Bay Company had been careless in not preparing the Métis for the many changes that were to come. He realized, too, that the demands of the Métis were far from unreasonable. On the other hand, the rebels had established an illegal government, had met a government official with armed resistance and had seized Hudson's Bay Company property. Despite these provoking circumstances, Macdonald believed that a peaceful settlement could be arranged. However, a particular incident was to change the orderly course of the Métis revolt.

Louis Riel enjoyed the support of the Métis, but a group of English-speaking settlers in the Red River district refused to recognize his provisional government. They ignored Riel's official decrees, they regarded him as a traitor and they tried to bring about the fall of his rebel government. Friction between the two parties became so bitter that Riel had a number of his opponents arrested and held prisoner at Fort Garry. Among them was young Thomas Scott, a former resident of Ontario who had settled in the Red River area.

Unfortunately, Scott was an outspoken man who taunted his captors and generally angered them by his uncontrolled violence and deep contempt. Finally, in a brief trial, in which he was accused of "insubordination and striking his guards," Scott was found guilty and sentenced to death. Although a number of Métis and Red River residents appealed to Riel to overrule the death sentence, Riel refused their pleas for mercy, remarking, "We must make Canada respect us." **Thomas Scott executed**

On March 4, 1870, Thomas Scott, his eyes bandaged with a white handkerchief, knelt in the snow facing a nervous firing-squad of six Métis. When the muskets fired, Scott fell forward, struck by three bullets. He moved slightly and groaned. A man stepped forward, raised a pistol and fired a final shot into his head.

This violent situation in the North-West disturbed officials both in Canada and in Great Britain. Some of the feeling in the mother country was expressed in an official letter sent by the British government to the Governor-General of Canada, Sir John Young:

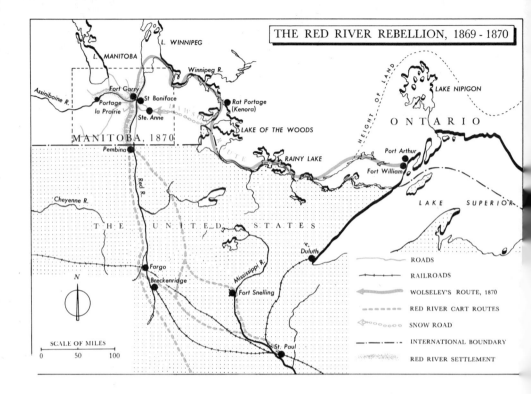

Legend:
- ROADS
- RAILROADS
- WOLSELEY'S ROUTE, 1870
- RED RIVER CART ROUTES
- SNOW ROAD
- INTERNATIONAL BOUNDARY
- RED RIVER SETTLEMENT

SCALE OF MILES
0    50    100

She [the Queen] relies on your Government to use every effort to explain whatever misunderstanding may have arisen—to ascertain the wants and conciliate the goodwill of the people of the Red River Settlement. . . .

The Queen expects from her representative that as he will be always ready to receive well-founded grievances, so will he exercise all the power and authority she entrusted to him in support of order and the suppression of unlawful disturbances.

If the position of the Dominion government was difficult before, it was infinitely worse after the execution of Thomas Scott. Unfortunately, the issues of both race and religion served to complicate the problem. Apart from everything else, the hard fact remained that French-speaking, Roman Catholic rebels had executed an English-speaking Protestant, formerly of Ontario. If the federal government took strong action against Riel and his followers, it

Upper Fort Garry was closely associated with the western fur trade, the Red River Settlement and the beginnings of what is now the city of Winnipeg, Manitoba. (There were actually two Fort Garrys—Upper and Lower—existing at the same time not many miles apart.) Upper Fort Garry was first built in 1822, rebuilt in 1835 and again in 1850. It was the first stone building erected in the western regions of British North America. The stone used in its construction was hauled in winter along the frozen surface of the Red River. In 1830, Hudson's Bay Company officials decided to abandon the original fort and build a replacement, Lower Fort Garry, farther down the Red River. The new fort was completed, but the older structure was never abandoned. Upper Fort Garry is here shown as it appeared in 1850.

would antagonize the French-speaking citizens of Quebec. If, on the other hand, nothing was done to punish the rebels, the angry citizens of Ontario would be in an uproar.

At this point, Alexandre Taché, the Roman Catholic Bishop of **Bishop** St. Boniface, performed a valuable service for the nation. Return- **Taché** ing from a visit to Rome, the Bishop reached Fort Garry a few days after Scott's death. With patience and skill, he persuaded Riel to release the prisoners, to restore the property of the Hudson's Bay Company and to accept the idea of union with Canada.

The Dominion government, in order to play safe, decided on action that displayed both sympathy and sternness toward the

The trek of Colonel Wolseley's force from Ontario to the Red River valley involved considerable difficulty and hardship. In addition to the troops, the expedition included numbers of boatmen and teamsters. The force travelled by steamer to Port Arthur and then set out over the partially constructed Dawson Road. Before reaching Fort Garry, the men were forced to cut fresh trails through the forests, make difficult portages and navigate dangerous waters. They completed the journey in just over three months at a cost to the government of approximately $500,000, a very large sum for that time.

rebels. A new province would be established within the Dominion but troops would be dispatched to ensure law and order.

**Creation of the Province of Manitoba, 1870**

In May, 1870, an act of the Dominion Parliament made the district of Assiniboia, still essentially a fur trade colony, into the province of Manitoba. In the new province, the French and

English languages were to be officially equal, and Protestants and Roman Catholics were to have separate school systems. Almost a million and a half acres were to be appropriated for the benefit of the families of Métis residents. However, by another clause of the Manitoba Act, the natural resources of the province were transferred to the Dominion. The Canadian government was already planning to build a railway across the prairies, and Macdonald and his cabinet members hoped that settlers would soon follow.

In June, 1870, several hundred British and Canadian troops under Colonel Garnet Wolseley made an exceptionally difficult ninety-five-day journey from Toronto to Fort Garry, travelling through Canadian territory the whole way. On learning of the approach of Wolseley's force, Riel fled to the United States. *Colonel Wolseley arrives at the Red River*

The Red River Rebellion was over.

When Riel fled to the United States, he relieved the Dominion government of the difficult duty of deciding on a suitable punishment. Had he been captured, many Ontario residents undoubtedly would have demanded his death.

The Red River rebellion achieved a certain success. The province of Manitoba was created out of part of the Assiniboia region and given its own legislature. Métis land rights were guaranteed by law. Separate schools and the official equality of the French and English languages were granted. After the approval of the Manitoba Act by the British Parliament, Manitoba and the North-West were incorporated in the Dominion of Canada. Thus, a definite start had been made in claiming the West for Canada. However, as future events were to demonstrate, Canada had not heard the last of Métis resistance to the advance of settlement. Canada had also not heard the last of Louis Riel.

# 33. The North-West Mounted Police

WHEN COLONEL WOLSELEY's force was withdrawn from Fort Garry, it was replaced by a fresh garrison of troops; however, this was not a real solution to the hard problem of maintaining order throughout the North-West. Believing that a civil police force rather than a military garrison would be a better organization for this purpose, the Dominion government, in 1873, created The North-West Mounted Police.

Recruits for the new force included "young men from the old Provinces, university graduates, younger sons of the nobility in the Mother Land, men of birth and breeding and social advantage." Horses selected for their use were matched in colour so that each division of the Police might have its own distinctive tone. The original group, consisting of only 300 men, was an astonishingly small force to undertake the policing of the whole North-West.

**The great march**

After a short period of training, the Mounted Police were ready to take up their duties. Posting the men in detachments across the North-West was not an easy operation. The distribution of the Force was only accomplished by an amazing overland march that began in southern Manitoba on July 10, 1874. It was not simply a column of horsemen that moved out on the plains, but a long train of men on horseback, with wagons, carts, cows, calves and a stock of farm implements. The column travelled a thousand miles across swamps, rivers and desolate prairies. Horses became lame, cattle died and men fell ill. Colonel George French, commander of the expedition, later reported:

A Canadian force, hastily raised, armed and equipped, and not under martial law, in a few months marched vast distances through a country for the most part as unknown as it proved bare of pasture and scanty in the supply of water.

A North-West Mounted Police constable of the 1870's. Half of the original police force was trained at Lower Fort Garry during the winter of 1873. Discipline was strict, and the rugged work of breaking and riding horses continued from six o'clock each morning until after dark. Only if the temperature dropped lower than thirty-six degrees below zero did the day's routine come to a stop. Pay was seventy-five cents per day. The British-made uniform consisted of a scarlet tunic, navy-blue trousers with white stripes down the outside seams, long brown boots or black Wellington top boots with spurs, a white helmet and white gloves. Although not issued by the Force, the men often acquired cowboy hats for use on patrol since the official headgear provided little protection from the sun. Revolvers and Snider-Enfield carbines were the weapons issued. An order of 1874 stated that constables might please themselves as to the wearing of whiskers, moustaches or beards, but if they chose to shave, they must do so every day.

After they had established themselves in their new posts, one of the first tasks of the Police was to clear out the ruthless traders who cheated the Métis and the Indians and provided them with a continual supply of liquor. These whisky pedlars, many of them Americans, had roamed the West unmolested before the Police arrived. **Whisky traders**

By December, 1874, the Force was able to report the "complete stoppage of the whisky-trade throughout the whole section of this country." The end of whisky-peddling brought a pleasant change

Whisky traders brought liquor from the United States to the North-West in barrels carried in covered wagons. In an attempt to cut off the flow of liquor, members of the North-West Mounted Police seized wagons after they had crossed the border. As a result, some spectacular chases and captures took place—as can be seen in the illustration. So bold were the whisky traders that they even fortified their trading posts with stockades and bastions. One of the most notorious of these liquor centres was Fort Whoop-Up in what is now the province of Alberta. The callousness and utter lawlessness of the area is revealed in a brief letter written by a resident of Fort Whoop-Up. It reads: *Dear friend—My partner, Will Geary, got to putting on airs and I shot him and he is dead—the potatoes is looking well. Yours truly, Snookum Jim.* In actual trading operations two tin cups of whisky bought a buffalo robe and three gallons of whisky purchased a good horse. Even greater profits were made when the whisky pedlars diluted liquor by adding water. The shrewd Blackfoot tribesmen, however, demanded that their whisky be strong enough to ignite when a match was put to it. The fact that whisky (and rum) would burn led to the invention of the term "fire-water" by the Indians.

for peaceful settlers. Until this time, they had lived in constant dread of attack and robbery by drunken, brawling Indians.

**Indian treaties**

It was fortunate that the North-West Mounted Police were on the scene to assist in treaty negotiations with the western tribes.

Increasing white settlement and the gradual destruction of the buffalo herds were making conditions difficult for many of the Indians. The situation was so serious that in the 1870's some of the tribesmen were in danger of starving to death. As a result, bands of Indians began raiding settlers' herds and hunting on American land.

It was obvious that something had to be done to assist the Indians and to prevent dangerous disturbances. Eventually, it was decided that the Indians should sign treaties in which they gave up claim to much of their old hunting-grounds and agreed to live on reservations. In return for these promises, the tribesmen would receive farming tools, seed, food stores and annual gifts of money. Before the end of the 1870's, the Indians had given up their claims to a great belt of land running through the southern part of the North-West.

In the difficult task of persuading the Indians to adopt a new way of life, the Police played an important part. They succeeded because they were respected and admired by the tribesmen of the plains. Chief Crowfoot of the Blackfoot, when signing the Black-foot Treaty in 1877, remarked: *Indian respect for the Police*

> The Police have protected us as the feathers protect the bird. I wish them all good, and trust that our hearts will increase in goodness from this time. I will sign.

The friendly attitude of the Indians toward the Force was astonishing. On one occasion, a constable wearing a blue overcoat encountered a band of American Indians that had wandered across the Canadian border. Thinking the rider was an American cavalry trooper, the Indians levelled their rifles and made hostile gestures. When the constable removed his blue coat and revealed his red tunic, the rifles were lowered and a friendly conference followed.

The famous Force was not always tracking down illegal traders, horse-thieves and murderers. There were other duties, not as excit-ing perhaps, but just as important in the development of the North-West. New settlers coming to the prairies were given aid and advice, and in time of fire, flood and famine the Police were *Work of the Police* there to help. On their regular patrols, the Police frequently dropped in on isolated ranches just to see that all was well. Many of the constables and officers were charming, well-educated men whose visits provided welcome breaks in the monotonous life of the settlers. There is also good reason to believe that the presence of the Police promoted an early interest in education and encouraged the erection of little schools on the prairies.

Twice since the founding of the Force, its name has been changed. In 1904, it was decided to honour its achievements by granting the title *Royal North-West Mounted Police*. In 1920, the Force absorbed the Dominion Police and was re-named the *Royal Canadian Mounted Police*, with headquarters at Ottawa rather than Regina. From that date on, the Police have undertaken duties in every part of Canada.

## SUMMARY—SECTION 7

In acquiring Rupert's Land from the Hudson's Bay Company and the North-West Territories from Great Britain, the Canadian government also acquired a gigantic problem of administration; the land areas were vast and their populations were scanty; there was a danger that eager American settlers would pour into the empty prairies and claim them as they had claimed Mexican territories.

In order to save the North-West for Canada, the Dominion government decided to promote fresh settlement in the newly acquired territories. This decision, however, proved disturbing to the Métis, who were already resentful that their existence had been ignored in the discussions that resulted in the land transfers. To the Métis, the sight of surveyors marking out townships in preparation for settlers meant that their old way of life was threatened with extinction.

In 1869, Louis Riel, the leader of the Métis, took action. After forming a "Provisional Government," he halted William McDougall, the new Governor of the North-West, at the international border, and then seized Fort Garry as his headquarters. Many of those who actively opposed Riel's rule were imprisoned. One of them, Thomas Scott, was tried and executed.

The Red River Rebellion of 1869-1870 created a crisis for the federal government. In Quebec, Riel was hailed as a hero; in Ontario, he was condemned as a traitor and a murderer. What could the government do with Riel that would not cause a storm of protest? The problem was resolved when Riel fled to the United States on learning of the approach of Colonel Wolseley and his force. In 1870, the Province of Manitoba was formed out of part of the old region of Assiniboia, and the new province was given it own legislature. Métis rights were guaranteed by law. Manitoba and the North-West were incorporated in the Dominion of Canada.

In order to ensure future peace and order on the prairies, the federal government, in 1873, created The North-West Mounted Police. The Police performed their many duties with such devotion and skill that they won the respect of the Métis, the Indians and the settlers.

# 8

## THE YOUNG NATION

Prime Minister Alexander Mackenzie ▪ The National Policy ▪ Macdonald returns to power, 1878 ▪ Tariffs ▪ Period of prosperity ▪ The Canadian Pacific Railway ▪ Financial problems of railway construction ▪ Driving the last spike ▪ Unrest among the Métis ▪ Return of Louis Riel ▪ The North-West Rebellion, 1885 ▪ Capture and execution of Louis Riel ▪ Results of rebellion ▪ Return to hard times ▪ Election of 1891 ▪ Death of Sir John A. Macdonald ▪ The Manitoba Schools Question ▪ Decline of the Conservative party ▪ Prime Minister Wilfrid Laurier ▪ Settlement of the Manitoba Schools Question ▪ Imperial Preference ▪ Queen Victoria's Diamond Jubilee ▪ A knighthood for Laurier ▪ Immigration to Canada ▪ The Yukon gold rush ▪ The Boer War, 1899-1902 ▪ Canada in 1900.

# 34. Macdonald Returns to Power

AFTER JOHN A. MACDONALD's political defeat in 1874, following the "Pacific Scandal," the Liberal leader, Alexander Mackenzie, became Prime Minister of Canada.

Mackenzie, a Scottish stone-cutter, immigrated from Scotland to Canada when he was twenty years of age. Being an ambitious, determined young man, he studied and read widely, providing himself with the education he had missed in boyhood. As a grown man, he was stern, industrious and rigidly honest in all his dealings.

Alexander Mackenzie

On coming to power, the Mackenzie government was faced with a number of serious problems. The Liberal party was not a united party. It lacked an overall policy for the government of the nation. Canada was suffering from a period of hard times marked by unemployment, falling sales and a general trade depression.

One of the major tasks facing Mackenzie was the unsolved problem of providing the railway that had been promised to the Province of British Columbia. The "Pacific Scandal" had brought previous planning to a stop and it was now necessary to make a fresh beginning. Mackenzie, being a cautious Scot, thought that the proposed railway to the Pacific could be built by the government in small sections on a "pay-as-you-go" basis. He also believed that large lakes and rivers could be used as water links in the long transportation route across the continent. There was such difficulty in finding companies willing to proceed on the terms offered that, by 1878, very little progress had been made.

The railway problem

Conservative members in Parliament criticized the Liberal railway policy, and the people of British Columbia demanded more vigorous action. The citizens of the Pacific province were, in fact, so disturbed that they threatened to withdraw from Confederation.

1          2

Gas was employed for various purposes in some large centres in the 1840's.   The city of Toronto began to use gas for street lighting in 1842 and continued to use it until 1910. In the 1880's, many of the better homes boasted gas fire-places like the ornate monster (1) shown here.   The ugly appearance of this specimen is a good example of the delight that people of this time took in mixed styles of design.   Such a fire-place (including the built-in mirror) could be bought pre-assembled.   The use of gas in cooking is shown in (2), a kitchen stove of the 1890's manufactured in Montreal.   It is interesting to note that this gas stove closely resembles the coal and wood stoves of the period.

Mackenzie was overly confident of winning the election of 1878 because he felt his party had provided the nation with sound and honest government.  In holding this attitude, Mackenzie was sadly underestimating the skill and the popularity of his Conservative rival, Sir John A. Macdonald.

The "Old Chieftain" was making careful plans for the election. Knowing that he must make a strong appeal to the voters, Macdonald created a new programme he cleverly called the *National Policy*. One important feature of the National Policy was a proposal to raise Canadian tariffs on imported goods. This measure would have the effect of increasing the prices of foreign products and, it was believed, would encourage Canadians to buy goods produced in Canada.

As well as high tariffs, Macdonald's National Policy included plans for the rapid construction of railways, the promotion of immigration and the settlement of the North-West beyond the boundaries of Manitoba. Macdonald was shrewd enough to know that these proposals would appeal to many Canadians.

Before the election of 1878, Macdonald and his followers proclaimed the merits of the National Policy. At many political conferences and gatherings, they underlined the necessity of protecting Canadian industry by means of tariffs and held out the prospect of making Canada a strong, unified and self-sufficient nation. In one address, the "Old Chieftain" said:

No country is great with only one industry. Agriculture is our most important, but it cannot be our only staple. All men are not fit to be farmers; there are men with mechanical and manufacturing genius who desire to become operatives or manufacturers of some kind, and we must have means to employ them; and when there is a large body of successful and prosperous manufacturers, the farmer will have a home market for his produce, and the manufacturer a home market for his goods, and we shall have nothing to fear.

So it was that the Conservatives entered the election of 1878 with a plan of action. The Liberals, on the other hand, were still divided among themselves and they depended upon the record of their government for re-election. However, many people were not satisfied with the Liberal record. They were inclined to blame the Liberals for not overcoming the difficulties created by the trade depression. Although this may have been an unfair criticism, it was a firm indication that the Liberals would have a hard fight at the polls.

Throughout the nineteenth century children were often dressed in clothes that were similar in style to prevailing adult fashions. An interesting variation of this trend was the "sailor suit," which, commencing about 1870, was worn in countless versions and styles by nearly all well-dressed young boys for the next quarter of a century. Although other clothing fashions for the young were available, the sailor suit remained most popular, appearing in long and short trouser styles and with an infinite variety of "middy" blouses (from midshipman) or tight-fitting tunic tops. Indeed, this particular costume had so much appeal that it continued to be worn, although on a lesser scale, until as late as the mid-1930's.

**Victory for Macdonald and the Conservatives**   The result of the election indicated how cleverly Macdonald had gauged the feelings of the Canadian people. In Ontario and Quebec, his party gained substantial majorities, while in Nova Scotia, Prince Edward Island, British Columbia and Manitoba the vote went almost solidly in favour of the Conservatives.

It was an overwhelming victory for Macdonald and his National Policy. When the new Parliament met, the victors had a majority of eighty-six seats in the House of Commons. So great was the appeal of the National Policy that the Conservatives remained in power for the next eighteen years—thirteen of them under the leadership of Macdonald.

# 35. The Canadian Pacific Railway

ONCE AGAIN PRIME MINISTER of Canada, Macdonald quickly set *Macdonald raises tariffs* about the work of putting the National Policy into operation. One of his first moves was to establish high tariffs on certain imported products. After consulting with Canadian manufacturers, the government raised duties on a number of imported articles that were considered a threat to home industry and agriculture. For example, the duty on imported cotton goods was raised from $17\frac{1}{2}\%$ to $30\%$ and on woollen goods from $17\frac{1}{2}\%$ to $35\%$. Substantial increases were made on the duties applying to imported boots, shoes, iron and steel goods. To provide some degree of protection for home agriculture, duties were placed on incoming shipments of corn, barley, wheat and farm animals. Although many people were pleased by the new tariff arrangements, Liberal members in Parliament complained that these measures assisted only manufacturers and farmers.

Macdonald and his government were fortunate in that the *Period of prosperity* period of hard times disappeared shortly after they took office. A time of prosperity followed, making it appear that the National Policy had worked miracles. Actually, it was a world-wide improvement in economic conditions that brought about the pleasant change. Canada's own economic recovery was also assisted to some extent by a series of excellent grain crops and by the renewal of a brisk timber trade with the United States.

In keeping with his election promises, Macdonald took care *Beginning the C.P.R.* to hasten the construction of the railway westward from Ontario to British Columbia. He still believed that the new line should be built, owned and operated by a private company rather than by the Canadian government. With this aim in mind, he devised a plan that he thought would prove attractive to a particular group of men with the capital and the experience to undertake the task.

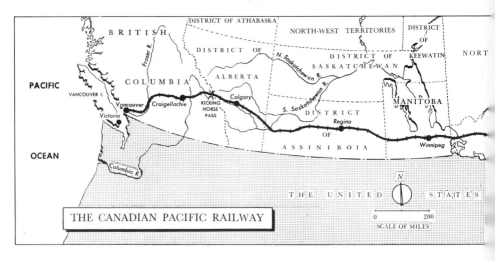

THE CANADIAN PACIFIC RAILWAY

0        200
SCALE OF MILES

After considerable negotiation, an association of Canadian, French and British financiers agreed to accept the plan. Among the Canadians were Donald A. Smith, an important official in the Hudson's Bay Company, George Stephen, President of the Bank of Montreal and James J. Hill, a native of Ontario. Along with other businessmen, they formed the Canadian Pacific Railway Company.

**Agreement with the C.P.R. Company**

The terms offered by the government were liberal indeed. In exchange for the construction and operation of the Canadian Pacific Railway, the Company was to receive several million dollars in cash and several million acres of land along the line of the proposed railway. In addition to this generous land grant, the Company was to receive, without charge, all land over which tracks were laid or buildings erected. As a further aid to the Company, it was agreed that all imported materials necessary for construction were to be admitted free of duty. It was also agreed that no other company would be permitted to build a competing railway line in the West for a period of twenty years.

The Canadian Pacific Railway Company, on its part, promised to build and operate a line from Lake Nipissing in northern Ontario to Port Moody in British Columbia. About 200 miles of

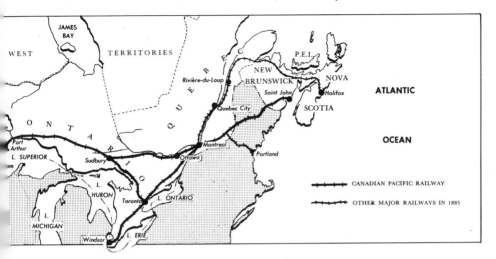

track had already been laid, and this was given to the Company as part of the bargain.

The contract between the Canadian government and the Canadian Pacific Railway Company was signed in London, England, in October, 1880, and a few months later came before the Canadian Parliament for approval. Sir Charles Tupper, then Minister of Railways, supported the contract in a moving address:

. . . the proudest legacy I would desire to leave is the record that I was able to take an active part in the promotion of this great measure by which I believe Canada will receive an impetus that will make it a great and powerful country at no distant date.

After Parliament had given consent to the building of the railway, work was pushed forward with great speed and vigour. William Van Horne, an American with wide experience in railway construction, acted as general-manager and chief engineer of the project. A man of great energy and ability, Van Horne played a vital rôle in the rapid progress that was made.

The many difficulties involved in railway construction included laying track through forests, and across swamps, prairies and mountain ranges. The wooded, rocky section north of Lake Superior was one of the more difficult stretches with its barriers

Difficulties of railway construction

of hard rock and areas of low, spongy muskeg. Blasting the unyielding rocks with dynamite was a slow and costly operation. Track laid on muskeg often sank and disappeared from sight. (One stretch of muskeg swallowed up track seven times, along with three locomotives.)

On the prairies, where there were fewer obstacles, lines were laid with less difficulty, but the problems of supply were more serious. Enormous quantities of food, timber, rails, spikes and equipment had to be transported to the "end of steel." On the plains, the railway was pushed forward at the rate of about two and one half miles per day, but on one memorable occasion a record of twenty miles in three days was established.

The C.P.R. charter stated that the railway would cross the mountains via the Yellowhead Pass, the route recommended by various engineers. When Van Horne saw the Pass, he remarked somewhat sarcastically:

Those [engineering] surveys will no doubt prove of great value to future alpinists. But I'm building a railroad!

Instead, he picked out a route farther south through the Kicking Horse Pass. Van Horne also ignored the charter statement that Port Moody would be the western terminal of the C.P.R. Seeing better harbour facilities farther east, he chose another spot on Burrard Inlet. Van Horne picked out the small village of Granville that lay next to a natural, almost landlocked harbour, the village that had once been called Gastown. He renamed it Vancouver.

**Work of the North-West Mounted Police**

To the credit of the North-West Mounted Police, there were no serious clashes between the prairie Indians and the railway workers. There were several attempts by hostile tribesmen to stop railway construction, but these were quickly dealt with by the Police. One chief, named Piapot, showed his displeasure with the railway by camping his followers directly on the right-of-way, thus bringing construction work to a stop. Piapot, however, moved his camp quietly and promptly when a Police sergeant and two constables walked among the Indian tipis and kicked down the

The *Countess of Dufferin* was one of the earliest locomotives employed on the Canadian Pacific Railway. Built in Philadelphia in 1872, it weighed 65,500 pounds and was fifty-one feet in length. The towering funnel at the front was a "spark-arrester" designed to reduce the danger of fire along the railway right-of-way. The locomotive carried a large kerosene headlight and used improved brakes. Air-brakes were just coming into use on trains at this time and were a vast improvement over the slower-acting hand-brakes of former times. The *Countess of Dufferin* enjoyed a long career in western service and pulled the official train bearing Sir John A. Macdonald and party on their first visit to the West and the Pacific coast. It is reported that during a portion of the trip through the mountains Lady Macdonald sat on a chair bolted to the cow-catcher of the locomotive. In this exciting, if rather hazardous position, she was able to view with ease the magnificent scenery on either side of the railway. The *Countess of Dufferin* can still be seen today on display outside the C.P.R. station in Winnipeg, Manitoba.

supporting poles. At times, there were also violent strikes and other disturbances among the railway workers, but these problems, too, were handled firmly by the Mounted Police.

The excellent work of the Force won the respect and admiration of all connected with the railway construction. This feeling was well expressed in a letter, written in 1882 by Van Horne, to the Commissioner of the Force.

Our work of construction for the year 1882 has just closed, and I cannot permit the occasion to pass without acknowledging the obligations of the company to the North-West Mounted Police, whose zeal and industry in preventing traffic in liquor and preserving order along the line of construction have contributed so much to the successful prosecution of the work.

Railway construction through the many mountain ranges between the prairies and the Pacific has long been regarded as one of the greatest engineering achievements of the nineteenth century. Before work could begin, survey parties explored the rugged regions, looking for routes suitable to track-laying, a task that at one time seemed impossible. It took months of dangerous, difficult blasting, filling, bridging and tunnelling to construct the twin tracks of steel through the mountains. This stupendous achievement is all the more remarkable considering the crude equipment available at the time, as can be seen in the illustration of the type of crane used for heavy work.

**Financial problems**

The cost of railway construction proved so high that, by 1884, funds available to the Canadian Pacific Railway Company were exhausted. As a result, the Canadian government issued a loan of several million dollars. Even this large sum was not sufficient to complete construction of the long line of steel. In the following year, the directors of the Company were forced to ask for more money. The situation became so desperate that Van Horne sent off a telegram to his head office:

> Have no means of paying wages, pay car can't be sent out, and unless we get immediate relief we must stop. Please inform Premier and Finance Minister. Do not be surprised, or blame me, if an immediate and most serious catastrophe happens.

Yet another request for funds created a most awkward situation for Macdonald. The Liberals were already complaining bitterly of high construction costs, and even Macdonald's own ministers could not all agree that more money should be released to the Company. The Prime Minister himself feared that members of Parliament might refuse to approve the loan. On the other hand, if the necessary funds were not provided immediately, construction would halt and all the energy, time and money invested in the railway would be lost. The prospect of such a gigantic failure was an appalling thought to Macdonald, for he could readily imagine what it would mean to Canada, to the Conservative party and to himself. Perhaps he remembered the remark of one of his cabinet members: "The day the Canadian Pacific busts, the Conservative party busts the day after!"

Under these conditions, it took courage for Macdonald to appear again before Parliament and ask for an additional five million dollars. However, such was the force of his personality that he won the required vote. At few other times during his political career did he show greater skill in leadership than on this occasion.

From that point on, railway construction advanced quickly and smoothly. By the late autumn of 1885, the task was complete.

On November 7, a simple ceremony was held at Craigellachie in the Rocky Mountains. It was there that Donald Smith, looking very dignified and solemn, personally wielded the heavy hammer that drove home the last spike in the line. Van Horne, other officials of the Company and a number of workers in a close-packed group watched the historic action. They were witnessing the completion of what was then the longest railway in the world.

The last spike, Nov., 1885

# 36. The North-West Rebellion, 1885

BEFORE THE CONSTRUCTION of the Canadian Pacific Railway was completed, serious trouble occurred in the Districts of Assiniboia, Saskatchewan and Alberta.

**Unrest among the Métis**

When Manitoba was established, the half-breeds of the province were given full title to their lands, but the same privilege had never been extended to the Métis living in other portions of the North-West. This led to discontent and unrest. The Métis could not understand why the Canadian government would not guarantee their property rights. In 1878, requests were sent to Ottawa from Métis settlements for "land grants as in Manitoba." While some Métis land claims near Edmonton had been recognized by Ottawa, other like claims in the Saskatchewan district were refused. The Métis of the Saskatchewan valley became more and more uneasy and watched with alarm what had happened to the Indians.

By 1880, the vast herds of buffalo—upon which the Indian depended for food and clothing—had been almost wiped out by white hunters. By 1880, the Dominion had moved many plains tribes into reservations where, as wards of the government, they were poorly treated. At the same time, the Indians, now living on reservations, watched as the westward march of the C.P.R. left to north and south of its tracks villages, towns, ranches and farming communities—on what had been Indian lands. The tribes began to feel that they had been robbed.

As the Canadian Pacific Railway moved farther and farther across the plains and settlement steadily followed it westward, the Métis and the Indians became increasingly uneasy. Tension was further increased as surveyors moved up the Saskatchewan River to divide land into townships.

In 1884, a small group of Métis under a noted buffalo hunter, Gabriel Dumont, rode southward 700 miles into Montana to consult the exiled Louis Riel. It seemed natural to them that they should once again turn to the man who, fourteen years before, had defied the Canadian government. Riel accepted their invitation to return to Canada, this time to lead Métis and Indians in their fight for freedom.

Return of Louis Riel

The North-West Mounted Police soon learned that Riel had returned. It quickly became clear to the Police that agents sent out by Riel were stirring up trouble among the prairie tribesmen. Métis agitators did not find it too difficult to persuade the restless Indians that, if they joined Riel in rebellion, the white men would be swept from the western plains. The Police lost no time in sending warnings of approaching trouble, but their messages made little impact upon the Canadian government. Macdonald and his cabinet were too preoccupied with the National Policy to pay attention to the North-West.

By Dominion Day, 1884, Riel had arrived at Batoche in the broad valley of the South Saskatchewan. Later that month, Riel spoke to his Métis followers at Prince Albert, his major plea being that they petition Ottawa for free title to their lands, for representation in the Dominion Parliament and for changes in the land laws. Unfortunately, as the next few months passed, Riel's many white supporters began to desert him. Western newspapers started to recall the death of Thomas Scott. The government in Ottawa steadily ignored Riel's existence and his speeches on behalf of his people.

Riel at Batoche, 1884-1885

By March, 1885, Riel, confused and embittered, had several times suggested that he return to Montana, but on each occasion the Métis pleaded with him to remain. Supported now only by a few hundred Métis, Riel decided to repeat the tactics of 1869-1870. He announced the formation of a provisional government, denounced as traitors all who would not ally themselves with him

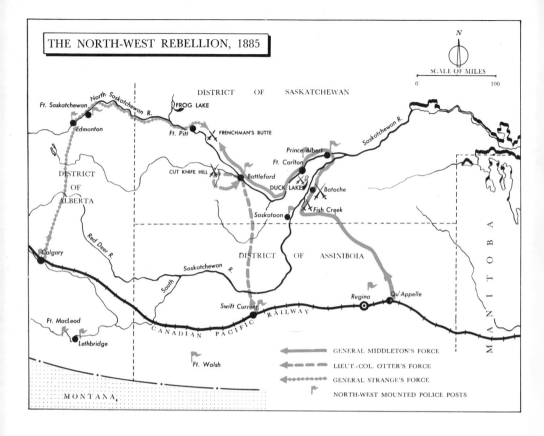

THE NORTH-WEST REBELLION, 1885

GENERAL MIDDLETON'S FORCE
LIEUT.-COL. OTTER'S FORCE
GENERAL STRANGE'S FORCE
NORTH-WEST MOUNTED POLICE POSTS

and arrested a number of "traitors."

**The clash at Duck Lake**    There was no doubt by this time that rebellion would break out at any moment. Accordingly, that same month, about 100 men of the North-West Mounted Police were moved from headquarters in Regina to Prince Albert. Unfortunately, they arrived too late to avert the first armed clash of the North-West Rebellion, a short engagement at Duck Lake. The Police had gone there to collect the contents of a government supply store—which included rifles—and bring them back to the Police post at Fort Carlton.

During the Duck Lake skirmish, fifty-three of the Mounted Police (aided by forty-one volunteers from Prince Albert) met a rebel force of about 400 Métis and Indians. Outnumbered as they were and fighting in the open against a partly hidden enemy, the Police and volunteers were placed in an impossible situation. After a courageous stand in which twelve men were killed and eleven wounded, they retired from the scene.

In 1885, the British Army began to discontinue the use of the scarlet coat in military uniforms. Battle experiences in India and Egypt had shown that this bright colour made troops far too conspicuous. As a result, khaki (a dull brown) soon became standard colouring in British uniforms, although during the period of change some dark green and blue were also worn. In 1868, the young Dominion of Canada began the formation of its own military forces with the establishment of militia units in major cities. With the single exception of Halifax, N.S., British troops ceased to perform garrison duties in Canada after 1871. Canadian militia uniforms kept pace with British developments and, as a result, were similar in design. The soldier shown here was a member of the Montreal Garrison Artillery Battalion. An important step in Canadian military affairs was taken in 1876 with the creation of an officers' training school at Kingston, Ont.—The Royal Military College of Canada. By 1886, this establishment was said—even by Americans—to provide better training than that of the famous United States Military Academy at West Point, New York State. The standard fire-arm of Canadian militia was the British-manufactured Snider rifle, a breech-loading weapon that fired a metal bullet. The Snider was actually the next development after the Springfield rifle used in the American Civil War. In the background is a novel military device of the time, a portable rifle-pit, consisting of a light-weight, moveable, metal shield with holes for sighting and firing.

The news of Duck Lake spread across the prairies. In the north, Chiefs Big Bear and Poundmaker began to talk war with their followers. Elsewhere, the plains Indians began to stir.

John A. Macdonald was entertaining guests in his home when he received a telegram reporting the Duck Lake incident. As his

Shock in eastern Canada

guests were leaving later in the evening, he whispered to a Canadian senator, "Mac, there's the very mischief to pay in the North-West."

If the government had been slow before to consider the problems of the North-West, it was now very prompt in responding to the emergency. General Frederick Middleton, commander of the Canadian militia, was ordered to proceed immediately to the North-West and crush the rebellion, particularly as the whole Indian population of the North-West might well join Riel and his Métis.

**Militia troops move west**

The Canadian Pacific Railway had not yet been completed between Manitoba and Ontario, and there were still some gaps in the line north of Lake Superior. Nevertheless, Van Horne offered to have troops in the West in eleven days. His offer seemed a ridiculous boast, but Van Horne actually improved on his promise. By using horse-drawn freight sleighs over the incompleted portions, the first militia troops were carried from Ontario to Winnipeg in just over a week.

On arriving in the West, General Middleton found a confused situation. Settlers, fearing Indian attacks, had crowded for safety into the towns. It appeared to Middleton that the best military plan was to divide his forces into three groups and to send these separately into the areas where the greatest danger threatened.

**Battle of Fish Creek, April 24**

On April 6, 1885, General Middleton, having left Qu'Appelle with a column of troops, advanced cautiously toward Riel's headquarters at Batoche. His advance was not a secret to the enemy because all troop movements were observed and reported by Métis scouts. Gabriel Dumont, anxious to strike at the advancing militia force, left Batoche on April 23 with a relatively small force of about 200 Métis and Indians. The following day, the rebels, concealed in rifle pits in the brush of a ravine where Fish Creek empties into the South Saskatchewan, waited for Middleton's force. The general had no better plan than to send the militia forward in frontal attacks on the ravine. The Canadians were twice repulsed by their hidden foes, and by nightfall the Métis withdrew at their leisure.

In the meantime, a second column of militia under Colonel Otter had left Swift Current and hurried northward to Battleford, which had been surrounded by Chief Poundmaker and his warriors. When Colonel Otter's column arrived, the people of Battleford raised shouts of joy as Poundmaker led his men away in sullen retreat.

Using this war drum, Chief Poundmaker summoned his followers to arms during the days of the North-West Rebellion. The wily chief and his warriors proved dangerous adversaries to the troops sent against them. This particular drum, standing as it does on four legs, is of unusual design. Note the extreme length of the drumsticks or beaters, which bear a remarkable resemblance to one type of Indian canoe paddle.

On learning that Poundmaker had withdrawn only a short distance and had camped at Cut Knife Creek, Colonel Otter made a swift over-night march and began to attack the Indian rebels at dawn. However, Otter allowed the surprised Indians to re-group and attack the column he was slowly reorganizing into a new battle formation. Colonel Otter was forced to break off the action and retreat to Battleford.

**Battle of Cut Knife Hill, May 2**

**Battle of Batoche, May 9-12**

General Middleton's attack on Riel's headquarters at Batoche was set for May 9. It became apparent when the fighting began that it would be a difficult task to dislodge Dumont's force from its well-constructed system of trenches and barriers. For more than three days, the fighting continued as the Métis put up an astonishingly strong defence. The rebel supply of ammunition, however, was not equal to that of the besieging militia, and the Métis were reduced to firing nails, bits of metal and small stones. On the fourth day, a direct assault on the rebel position put the Métis to flight. Gabriel Dumont made his escape across the American border, but Louis Riel surrendered on May 15.

**Surrender of Poundmaker**

General Middleton followed up this success by pushing on to Battleford from which he sent a note to Poundmaker, demanding that he surrender. Knowing full well that further resistance was futile, the chief appeared at Middleton's camp and surrendered.

**Action against Big Bear, May 27**

Even then the North-West Rebellion was not over. In what is now the Province of Alberta, a third column of militia was still fighting Chief Big Bear. This column was under the command of General Strange. It was vitally necessary to defeat and capture Big Bear because some of his warriors had attacked the little settlement at Frog Lake, killing nine persons and taking three prisoners. General Strange led his column down the North Saskatchewan River toward Fort Pitt in the hope of meeting Chief Big Bear.

On May 27, fifteen days after the fall of Batoche, the third column of militia clashed with the Indian rebels at Frenchman's Butte, which lay a short distance from Fort Pitt. By this time, Chief Big Bear knew that Louis Riel and Poundmaker were prisoners, but he was determined to make what he realized might be his last stand. As it turned out, his warriors offered such fierce resistance that Strange decided to withdraw.

**Surrender of Big Bear**

General Strange urged General Middleton to join forces with him and carry out a full-scale campaign to capture Big Bear. Middleton, however, refused this suggestion (as he did an offer of help from the Mounted Police).

Deciding to act alone, Middleton set out with his own column after Big Bear. The shrewd old chief refused to engage in battle.

The Cree Indians responsible for the massacre at Frog Lake in 1885 were a restless, discontented band who had caused trouble in the district the previous year. They stole horses from settlers and created a number of minor disturbances. These Indians were poorly clothed, wearing costumes that included such articles as felt hats and woollen blankets. They were, however, well-armed, some of them even possessing the American Winchester rifle. Unfortunately, the official view of the situation was that the tribesmen were not liable to attack settlements or commit murder. Thus, a Mounted Police detachment located at Frog Lake that might have prevented the massacre, was withdrawn to Fort Pitt, thirty miles away, only days before. The transfer was also made in the belief that the presence of the Police tended to provoke the Crees.

Since he knew the region well, it was a simple matter for the Indian leader to evade the pursuing militia. Eventually, Middleton gave up the fruitless hunt and returned to Battleford. Big

Bear, however, was having troubles of his own, for his followers, growing weary and discouraged, had drifted away to their homes. Regretfully, the proud old chief surrendered to the Mounted Police at Fort Carlton.

The North-West Rebellion was over.

The punishment meted out to the rebels was not too severe. Although a few Indian chiefs were hanged, Poundmaker and Big Bear were both given prison sentences. Of the Métis, a number were imprisoned. However, Louis Riel was taken to Regina to await trial.

**Trial of Louis Riel**

On July 20, 1885, Louis Riel, guarded by two scarlet-coated members of the Mounted Police, stood in the prisoner's dock of a tiny courtroom. He was charged with high treason. Riel pleaded "not guilty," and his counsel based their defence on the argument that the Regina court had no proper jurisdiction and that Riel was insane (between 1876 and 1878 he had spent twenty months in Quebec asylums).

Medical authorities differed in their opinions of the accused's sanity. The jury then concentrated on the question of whether or not Riel had stirred up and led an armed rebellion. After hearing all evidence, the jury deliberated and returned a verdict of "guilty"—with a recommendation for mercy. Riel was sentenced to hang on September 18.

By November 12, Riel had twice been reprieved. Ontario was shouting for the death of the murderer of Thomas Scott, while petitions for clemency were pouring into Ottawa from Quebec and from French-speaking communities in Ontario, Manitoba and the North-West. However, Macdonald and his cabinet decided that the court's sentence could no longer be postponed. At Regina, on the morning of November 16, Louis Riel was hanged.

**Results of Rebellion**

It should be remembered that many Métis and the vast majority of the Indians took no part in the North-West Rebellion. After the hostilities were over, the rebel tribesmen returned to the reservations where they lived peacefully in later years. Although the Métis were granted title to their lands, many of them squandered their rights by selling land cheaply to incoming settlers. A number of Métis, seeking greater solitude and freedom, moved northward into the wide lands of the Peace River region.

The execution of Riel revived old race hatreds in Quebec and Ontario that carried over into the twentieth century. Riel became —in the eyes of people who had shown little sympathy for the Métis cause whilst he was alive—a martyred champion of French-Canadian tradition and culture. His death remained a source of bitterness that affected Canadian political life for many years afterwards.

# 37. The Decline of the Conservatives

Return to
hard times THE SUCCESSFUL COMPLETION of the Canadian Pacific Railway probably represents the high point in the career of Sir John A. Macdonald. From then on, he retained much of his old popularity, but his government received less support from the Canadian people. There were a number of reasons for this development. The Conservative party was severely criticized for its mishandling of the North-West Rebellion. National prosperity was gradually fading as trade and industry slowed down. The country was not enjoying the swift, flourishing progress that had been expected. Thousands of Canadian citizens were emigrating to the United States.

Not even Macdonald's National Policy was able to stem the tide. By 1890, the United States had begun to protect its own industries with high tariffs. Canada's small population did not form a large enough market to absorb all the farm products and manufactured goods produced in the country. Under these circumstances, the nation seemed to be drifting toward economic depression.

Election
of 1891 The election of 1891 threw both the Liberals and the Conservatives into a fever of excitement. Both parties realized that it would be a close contest and that victory could turn either way.

At political meetings before the election, Liberal orators promised the people that their party, if elected, would bring back prosperity by establishing free trade with the United States. This policy of closer trade relations with a rich, powerful neighbour appealed to many Canadians who were fearful of their country's future. Some were even ready to turn away from Great Britain and make Canada a part of the United States.

Conservative speakers pointed with pride to the achievements

People of the Victorian period were very fond of a massive, solid style in architecture and home furnishings. Their preference is eloquently demonstrated in this huge, ugly bed of the period 1880-1890. By this time, factory-produced furniture had largely replaced the superb hand craftsmanship of former years. Compare this bed with the earlier one on page 195. Manufacturers, as if to show what their machines could do, worked wood—chiefly walnut—into a tangle of patterns, sometimes leaving no surface free of design. This tendency was also evident in the production of other household items, as has been already noted in the fire-place and stove on page 366.

of the Conservative government and those of the "Grand Old Man." In spite of his seventy-six years, Macdonald conducted a vigorous election campaign, speaking with all the humour and enthusiasm that his followers loved. He scoffed at the very idea of free trade with the United States and ridiculed all suggestions of a political union. Speaking of the old ties with the mother country, he shouted, "A British subject I was born and a British subject I will die!" Following his lead, the Conservatives linked the Union Jack with the National Policy, shouting the slogan, "The old flag, the old man, the old policy!"

**Death of Macdonald, 1891**

Macdonald's great popularity and his rousing speeches undoubtedly had a marked effect upon election results. Although he and his party were returned to power, they held a reduced majority in the House of Commons. Unfortunately, the rigours of the campaign were too much for a man already weakened by years of physical and nervous strain. Early in June, 1891, three months after the election, Canadians were shocked to learn that Macdonald was dying. No last message came to the Canadian people from the old warrior. None was needed. He had sacrificed wealth, health and life to give some substance to his dream of a Canadian nation. It was now left to others to complete his work.

Macdonald's body lay in state for some days in the Senate Chamber of the Parliament Buildings in Ottawa. On June 10, his funeral procession wound its way down Parliament Hill to the railway station where a C.P.R. locomotive, draped in purple and black, waited to bear the body to Kingston for burial.

Many tributes were paid to the dead leader, but perhaps the greatest was offered by a political rival, the leader of the Liberal party, Wilfrid Laurier. In an address to the House of Commons, Laurier said:

> The place of Sir John Macdonald in this country was so large and so absorbing that it is impossible to conceive that the political life of this country, the fate of this country, can continue without him. I think it can be asserted that, for the supreme art of governing men, Sir John Macdonald was gifted as few men in any land or in any age were gifted—gifted with the highest of all qualities, qualities which would have made him famous wherever exercised. . .

**Difficulties of the Conservative party**

Following the death of Macdonald, the Conservative party suffered a succession of handicaps and disappointments. To begin with, it was not a simple matter to find a leader who could take the place of the "Old Chieftain." The party, which for so many years had depended upon the guidance of Macdonald, now felt the full force of its loss.

Sir John Abbott, a Montreal lawyer, succeeded Macdonald as prime minister and leader of the Conservative party. His was a short and unhappy term of office because the Liberals in Parliament brought forward a number of serious charges of bribery and inefficiency against the government. It was said that officials in the Department of Public Works had received money from contractors doing business with the government.

During the 1880's, the housewife looking for the latest in household appliances could buy a washing-machine, such as the one illustrated, for $8.50. Although it appears much more advanced in design and operation than the machine on page 78 and possesses a wringer, it was still a hand-operated unit. Washing action depended on turning the crank— a slow and laborious procedure. All domestic appliances of this time, many of which were quite imaginative, were awaiting the great boost that electricity was to give them in the twentieth century.

The following year, Sir John Abbott resigned and was succeeded by Sir John Thompson. During his term of leadership, Canada and the United States settled a dispute over the rights of seal hunters in the Bering Sea. Friction had arisen between the two countries when the United States declared the Bering Sea to be a "closed sea" completely under American control. What really annoyed the Canadian and British governments, however, was the seizure by Americans of several Canadian sealing ships operating

Sealing agreement, 1892

seventy miles off the coast of Alaska. Strong protests were made to the United States government. In 1892, it was agreed that the United States controlled sealing only in waters as far as three miles from the Alaskan coast. Even more important were the regulations imposed upon the sealing industry itself. A definite season was established, and limitations were placed upon the equipment to be used by the sealers. In later years, further international sealing agreements were reached.

Another problem facing the Conservative government was much more difficult to solve—the question of Roman Catholic schools in Manitoba.

"Manitoba Schools Question"

According to the terms of the British North America Act, no provincial government had the authority to interfere with the rights or privileges of denominational schools in the provinces at the time of union. This provision protected the established rights of Roman Catholic and Protestant minorities, a provision that ensured that Roman Catholic schools would receive support from provincial funds as well as from local taxes. When the Province of Manitoba was created in 1870, the educational system of Assiniboia had been continued—local schools, classified as Protestant or Roman Catholic, were maintained, and grants from the provincial government were divided up among the schools. By 1890, however, immigration from eastern Canada, notably Ontario, had made Manitoba predominantly English-speaking and Protestant. That same year, a provincial statute abolished French as an official language. Another statute introduced a single system of provincially supported, non-denominational public schools. No provision was made in the School Act for the support of Roman Catholic separate schools with public funds.

Roman Catholic authorities protested against the School Act and appealed to Ottawa for assistance. Sir John Thompson and the Conservatives were placed in a most difficult position, for by this time the "Manitoba Schools Question" had caught the attention of the entire nation. Another election was approaching, and the very last thing the Conservatives desired was to become involved in a dispute that was both religious and racial.

Canadian nineteenth-century architecture came to a spirited but pompous climax in this "High Victorian" house of 1880. That architects of the time "borrowed" ideas is clearly in evidence. The narrow, elongated windows are Romanesque. The unusual, sloped-back roof is a seventeenth-century French style created by one, Francois Mansart. This style was so widely imitated during the nineteenth century that the name Mansard was given to any architectural fashion employing this type of sloped roof. One feature of the Mansard building was the use of projecting, half-size dormer windows. Three such windows can be seen in the illustration. Bay windows, as depicted, were also very popular. Elaborate designs were worked directly into the brickwork of the house, and intricate patterns were woven into the trim on the verandah. Interiors were gloomy in comparison with those of modern homes. Dark woods, dark wallpapers and heavy window drapes created a feeling of perpetual twilight within the house.

Disputes flared up across the nation—between French and English, between Liberals and Conservatives, between Roman Catholics and Protestants. To make matters worse, Sir John Thompson died suddenly while visiting in England and was succeeded by Mackenzie Bowell, a man lacking in leadership.

Finally, in the spring of 1895, Bowell's Conservative government ordered Manitoba to change its law of 1890 so that Roman Catholic schools might be given a share of provincial grants. When the Manitoba government refused to obey the order, the federal government prepared a bill to force a change in Manitoba school law. In the meantime, the Conservative cabinet ministers in Ottawa had become so dissatisfied with Bowell's leadership that some of them resigned and Bowell was forced to retire from office.

**Defeat of the Conservatives, 1896**

The Conservative government now faced a frightening crisis. It was without a leader, the Manitoba question was still unresolved and another election was approaching. A hasty appeal for help was sent off to that gallant old veteran of the Conservative party, Sir Charles Tupper. It reached him in London, England, where he was at that time serving as Canadian High Commissioner. Returning to Canada, Tupper took up the reins of government. He must have known that his party could not be saved. When attempts to solve the Manitoba problem failed, he dissolved Parliament and called an election.

The results of the election of 1896 clearly indicated that the nation was ready for a change in government. Not even the great respect accorded by Canadians to Sir Charles Tupper, a Father of Confederation, could save the Conservative party from defeat. On a rising tide of Liberalism, particularly in a Quebec that remembered the execution of Riel and was now further angered by the treatment of Roman Catholics in Manitoba, Wilfrid Laurier and his followers were swept into power.

# 38. Sir Wilfrid Laurier

A FRENCH-CANADIAN, Roman Catholic prime minister was something fresh and new in the life of the young nation.

Wilfrid Laurier was born in 1841 at St. Lin, in what is now Quebec. His ancestors had come to Canada before James Wolfe captured Quebec. Young Wilfrid began his education in a local French-speaking school, but later, for a time, he attended a Protestant academy located in the Scottish community of New Glasgow, not far from St. Lin, and boarded at the home of a Presbyterian family. So it was that the boy grew up with both French-speaking and English-speaking people, Roman Catholics and Protestants. He admired and respected them all. *Laurier's early life*

As a young man, he studied law at McGill University and, on graduating, gave the valedictory address of his class. In the course of his remarks, he said:

> I pledge my honour that I will give the whole of my life to the cause of conciliation, harmony and concord amongst the different elements of this country of ours.

The young lawyer meant exactly what he said, for during his brilliant career he strove to bring about a greater unity and understanding among Canadians.

It was inevitable that Laurier, with his gift of oratory and his love of humanity, should enter political life. After becoming a Liberal member of the federal Parliament in 1874, he rose quickly in the ranks of the party, becoming leader in 1887 when he was forty-six years of age. He became prime minister on the defeat of the Conservatives in the election of 1896. *Entry into politics*

Prime Minister Laurier was an impressive figure in the House —tall, slight, dignified, with white hair framing a pleasant face. When he spoke, members of Parliament—followers and rivals alike—listened with attention.

Towards the end of the nineteenth century, the western prairies were being settled by an ever-increasing number of homesteaders. The Canadian Pacific Railway was rather slow in extending branch lines into prime agricultural districts, and thus it often became necessary for new settlers to travel great distances by cart or wagon. The settler's immediate task was to plough land and sow a crop, with the result that there was no time to erect a dwelling. For the first few months, a tent or a wagon often served as a home. In the West, largely a treeless area, there was only one thing with which the homesteader could construct his first home—the prairie sod. At the left is one such sod hut—low, thick-walled and fitted with one tiny window. For all their crudeness and discomfort, sod huts were sturdy structures, some of which can still be seen in western Canada. If time were desperately short, the settler might even construct a more primitive dwelling—a dugout house roofed with sod. When timber was available, the settler constructed a shack, such as the one shown on the right of the drawing. However, the small, slim trees of the prairies could not provide the sturdy, solid, log cabins that were common in eastern Canada in pioneer days. Early prairie shacks were often replaced by larger ones with walls made from lengths of short logs set between uprights.

**Laurier as Prime Minister**

In addition to being an able speaker, Laurier was a courageous man who dared to speak and act as he saw fit. He was of French descent, but above all he was a Canadian, a citizen of the Dominion of Canada. His broad vision went far beyond the province in which he was born. Because of this attitude; he was sometimes in trouble with his fellow French Canadians and with English-speaking Canadians. Even before becoming prime minister, Laurier had declared in the House of Commons:

So long as I have a seat in this House, so long as I occupy the position I do now, whenever it shall become my duty to take a stand upon any question whatever, that stand I will take, not from the point of view of Roman Catholicism, not from the point of view of Protestantism, but from a point of view which can appeal to the conscience of all men. . . .

One of the pressing problems to be solved was the touchy matter Settlement of the Manitoba Schools Question of the Manitoba Schools Question. Because Laurier believed this could be settled in a friendly, peaceful manner, he arranged a series of discussions between federal and provincial officials. A compromise was worked out by which the Manitoba government, of its own will, made changes in school law. The provincially supported, non-denominational public school system remained in effect but provision was made for the teaching of religion by any denomination at certain times and under certain conditions. In addition, if a certain number of pupils spoke French as their native tongue, a bilingual teacher was to be hired. These agreements were not entirely satisfactory to many inhabitants of Manitoba, but the school question ceased to be a prime political issue.

During the nineteenth century a broad variety of farm machinery was invented, beginning with a mechanical reaper in 1831 and a threshing-machine in 1837. Until the 1880's, these machines were hand- or horse-operated. However, about this time steam-power, following its success in steamships and locomotives, was utilized to power engines that gave the prairie farmer the means to cope with his large acreage. The operation shown here illustrates one of the early (1895) wood-fired, iron giants driving a threshing-machine from a considerable distance by means of pulleys connected with a long leather belt. Frequently, farmers did not own such heavy machinery but rented it (along with a crew) when required. Due to climatic conditions, prairie farmers required a hardier strain of wheat than that grown in the East. Above all else, they needed a wheat that would mature ahead of the killing prairie frosts of September—and sometimes of August. From 1882 until about 1908, a famous strain of wheat known as *Red Fife* met this need and thus proved to be a tremendous boon to western farmers. Since 1908, a number of even hardier and quicker-maturing wheats have been discovered and have yielded even greater results.

For some years, the Liberal party had been urging lower tariffs Imperial Preference and the gradual establishment of a free trade policy. While Laurier was interested in such ideas, he thought it wise to proceed cautiously. Nevertheless, new laws introduced by Laurier's government had a lasting effect upon trade with Great Britain, one really important development being the policy whereby Canada gave preferential trade treatment to members of the British Empire. The policy also implied that members of the Empire would, in turn, offer preferred treatment to Canadian exports. In supporting such a policy, Laurier and his ministers stated that *Imperial Preference* would stimulate trade and would create a strong bond among the nations and colonies of the Empire.

The new trade decision was sharply criticized by manufacturers who complained that the arrival of large quantities of Empire goods would handicap Canadian industry. Despite many such gloomy warnings, increasing trade and expanding industry followed the introduction of imperial preference. Quite naturally, the Liberals took credit for this—probably more credit than they deserved, because other factors were also contributing to business progress. These factors included good markets in other countries, the Yukon gold rush and an increase in the Canadian population.

In 1897, Laurier crossed the Atlantic to attend Queen Victoria's Queen Victoria's Diamond Jubilee, 1897 Diamond Jubilee — an Imperial celebration in honour of the Queen's sixtieth year on the throne. Millions of excited visitors from all parts of the globe met and mingled in London. The Diamond Jubilee was a glittering affair that lasted for days and was climaxed by a gigantic parade of bands and troops from the scattered lands of the Empire. In this great Jubilee Procession, through London's cheering throngs, a Canadian contingent composed of Mounted Police, troopers of the Governor General's Bodyguard and soldiers of the Canadian Grenadiers and Highlanders followed behind Laurier's carriage.

Among the statesmen attending the Jubilee, none was more dignified or more distinguished in appearance than the silver-haired Prime Minister of Canada. His graceful manner, eloquence and personal charm quickly made him a popular figure. Lavish entertainments and honours were pressed upon him. A British association, the Cobden Club, presented Laurier with a medal for his part in the promotion of Empire trade. Even more important than this fine honour, however, was the knighthood bestowed upon him by Queen Victoria. The excellent impression made in Britain by the Prime Minister and his countrymen undoubtedly increased interest in Canada throughout the world.

**Flow of immigration**

The new interest in Canada had a pleasing effect upon the flow of immigration. Europeans in particular were becoming increasingly aware of the opportunities in North America, and newer methods of transportation—steamship and railways—were making travel more rapid and comfortable. Much of the best land in the western part of the United States had been occupied, but in the Canadian North-West there were thousands upon thousands of acres of untouched, rich soils.

The Laurier government was intensely interested in the prospects of immigration and did everything possible to encourage it. The success of its programme was in large measure due to the efforts of Sir Clifford Sifton, Minister of the Interior. Advertising free land and assisted passages in literally thousands of newspapers and magazines, he attracted a flood of American, British and European immigrants. This sweeping tide continued from 1897 until the beginning of World War I in 1914. In those seventeen years over 3,000,000 newcomers arrived in Canada. The western portions of Canada received a major share of the immigrants, but the eastern provinces also added to their population.

**Yukon gold rush, 1897**

In 1897—the year of the Diamond Jubilee and the beginning of large-scale immigration—another colourful development was taking place in the North. It was the Yukon gold rush. This gigantic scramble for gold was even greater than the earlier rushes that had taken place in California and the valley of the Fraser River. Men from all over the world hurried eagerly to the mining area that lay on Canadian soil within Yukon Territory. Tough miners and hardy prospectors mingled with inexperienced men in

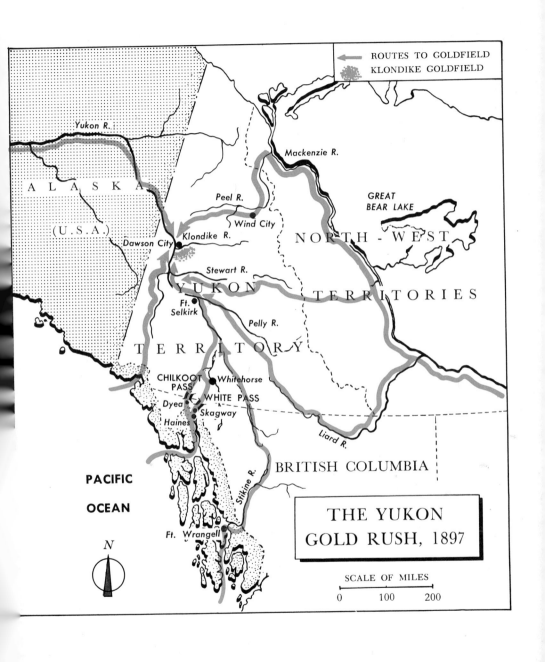

ROUTES TO GOLDFIELD
KLONDIKE GOLDFIELD

Yukon R.

Mackenzie R.

A L A S K A

(U.S.A.)

Peel R.

GREAT
BEAR LAKE

Wind City

Dawson City    Klondike R.

NORTH - WEST

Stewart R.

Y U K O N    T E R R I T O R I E S

Ft.
Selkirk

Pelly R.

T E R R I T O R Y

CHILKOOT
PASS    Whitehorse

WHITE PASS

Dyea

Haines    Skagway

Liard R.

BRITISH COLUMBIA

PACIFIC

OCEAN

Stikine R.

THE YUKON
GOLD RUSH, 1897

Ft. Wrangell

N

SCALE OF MILES

0        100        200

the surge northward. They travelled by ship to Skagway and then made terrible, winter journeys over the Chilkoot Pass or the White Pass and on down the Yukon River. Others made the long trek overland from the provinces of Canada, or came from Alaska by river steamer up the Yukon River.

A tiny settlement at Dawson expanded into a hustling gold rush centre complete with stores, banks, hotels, dance halls and newspapers. Tens of thousands of men took part in the journey north and the frantic search for the precious metal. As in all gold rushes, a fortunate few did extremely well, while thousands could not even meet their expenses for travel, provisions and equipment. Millions of dollars worth of gold were removed from river and creek beds, but the full glory of the rush was of relatively short duration. After the free surface gold had been removed by panning and placer mining, operations were taken over by mining companies with dredges and heavy machinery.

Just as the earlier gold rushes in California and British Columbia had brought lasting benefits to those regions, so the Yukon rush brought improvements in the North. The Yukon River was opened up to navigation by steamship, and a railway was constructed to connect Skagway on the coast with Whitehorse in the Yukon Territory.

# 39. The Boer War, 1899-1902

IN 1815, AT THE CLOSE OF THE WAR WITH NAPOLEON BONAPARTE, Origins of the war Great Britain had secured control of South Africa, which was then occupied by Dutch settlers known as Boers.

The Boers were a religious, hard-working people, interested primarily in farming. They had very little in common with the eager, bustling British who established businesses in South Africa. In time, various developments led to friction between the two people. When, in 1833, Great Britain abolished slavery within the Empire, the Boers resented the loss of slave labour on their farm lands. The British grant of land and political rights to certain native groups in South Africa further antagonized the Boers, who moved north to found their own republics. However, several native wars forced Britain to annex Boer territory, a move that caused the Boer War of 1881. The British were defeated and forced, in 1884, to recognize the independence of the Boer Republic of the Transvaal. Unfortunately, disagreements and misunderstandings between British and Boer settlers led to the outbreak of war in 1899 between Britain and the Boer republics of the Transvaal and the Orange Free State.

The conflict in South Africa posed a problem for Sir Wilfrid A problem for Laurier Laurier and his Liberal government. The question was—should Canada as a member of the British Empire assist the mother country in her struggle against the Boers?

Great Britain was even more to blame for the war than the Boers, but at the time the British cause seemed just. English Canadians, proud of their new place in the Empire, urged the government to raise troops and send them off to South Africa. There were mass meetings, petitions and editorials in newspapers, all expressing a strong, emotional urge to aid the mother country.

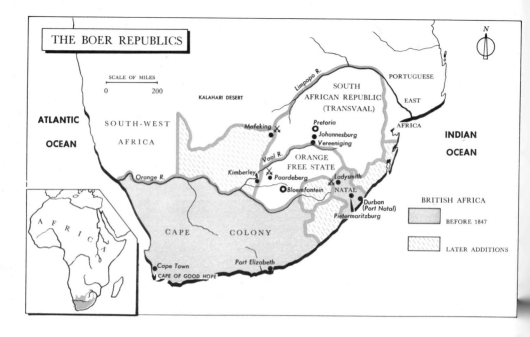

THE BOER REPUBLICS

SCALE OF MILES

0     200

ATLANTIC

OCEAN

SOUTH-WEST

AFRICA

KALAHARI DESERT

Limpopo R.

SOUTH
AFRICAN REPUBLIC
(TRANSVAAL)

PORTUGUESE

EAST

AFRICA

INDIAN

OCEAN

Pretoria

Mafeking

Johannesburg

Vereeniging

Vaal R.

ORANGE
FREE STATE

Kimberley

Paardeberg

Ladysmith

NATAL

Orange R.

Bloemfontein

Durban
(Port Natal)

Pietermaritzburg

BRITISH AFRICA

BEFORE 1847

LATER ADDITIONS

CAPE    COLONY

Port Elizabeth

Cape Town

CAPE OF GOOD HOPE

AFRICA

N

In the Province of Quebec, however, there was little enthusiasm for war, particularly a war that had no direct connection with Canada. The French Canadians were quite willing to fight for their native land, but they could see no reason why Canadian troops should be sent to fight men who were not enemies of Canada.

It was this difference of opinion between French-speaking and English-speaking citizens that made the war situation so difficult for Sir Wilfrid Laurier. How could his government support the Empire and still retain the support of Quebec?

**Canada's contribution**

Laurier decided to follow a middle-of-the-road course which, he hoped, would be reasonably acceptable to everyone. He decided to send a limited number of volunteers to South Africa, but not in such large numbers as to anger the people of Quebec. The first contingent of troops, numbering 1,141 infantrymen, sailed from Quebec City in October, 1899. A second contingent, composed of about 1,300 cavalrymen and artillerymen, sailed the following year. These contingents included men of the Royal Canadian

The Boer War was a fast-moving conflict fought by the elusive Boers against British and Imperial troops. Boer forces, although heavily outnumbered, were skilful "commandos," groups of guerrilla fighters who knew the rugged terrain of South Africa and used it to their own fighting advantage. The British, at first, had considerable difficulty in maintaining contact with enemies that appeared so abruptly, battled briefly and then disappeared so quickly. To make matters worse, Boer fighting men wore no uniforms and at times masqueraded as peaceful farmers. To offset the tactics of such a wily foe, the British eventually came to rely upon the frequent use of large bodies of hard-riding mounted troops. Canadians, particularly those from the West, proved ideal for this type of warfare. When the second Canadian contingent was being organized, army authorities recruited first among members of the Mounted Police and then among prairie cowboys because both groups of men were thought to ride and shoot as well as any cavalry in the world. In addition, if it was necessary, these men could stay in the saddle for thirty-six hours at a stretch. Shown above is a British patrol, skirmishing with a Boer patrol that it has just encountered.

Regiment, the Canadian Mounted Rifles and the Royal Canadian Artillery. This was Canada's official contribution to the war effort.

Other Canadians, however, managed to participate by volunteering for service in the British Army. Nearly 600 others joined a cavalry unit, Lord Strathcona's Horse, which was raised and financed by Lord Strathcona (Donald Smith, formerly of the

Despite the fact that fire-arms first appeared in Europe about 1400, their development as late as the mid-nineteenth century had been a slow one. Minor changes had occurred over the years but few new principles had been put into actual practice. Even during the American Civil War, cannon were still being loaded at the muzzle as they had been for centuries. The muzzle-loading rifle, too, was still a common weapon. However, from about 1865 on, the development of fire-arms was quite rapid. The breech-loading cannon, which greatly reduced the time required to load and fire, made its appearance. The discovery of the breech-loading principle quickly resulted in the invention of the machine-gun. A number of machine-gun designs came into use. Perhaps the most famous of these was the Gatling gun. By 1885, the *Maxim* gun, too, had appeared—a Boer War version of which is shown above. All earlier machine-guns had been manually operated, using cranks or handles. The Maxim was unique in that it could be fired by trigger pressure alone. Its ammunition was carried in a separate box at the side and fed into the breech on a continuous belt. In order to counteract the heat generated by sustained fire, the barrel was cooled by means of a metal jacket filled with water.

Hudson's Bay Company and the Canadian Pacific Railway). In all, it is probable that about 7,000 Canadians—all volunteers—took part in the war.

**Canadians in action**

During the first months of fighting in South Africa, the British suffered a series of defeats, but as troops from various parts of the Empire arrived, the situation changed. Canadians held a forward position among British forces that surrounded and defeated a

Boer army in the decisive Battle of Paardeberg in February, 1900. Lord Roberts, the British commander-in-chief, reported after this decisive engagement that "a most dashing advance made by the Canadian Regiment and some engineers . . . apparently clinched matters." As a direct result of Paardeberg, the British garrison besieged in the town of Ladysmith was relieved. Advancing into Boer territory, the Imperial forces captured Bloemfontein, capital of the Orange Free State, and Pretoria, capital of the Transvaal. These successes, however, were followed by a prolonged period of guerrilla warfare.

The Boer War came to an end in May, 1902, with the Treaty of Vereeniging. By this agreement, the Boer republics became part of the British Empire, although self-government was promised the Boers for the future.

Canada's military achievement in the war was small but distinguished. Canadian newspapers and English Canadians of the time were inclined to over-exaggerate the exploits of the nation's tiny fighting force. Some American newspapermen, noting this tendency, made sport of Canadian enthusiasm and pride. One American reporter, with tongue in cheek, wrote that British generals would not dare begin a military engagement unless supported by Canadians. However, the very fact that Canada participated at all won the nation new attention and respect abroad. Canadians themselves were, of course, proud of their part in the war and felt a gratifying sense of national accomplishment.

*Results of the war*

# 40. Canada in 1900

IN 1900, the Dominion of Canada consisted of the North-West Territories, the Yukon Territory, the Arctic islands, the Districts of Athabaska, Alberta, Saskatchewan and Assiniboia, and the provinces of Nova Scotia, New Brunswick, Prince Edward Island, Quebec, Ontario, Manitoba and British Columbia. Newfoundland remained a British colony, and the two provinces of Saskatchewan and Alberta had yet to be created.

**Population**   Between the years 1800 and 1900, the population of Canada multiplied more than ten times—from 500,000 to 5,300,000 people, yet this was a most disappointing growth. Other nations had done much better.  (The United States, for example, with a population in 1800 of 5,000,000, had a population of 70,000,000 by the end of the nineteenth century.)

One reason for the relatively small growth was the loss of Canadians to the United States.  Thousands of them, attracted by opportunities and prosperous conditions, crossed the border and took up residence in nearby states.  This was an unfortunate development from Canada's viewpoint, for a host of able, industrious people was lost to the southern neighbour.  It has been estimated that if Canada had been able to retain all the people born here and all those who had immigrated, the Canadian population by 1900 might well have been 8,000,000 people.

**Cities**   In 1900, Montreal was the largest city of the Dominion, boasting a population of 230,000.  Toronto, with more than 200,000 citizens, followed close behind.  Other large Canadian centres included Halifax, Saint John, Quebec City, Ottawa, Hamilton, London and Winnipeg.  In the North-West there were still no towns with a population of over 5,000.

**Farming**   Farming remained the most important industry.  Great changes, however, had been made in the methods of agriculture since the days of the first pioneers. By the end of the century new machinery was taking the place of the scythe, the sickle, the hand rake and the flail. Farm implements in the form of hay-rakes, hay-loaders, cultivators, binders, reapers and steam-driven threshing machines eased the farmer's task and increased production.

Other technical and mechanical developments were also assisting the farmer to find new markets for his products. The invention of the cream separator enabled farmers to separate cream from milk, and the sale of cream led to the making of butter in local creameries. The use of ice for refrigeration in freight trains and ships made it possible for perishable farm products to be transported long distances with little danger of loss.

During the latter part of the century, railways and immigration brought a rapid expansion of wheat-growing in the West. By 1900, the Canadian prairies were producing 25,000,000 bushels a year, forty per cent of the nation's annual wheat crop. New railway construction enabled western farmers to move their crops easily and quickly to market. During the last four years of the century, extra railway lines were being constructed at the rate of two miles per day. **Wheat growing**

Mineral production increased at a slower pace than that of agriculture, but significant developments were taking place. Coal and iron were being mined in Nova Scotia, and this led to the birth of a steel industry shortly before 1900. There was some nickel-mining in the newly discovered fields at Sudbury in northern Ontario and some copper and asbestos-mining in southern Quebec. In British Columbia, people were just becoming aware of their mineral wealth in gold, silver, lead, copper and coal. In Alberta, coal-mining was expanding in a remarkable manner. However, the large base metal mining operations for which Canada was to become famous did not really begin until after electric power became readily available in the early years of the twentieth century. **Mines**

In 1900, Canadians were just beginning to use electricity, but it was still very much of a novelty. One of the first uses of electricity was in electric street cars, which were beginning to appear

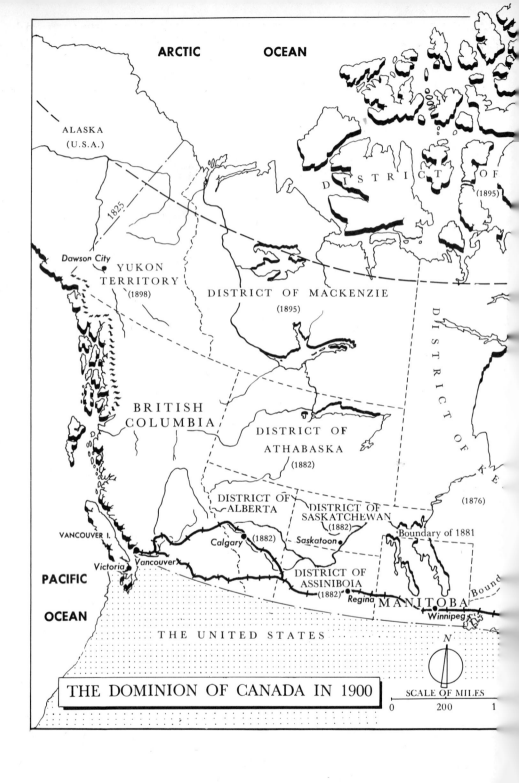

ARCTIC OCEAN

ALASKA
(U.S.A.)

D I S T R I C T    O F
(1895)

1825

Dawson City
YUKON
TERRITORY
(1898)

DISTRICT OF MACKENZIE
(1895)

D
I
S
T
R
I
C
T

O
F

BRITISH
COLUMBIA

DISTRICT OF
ATHABASKA
(1882)

D
I
S
T
R
I
C
T

O
F

DISTRICT OF
ALBERTA

DISTRICT OF
SASKATCHEWAN
(1882)

(1876)

Boundary of 1881

VANCOUVER I.

Calgary (1882)    Saskatoon

Victoria    Vancouver

DISTRICT OF
ASSINIBOIA
(1882)

MANITOBA

PACIFIC

Regina

Bound

OCEAN

Winnipeg

THE UNITED STATES

N

THE DOMINION OF CANADA IN 1900

SCALE OF MILES
0          200          1

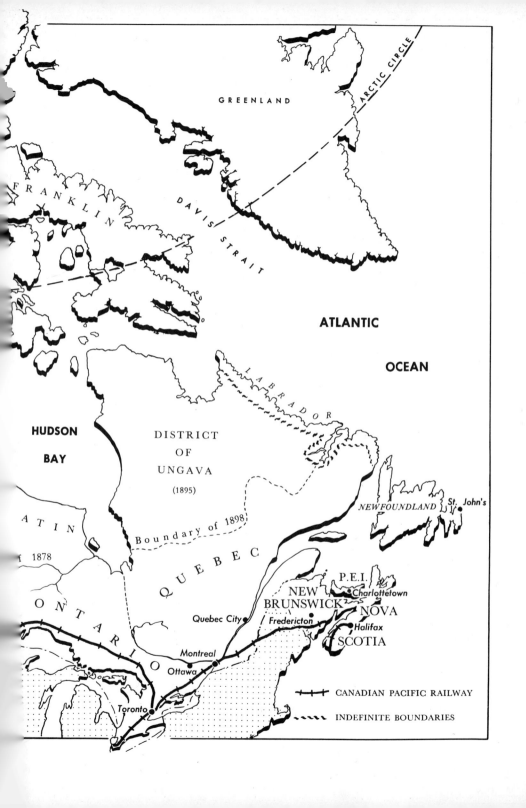

ARCTIC CIRCLE

GREENLAND

FRANKLIN

DAVIS STRAIT

ATLANTIC

OCEAN

HUDSON

BAY

LABRADOR

DISTRICT

OF

UNGAVA

(1895)

ATIN

Boundary of 1898

f 1878

QUEBEC

NEWFOUNDLAND

St. John's

ONTARIO

P.E.I.

NEW

BRUNSWICK

Charlottetown

NOVA

Quebec City

Fredericton

Halifax

SCOTIA

Montreal

Ottawa

Toronto

╫╫╫ CANADIAN PACIFIC RAILWAY

✦✦✦✦ INDEFINITE BOUNDARIES

in the major cities at the turn of the century. Telephones were also coming into use, although they were very little more than a plaything at the time. Canada was to become dependent on electrical energy as the twentieth century progressed, but at the beginning of the century its importance was foreseen by only a few.

**Manu-facturing**

Manufacturing was growing slowly. The early activities involved in the making of flour, lumber, leather, woollens, whisky and iron goods continued, and to these were now added the production of steel, cotton goods and paper. It was fortunate that, at a time when the wooden sailing ship was fast disappearing, a new market was found for forest products in the paper-making industry.

**Education**

Opportunities for young people to acquire an education were much greater in 1900 than they had been in 1800. The early common schools and grammar schools had given way to public schools, separate schools and high schools. Many of the teachers were fully qualified, and good textbooks were plentiful. School buildings were more attractive and much better equipped than those of the pioneer period. Secondary and higher education were no longer considered to be the right of wealthy people alone. By 1900, the people of Ontario were boasting that they possessed the finest educational system in the world. Universities and colleges thrived in five of the seven provinces.

**Cultural development**

Before the century's end, Canadians were displaying a new interest in cultural affairs. Most towns and cities had a theatre or "opera house" where travelling companies performed plays and musical programmes. Noted singers from abroad, such as the famous Jenny Lind, attracted enthusiastic audiences in the cities. Local musical groups held regular rehearsals and presented annual concerts.

Canadian art was also developing and was being given encouragement and assistance by the Royal Canadian Academy of Arts, which had been founded in 1880. By 1900, such painters as Horatio Walker (1858 - 1938) and Homer Watson (1855 - 1936) were earning praise beyond Canada's borders. James Wilson Morrice (1864 - 1924), although famed for winter landscapes of

The horse-car was a common sight in urban communities during the period 1860-1890. In Toronto, the first of these vehicles was put into service in 1861. The contract arranged between city authorities and the transportation company required that horse-cars be operated sixteen hours per day in summer and fourteen in winter. Cars were to run at intervals of not more than thirty minutes and at speeds not exceeding six miles an hour. The passenger fare was set at five cents. During the early years of operation, horse-cars frequently ran off the tracks. Luckily, the passengers were usually willing to push them back onto the rails. In winter no means of heating was provided in the horse-cars—just some straw on the floor into which the passengers pushed their feet for warmth. The daily work of drawing the heavy vehicles was so hard on horses that the animals rarely lasted more than one year in service.

his native Quebec, was better known in Europe than in Canada for the hundreds of canvases he painted in Europe, Africa and the West Indies.

There now appeared the first signs of a native literature that reflected Canadian thought and feeling. In English-language works, Sir Charles G. D. Roberts (1860 - 1943) published in 1880 his *Orion and Other Poems* — a collection that brilliantly interpreted Canadian scenes. Archibald Lampman (1861 - 1899), "Canada's nature poet," contributed a freshness and genius for observation quite new in Canadian literature, Bliss Carman (1861-1929) and Duncan Campbell Scott (1862 - 1947), both lyric poets, won much admiration for their work.

Before 1900, French-language literature was largely devoted to the theme of the racial and religious survival of a small people separated from the rest of the country by the barrier of language. Around 1900, a new trend developed—the discovery and inquiry into general human problems rather than specific, racial ones.

By the end of the century, most Canadians still lived in rural areas, working on farms or in the many small towns that served as the centres of farming communities. These towns were remarkably similar in appearance. There was an unpaved Main Street, lined with stores, and at intervals along the wooden sidewalks were horse-troughs and hitching posts. (This was still the age of horse transport; the "new-fangled horseless carriage" was a rich man's plaything.) The general store was a popular meeting-place. Here, farmers and their wives mingled with townsfolk and exchanged local news. In the store, food stuffs vied for space with such items as clothing, farm supplies, harness and hardware (hanging from the ceiling) and chinaware. While the women chatted about their families and household problems, the men talked and argued about the weather, their crops, politics and, of course, the latest reports from the front in South Africa.

Canada in 1900 was a very different land from the British North America of 1800. Canadians might be jealous of the progress made in the United States, but they had every reason to be proud of the great strides their own country had taken. Pioneer settlements had become cities and towns; industry, transportation and trade had developed. Britain and the United States began to take a greater interest in Canada's future, particularly in her railways, forests, mines and factories; at the end of the nineteenth century, millions of dollars worth of British investment funds were pouring into the Dominion, and large amounts of money were being brought into the country by British and American settlers. By 1900, the new nation of Canada had passed through its first crucial years, and the few widely separated colonies of 1800 were entering the twentieth century with courage, hope and determination as one dominion.

## SUMMARY—SECTION 8

After the defeat of Macdonald's government in 1873, Alexander Mackenzie became prime minister of a Liberal government. Mackenzie was a hard-working, conscientious leader, but he lacked the popularity and political skill of Macdonald.

In preparation for the elections of 1878, Macdonald created a new programme, which he called **The National Policy**. It caught the imagination of the electors and helped Macdonald and his Conservatives to regain power. Once back in office as prime minister, Macdonald put his "National Policy" into effect; tariffs were raised, and the construction of the Canadian Pacific Railway was renewed and pushed to completion by 1885.

Several months before the last spike of the C.P.R. was driven home, the railway demonstrated its usefulness by transporting troops from eastern Canada to quell a second uprising among the Métis led by Louis Riel, the North-West Rebellion. Under the command of General Middleton, troops eventually put down the insurrection. Riel was tried, found guilty and condemned to death. Again the rebel leader presented the government with a problem, but despite great pressure from Quebec, Macdonald and his cabinet refused to overrule Riel's death sentence.

After 1885, economic conditions in Canada worsened, and the Conservatives, having lost the confidence of Quebec over Riel, had great difficulty in winning the election of 1891. The campaign proved too exhausting for Macdonald himself and within three months he was dead. His passing was a shock to the nation, but it was a particularly hard blow to the Conservative party, which was unable to find a successor. Plagued by a number of difficult political problems, including the **Manitoba Schools Question**, the Conservatives were defeated in the election of 1896.

With the Liberal victory of 1896, the charming and brilliant Wilfrid Laurier became prime minister. The new leader concentrated on unifying the Dominion. Two of his greatest achievements were the settling of the Manitoba Schools Question and the establishment of a new trade policy known as **Imperial Preference**.

Between 1896 and 1914, Canada's development proceeded at a quick pace. As a result of the Laurier government's immigration policy, several million new settlers came to Canada, in particular to the North-West. At the same time, the discovery of gold in the Yukon brought a certain amount of industry and settlement to that area. Together, these two developments show the important combination of government action and private effort that has been so important in the growth of Canada.

The final year of the century revealed an unhappy feature of Canadian political life, the antagonism between French-speaking and English-speaking Canadians. Upon the outbreak of the Boer War in 1899, Ontario demanded that help be sent to Great Britain, while Quebec voiced its suspicions that this was simply another Imperial war in which Canada should have no part. However, by way of compromise, a small military force of volunteers was sent to South Africa and its contribution to the Imperial war effort brought considerable pride to a young nation fighting in its first foreign war.

Canada's participation in the Boer War came almost one hundred years after the War of 1812. The contrast between the scattered British colonies of 1812, scarcely able even to assist in their own defence, and the young nation taking its first hesitant steps into the world of international affairs, symbolizes the important changes that had taken place during the nineteenth century. British North America had emerged as one dominion, the Dominion of Canada, eager to take its place among the nations of the world in the twentieth century.

# 9

## CANADA IN A TROUBLED WORLD

New prosperity ■ Reaching for independence ■ Alaskan Boundary Dispute ■ International Joint Commission ■ Proposal for a Canadian Navy ■ Reciprocity Agreement ■ Election of 1911 ■ Kaiser William ■ European alliances ■ Naval race ■ Archduke murdered ■ Britain declares war ■ Canada joins the conflict ■ The war in Europe ■ The Empire at war ■ Conflict at sea ■ Canadians in combat ■ Problems at home ■ The Conscription Crisis ■ United States enters the war ■ Battle in the air ■ War weariness ■ Russian Revolution ■ Vimy Ridge ■ Discouragement on both sides ■ The spring of 1918 ■ Counterattack by Marshal Foch ■ Treaty of Versailles ■ League of Nations ■ High cost of victory ■ Conditions in Canada ■ The Winnipeg Strike ■ Agricultural problems ■ William Lyon Mackenzie King ■ Returning prosperity ■ Electrical power ■ The Canadian Shield ■ Conditions across Canada ■ Automobiles ■ Early flyers ■ Entertainment ■ Radio ■ The Jazz Age ■ Group of Seven.

# 41. Challenge of a New Century

Lack of
unity and
cohesion

ALTHOUGH AT THE beginning of the present century Canada was showing signs of great promise, the country lacked the unity and cohesion essential for a strong nation. Cross-country transportation and communication presented major problems. Canadians living in regions spread from the Atlantic shores to Vancouver Island, were still divided by race, culture, religion and economic interest. It was during the slow unrolling of the twentieth century that the people of Canada began to see themselves as citizens of a nation distinct from Great Britain, France, the United States and other countries from which they had come, and as uniquely Canadian.

New
prosperity

Fortunately, between the years 1900 and 1914 Canada achieved a prosperity unknown in previous centuries. Further development of railways and mail service; settlement of the prairies; increased wheat harvests; growth of industry, lumbering and mining; all contributed towards an economic boom. Political progress came as well in 1905, when the two new western provinces of Saskatchewan and Alberta were created from the southern portion of the Northwest Territories.

Reaching for
independence

It was not surprising, therefore, that a growing feeling of confidence and independence began to assert itself among the national leaders. By 1908 Canada had secured the agreement of Britain that no imperial treaty would be binding on Canada without Canada's specific consent. A year later, in Ottawa, the government established its own Department of External Affairs. Just as important as these developments was

300

The first airplane flight in Canada was made on February 23, 1909, by a young Canadian pilot, John McCurdy, who flew his fragile plane *Silver Dart* over half a mile across the frozen surface of Bras d'Or lake in Nova Scotia. The plane, designed by McCurdy and some associates, had a 49-foot wing span and weighed 800 pounds fully loaded, including fuel and pilot. McCurdy was one of the most celebrated figures in the early days of flying, and his exploits brought him international fame. In 1914 he tried to persuade the Canadian government of the military value of an air force, but was told by the Militia Minister Sam Hughes that the airplane was "an invention of the devil" and had no place in military operations!

the step taken in 1910 when the nation assumed control of Canadian immigration—even the admission of British subjects. This action, of course, signified that Canadians were not just British subjects but something more.

While the ties between Canada and the Mother Country were grad-

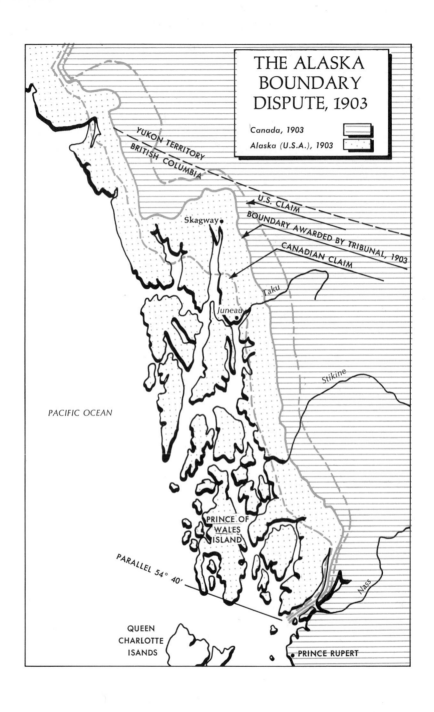

# THE ALASKA BOUNDARY DISPUTE, 1903

Canada, 1903

Alaska (U.S.A.), 1903

YUKON TERRITORY

BRITISH COLUMBIA

U.S. CLAIM

Skagway

BOUNDARY AWARDED BY TRIBUNAL, 1903

CANADIAN CLAIM

Taku

Juneau

Stikine

PACIFIC OCEAN

PRINCE OF WALES ISLAND

PARALLEL 54° 40'

Nass

QUEEN CHARLOTTE ISANDS

PRINCE RUPERT

ually being loosened, the process was orderly and friendly, causing little ill-feeling between Britain and her former colony. Canada still retained many of its constitutional, cultural and commercial bonds with Britain and in addition remained a senior member of the British Empire.

Friendly relationships with the United States, however, suffered a setback early in the century because of various misunderstandings concerning fishing rights, seal hunting and the true location of the Alaskan boundary.

**Alaskan Boundary Dispute**

The boundary dispute proved to be the thorniest issue of the three, because the Canadian and American governments disagreed on the interpretation of the old Anglo-Russian Treaty of 1825, a treaty that first set out the nature of the boundary line. Discussion focused on the amount of territory legally included in the "Alaskan Panhandle," a narrow land strip stretching southward along the Pacific coast from the main body of Alaska. With the discovery of gold in the Klondike, both Canadians and Americans were especially eager to control the profitable Yukon trade, which reached the sea through the Panhandle. The mountainous nature of the region and the indented coastline made boundary definition a most difficult task.

Friction between the two nations increased when it became clear that the United States was determined to claim more land than Canada thought was justified. Indeed, it appeared that President Theodore Roosevelt was prepared to place his troops in Alaska to defend the American claims.

This unpleasant dispute was settled in 1903 by an international commission made up of three Americans, two Canadians and one Englishman. The commission granted most of the American territorial demands.

Canadians were enraged by the decision and especially by the role of the British member of the commission who seemed to side with the Americans. Prime Minister Laurier in a report to Parliament complained that the Americans were "determined on every occasion to get the best in any agreement." The Alaska boundary dispute strengthened Canada's desire to determine its own affairs. The spirit of Canadian nationalism was increasing.

One very good thing did come out of the dispute with the United States over international boundaries. In 1909 Canada and the United States formed a permanent International Joint Commission responsible for the settlement of questions related to boundaries, rivers and coastal waters. The commission is still very active. Since its establishment, it has solved numerous problems of deep concern to both countries and so has contributed significantly to their peaceful relationship.

In the meantime Prime Minister Laurier had become alarmed by the rise of German military power in Europe. His alarm was so great that he became concerned about Canadian defence. It is true there was a small army of trained troops but there was no navy to guard Canadian shores. Up to this time Canadians had been content to leave their maritime defence in the capable hands of the British Royal Navy.

As the result of Laurier's promptings, Parliament in 1910 passed a Naval Service Bill, establishing a navy under direct control of the Canadian government. Naval bases were to be set up at Esquimalt in British Columbia and Halifax in Nova Scotia. Orders went out for the construction of five cruisers and six destroyers, all to be built by Canadians in Canada. But shortly after the passing of the Naval Service Bill, political fate was to interfere with the birth of a Canadian navy.

Laurier had not expected the protest that was aroused by his plans for defence. Some citizens feared his ideas would lead to the loss of British protection and perhaps complete separation from the Empire. Others, less concerned with imperial connections, believed Canada might become directly involved in Britain's wars. And some unkind critics referred to the proposed service as Laurier's little "tin-pot navy" and demanded instead direct Canadian contribution to the British fleet.

Another troublesome problem appeared for the Prime Minister in connection with trade between Canada and the United States. From both sides of the border came insistent demands for freer trade in certain goods, trade unhampered by the high cost of government tariffs imposed on imports. Farmers in western Canada were eager to sell their wheat in the United States and American manufacturers were just as eager to export their goods to Canada.

Frail and balky, costly, dirty and noisy, spitting oil, fire and smoke, the automobile made its first Canadian appearance in 1898, and was dismissed as a rich man's plaything, a fad. By 1912, there were 50,000 of these "fads" across the Canadian scene and by 1920 the number was up to 250,000. It was obviously here to stay, and perhaps more than any other single thing, to transform the face and the life style of the nation. In 1910, outside the cities and towns, there were practically no paved roads, only roads of dirt or gravel. Early motorists ventured into the country at their own risk and as often as not ended up stuck in the mire, ruts or potholes of horse and buggy trails. Direction signs were practically unknown. Before taking to the road the pioneer motorist usually decked himself out in cap and goggles, duster (a large cloth coat) and gauntlets. Women secured their straw hats with cheesecloth auto veils which also helped to keep the dust from their faces and their hair. The duster was equally popular with them, and they often wore them with high button boots. Today Canada has many thousands of safe and well-paved roads, but the most spectacular is the 4,860-mile Trans-Canada Highway, opened in 1962 and stretching from St. Johns in the east to Victoria in the west.

Such demands roused interest in the idea for a reciprocal trade agreement by which both countries would allow the importation and exportation of certain goods some with only low tariff payments and others completely free of them.

**Reciprocity Agreement**

During the winter of 1910 Prime Minister Laurier and President Taft of the United States negotiated just such an agreement. By the proposed plan there was to be free trade in meats, fish, fruits, vegetables and grains. In addition, Canada agreed to lower her import duties on some manufactured goods, such as agricultural machinery and building materials.

Before the new trade agreement was approved by the Canadian Parliament, Laurier went off to England to attend the coronation of King George V. While enjoying the pomp and splendour of the ceremonies there, he did not realize that a political storm was brewing at home.

**The election of 1911**

On his return to Canada, the Prime Minister soon discovered that the Conservative Party under Robert Borden was campaigning across the country against the plan of free trade with the United States. It became clear that there were Canadian manufacturers, railwaymen, bankers, meat-packers and fruit-growers who could see no value in the proposed agreement negotiated with President Taft. There was a feeling among many that Canada would eventually be absorbed into the United States if the trade agreement came into effect.

Laurier was surprised, disturbed and discouraged. With reluctance, he called the federal election of 1911.

It was a tense and bitter election campaign centring mainly on the two issues of free trade and the Naval Service Bill. Conservative speakers hammered steadily on the theme NO TRUCK OR TRADE WITH THE YANKEES, and in this effort they were supported by manufacturers and industrialists based mainly in Ontario and Quebec.

In the Province of Quebec the question of free trade was much less important than the Naval Service Act, which was viewed with both anger and alarm.

The Prime Minister and his Liberal Party were badly beaten in the election. The Congress of the United States was very disappointed. One American newspaper, the *New York World*, concluded that the benefits of free trade had been lost through the exercise of "popular stupidity" on the part of Canadian voters.

The new Prime Minister was Robert Laird Borden, who for ten years had been leader of the Conservative Party. Although he lacked the brilliant speaking ability of Wilfrid Laurier, he possessed a quick mind and powers of logical reasoning, which made him a formidable opponent in parliamentary debate. Like the former Prime Minister, he was concerned with Canadian defence, with suitable ties with the Mother Country and with the continued prosperity of the British Empire.

*Robert Laird Borden*

In Europe, tensions were rising. Most countries, and many national groups which lacked their own governments, were experiencing a surge of nationalism. Unfortunately many expressed their nationalism in a bullying and domineering way. The atmosphere was filled with suspicion and hostility.

*European nationalism*

The newly established German Empire was rapidly developing into a major economic power. The former agricultural economy was, by 1900, producing as much iron and steel as Britain, and this economic rivalry led to friction between England and Germany.

*Economic rivalry*

The German Emperor, William, a proud and arrogant leader with almost total power and authority, wanted a "place in the sun" for Germany. To achieve this, he too sought a colonial empire overseas, a powerful navy, and the expansion of his influence in Europe.

*Kaiser William*

European countries had always formed alliances among themselves —in times of peace as well as war. The motives of nations involved in partnerships were usually complex. By 1914 the major European countries were divided into two armed camps, each eying the other with hostility and suspicion.

*Alliances*

The members of the *Triple Alliance* were Germany, Austria-Hungary and Italy. *The Triple Entente* consisted of Britain, France and Russia. Members of each group were pledged to come to each others' defence if war broke out. If the delicate balance was tipped, all of Europe would be at war.

There were strong feelings of uneasiness in Great Britain due to uncertainty over imperial defence. Britain had an army of some 250,000 men but in comparison with the massive body of German soldiers it

*Concern in Britain*

Today we have become so completely accustomed to the push-button conveniences of our homes that it is hard to imagine what it was like living in homes at the turn of the twentieth century, before the use of electricity became widespread. It was a rare Canadian kitchen that did not have a stove of this type, a big, black cast-iron wood or coal-burner, elaborately decorated and trimmed with nickelplated hardware. In 1902 a stove such as this one sold for $42.75. In addition to cooking, such stoves were a welcome source of heat in cold weather, as many homes had no central heating systems. Working over such a stove in warm weather, however, could be quite a task.

was a small force. Britain did possess the most powerful navy in the world, a navy defending not only the homeland but the long sea routes leading to distant parts of the Empire. Nevertheless, the British had become alarmed by the power of the German Navy which was growing so swiftly that it threatened in a few years' time to surpass the British fleet.

In 1909 the British cabinet decided to order the construction of four new super-battleships, known as dreadnoughts. The public wanted more. This strong feeling was expressed in the cry of:

Naval race

> "We want eight
> And we won't wait."

The Germans reacted by trying to match British shipbuilding, dreadnaught for dreadnaught. Each country accused the other of having a threatening naval program, and defended its own shipbuilding as necessary for its security. The race was on.

During a visit to England in 1912, Borden was startled by the deep animosity that was growing between Great Britain and Germany. It was evident that the European situation was reaching a dangerous condition.

On his return to Canada, the new Prime Minister introduced in Parliament the Naval Aid Bill of 1912. The bill called for a Canadian contribution of $35,000,000 for building three battleships for the Royal Navy. To get the support of Quebec, the bill provided that Canadian sailors could train on these ships and that these ships might, in the future, become a Canadian unit within the British Navy.

Naval Aid
Bill

Robert Borden believed that this proposal would be accepted by the Canadian people but developments proved that he had misjudged the situation.

Some of his own cabinet ministers uttered fiery protests, while others demanded the question be voted on by the Canadian public. There were bitter wrangles lasting through long days and nights of parliamentary debate. Eventually the Naval Aid Bill was passed by the House of Commons, but went down to defeat in the Senate, which had a large majority of Liberal members. The problem of Canadian naval defence still remained unsolved. When war broke out the new Canadian Navy had two cruisers, one light and one heavy. No concrete plans had been made for further development of the navy, or for contributing to the British fleet.

An international incident finally tipped the scales in Europe. That incident came on Sunday, June 28, 1914, when an Austrian Archduke,

Archduke
murdered

Although electricity was used for lighting in a few Canadian homes before 1900, it was not until the second decade of the twentieth century that the convenience of electricity began to find application in new forms of labour-saving household appliances. Housewives began cooking with electric ranges, using electric irons and washing machines, electric hot water heaters and vacuum cleaners. This early vacuum cleaner is advertised as being "so superior in power, durability and construction that it is in a class by itself." It is "built to last a lifetime"—a claim rarely made of appliances manufactured today.

heir to the throne of Austria-Hungary, was shot to death in the tiny country of Bosnia (now a part of Yugoslavia) by a Serbian anarchist. Austria-Hungary, backed by its ally Germany, demanded humiliating concessions from Serbia. Serbia, backed by its supporter Russia, accepted all but two of Austria's demands. Austria would settle for nothing but complete acceptance of its terms.

The whole world held its breath. Events followed swiftly, with the staccato beat of exploding fireworks. Austria declared war on Serbia, the nation blamed for the death of the Archduke; Russia mobilized her troops; Germany declared war on Russia and France; and then German troops marched through the Belgian countryside on their way to France.

Invasion of neutral Belgium brought Great Britain unhesitatingly into the conflict, because the defence of this European country had been guaranteed by treaty. Just thirty-seven days after the killing of the Austrian Archduke Britain declared war, and in so doing ordered the Royal Navy to commence hostilities against the Germans.

*Britain declares war*

Curiously, in England the start of war in Europe was taken in a rather light-hearted way. Young men saw an opportunity for action and adventure; merchants dreamed of making fortunes, and no one believed the coming land and sea battles could last more than a few months.

In Canada, the news that Britain was at war burst on a nation enjoying the pleasant warm weather of August, 1914. Schools were closed, families were on vacation, the fishing was good and the beaches lively. It was difficult in such circumstances to visualize the startling events then taking place in Europe.

*Canada joins the conflict*

Immediately after the first shock of realization a spirit of patriotism raced across Canada. Once Great Britain had declared war, Canada was legally bound to be at war too.

The call to battle brought an extraordinary feeling of unity and determination throughout Canada, as political and regional differences were set aside in an eagerness to get on with the task. Both Wilfrid Laurier and Robert Borden urged citizens to put forth a supreme effort in support of Britain and the Empire. Parliament unanimously passed a War Measures Act which gave the government special powers to carry out the war. Just six days had passed since the invasion of Belgium, when the government ordered Colonel Sam Hughes, Minister of Militia and Defence, to organize an expeditionary force for service in Europe.

*Canadians support the war effort*

An enormous military camp was established at Valcartier near the City of Quebec and into this military centre poured a steam of volunteers from all over Canada; farmers, fishermen, lumbermen, railway men, miners, teachers, clerks, factory workers, storekeepers, men of business and the professions.

Six thousand volunteers reported at Valcartier during the first seven days after the camp's opening and two weeks later the total had swelled to 25,000. In less than two months' time the 1st Canadian Division of 33,000 men was sailing eastward across the Atlantic aboard a fleet of luxury liners.

When the phonograph was invented in 1877 by Thomas Edison, it was regarded as the most brilliant creation of its era. By 1900 its thin, reedy sound was invading many of the parlours of the nation, bringing with it, on fragile wax discs or cylinders, music and voices from around the world. Advertised as a "talking machine," one such as this could be bought in 1910 for $19.00 through Eatons mail order catalogue.

In spite of her admirable patriotism and energetic preparation for war, Canada was not really ready for a major conflict. To begin with, Canadians underestimated the seriousness of the international struggle and the cruel sacrifices necessary for the winning of eventual victory. Like the citizens of Britain, Canadians tended to believe that the war would be a brief affair.

Adding to the nation's difficulty, was the fact that just one year before, Canada had moved into a period of economic depression resulting in unemployment, dropping prices, lower incomes and a reduced rate of construction. Canada now faced the costly procedures of assembling troops, establishing a navy, manufacturing arms and raising sufficient food for Canadians and allies abroad.

**Economic problems**

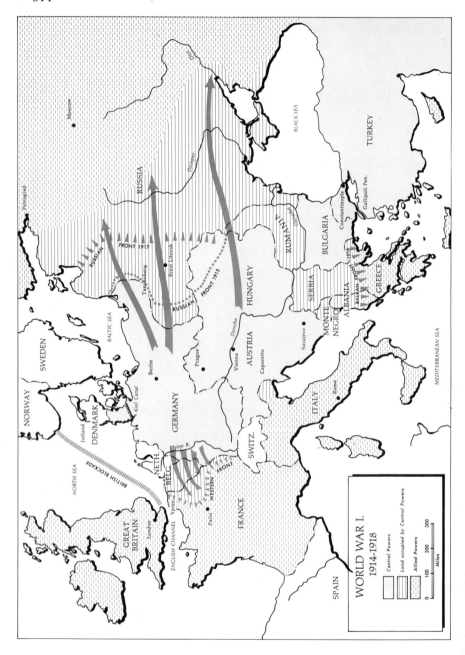

Moscow

Petrograd

RUSSIA

RUSSIAN FRONT 1917

Tannenberg

Brest Litovsk

RUSSIAN FRONT 1915

BALTIC SEA

Berlin

Prague

GERMANY

Kiel Canal

Rhine R.

Ypres

Paris

London

GREAT BRITAIN

ENGLISH CHANNEL

WESTERN FRONT

FRANCE

SPAIN

NETH.

BELG.

SWITZ.

NORTH SEA

BRITISH BLOCKADE

Jutland

DENMARK

NORWAY

SWEDEN

Vienna

AUSTRIA

Caporetto

HUNGARY

Sarajevo

MONTE NEGRO

SERBIA

ALBANIA

BALKAN FRONT 1916

Danube

RUMANIA

Danube

BULGARIA

GREECE

Constantinople

Gallipoli Pen.

TURKEY

BLACK SEA

Dnieper

Don

ITALY

Rome

MEDITERRANEAN SEA

WORLD WAR I.
1914-1918

Central Powers

Land occupied by Central Powers

Allied Powers

0   100   200   300
Miles

# 42. *World War I*

GERMAN MILITARY STRATEGY was based on the so-called "Schlieffen Plan," named for the general who developed it. This called for a quick strike through Belgium against Germany's western enemy, France, before Russia, the eastern enemy, could reach Germany. But after a series of desperate battles the German thrust was stopped and held by the stubborn resistance of the British and French.

The War in Europe

The war of movement then settled into a static condition, as both sides dug into a vast network of trenches and barbed wire which eventually stretched from the English Channel to the borders of Switzerland. Attacks made from these strong, defensive positions were costly in human lives and, in most cases, resulted in little change along the long, twisting line known as the Western Front.

The Western Front

Life in the trenches was horrible for the men on both sides of the Western Front. They fought in mud, water, rain and snow. They died of disease, bullet wounds and bursting shells. They were mowed down by the thousands in savage attacks across the ravaged land between the trenches. And some became mentally unstable in the inferno of pain, death and ear-shattering sound.

The main theatre of land operations was in Europe but World War I was a global conflict reaching out across the oceans and continents. Other nations became involved in the struggle and so joined forces with one side or the other. In 1914 Japan joined Britain, France and Russia in a group that came to be known as the Allies. In the same

Allies vs. Central Powers

315

Within a few weeks of the beginning of the war both sides dug in, taking up positions which they would occupy for the next four years. Along a front of 350 miles the opposing armies went below ground, constructing a vast network of trenches and dugouts which would offer some protection from the withering fire of the newest scourge of the battlefield — the machine-gun. Life in the trenches was an uncity-like system of interconnecting arteries stretched across France from the North Sea to Switzerland in the south. Rain turned the trenches into muddy pits, and despite the wooden walks — "duckboards" as they were called — troops were

sometimes knee deep in water. Rats were as numerous as the enemy and ran freely everywhere, into food, clothing, haversacks and even beds. Men were known to burn the crosses from graves to keep warm, and tea could be made by boiling water in the cooling systems of machine-guns. Beyond the trenches — often no more than a few hundred feet away — were the enemy's trenches. Raids between trenches were constant, and "no mans land," the short distance separating the lines, was often littered with dead or dying men from both sides — while not even an inch of ground might change hands for months at a time.

year Turkey joined Germany, Austria-Hungary and Italy in an alliance which would be known as the Central Powers. In 1917 Italy shifted to the side of the Allies.

The war took a fresh turn during 1914 when Russian troops thrust westward across the border of Austria-Hungary and Germany, thus opening up a new battle line known as the Eastern Front, running from the Gulf of Riga to the Black Sea.

**The Empire at war**

Kaiser William had hoped the British Empire might fall apart because of the heavy pressure of warfare, but members of the imperial family of nations rallied to the support of Britain and the Allies. Australia, New Zealand, South Africa, India and smaller dependencies rushed troops to action in the South Pacific, Africa, the Near East and Europe. German colonies were seized and German movements hampered by the solid front presented by the Empire.

**Conflict at sea**

It was most fortunate that Britain's Royal Navy was in a powerful position at the beginning of war. Her fleets hunted down scattered enemy units and kept the main naval force of Germany bottled up in the North Sea. The war at sea was a risky one for Britain because a serious defeat could result in an invasion of the British Isles by German land forces. The only major clash at sea, the Battle of Jutland, 1916, was a disastrous victory for the British. The British Navy suffered greater losses, but the German fleet did not again put to sea. The major task of the Royal Navy was to keep Germany and her allies cut off from supplies. The Germans responded to the blockade with the submarine, which remained a serious threat to Allied war craft and to merchant vessels carrying food supplies and materials of war. Finally the blockade of the Royal Navy was so successful that the enemy responded by declaring unrestricted submarine warfare on the ships of all nations sailing the waters off Allied coastlines.

In desperation, the British looked about for some means of fighting off the underwater menace, and protecting their vital lines of supply. An effective convoy system, by which merchant ships sailed under the protection of light and speedy war craft, was organized. A crude warning device was developed for detecting the sound of approaching raiders. And a destructive new weapon, the depth charge, was developed.

If dropped properly into the sea, it exploded and cracked the hulls of enemy submarines.

The submarine threat was not entirely eliminated during the course of the war but its thrust was blunted so that the flow of Allied men and materials continued to supply the theatres of battle.

In an attempt to break through Allied lines in April 1915, the Germans used poison gas as an offensive weapon. A Canadian regiment, The Princess Patricia's Canadian Light Infantry, was among the first to stand against it, using makeshift gas masks from strips of dampened cotton tied across the nose and mouth. Poison gas — of which there were many types — could be discharged from cylinders and carried by prevailing winds, or fired in bombs or shells. Gas masks were designed to clean the air by passing it through chemical purifiers contained in the bag beneath. The mask fitted the face and neck closely, vision being provided through mica eyeholes. Such masks successfully neutralized the tactical advantages hoped for in gas warfare, and although it remained a ghastly weapon, it never became a decisive factor in the war.

By February, 1915, Canadian troops were in France to participate in the grim struggle along the Western Front. They were stationed in a hazardous position near the French city of Ypres, close to the Belgian border, in a region at the northern end of the long battle line.

Canadians in combat

In this region, near St. Julien, in April, some of the Canadians encountered a fog of greenish, chlorine gas drifting from the German positions. Although some of the Allied troops fell back before the advance of the deadly gas, the Canadians stood firm, improvising crude masks out of wet handkerchiefs. Quickly they filled up the empty gaps in the line and hung on stubbornly until relieved three days later.

Years before, the use of poisonous gases had been outlawed by international agreement, yet the Germans added them to their stock of weapons. The German High Command believed that gas might be the one fearsome factor that could break up the stalemate of trench warfare. But the effect of poison gas would soon be neutralized by the development of the respirator, an early form of gas mask.

Canadians won high respect for their bravery in action at Ypres, but the cost was high. Thousands died of wounds, fell before rifle bullets or disappeared in the shattering blast of artillery shells. One of several units hit particularly hard was Princess Patricia's Canadian Light Infantry, a regiment almost completely wiped out after six months' fighting on the Western Front.

By 1916 men of the 2nd and 3rd Canadian Divisions had joined their comrades of the 1st Division in France and all three divisions formed into the famous Canadian Corps.

Canadians enhanced their fighting reputation still further in the big Allied offensive of 1916, south of Ypres in a region near the Somme River.

Here they won a reputation as outstanding assault troops, with the fighting spirit to lead vigorous attacks on enemy positions. For this reason, in some future battles they were to be placed in extremely dangerous and responsible positions.

**Problems at home**

The government in Canada was deeply involved in planning for the war effort. Industry was reorganized for the manufacture of armaments, explosives and airplane parts. Six hundred munition factories poured out an endless stream of artillery shells. Shipyards in the Maritime Provinces constructed vessels to replace those lost to German submarines in the North Atlantic. Farms across the nation produced enough food stocks for Canadian use and for the partial supply of the Allies abroad.

**Dissatisfaction**

In spite of the notable progress achieved, there was criticism of the total war effort. In the beginning there had been much confusion connected with the early stages of preparation. Quebecers complained

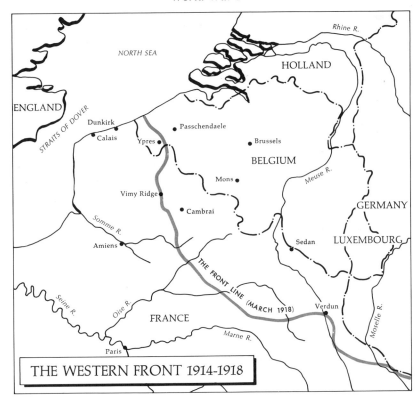

THE WESTERN FRONT 1914-1918

of recruiting methods and of military manuals printed in English. Among military men there was dissatisfaction with the Ross rifle, a weapon which, it was said, heated up and jammed under battle conditions. The man responsible for adopting the Ross rifle was Sam Hughes. There was widespread grumbling about several of Hughes' actions. He was accused of acting without proper authority, of interfering with the orders of commanders and of scoffing at British wartime policy. In 1916 he left the cabinet.

By the spring of 1917 it had become clear that Canada's military manpower could no longer be maintained solely by the number of men volunteering for overseas duty. The sad fact was that Allied losses on the battlefields were greater than the numbers of new recruits arriving for military service. In order to maintain the flow of Canadian troops, it seemed necessary to adopt a policy of compulsory recruitment, a policy already established in Britain.

**The Conscription Crisis**

Prime Minister Borden hesitated to introduce conscription into Canada, for he had promised that no Canadians would be forced to engage in battle. But the pressure for action became so great that in 1917 he brought the Military Service Bill before Parliament. He explained his action in the following words:

"To the state, each citizen owes a duty of service, and the highest duty of all is the obligation to assist in defending the rights, the institutions and the liberties of his country."

He hoped that the measure would be accepted calmly, but at the same time he realized the chances of protest were extremely high.

Passing of the Military Service Bill in the summer of 1917 brought about a condition dangerously close to civil war. Canadians were sharply divided into groups, separated by various opinions either for or against the idea of conscription. Scattered opposition came from all parts of Canada but most vigorously from the Province of Quebec. Henri Bourassa, a French-Canadian leader, stated that, in doing what it saw as its duty towards the Empire and humanity, the government was

"...preparing to increase the sufferings of the Canadian people, to make Mothers weep, and to reduce to misery thousands of homes by depriving them of their natural sustenance."

He warned the government to be careful

"...that the people do not rise against you and against the vultures who are gorging themselves with millions torn from the vitals of the nation."

Old racial and religious frictions, largely forgotten at the beginning of war, burst out again with flaming passion.

**United States enters the war**

As World War I progressed, the people of the United States became uneasy about events taking place abroad. They were upset by the German invasion of neutral Belgium and the sinking of unprotected ships in the North Atlantic. German torpedoing of the passenger vessel *Lusitania* horrified the American public. When Germany began unrestricted submarine warfare in 1917 the destruction of American ships by undersea raiders finally brought loud demands for action, and an official declaration of war on Germany, April 6, 1917.

**Battle in the air**

In addition to fighting on the land and at sea, the European adversaries faced increasing action in the air, a form of combat unknown in previous wars. In the early stages Germany had used huge, gas-filled dirigibles known as Zeppelins for bombing raids on Britain. The big airships were slow but they could carry an effective load of explosives to enemy targets. As a result of the Zeppelin raids, several thousand persons were killed in England and much property was destroyed.

As the war proceeded, however, the cumbersome airships were gradually replaced by small, speedy airplanes, which at first were used for observing enemy positions, scattering leaflets and guiding the fire of ground artillery.

Once the airplane had proved itself, both sides in the struggle began to refine the machine as an actual weapon of war. Fighter planes were equipped with machine-guns firing directly ahead through the rotating blades of propellers.

The coming of fighter planes, made it possible to attack ground positions and fight spectacular duels in the sky.

Many young Canadians took to the air and became skilled pilots in the Royal Flying Corps and the Royal Naval Air Service. Twenty-five thousand of them eventually flew in combat in Europe and won great respect. Before the end of the war almost one-third of the pilots in the British flying service were Canadians.

Among the Canadian fliers were several who became famous as pilots of extraordinary achievement: Raymond Collishaw, W.C. Barker and "Billy" Bishop. Bishop during his amazing flying career shot down seventy-two enemy planes and won an impressive series of military honours, including the Victoria Cross. Many of these pilots returned to Canada and, as the famous "bush pilots," helped to open Canada's North.

After two years of unrelenting conflict, both the Allies and the Central Powers had become weary of war, discouraged by the stalemate on the Western Front and disheartened by the shocking losses in men and materials. **War weariness**

In the meantime on the Eastern Front, the poorly equipped, ill-trained Russian Army suffered defeats marked by appalling death and injury. In the fighting of the summer of 1916 alone, Russia had lost nearly a million men. Restless conditions within Russia, sharpened by the disasters of war, burst into violent revolution in 1917. The autocratic Tsar Nicholas II was overthrown and a provisional government took over. **Russian Revolution**

But soon Vladimir Ilyich Lenin and his Bolsheviks, promising to take the exhausted country out of the conflict, gained control. By the

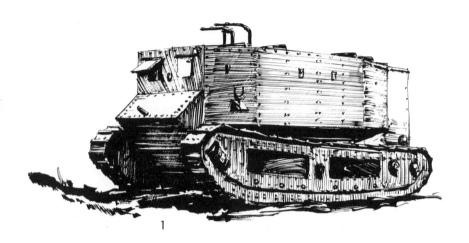

1

2

Although Leonardo da Vinci, the sixteenth-century Italian genius, designed a heavily armoured military vehicle, the modern tank was developed between 1914 and 1915 by the British, as a result of a number of independent inventions. In the early stages of development, the tank was supported by Winston Churchill, then First Lord of the Admiralty, who saw it as a bullet-proof steam tractor carrying small armoured shelters housing men and machine-guns. After months of experiment the first functional machine (1) was built. Nicknamed "Little Willie," after the German Crown Prince, it was gasoline-powered, steam-power having been dropped in the early planning stages. Its 105-horse-power, six-cylinder engine gave it a speed of 3.5 m.p.h. Although never used in action, it provided valuable information that helped build a larger and more highly developed machine, "Big Willie," the first tank

Treaty of Brest-Litovsk, Russia made peace with Germany, and gave up a large portion of its territory. The disappearance of the Eastern Front was a serious blow to the Allies, for Germany and Austria were now free to send additional troops into western and southern Europe.

By the spring of 1917, the Allies were organizing a powerful offensive to break through German positions along the Western Front. But the Germans, foreseeing such action, fell back on a well-prepared defensive position known as the Hindenburg Line. British and French assaults on this tough, new line achieved little and brought still further losses.

The Hindenburg Line

Another offensive of 1917 involved an Allied attempt to thrust through enemy-held territory in Belgium in order to seize German submarine bases on the English Channel. The Canadians played an extremely important role in this campaign. One vital task given to the Canadian Corps was the capture of Vimy Ridge, an elevation of land protected by a German network of trenches, pillboxes, concrete emplacements, machine-guns, mortars and shell-proof dugouts. Vimy Ridge was strategically important to the Germans, since from its summit their artillery was able to dominate the surrounding countryside.

Vimy Ridge

At dawn on Easter Monday, 1917, nearly one thousand Allied guns opened fire on Vimy Ridge. Along the long artillery line, the guns thundered and spouted flames as they hurled shells on the defenders, filling in trenches, smashing concrete slabs and wiping out observation posts.

Then up the muddy slopes came the waves of khaki-clad men of

---

used in battle. Somewhat boat-shaped, its sides were completely encircled by tractor treads. However, its thickest armour was only two-fifths of an inch, very light by modern standards and effective only against standard small-arms fire (bullets striking the armour caused small white-hot metal fragments to fly off within the tank). "Big Willie" crawled along at anything up to 3.7 m.p.h., armed with two six-pounder naval guns and four machine-guns or with six Lewis guns. Its baptism of fire was September 15, 1916, during the Battle of the Somme, when forty-nine of the machines were unleashed against the surprised Germans. "Big Willie" soon became officially known as the Mark 1 and underwent constant development and improvement throughout the remainder of the war. In the Mark V (2) the armour was slightly heavier and a more powerful engine gave it a top speed of 4.6 m.p.h. The range of the Mark V, although only twenty-five miles, was twice that of the Mark 1. The Mark V could also fire to the rear, another improvement over its predecessor. Since such items as springs, shock absorbers and mufflers were still lacking, crew comfort was at a minimum.

The firepower of the opposing armies in World War 1 was staggering. Weapons'
designers and armaments' makers poured enormous energy and ingenuity into
devising more powerful and sophisticated guns with which to annihilate the enemy.
One such was the German's Paris Gun, which even today holds something of a
record for long-distance shooting. In March of 1918 it began shelling Paris from
a distance of sixty-seven miles away and kept this up at a rate of one shell every
twenty minutes — barring interruption — for 140 days. The 228-pound shell took
three minutes to cover the distance, and the gunners had to calculate the forty
miles of the earth's rotation when aiming. The truss along the top of the gun was
necessary to keep the enormously long barrel from drooping.

four Canadian divisions and a British brigade. They advanced over the
churned-up earth of no-man's-land. Some were struck by bullets,

dropping and dying where they lay; others were seriously wounded, and slid into deep shell holes, drowning in icy water. It was desperate, bloody fighting but by noon the attackers had reached the top and stood as victors on the German stronghold.

The Canadian Corps took part in other bitter battles in this campaign at Arleux, the Scarpe, Hill 70 and Passchendaele. At Passchendaele, the Canadians, in two weeks of fighting, won two miles — a remarkable achievement on the Western Front. However the cost in human lives was a thousand men a day.

As 1917 drew to a close, there was still no real promise of an early end to the struggle. There had been some British successes against the Turks in the Near East but the total picture was gloomy. Morale was low. Only the recent entry of the United States into the global confrontation raised hopes of possible victory. It was expected that, when the full weight of American power reached the battlefields of Europe, the course of conflict would change. *Discouragement on both sides*

The Central Powers, too, were becoming discouraged and apprehensive. German submarines had not destroyed the Royal Navy, had not stopped the flow of men and supplies across the North Atlantic, and had not broken the British blockade of the continental ports. Stocks of food and clothing were running low. The German people were slowly losing faith in their wartime leaders.

Realizing that powerful American help for the Allied cause was on the way, the German High Command decided on a massive campaign to break through on the Western Front, a great, crushing blow to send the Allies reeling. A million troops were moved from eastern Europe to bolster the forces along the Western Front.

During March, 1918, the German flood of men flowed westward with such force it swept the British lines backward in the region of the River Somme. *The spring of 1918*

At this time the Allies appointed a brilliant French officer, Marshal Foch, as Supreme Commander of all their forces. The British and French stopped the German Army short of its objective, the town of Amiens.

In April came another German push a little further south, below Ypres, aimed at reaching Allied ports on the English Channel. They managed to crack the British lines but were hindered by British stubbornness and their lack of reserve troops. The German thrust again was halted.

The Germans then moved southwestward against the French and in so doing had considerably more success. They smashed through their lines and during the following weeks pushed on to a point fifty-six miles from Paris.

Six weeks later the Germans were less than forty miles from the French capital and threatening to close that short distance. It was a critical time of the war, for the loss of France and the Channel ports had become a strong possibility.

**Counterattack by Marshal Foch**

At this point, July 1918, Marshal Foch put into action his own plan for a counter-stroke, involving the elements of power and surprise. With the aid of light tanks and masses of American troops, Foch struck at the Germans with such force that the invaders reeled back, retreating in the direction of Germany.

Further north along the River Somme, a few weeks later, British, Canadian and Australian troops aimed a second blow at the German lines. Tanks and armoured cars employed in this offensive shocked the enemy, whose bullets were useless against the "roaring, smoke-belching, invulnerable, steel monsters."

The tide of war turned in startling fashion as Marshal Foch maintained steady pressure on the enemy, keeping them off balance with a series of bewildering attacks at numerous points along the Western Front. Fresh American troops were arriving in France at the rate of 25,000 a month. The Germans were in final retreat. Allied troops seized enormous stocks of war materials and captured many prisoners. The German military situation was now hopeless.

During the last weeks of conflict in Europe, American forces under General Pershing played a vital role in breaching the Hindenburg Line and marching on Germany.

Resistance of the Central Powers collapsed in eastern Europe. The German navy mutinied, and Germany itself was on the brink of revolution, as a general strike hit the country on November 9. On that day the Kaiser abdicated and fled to Holland.

**Armistice**

On the morning of November 11, 1918, Marshal Foch and the German delegates gathered in a special coach standing on a railway siding and there they signed the Armistice terms dictated by the Allied nations. At 11:00 on that morning World War I was officially over.

# 43.   A Restless Peace

THE END OF war brought a feeling of vast relief to a world sickened by the horrible slaughter. This was followed by a sober pondering of the many problems awaiting solution.

Treaty of Versailles

The first of these were the problems of negotiating peace treaties and establishing some method of ensuring that there would never be another war.

The major victorious powers, Great Britain, France, the United States and Italy, arranged the general settlement of war affairs through *The Treaty of Versailles*, 1919. Germany was stripped of much of its former power and possessions. By this agreement, Germany lost all its overseas territories and suffered changes in its own European boundaries. The navy was to be destroyed and the size of the army severely limited. There was to be no German submarine service or air force. The Germans had to sign a statement agreeing that they were to blame completely for the war. Stiff payments for the damages of war were to be made by Germany to the victorious countries.

Allied leaders believed the terms at Versailles provided punishment for a nation that had triggered the long conflict. In reality, the guilt for World War I could not be limited to Germany, or any one country. In Germany the treaty seemed harsh and severe, an indignity forced on a proud people. The Germans had expected to be partners in the discussions leading up to the peace treaty but they had been ignored, and now faced a series of decrees dictated by the enemy powers.

As a result, the Treaty of Versailles was remembered in Germany

The styling of women's clothing in the twentieth century has been as spectacular as the times and technical achievements it reflects. From 1900 to 1908, women were still wearing costumes inspired by the Victorian era. Typical of these years is (1) a 1903 spring dress with diamond-shaped satin insets and a lace blouse. Also typical is the very large hat, the very narrow waist, the trumpet-shaped skirt trailing the ground and the dress's full sleeve. Male costume in 1900 more closely resembled that of today—dramatizing all the more the revolution in women's clothing. (2) a business suit of 1904 differs little from today's mens wear except for a slightly longer jacket. By 1910, a major change became evident in women's dress styles. Skirts were much more narrow at the hem line, and became known as "hobble skirts." A strong fashion movement demanded a return to more basic

forms. Fashion was echoing developments in other fields of design (architecture, furniture) where simplicity was again being sought. (3) is a 1914 style which managed quite successfully to hide the shape of the body in a somewhat tubular creation. Hats had shrunk by 1912, and now the large crown was being accentuated. Silver fox fur, monkey fur, flared coats and fur borders became increasingly popular. Colours were more sombre, greys, browns, blacks and navy blue being favoured. (4) is a fashionable dress of 1923, which although more of a gay print, is still basically simple in its lines. The twenties was a fast-changing decade for the woman who wanted to stay in style. Designers were moving quickly toward a "straight line" dress. By 1926 this design dominated the world of fashion.

with bitterness. Indeed, German resentment grew, and so, with the passage of time, shaped conditions for another world war twenty years later.

League of Nations

Woodrow Wilson, President of the United States, was a key figure at the Peace Conference. Among his suggestions was one to establish a "general association of nations" whose function it would be to pre-serve world peace. Wilson realized that many international disputes would inevitably come up in the aftermath of war and that proper settlement of these would increase chances for permanent peace.

In consequence of Wilson's plea, the League of Nations came into being during the spring of 1919. It represented an important advance, since it bound nations together in an agreement for mutual security and the maintenance of peace. One of the vital elements of the Cove-nant of the League of Nations was the clause stating that member nations would submit dangerous questions for arbitration. Yet the League did not have the necessary machinery to act against a military aggressor and keep peace.

Germany, Austria-Hungary, Turkey and Russia were not allowed to become members but provision was made for their entry. Unfortunately, at this time the United States was swept by a spirit of isolationism, and even though the league had been the inspiration of their own president, the American Congress voted against joining.

A nation among nations

Prime Minister Borden had led Canada and the other self-governing Dominions of the Empire in demanding representation as sovereign nations at the Peace Conference and in the League. The Treaty of Versailles, which included the provision for the League of Nations, was signed by Great Britain for the Empire, but Canada and the other Dominions signed separately. At the first session of the League in 1920, Canada and the Dominions each took their own seats.

The high cost of victory

During the course of the conflict the nations involved had been so intent on the immediate problems of war that they had not realized the total cost and sacrifice. The terrible nature of so much of the fight-ing made it difficult to get exact figures on the number of war dead. But the number of losses which could be accounted for were appalling.

Altogether 65,000,000 men had been called to arms and of this total nearly one-seventh had lost their lives. Russia lost at least 1,700,000

## ARMIES MOBILIZED AND CASUALTIES IN WORLD WAR I[*]

| Countries | Total mobilized forces | Killed and died | Wounded casualties | Prisoners and missing | Total Casualties | Percentage of mobilized forces in casualties |
|---|---|---|---|---|---|---|
| **Allies and Associated Powers:** | | | | | | |
| Russia.......... | 12,000,000 | 1,700,000 | 4,950,000 | 2,500,000 | 9,150,000 | 76.3 |
| France.......... | 8,410,000 | 1,357,800 | 4,266,000 | 537,000 | 6,160,800 | 73.3 |
| British Empire... | 8,904,467 | 908,371 | 2,090,212 | 191,652 | 3,190,235 | 35.8 |
| Italy .......... | 5,615,000 | 650,000 | 947,000 | 600,000 | 2,197,000 | 39.1 |
| United States ... | 4,355,000 | 126,000 | 234,300 | 4,500 | 364,800 | 8.2 |
| Japan ......... | 800,000 | 300 | 907 | 3 | 1,210 | 0.2 |
| Romania........ | 750,000 | 335,706 | 120,000 | 80,000 | 535,706 | 71.4 |
| Serbia ......... | 707,343 | 45,000 | 133,148 | 152,958 | 331,106 | 46.8 |
| Belgium........ | 267,000 | 13,716 | 44,686 | 34,659 | 93,061 | 34.9 |
| Greece......... | 230,000 | 5,000 | 21,000 | 1,000 | 27,000 | 11.7 |
| Portugal ....... | 100,000 | 7,222 | 13,751 | 12,318 | 33,291 | 33.3 |
| Montenegro..... | 50,000 | 3,000 | 10,000 | 7,000 | 20,000 | 40.0 |
| Total....... | 42,188,810 | 5,152,115 | 12,831,004 | 4,121,090 | 22,104,209 | 52.3 |
| **Central Powers:** | | | | | | |
| Germany........ | 11,000,000 | 1,773,700 | 4,216,058 | 1,152,800 | 7,142,558 | 64.9 |
| Austria-Hungary ...... | 7,800,000 | 1,200,000 | 3,620,000 | 2,200,000 | 7,020,000 | 90.0 |
| Turkey ........ | 2,850,000 | 325,000 | 400,000 | 250,000 | 975,000 | 34.2 |
| Bulgaria ....... | 1,200,000 | 87,500 | 152,390 | 27,029 | 266,919 | 22.2 |
| Total........ | 22,850,000 | 3,386,200 | 8,388,448 | 3,629,829 | 15,404,477 | 67.4 |
| Grand Total .... | 65,038,810 | 8,538,315 | 21,219,452 | 7,750,919 | 37,508,686 | 57.6 |

[*]As reported by the United States War Department in February, 1924

333

men; Germany almost 1,800,000; France almost 1,400,000; the British Empire almost 950,000; Austria-Hungary 1,200,000; the United States 116,000. Among the losses sustained by the British Empire were 60,000 Canadians.

In addition to the sacrifice in human lives there had been widespread destruction of property, wastage of agricultural land, sinking of ships, disruption of trade and the incredible expense of maintaining armies, navies and air forces.

The world-wide task of reconstruction and rehabilitation was enormous.

**Conditions in Canada**

Canadians came out of World War I with fresh confidence and the expectation that they were entering a new era of peace and prosperity. This feeling was justified to a degree, but certain conditions resulting from war held back rapid progress.

Canadian industry had yet to shift from the manufacture of munitions and uniforms to the production of items required in everyday living, a shift which required time. During this period of transition unemployment rose sharply, so that many young Canadians recently returned from the war found themselves without work.

Wages were not keeping up with the cost of living. A feeling of unrest and dissatisfaction swept across the nation, particularly among the workers, and so brought about rising demands for higher pay and shorter working hours. Labour unions grew stronger and strikes increased.

**The Winnipeg strike**

A dramatic climax came in 1919 with a spectacular strike in the city of Winnipeg. Beginning with demands from construction and metal workers for shorter hours and more pay, the strike snowballed into a general strike supported by many others, ranging from firemen and street cleaners to butchers and government employees—35,000 in all. The work stoppage was so effective that Winnipeg was brought to an almost complete standstill.

Rioting caused by the arrest of some strike leaders led the Canadian authorities to send in the militia and members of the Royal North-West Mounted Police to restore order.

To most strikers their own protests meant no more than a demand for better living conditions but to many Canadians such massive strike action seemed to have a more sinister motive. An editorial in a Winnipeg newspaper, the *Citizen*, proclaimed that workers were out to change "the industrial and governmental system" of the nation. There was some fear that striking Canadians were imitating the behaviour of Russian workers during the revolution of 1917.

Eventually, under the sharp disapproval of Canadian citizens and government, the Winnipeg strike faltered and broke down. The original striking unions did earn the right to bargain together for better conditions and pay. But a section was introduced into the criminal code allowing the government to act strongly against labour unions it considered unlawful. Important leaders of the strike were brought to trial and found guilty on charges of sedition.

Between the years 1920 and 1923 difficulties were encountered not only in industry but in agriculture as well. During the war Canadian farm production had been expanded remarkably to meet the urgent needs of the nation and her allies. This quick expansion had been encouraged by the federal government through the use of special farm bonuses and guaranteed prices for agricultural products. With the arrival of peace, however, food stocks became greater than demand required, so prices fell and farmers suffered a reduction in their incomes. **Agricultural problems**

Dissatisfaction among the farming population in the West led to the establishment of organizations through which the crops were pooled and sold cooperatively. This movement was strongest in the Prairie Provinces where wheat pools were formed in all three provinces.

In order to achieve their economic and political aims farmers founded political parties, and elected provincial governments in Saskatchewan, Alberta and Ontario. Having done so well at the provincial level, farming groups established a nation-wide party known as the National Progressive Party which became very much interested in freer trade conditions with the United States. **National Progressive Party**

In the federal election in 1921 Canadian voters had a choice between two new political leaders of the major parties. Prime Minister Borden, worn out by his wartime duties, had resigned from office and was succeeded as leader of the Conservative Party by Arthur Meighen. And a year before that Wilfrid Laurier had died, leaving leadership of the Liberal Party to William Lyon Mackenzie King.

In the election campaign Liberals, Conservatives and the National Progressive Party each presented their plans for the future. King kept a middle course between Meighen and the Progressive leader, and the Liberal Party won the greatest number of votes.

**William Lyon Mackenzie King**

William Lyon Mackenzie King, the new Prime Minister, was a grandson of William Lyon Mackenzie, the colourful leader of the rebel uprising in Upper Canada during the year of 1837.

Mackenzie King was not a radical leader seeking revolutionary changes in government. He had studied economics, social science, law and political science in university. In addition, he had been employed in the Canadian civil service and had worked in the United States as a director of industrial research. He was respected, too, for his skill in settling disputes between labour and management.

Mackenzie King was not an exciting or colourful personality, but he was a man of intelligence, judgment and integrity. No one, in 1921, dreamed that he would dominate the Canadian political scene for the next thirty years.

King's first term as Prime Minister was difficult because his party lacked a majority of members in Parliament. Only the support offered by the Progressive Party enabled him to keep his government in office. This unsatisfactory condition made King's task a frustrating one, marked by slow progress in achieving the changes he wished for the nation. He did manage, nevertheless, to secure passage of a bill introducing old age pensions to provide assistance for elderly people. A feature of this period was the intense rivalry between King and Meighen.

In the election of 1926 King gained the majority he needed and so had far more power than before. He proceeded to legislate changes in trade, taxes, immigration and social welfare.

**Returning prosperity**

The difficult economic period of the years just following World War I had given way to an era of prosperity. By 1924 western farmers were enjoying lower production costs and higher selling prices on the grain markets of the world. Wheat pools were operating numerous storage elevators on the prairies and some enormous ones on the Great Lakes and the Pacific coast. A Central Selling Agency was, by 1926, handling most of the wheat crop of the prairie. High quality Canadian wheat was being exported to many foreign countries.

Canada was fortunate in having numerous rivers and waterfalls which could be harnessed to produce electricity. So, in the 1920's the development of inexpensive electrical power gave a strong push to industrial expansion. Electrical power

One dramatic example of electrical power used in manufacturing was the Arvida aluminum plant on the Saguenay River in Quebec. Although all the necessary bauxite ore had to be imported into Canada, it was still possible to manufacture aluminum profitably because of the cheap electricity provided by the Saguenay River, which drops over three hundred feet in its first thirty miles. Arvida became the largest aluminum smelting plant in the world.

Electrical power was responsible for dramatic growth in the pulp, paper, chemical and steel industries and in the manufacture of a long list of goods required for domestic use and foreign export. New manufacturing plants appeared across Canada but the greatest concentration of them dotted the shores of the St. Lawrence River and lower Great Lakes, expanding the economic prosperity of Quebec and Ontario.

The Canadian Shield, a rugged, rocky region stretching across northern Ontario and reaching out northwestward to the valley of the Mackenzie River, had been regarded only as a source of fur and timber. Now this vast territory became vital because of its extensive deposits of mineral wealth. The Canadian Shield

Prospectors roving the lonely lands of the Canadian Shield gradually uncovered an unexpected treasure of minerals of astonishing variety and quantity.

Gold mining had been established at Porcupine in 1912 and shortly afterward at Kirkland Lake, but it was not until the 1920's that mining was in full swing. Then came copper mining at Noranda, nickel mining at Sudbury, iron mining in northern Quebec and copper-zinc mining at Flin Flon in northern Manitoba.

The return of prosperity reached across Canada. As already noted, manufacturing and mining were major industries in Ontario and Quebec, while the Prairie Provinces were thriving because of the pro- Conditions across Canada

In the 1920's the automobile brought about a revolution in Canada in the way people lived. In the country, improving roads ended the long and lonely isolation of the farmer, while in the cities, the auto made it possible for workers to travel long distances to their jobs, giving rise to the growth of suburbs as well as decentralized industry. With more than one million cars on the road by 1930, the car manufacturers had become vast consumers of goods and materials such as steel, lead, rubber, and nickel while car owners of course used gasoline. Many of the cars of the late twenties were impressive machines. This 1929 Packard Super 8 sport Phaeton gives the impression of rakish elegance and restrained power. Hydraulic brakes, balloon tires, better suspension and seating, all combined to enhance the appeal and reliability of vehicles of this day and to lure Canadians onto the highways. Today there are approximately eight million motor vehicles in Canada and the automobile accounts for roughly 83 per cent of all the passenger miles travelled annually.

duction and exportation of wheat.

British Columbia was prospering through the industries of lumbering, salmon fishing, fruit growing and mining. Transportation developments made Vancouver a port of vital importance. With the opening of the Panama Canal in 1914, it became possible to transport wheat, lumber and canned fish economically to ports in the British Isles and Europe. As a direct result, Vancouver was not only a centre of sea transport but developed into a thriving city.

The Maritimes were making progress in manufacturing, mining, shipbuilding and sea transportation, but toward the end of the 1920's concern was growing for the future of coal mining and steel making. The completion of settlement of the Canadian West had reduced the need for railway cars and steel rails. Then, too, the increasing use of electricity for industrial purposes was looming as a threat to the sales of Maritime coal. In general, conditions in the Maritimes were far less prosperous than those in the other regions of Canada.

The boom of the 1920's brought about a series of fascinating changes in the Canadian way of life, most of them dictated by new ideas and inventions.

An outstanding example was the mass production of inexpensive automobiles. The Ford Motor Company of Detroit was the leader during the era. An American inventor-genius, Henry Ford, conceived the idea of manufacturing a "people's car" which would sell so cheaply that almost any family could afford to own one. It soon became apparent that North Americans agreed with Ford's plan and eagerly purchased the motor vehicles.

Automobiles

The famous Model T. Ford, or "Tin Lizzie," created in 1909, became the most popular auto on the continent and continued to sell briskly into the 1920's. During this period 15,000,000 of them were rolled out of Ford factories and whisked away to distant points. Its popularity fell only when the Ford Company introduced an improved version, the Model A Ford, of 1928.

The widespread use of automobiles and trucks brought great changes in the everyday lives of the Canadian people. A man who owned an automobile could drive long distances to work, so suburban communities blossomed on the outskirts of cities. The sales of manufactured goods became easier and more efficient because salesmen were able to visit their territories more quickly and easily. Perishable agriculture products were transported swiftly from farms to city markets. A whole new series of industries and businesses appeared: the manufacture of auto parts, tires and gasoline; the operation of service stations and repair shops; the construction of highways; and the provision of facilities for a flourishing tourist trade.

Back in 1909 at Baddeck, Nova Scotia, a young Canadian, J.A.D. McCurdy, made the first airplane flight in the British Empire. The flying machine developed rapidly during the war years. In 1919 two Royal Air Force men, John Alcock and Arthur Whitten-Brown, flew eastward across the Atlantic from Newfoundland and landed in Ireland. This event proved beyond a doubt that the improved machines could cover long distances quickly and reliably.

At the close of war, conditions in Canada were ripe for the development of the airplane as a major means of transportation. Hundreds of Canadians with experience in the Royal Flying Corps were eager to turn their skills to peacetime use. And certainly there was need for a Canadian air service, particularly in the northern regions still untouched by railroads and highways.

An encouraging push to the promotion of air flight came with the establishment in 1924 of the Royal Canadian Air Force. In addition to its military duties, the RCAF helped in fighting forest fires, assisted the Royal Canadian Mounted Police, inspected coastal fisheries, participated in weather studies and engaged in aerial photography.

Some of the first endeavours in Canadian commercial flying were related to the transport of mail between cities. These operations were handicapped in the beginning by a lack of suitable airports, weather forecasts and wireless communication. In some regions, too, high mountains formed barriers for planes lacking the power to rise above certain altitudes.

Undoubtedly the most colourful flyers of early days were the amazing bush pilots who have found their place in Canadian legend. These daring men flew planes fitted with floats in summer and skis in winter. Their landing strips were the waters and ice of countless wilderness lakes dotted across the North. Their cargoes were everything from flour and sleigh dogs to coffee pots and drilling machines.

It was these bush pilots who carried prospectors into the Canadian Shield and brought isolated mining camps supplies, equipment and machinery.

Bush pilots had to be instinctive flyers, navigating dangerous courses

In the 1920's thousands of square miles of Northern Canada were unmapped and virtually unknown. Here and there were isolated settlements of Indians or Eskimos, mining camps, and trading posts, accessible only by canoe or dog team. The daring bush pilots of the postwar years were the link between these communities and the rest of Canada. Without them, little development of the North would have taken place. Flying with primitive navigational instruments and often without charts or guides and without radio equipment, these men had to be resourceful and ingenious merely to survive. Rivers and lakes usually provided the landing strips; in winter the plane replaced its pontoons with skis. Winter flying had its peculiar problems. On overnight stopovers, the oil had to be drained from the engine and re-heated over a stove or primus, such as seen here, before starting the engine next morning. The engine itself was carefully heated with a gasoline fired blowtorch. Although improved planes and charts made bush flying less hazardous by the 1930's, to these aerial "voyageurs," danger was always an inescapable part of the job.

by their own good judgment, sense of direction and accumulated knowledge of northern geography. They flew, as they said themselves, "by the seat of their pants." They met great difficulties and improvised solutions to the most puzzling problems.

**Entertainment**    Perhaps as a reaction against the grim days of war, people of the 1920's were ready to be amused and entertained, and a steady supply of entertainment appeared to fill the need. Among the most popular of the available pleasures were the motion pictures which came from the American studios in Hollywood. The first "silent pictures" flickered unsteadily and showed actors performing in a very artificial way, but they did have movement, excitement, romance, adventure and humour.

**Radio**    At the same time as movies were attracting mass attention in theatres, the radio emerged as the most popular home entertainment.

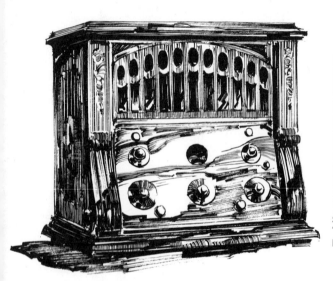

No single product of the postwar decade enjoyed a more brilliant success than radio. From its beginning as a barely audible plaything listened to by determined hobbyists, it grew within ten years into an entertainment giant. In its early days attemps were made to keep programs free of advertising, but this soon proved to be a lost cause, and commercial sponsorship of the broadcasting began its long ascendancy. Shown here is a 1924 RCA Radiola X, a table model in a mahogany cabinet, powered by dry batteries and selling for approximately $250. The advertisement reads: "Tune in! Turn the knob and pick your programme out of hundreds — all clear — loud — and *real* with Radiola X."

During the war a means of communication known as "wireless telephony" had been developed, chiefly to transmit messages from ship to shore. The system was adapted for broadcasting news, sporting events, music, lectures, plays and other items of interest.

The first really useful receiving sets for use at home came in bulky, heavy, wooden cases fitted with big knobs, dials, switches, and sometimes earphones. The quality of sound was rather poor and frequently interrupted by "static" squeaks, groans and squawks caused by atmospheric interference.

With the opening of public broadcasting stations and the improvement of radio receiving sets, radio listening became a favourite evening pastime. The most exciting radio programs of the 1920's were American. Comedy programs were especially appealing. Radio characters like "Amos n' Andy" were followed each week by eager audiences. Equally well known were such performers as Eddie Cantor, the comedian-vocalist, and Rudy Vallee, a singer of popular songs and many others.

In time, the Canadian government became concerned by what seemed to be an ever increasing "Americanization" of the Canadian people through radio broadcasting. A Canadian Radio Commission was established in 1932 to regulate Canadian broadcasting by maintaining Canadian control and Canadian character. The Canadian Broadcasting Corporation was established by Parliament in 1936. The newly formed CBC was given authority to establish a chain of radio stations across Canada and to regulate all broadcasting operations. *Founding of the CBC*

Popular music of the period took an original turn with the introduction of "jazz," a musical form originating among the musicians of New Orleans, with its roots in the music of the American blacks. *The Jazz Age*

And to accompany the new rhythm of jazz, came such energetic dances as the "Black Bottom" and the "Charleston."

In painting, the work of the Group of Seven caused great excitement. These Canadian artists emphasized the unique features of Canada — its mountains, cities and countryside. Rich colours, clear light and strong outlines characterized their style. Canadians began to appreciate and buy Canadian art. *Group of Seven*

## SUMMARY — SECTION 9

Canada began the twentieth century as a relatively prosperous country with great promise, but still lacking the necessary unity and cohesion. The nation was reaching for complete independence and equal status with

Britain within the structure of the British Empire. In spite of a few minor disputes, Canada was on good terms with its powerful neighbour, the United States.

Prime Minister Laurier was defeated in the election of 1911 and was succeeded by the Conservative leader, Robert Borden. The new Prime Minister soon became alarmed by the rising military power of Germany and increasing tension between the European alliances: Germany, Austria-Hungary and Italy on one side; Britain, France and Russia on the other.

World War I began in 1914 when German troops invaded Belgium on their way towards France. Canada and other members of the Empire rallied quickly to the support of Britain. Canada was at war.

When the war began a feeling of unity and determination spread across Canada, as political and regional differences were set aside. A huge, military camp was established at Valcartier, Quebec, and thousands of willing recruits poured into this centre. In less than two months the 1st Canadian Division was on its way overseas.

In Europe what had begun as a conflict of movement settled down into grim, trench warfare along a north-south line known as the **Western Front**. Men died of disease, bullet wounds and bursting shells. They were mowed down by the thousands during savage attacks across the ravaged land between enemy trenches.

The war at sea was just as grim. The British Royal Navy hunted down scattered enemy units and kept the main mass of the German naval force bottled up in the North Sea, enforcing a blockade on Germany. Nevertheless, German submarines were a serious threat to Allied war vessels and merchant ships carrying food and war materials. German torpedoes sank many unprotected ships.

By February, 1915, Canadian troops were in France. In battles at Ypres, St. Julien, the Somme and others, they gained a high reputation as courageous, tough assault forces.

Meanwhile at home the government was experiencing difficulties in supplying the enormous requirements of arms, equipment, food stocks and men needed in the war effort. Some military men and leaders in government were unhappy because Canada and other members of the Empire still had no real voice in the direction of war affairs. Army officers declared that the Ross rifle used by our men in France was an inefficient weapon. The anger in Quebec when Borden introduced conscription led to great tension and almost tore the nation apart.

The European adversaries fought in the air, a form of combat unknown in previous wars. In the early stages the Germans used huge gas-filled airships, the Zeppelins, for bombing raids on Britain. As the war proceeded, however, the cumbersome airship gave way to small, speedy airplanes fitted with light bombs and machine-guns. Many young Canadians became skilled pilots in the Royal Air Force and the Royal Naval Air Service, winning high respect for their skill and bravery. Before the end of the war almost one-third of the pilots in the British flying services were from Canada.

The situation was difficult for the Allies along the **Eastern Front**, where Russians were fighting the Germans. Long-simmering discontent within Russia finally burst into revolution, toppling the Tsar and leading to the Communist government. Russia dropped out of the war.

During an Allied offensive in 1917, Canadian troops took a leading part in the Battle of Vimy Ridge, capturing a well-fortified elevated position from the Germans.

During 1917 the United States entered the war on the side of the Allies. In the spring of 1918 Germany launched heavy offensives along the Western Front, fearing the growing strength of the American military effort. The German forces succeeded in reaching a point just forty miles from Paris.

But at this point the Allied Supreme Commander, Marshal Foch, began a series of counterattacks, using light tanks and masses of American troops. The tide of war was turning. Foch kept up steady pressure on the Germans, keeping them off balance with attacks on numerous points.

At 11:00 A.M. on November, 1918, Marshal Foch and German representatives gathered to sign the Armistice terms decided upon by the Allied nations. World War I was over.

During the course of 1919 a peace treaty known as the **Treaty of Versailles** was arranged and the **League of Nations** was established to help keep world peace.

Canadians came out of World War I with fresh confidence, expecting that they were entering a new era of prosperity. Unfortunately, during a period of readjustment, unemployment and hardship developed. Discontent increased among war veterans and others lacking jobs. Farmers were unhappy when the over-supply of agricultural products caused prices to fall.

The Liberals won the election of 1921 and William Lyon Mackenzie King became the new Prime Minister.

The difficult economic problems of the years directly after World War I slowly gave way to a period of prosperity, during which industry, mining and the development of hydro-electric power grew. It was a lively time, during which Canadians fell in love with the automobile, watched Hollywood movies and listened intently to radio programs. Jazz was the new popular music, and in the field of painting The Group of Seven caused great excitement.

# 10

## THE GREAT DEPRESSION AND WORLD WAR II

Reaching for equal status with Britain ■ The Empire ■ The British Commonwealth of Nations ■ The market crash of 1929 ■ The speculators ■ The Great Depression ■ The Hungry Thirties in Canada ■ Prime Minister R.B. Bennett ■ J.S. Woodsworth and the CCF ■ William Aberhart and Social Credit ■ Maurice Duplessis and the Union Nationale ■ World-wide despair ■ Japan ■ Invasion of Manchuria ■ Italy and Benito Mussolini ■ Invasion of Ethiopia ■ Germany ■ Weimar Republic ■ Adolf Hitler and the Nazi Party ■ Nazi propaganda ■ Hitler's rise to power ■ Germany rearms ■ Invasions of the Rhineland, Austria and Czechoslovakia ■ Partnership of the dictators ■ Invasion of Poland ■ Britain and France declare war ■ Invasion of the Low Countries ■ Rescue at Dunkirk■ France surrenders ■ Winston Churchill as Prime Minister ■ Canadian contribution to the war ■ Battle of Britain ■ Defeat of the Italians in North Africa ■ German invasion of Russia ■ Japanese attack on Pearl Harbour ■ The Dieppe Raid ■ Americans and British defeat "The Desert Fox" ■ Allied invasion of Sicily ■ The Italian campaign ■ Allied invasion of France ■ Germany surrenders ■ End of war in the South Pacific ■ Atomic bombing of Japan ■ World-wide conditions when peace came ■ Formation of the United Nations ■ Structure of the United Nations.

# 44.  Depression and Dictatorships

Reaching for equal status

FOR YEARS CANADIAN political leaders had been suggesting a more significant role for the nation within the framework of the British Empire. Canadian experiences in World War I — the battlefield accomplishments of Canadian service men; Canada's role in peace making — further strengthened determination to achieve equal status with Great Britain.

During the 1920's a vigorous thrust for independent Canadian action developed under the leadership of Prime Minister William Lyon Mackenzie King. When tension arose in Turkey, Britain requested that the Dominions offer support if war broke out. The Dominions were not consulted; King refused to guarantee that Canada would give aid without first discussing the matter in Parliament. Canada would not automatically support British foreign policy.

In 1923 the Prime Minister insisted that an agreement between Canada and the United States regulating fishing on the Pacific coast (the Halibut Treaty) be signed by the Canadian Minister of Marine and Fisheries. When Britain requested that the British ambassador to Washington sign as well, King refused. It was clear that Mackenzie King was determined to bring Canada forward as an independent nation, with the power to negotiate and sign treaties.

Another step forward on the road to Canadian autonomy was the appointment in 1927 of Vincent Massey as the first Canadian Minister to the United States. Canada now had demonstrated its power to appoint its own representatives in foreign countries.

Following World War I a new relationship between Great Britain and the self-governing members of the Empire — Canada, South Africa, Australia and New Zealand — was evolving. A new organization was needed to replace the Empire, one in which nations would be bound together in mutual co-operation.

Through the famous *Statute of Westminster*, passed by the British Parliament in 1931, the self-governing Dominions of Canada, Australia, New Zealand, South Africa, and the Irish Free State could pass any legislation they wished, without regard to English law. No act of the British Parliament would extend to the Dominions, unless the Dominion requested it. These nations became members of the British Commonwealth of nations.

"...autonomous communities within the British Empire, equal in status, in no way subordinate one to another in any respect of their domestic or external affairs, though united by a common allegiance to the Crown and freely associated as members of the British Commonwealth of nations..."

Formerly the Canadian Governor-General had been both agent of the British government and representative of the Crown, but he now became simply the representative of the British Crown. After the Statute of Westminster, it was possible for the Prime Ministers of Canada and Great Britain to communicate directly and informally with one another on matters of common interest.

The process which had begun almost eighty years earlier, when Canadians had won responsible government, had been completed with the achievement of complete legislative independence. Canada was now an autonomous nation, and member of a new, unique organization, the British Commonwealth.

At the end of October, 1929, the world was rocked by news of a stock market "crash" in New York City, financial centre of the United States. The value of shares fell by the minute as bewildered stockholders saw their expected profits melting away. During the next six weeks it is probable that American investors lost more than forty billion dollars in the value of their stock holdings. And still the market fell.

Many people had speculated in the shares or stock of companies engaged in manufacturing, mining, oil production, transportation and banking. They had bought shares in the hope that prices would rise and large profits follow. The brisk demand for company shares did force a rise in prices but too often these became higher than the shares were actually worth.

When nervousness developed, too many stockholders began selling their shares at one time. Then, genuine panic set in, as everyone tried to get rid of their shares on the stock markets. It was such action that led to the "crash." A shudder of apprehension ran through the United States and rippled out across the world.

The sudden collapse of the New York stock market signalled the climax of a serious financial situation that had been building up in North America during the boom years of the late 1920's. It resulted from no single cause but from several which in combination brought about the Great Depression of the 1930's.

**The Great Depression**

One cause of the Great Depression had been overproduction. Manufacturing, encouraged by prosperity, had expanded to a level where more goods were being produced than could be sold at home or abroad. In the course of time such oversupply could only lead to falling prices, cutbacks in manufacturing production and the layoff of men employed in factories, stores and warehouses.

Prosperity had encouraged risky financial practices. Because work was plentiful and wages high, many families had bought new things like houses, furniture, clothing, radios, electrical appliances, summer cottages, boats and automobiles, on credit, and so burdened themselves with heavy instalment payments and house mortgages. They believed that there was no need to worry, that good times would go on forever.

But good times did not go on forever — during the Great Depression, when unemployment became widespread, many people had no money to keep up with instalment payments and big house mortgages. Families lost homes, automobiles and furniture.

In Canada, the period of depression was known as "The Hungry Thirties" and with good reason. There was much unemployment at home and a severe loss of trade abroad. As world trade fell off, the prices of all Canadian staple goods — newsprint, metals, lumber — fell drastically. Canada's national income from exports fell 67% between 1929 and 1933. The Canadian wheat farmer was especially hard

**The Hungry Thirties in Canada**

In the West the depression was made even more disastrous by the effects of prolonged drought. Lack of rain turned the once prosperous wheatfields into dust bowls, as weakened crops succumbed to the effects of grasshoppers, Russian thistle and wheat rush. Whole towns and communities went bankrupt as jobs almost seemed to blow away along with the topsoil. Often driven by high winds, the dust seemed to be everywhere. It got into the houses and formed little drifts around doors and windows. It got into the food, the furniture, the beds, and lay as a thin film on everything indoors.

hit. A world surplus of wheat, plus new high tariffs in the United States and Europe combined to lower the price of wheat from $1.60 to 38¢ per bushel. To further the despair in the prairies, severe droughts wiped out crops. In general, the effects of the depression were not devastating in the West.

Throughout the nation factories closed, railway profits dropped, seaports became quiet, building construction slowed and unemployment reached a frightening level.

The times were grim. People not getting food from government relief offices bought the least expensive kinds they could purchase. They patched their old clothing and worn shoes. Furniture was sacrificed and fine old trees cut down to provide firewood to heat homes. Some farmers, unable to pay the cost of gasoline, travelled in what were called "Bennett Buggies" (named for the Prime Minister of the early 1930's. Thousands and thousands of single, jobless men moved about Canada, travelling on freight trains, in an endless search for employment.

**Prime Minister R.B. Bennett**

William Lyon Mackenzie King did not seem to realize the seriousness of the situation and insisted that the federal government had no legal right to help the victims of the depression.

When asked in the House of Commons if his Liberal government would grant aid to provincial governments for unemployment relief, he replied:

"With respect to giving monies out of the federal treasury to any Tory government in this country for these alleged unemployment purposes, with these governments situated as they are today, with policies diametrically opposed to those of this government, I would not give them a five-cent piece."

In the election of 1930, King was defeated by the Conservative leader, Richard Bedford Bennett. The new Prime Minister, a wealthy lawyer, believed prosperity could be recovered by protecting Canadian business and industry from the competition of foreign imports.

Bennett negotiated an Empire trade arrangement in 1932 by which Great Britain and the Dominions agreed to give "preferential" trade treatment to certain products manufactured and grown within the Empire. As part of this agreement, Canada was to receive special treatment in connection with the export of food, lumber and metals, while at the same time Britain was to receive special treatment in connection with the export of numerous manufactured products. The

# UNEMPLOYMENT IN CANADA, UNITED STATES AND BRITAIN, 1929-1943

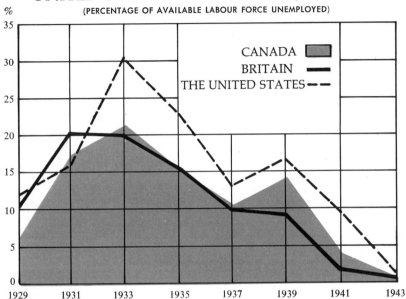

(PERCENTAGE OF AVAILABLE LABOUR FORCE UNEMPLOYED)

CANADA
BRITAIN
THE UNITED STATES

new trading arrangement would be valuable during the coming years, but it failed to solve the problem of the depression.

Shocked by the desperate circumstances of the 1930's, and the failure of the government to improve conditions, many Canadians, especially in the most severely hit regions, began to question the existing political parties. Such feeling led to the formation of new political parties with definite proposals concerning the management of provincial and national affairs.

A new political party, national in scope, appeared with the birth of the Co-operative Commonwealth Federation or CCF. Its leader, J. S. Woodsworth, an idealistic Methodist clergyman from the West, hoped to develop a powerful party organization supported by farming and labour groups.

**J.S. Woodsworth and the CCF**

The CCF was devoted to seeking security and justice for the common man. It proposed that the national government should take over nation-wide operations in banking, transportation and electric power. The party believed that the government should support agriculture and conservation, as well as an extensive program of social welfare. The party proposed that public works projects, like slum clearance and bringing electricity to rural areas, should begin immediately to provide jobs and improve living conditions.

The fact that labour groups failed to give full-hearted support to the CCF movement was a keen disappointment to J.S. Woodsworth. The party was accused by some of being a Communist organization. In fact, its policies were very similar to those of the British Labour Party.

The party explained its goals in The Regina Manifesto.

"...to replace the present capitalist system, with its inherent injustice and inhumanity, by a social order from which the domination and exploitation of one class by another will be eliminated, in which economic planning will supersede unregulated private enterprise and competition, and in which genuine democratic self-government, based upon economic equality will be possible."

The CCF did not gain enough parliamentary seats to control the government in Ottawa, but some of its ideas caused serious thought across the nation. Indeed, in future years both the Liberal and Conservative parties were to adopt proposals made in the 1930's by J.S. Woodsworth and his party followers. Out of the CCF grew the present-day New Democratic Party.

**William Aberhart and Social Credit**     In Alberta, William Aberhart, a Calgary teacher and radio evangelist, founded the Social Credit Party. Aberhart maintained that the depression could be beaten if citizens were given more buying power. He would, he said, provide all Albertans with a monthly dividend of $25.00 in order to survive the hardships of the period. In addition, he proposed major changes in banking and financial operations across Canada. The impoverished Alberta farmers responded to his ideas and in 1935 swept the Social Credit Party to power in the provincial elections. Since issuing money and controlling banks were responsibilities of the federal government, Premier Aberhart could do little to put his theories to work in Alberta. His party did elect a small number of members to parliament, but Social Credit did not develop into a major force on the national scene.

In Quebec, a new party, the Union Nationale, led by a clever, strong-willed lawyer, Maurice Duplessis won a sweeping victory in the provincial election of 1936. Although originally proposing a reform program, Duplessis instead became a strong supporter of Quebec's rights and, with his enormous power, put down any opposition to his government. His 25-year rule in Quebec held back much economic and cultural development within the province.

*Maurice Duplessis and the Union Nationale*

The depression was worldwide, causing feelings of despair and a sense of desperation in many nations. The unsettled, disturbing conditions led many people to support dangerous political ideas because these seemed to hold some chance of bringing a return to prosperity.

*Worldwide despair*

Japan, a small country, with a large population and a highly industrialized economy, was especially hard hit by the disruptions of the depression. Even in the 1920's some Japanese businessmen had looked longingly at China—both as a source of much needed raw materials and as a huge market for Japanese goods. Now many Japanese army officers favoured this plan to extend the territory and power of Japan and, by the early 1930's their influence in Japanese affairs had grown strong.

*Japan*

In September, 1931, Japan invaded the province of Manchuria in northeastern China.

*Invasion of Manchuria*

Outraged by this sudden invasion of her lands, China appealed to the League of Nations to take strong action against the Japanese aggressors. But the League members discussed the matter for several years and in the end did no more than send off protests to the government of Japan. In 1933, Japan withdrew from the League. It is not surprising that these weak, bumbling actions caused a worldwide loss of confidence in the ability of the League of Nations to deal with an aggressive action.

Italy, by the 1930's, was firmly under the control of Benito Mussolini and his Fascist Party. The stocky, square-jawed Mussolini was an all-powerful dictator hailed by Italians as *Il Duce* (the Leader). Political opposition was eliminated — only the Fascist Party was permitted. The press was controlled and opposition newspapers banned. The government's policy of secrecy, with its network of spies and informers, silenced any criticism, often by violence.

*Italy and Benito Mussolini*

During the early years of his rule, Mussolini, through his complete

The fashion emphasis in the twenties was on "functionalism," seen in the increasing simplicity of all designs and goods of the period, whether buildings, furniture, household appliances or anything else. The "straight line" dress of (1) was "functional," but also daring for those days: dresses became shorter than at any previous period in western history and also bared the entire arm, something unknown since ancient times. Note the artificially lowered waistline, very typical of this fashion period. These short dresses were excellent for dancing to a step that was all the rage at this time — "the Charleston." Another garment that is closely connected with the history of this period is (2) the raccoon skin coat, which signified the independence and the desire to be different so characteristic of the twenties' generation. The early thirties saw a return of a more conservative skirt length and of the waistline to its normal position. (3) is a "costume suit" of 1936, the overcoat and jacket both being of matching colours, whereas the skirt was made of contrasting material.

control of the economy, was able to achieve many national improvements, such as the construction of power dams, highways, factories and schools. Health services were expanded, swamps drained to provide farming land and homes erected for workers.

Il Duce, nevertheless, dreamed of doing much more. He saw himself as the supreme ruler of a mighty Italian state rivalling the glories of the old Roman Empire. When the hardships of depression arrived in Italy, Mussolini realized that he had to distract the attention of his people from their economic misfortunes before they became restless and dissatisfied with their own government.

Mussolini had seen the ease with which the Japanese had invaded Manchuria and the lack of any punishment by the League of Nations. It seemed, therefore, that it would be quite safe for Italy to seize an African colony. The ideal victim, appeared to be the unprotected nation of Ethiopia, where the Italians had suffered a humiliating defeat in 1896. **Invasion of Ethiopia**

In 1935, Mussolini hurried ships, troops and arms to Somaliland a neighbouring Italian colony, and began active preparations for the coming invasion. In October, without declaring war, the heavily armed battalions, tanks, artillery and airplanes crossed the border to confront the poorly armed forces of Ethiopia.

Haile Selassie, Emperor of Ethiopia, appealed to the League of Nations but, again, members of that organization did little more than discuss, argue and impose a useless embargo. The embargo meant that league members would not sell certain goods to Italy. But the goods which were embargoed were not important to Italy's economy.

By early 1936 Ethiopia was under Italian control, and the valiant Haile Selassie was in exile in London.

Germany's economy and political institutions were shattered by World War I. Some disillusioned Germans looked to the example of the Russian revolution as a hope for the future. A small group of radicals, calling themselves "Spartacists," worked to overthrow the government and establish a Communist system in Germany. The Spartacists were bloodily suppressed in 1919 by organizations representing industrialists and landowners. **Germany**

The Weimar Republic was the name of the democratic government

Weimar
Republic

which ran Germany in the 1920's. Unfortunately, after a few brief years of success, it failed. The downfall of the Weimar Republic was largely due to a devastating period of inflation in the early 1920's, and the depression, both of which were blamed on the government. Of all European countries, Germany was hardest hit by the depression. Unemployment reached six million and at least half the population suffered extreme poverty.

The middle class was losing faith in the economic and political system. They feared the solutions proposed by the Communists, and were attracted by the promises of a new party and its leader. Up to this time few middle-class Germans had paid much attention to Adolf Hitler, the forty-year-old leader of the National Socialist German Workers' Party, more commonly known as the *Nazi* Party. His aggressive, swaggering followers believed in military might and a strong Germany and were violently opposed to democracy and communism.

Adolf
Hitler
and the
Nazi
Party

Adolf Hitler was a poorly educated, unbalanced person, and a bitter misfit. As a young man, he had drifted about Austria and Germany barely supporting himself by such odd jobs as painting postcards, shovelling snow and carrying luggage in railroad stations. During World War I he had been decorated several times for bravery but had never risen above the rank of lance-corporal. He was unpopular, self-centred and argumentative.

Hitler and his party had a violent hatred of the Jews. Jews had been persecuted in Europe since the Middle Ages. During the nineteenth century, except in Russia, persecution had declined and was replaced by less vicious forms of discrimination. The Nazis blamed the Jews (who made up less than one per cent of the German population) for defeat in World War I; for the depression; for plotting to take over the country, and so on. Through the use of propaganda and shrill speeches, Hitler and his party roused the emotions of millions of Germans. It seemed an easy answer to the humiliation of the war, to the economic turmoil — the Jews were responsible. Millions of Germans accepted this conclusion.

Nazi
propaganda

Adolf Hitler had remarkable speaking powers and the ability to whip up the emotions of his listeners. He was the master of the "Big Lie." He guessed, correctly, that sweeping lies, repeated over and

The furniture of this period takes on a new simplicity.   Lines are long and low—
the emphasis now being on the horizontal rather than the vertical.   On sofas, lounge
chairs and beds, the legs which were so typical of period furniture are eliminated
and these pieces sit on a pedestal base reaching straight to the floor.   A conscious
attempt was made to eliminate all unnecessary decoration and to leave the basic
lines and shape of the furniture clean and uncluttered in appearance.   New materials such as metal, glass, cork and even plastic, are in increasing use.

over again, would impress and eventually convince the public. His
organization of propaganda was highly skilled.

Realizing that the troubled conditions in Germany provided an excellent opportunity for seizing power, Hitler energetically promoted

his own ideas for government. In this effort he was supported by many wealthy men of industry who feared communism and who thought they might use the Nazi leader for their own purposes. They did not realize their mistake until it was too late.

**Hitler's rise to power**

In 1933 Hitler, held a strong position in the German Reichstag (parliament) but his party had not won a majority in the election. By plotting and using force, he managed to achieve the necessary majority. He was appointed Chancellor of Germany, a position similar to that of a president.

Making swift use of his newly won authority, Hitler proceeded in ruthless fashion to dominate the German people. He abolished other political parties, removed the right of free speech and took over control of all things that might be used to influence the thinking of the public: schools, universities, newspapers, books, radio broadcasting motion pictures. Bands of brown-shirted Nazi hoodlums known as the SS employed strong-arm tactics against any persons who dared to protest the action of the party.

In spite of their loss of personal freedom, the Germans remained spellbound under the fiery oratory and the driving force of their Nazi leader.

**Germany rearms**

By the autumn of 1933, Adolf Hitler was busily engaged in the military rearmament of Germany, an operation which was in direct defiance of the Treaty of Versailles. In 1935 he announced compulsory military service and the establishment of a new air force.

Great Britain, France, Canada and other nations of the world were aware of Hitler's threatening activities but none took determined steps to intervene. Many believed that the possibility of Germany becoming another Communist country was worse than Germany under the dictatorship of Hitler. Many, remembering the horrors of World War I, were prepared to make many compromises, if peace could be maintained.

In the British Parliament, only Winston Churchill and several colleagues spoke of the rising danger. On one occasion Churchill said, "We hear the deep repeated stroke of the alarm bell. Will it be a call to action or the knell of our race and fame?"

# 45.  *World War II*

ENCOURAGED BY THE lack of bold countermeasures by other nations, Hitler occupied the Rhineland in 1936 and took over Austria and Czechoslovakia during 1938.

Realizing that open conflict with other nations was inevitable, he signed a treaty with Mussolini, a treaty by which the two dictators promised to support one another when war broke out. A month later, Japan joined the alliance. In a very surprising move, Hitler signed a friendship pact with the Soviet Union, which included a secret agreement to divide up eastern Europe between the two countries.

On September 1, 1939, Hitler invaded Poland with a massive striking force of infantry, tanks, armoured cars and troop carriers supported by bombers and fighting planes. This new form of mechanized warfare requiring close coordination between tanks and airplanes, caused widespread confusion and terror. It was known as *Blitzkrieg* ("lightning war").

On September 3, France and Britain declared war. The members of the Commonwealth rallied in support. In contrast to 1914, Canada was no longer bound to act automatically with Britain but had freedom of choice. The debate in Parliament was brief, and the vote almost unanimous. As Mackenzie King explained "It is for all of us on this continent to do our part to save its privileged position by helping others . . . " On September 10, King declared war on behalf of Canada. World War II had begun.

There was very little fighting on land in western Europe during the

361

These three planes are fighter aircraft of World War II. (1) the famous Supermarine Spitfire, was probably the finest and the most widely used of all British fighter planes. Its design was begun in 1935 and by 1945 the plane had gone through twenty-two versions. The later models were armed with cannon and machine-guns mounted in the wings and flew at about 400 m.p.h. The outstanding German fighter of the war was the Focke-Wulf 190A 3 (2). A very fast, heavily armed plane, it carried machine-guns in both the wings and the fuselage and also two 20-mm. wing cannon. The Spitfire and the Focke-Wulf more or less exhausted the limits of propeller-powered flight, and by 1940, Italy, Germany and Britain were designing jet aircraft. The first combat jet was (3) the German Messerschmitt ME 262. Had Adolf Hitler not delayed production of this aircraft for six months, it might have regained German mastery of the skies over Europe in 1944 and 1945. The two turbo-jet engines, slung beneath a slender, swept wing and fitted to a beautifully streamlined fuselage, gave it speeds of over 560 m.p.h. — at least 120 m.p.h. faster than most Allied fighter planes of that time. Its ejector seat, radar, rocket armament, power-operated controls and special parachute harness (with oxygen supply attached) for bailing out at great heights made it the most advanced aircraft of its time. Some four hundred ME 262s saw action in the closing months of the war, but they were crippled by crucial shortages of spare parts after their production plant was destroyed by Allied bombing. In addition, Allied fighter planes shot up their airfields day and night and many ME 262s were destroyed while landing to refuel.

winter of 1939 and into the early spring of 1940. Britain began a blockade of Germany, as they had in World War I. They hoped to stop all German shipping in the North Sea.

In May, 1940, Hitler's forces smashed into Denmark and Norway. Next, the Germans invaded neutral Holland and Belgium, overwhelming their armies within days.

**Invasion of the Low Countries**

The Germans then moved into northern France, going around the massive defence works known as the Maginot Line which France had built along its eastern border. Allied troops were pushed back to the harbour of Dunkirk on the English Channel, trapped between the enemy and the sea. Then came the "miracle of Dunkirk." Hundreds of boats from southeastern England sped across the Channel to pick up the troops on the French coast. Naval ships, tugs, ferries, cabin cruisers, fishing boats, open motor boats, scows and dinghies all took part in this bold venture. The heroic rescue was a magnificent success in terms of saving human lives, but the loss of war materials was a serious matter. Behind in France lay piles of supplies, equipment and arms.

**Rescue at Dunkirk**

In June, 1940, the new French President, Marshal Pétain, signed a humiliating peace with Adolf Hitler. France officially dropped out of World War II. But General Charles de Gaulle refused to recognize the surrender, or the puppet Vichy government set up by the Nazis and headed by Pétain. He, along with French troops evacuated from Dunkirk, went into exile in Britain. At first, De Gaulle's Free French National Committee had few followers, as most Frenchmen were too discouraged to resist the Nazis. As the war progressed, members of the French overseas empire recognized De Gaulle's authority. The Vichy government grew more and more unpopular and the French Underground developed strength. By 1943 De Gaulle was to be acknowledged as commander in chief by almost all French Resistance forces. But in the summer of 1940 Britain and the Commonwealth were left to fight on alone.

**France surrenders**

Fortunately, at this desperate time Winston Churchill had become Prime Minister of Great Britain. The new Prime Minister had gained fame as a soldier, journalist, and parliamentary leader. Churchill was a highly skilled speaker who inspired the nation with his ringing words.

**Winston Churchill as Prime Minister**

When it became obvious that the next step might be the German invasion of Britain itself, Churchill delivered his famous speech of defiance in which he said:

"We shall fight on the seas and oceans, we shall fight with growing confidence and with growing strength in the air, we shall defend our island, whatever the cost may be, we shall fight on the beaches, we shall fight on the landing grounds, we shall fight in the fields and in the streets, we shall fight in the hills; we shall never surrender . . . . "

**Canadian contribution to the war**

When war had broken out, Canada had not been prepared. The permanent army was made up of four thousand men, and the air force and navy were just minor branches of the military force. Britain and Canada agreed that the Canadian contribution would be mainly providing war supplies and food and special air and sea services. But as country after country fell to the Nazis, this limited role was to expand dramatically.

**Air training**

Canada, having miles of open spaces and being located so far from the battlefields, was a natural choice for the home of the British Commonwealth Air Training Plan. At sixty-four flying schools across Canada were trained tens of thousands of pilots, navigators, gunners and radio operators from Commonwealth nations and, as the war went on, from other Allied countries.

**The Canadian Army**

The first Canadian troops landed in Britain in December, 1939. This 1st Division was soon joined by the 2nd Division. The Canadian commander, General McNaughton, insisted that his men be kept together, rather than spread amongst the Allies in various battle areas.

Mackenzie King had promised Parliament that the war would be fought by volunteers; conscription would not be used. However, as casualties mounted during the Allied invasion of France in 1944, King was forced to propose a Conscription Act, which sent 13,000 Canadians to fight in Europe. The support of Louis St. Laurent, King's leading minister from Quebec, contributed to lessen somewhat the hostility of French Canada towards conscription. And, most important, the crisis was less severe than King had feared because the war was drawing to an end.

**The Canadian Navy**

The Royal Canadian Navy expanded from seventeen to over nine

WORLD WAR II (1939-1941)

| | Allied or occupied by Germany | | Conquered by Germany |
| :-- | :-- | :-- | :-- |
| | Neutral | | |

hundred ships, more than a third of which were combat ships. But the main duty of the navy was to act as convoy escorts, protecting ships sailing between North America and Britain and Europe. In the final days of conflict, Canadians escorted eighty per cent of the ships crossing the North Atlantic. Canadians sailors also served in the Mediterranean, off the Aleutian Islands and in other scattered areas. From a prewar strength of five thousand, the navy grew to over ninety thousand.

Beginning in July, 1940, the German Luftwaffe engaged the Royal Air Force in a series of mammoth aerial battles, designed to destroy British air power and allow the Luftwaffe to dominate the skies over England. Throughout "The Battle of Britain," as this engagement is called, losses on both sides were heavy, but German losses were especially so, and eventually the Luftwaffe turned its attention to a new target — the British cities. Throughout the fall and winter massive bombing raids were made against most of the major cities of England, with London, the coastal ports, and the manufacturing towns in the Midlands taking the brunt of the attacks. From September 7 and for every night but one for eight weeks, 200 or more planes bombed London alone, shattering docks, factories, houses, schools, railways and historic buildings. On November 14, in the worst single raid of the battle, the city of Coventry was hit by 500 planes, causing terrible devastation to the city's centre. Despite the injuries, casualties, and widespread destruction, people carried on. Later in the war the Allied air forces carried out assaults against German cities that equalled or surpassed in fury and intensity the raids of the Battle of Britain.

With the fall of France, Hitler had hoped that Great Britain might be frightened into surrender. It soon became apparent, however, that the British people under the leadership of Winston Churchill would stand firmly and fight.

Hitler then turned the full power of his air force, the Luftwaffe, against Britain, believing that continued bombing would break British will to continue. But the brave fighting of the Royal Air Force (which included two Canadian squadrons) met the challenge. Tons of German bombs fell, searchlights stabbed the darkness, sirens screamed, people rushed to air raid shelters, anti-aircraft guns thundered and bombs levelled whole blocks of buildings. This was the Battle of Britain.

**Battle of Britain**

With outstanding calmness the British people carried on during those terrible days, still confident that victory would come in the end. The Luftwaffe lost hundreds of aircraft to the Commonwealth pursuit planes and anti-aircraft guns. The losses were so severe that Hitler was forced to suspend his plans for invading England. Nazi Germany had received its first defeat — delivered by the RAF.

Mussolini, still dreaming of a new Roman Empire, embarked on adventures of his own. He felt confident of his own power because he had armies in Europe, a strong fleet in the Mediterranean and troops in North Africa. His first military campaign, the invasion of Greece, was stopped decisively by the tough Greek troops. His armies were forced back into Albania. He attempted to take over North Africa from Egypt and the Sudan, but the torpedoing of several large naval craft by the British and the strong offensives launched by the British general, Wavell, in North Africa defeated his ambitions.

**Defeat of the Italians in North Africa**

Rumania, Hungary and Bulgaria were taken under Nazi "protection." Hitler was free to make extensive demands on the powerless countries, in return for protecting them from the Soviet Union. The

**Nazis dominate the Balkans**

next victim was Yugoslavia which had been created in 1919 by joining together various national groups. The state had been torn by ethnic rivalry and bitterness for years. When the weakened government agreed to come under Nazi domination, a group of nationalist Serbs took over, deposed the ruler and renounced the arrangement with Hitler. Within ten days, the German tank divisions were in position. It took the Nazi Blitzkrieg eleven days to destroy the Yugoslav Army. The tanks then rolled down to Athens and the Greeks soon signed a peace treaty. Hitler held the Balkans under his control. He was ready to turn his attention to the east.

**German invasion of Russia**

In June, 1941, one month after Mussolini's defeat in North Africa, Adolf Hitler shocked the world by invading the vast territory of his ally, Russia. During the dry months of summer and early autumn German armoured forces made such rapid progress across the country that by November advance units were within thirty-five miles of Moscow. But with the coming of cool weather and heavy rains, the advance was slowed.

Hitler had counted on his Blitzkrieg leading to rapid victory. His men were not equipped or clothed for the approaching winter. By December, snow blocked the routes of advance, troops suffered from frostbite and the long German supply lines were a shambles. Hundreds of Germans died of starvation or froze to death. Hitler had also under-rated the tough, determined Russian Army and the brave spirit of the Russian people.

**Japanese attack on Pearl Harbour**

The second great shock of 1941 came on December 7, when Japanese planes struck suddenly at Pearl Harbour, an American naval base in the Hawaiian Islands. This bombing attack, combined with the German invasion of Russia, changed the nature of the conflict. Within twenty-four hours of the disaster at Pearl Harbour the United States declared war. Now Germany, Italy and Japan faced the combined strength of Britain, the Commonwealth, the United States, Russia and China.

**War in the Pacific**

During late 1941 and early 1942, conditions in the South Pacific grew more serious, as the Japanese overran Hong Kong, Thailand, Malaya, Singapore, Burma, the Philippines, the Dutch East Indies, New Guinea and a large number of islands in the western Pacific.

At the last moment, in reply to a British request, two Canadian regiments, the Royal Rifles and the Winnipeg Grenadiers had been sent to reinforce the garrison at Hong Kong. The casualty rate was enormous. Japan now held control over a million square miles with a population of more than 100,000,000. This conquest provided the Japanese with an empire rich in minerals, oil, rubber and food resources.

In order to test German land defences in Europe, the Allied Command decided, during the summer of 1942, to raid the occupied coast of France. Five thousand Canadians along with British commandos launched the surprise attack at Dieppe. The raiders battered their way ashore but their artillery and tank support was not strong enough to break through the German defences. More than 3,000 Canadians were killed, wounded or reported missing, and 1,946 Canadians were left behind as prisoners of war. This costly experiment seemed to show that the German-held coast of Europe could be successfully invaded only by an overpowering mass of men and machines.

The Dieppe Raid

In North Africa fierce, desert battles were raging between the British Eighth Army under General Montgomery and the Afrika Korps under General Rommel, "The Desert Fox." Rommel was a brilliant general, but Hitler lost interest in North Africa and did not send him the necessary reinforcements. British planes, taking off from the island of Malta, sank ships with supplies for Rommel's men. Some of these planes had Canadian crews. A British victory at El Alamein forced the Germans to retreat into Tunisia.

Americans and British defeat "The Desert Fox"

A strong invasion force of American and British troops, under the American commander General Eisenhower, landed in Morocco and Algeria. The Allies had to overcome the obstacle of the French army units in North Africa who were loyal to Pétain's Vichy government. A deal was arranged, giving a French admiral control of French Northwest Africa in return for his cooperation. Too late Hitler began to pour men and materials into North Africa. The last German and Italian soldiers in North Africa were cornered in the northeast tip of Tunisia. In May 1943 these soldiers surrendered.

Although Canada's role in the North African campaign was limited, a small number of Canadian soldiers gained valuable experience in Tunisia, with the First British Army.

The beginnings of the tremendous, present-day programmes of missile development and space research occurred in Germany in 1929 with a series of rocket experiments. At about the same time, Paul Schmidt, a German engineer, patented a design for a simplified form of jet engine known as an induction engine. These events marked the beginnings of a technology that by 1944 had put into the hands of the German High Command weapons that existed only in the minds of Allied scientists. First to appear was the V.1 (1) commonly called the "Buzz Bomb." The V.1 was just over twenty-five feet in length with a wing span of about 17-1|3 feet and a weight of two and a half tons when loaded. Its speed of 360 m.p.h. (at 2,000 feet) put it just within reach of the Allied fighter planes of 1944, the year in which this flying bomb was first used against Britain. It was launched from a fixed, inclined ramp aimed at the target zone. When over the target area (anywhere within a range of 150 miles) the engine cut off — this was predetermined and set before launching — and the bomb fell to earth. Most of these machines were directed against London, about 8,000 being successfully launched altogether. Almost 4,000 of the flying bombs were destroyed in flight by fighter craft and anti-aircraft guns or caught and brought down by defence balloons. Although only 2,240 of them actually got through to the London area (the remainder falling all over England's southeastern counties), they killed nearly 6,000 people, injured over 17,000 and damaged or destroyed nearly 75,000 buildings. It must be emphasized that the flying bomb was not a true rocket. Its motor was a form of jet called a pulse jet which alternately fired and shut off over the length of the flight. The V.2 (2) was the first of the rockets we know today. German scientists and special personnel — about 12,000 in all — had been working for many years at a huge rocket research centre on the Baltic Sea. Due to the complexity of the V.2 their work was marked by numerous failures. However, after a number of successful tests, the V.2 rocket was in mass production by 1943. This massive weapon was forty-six feet long and weighed twelve tons. Although its range of 190 miles was not much of an improvement on the V.1, it reached speeds in excess of 3,400 m.p.h. and attained heights of sixty miles or more by burning a fuel largely made up of liquid oxygen and alcohol. The V.2 took less than four minutes to reach an English target from the time of launching and was thus impossible to destroy en route. Until the launching sites were overrun and captured, more than 2,000 V2s were loosed upon southeastern England and another 2,300 against cities in liberated Europe.

**Allied invasion of Sicily**

The Allies could now proceed northward from Africa against the weaker side of the Axis defences in Europe. In the early summer of 1943 an immense fleet sailed from North African ports to invade the Italian island of Sicily. They were joined by ships from the United States carrying fresh troops, and British ships from England carrying Canadian infantry and tanks. In little more than a month, Sicily was in Allied hands. The campaign, fought in the sticky, summer heat, over hilly terrain and dusty roads, had been violent and exhausting. An outstanding Canadian unit in the Sicilian campaign had been the Nova Scotia Highlanders.

While the Sicilian campaign was still in progress, Benito Mussolini was arrested by some of his disillusioned followers. A new Italian gov-

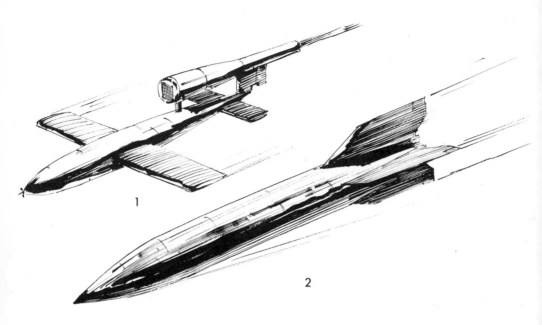

1

2

ernment sought peace and surrendered to the Allies. Italy was out of
the war.

Adolf Hitler, however, had no intention of giving up Italian terri- **The Italian**
tory. The long, boot-like peninsula formed a protective barrier for **campaign**
the land mass of central Europe. He sent German troops in to defend
Italy against the invading Allies. The Allied invasion of Italy was slow
and difficult. Rivers, mountains, bad weather and the stubborn defence of German troops held them back. Canadian soldiers captured
the town of Ortona, and established a key position in the drive up the
peninsula to Rome. Again, casualties were high in the series of bloody
battles.

The position of Hitler had greatly changed. He could not invade **Allied invasion**
Britain; the Allies held the Mediterranean Sea and were moving north- **of France**
ward into central Europe; the Russians were advancing westward. Only

1

2

In the early stages of World War II the Germans developed the use of the tank to the point of near perfection. Self-contained armoured divisions called Panzer divisions were created; operating as independent striking forces under their own leaders. A Panzer command was built around a core of 400 tanks — light, medium and heavy. To this was added a motorcycle unit, a regiment of field artillery, an anti-tank battalion, engineer battalions (bridge and road repairs), mobile supply and tank repair units, motorized brigades of infantry and a squadron of reconnaissance and dive-bomber aircraft, a total of about 3,000 vehicles to the division. Panzer strategy was simply to outflank an opponent or to probe his defences for weaknesses, using the crushing weight of tanks to smash through any weak spot discovered. Once around or through the oppostion, the tanks, followed by the rest of the division, fanned out, shooting up the remains of the defence line, blasting communication lines and creating havoc everywhere. Poland, Holland, Belgium, France and the Balkans were easily overrun largely because conventional "fixed" lines of defence were useless against the Panzer divisions. Allied armies were slow to adjust to this new concept of powerful, mobile, self-contained, armoured forces. The lesson was eventually learned, however, and as the war progressed, the Allies used heavier armour with an imagination and daring equal to that shown by the Panzers. (1) is a British Crusader Mark II of World War II, an eighteen-ton vehicle with a speed of twenty-six m.p.h. Its armament usually consisted of one two-pounder gun (too small to be effective against the normally heavier German tanks) and a 7.92-mm. machine-gun. The most famous American tank of World War II was (2) the "General Sherman." The Sherman was equipped with a power-operated, rotating turret that had a 360° field of fire and mounted a 76-mm. high-velocity gun. It also carried F.M. radio equipment. The Sherman was a medium tank and was probably overrated in terms of its total effectiveness. Its armour was too easily pierced by enemy shells and it was originally armed with a low-velocity 75-mm. gun that was relatively ineffective against such German tanks as the Mark IV. The Sherman's high silhouette presented a better-than-average target to enemy gunners.

(3) is a German Mark IV tank of World War II. Weighing twenty-three tons and mounting a long-barrelled 75-mm. gun and two machine-guns, its 300 h.p. engine

3

4

*J. MOULD*

gave it a speed of twenty-two m.p.h.   Some of the greatest contributions to World War II tank design were made by Russians, whose designs sacrificed crew comfort and safety to increase fighting performance.   Russian tanks made a brilliant show-ing against German armour.   Many military experts regarded their wartime tanks as the best in operation.   (4) the Russian heavy tank, "Joseph Stalin III," was a model that appeared towards the end of the European war.   It had a welded hull and turret and carried, in addition to lighter machine-guns, a very powerful 122-mm. gun.

in western Europe did the German dictator remain behind strong de-fences.

On June 6, 1944, in the greatest combined land, sea and air opera-tion ever, the Allies invaded France along the Normandy coast. As-sault troops waded ashore, ran over sandy beaches, past barbed wire and concrete gun emplacements and fought their way onto French soil. As they raced across the beaches, the first Canadian assault troops — Regina Rifles, Royal Winnipeg Rifles, Queen's Own Rifles and North Shore (New Brunswick) — were met by blazing German guns. Despite the bombardment, the crush of men and equipment, and the stormy weather, the 3rd Canadian Infantry Division reached almost seven miles inland on the first day, the farthest of any of the assault divisions. As the Allies fought their way inland, they met fierce German resistance around the town of Caen. The Canadians and the Second British Army were given the task of pinning down the Germans in Caen, while the Americans swept around to attack unexpectedly from the west. One hole for German retreat remained in this quickly closing trap — the Falaise Gap A small detachment of the 4th Canadian Armoured Division fought their way into a village close to one of the last roads of escape. It was not closed in time, and thousands of Germans rushed through to safety.

The American forces under General Patton and those under the British General Montgomery headed for the Rhine. The Canadians' job was to capture the channel ports, occupy the Scheldt River area, and free Antwerp. With the ports secure, supplies could be rushed to the Allied soldiers as they crossed into Germany. With little help from the Allied generals, who were occupied with the thrust across the Rhine, the Canadian forces bravely overcame German resistance.

Hard fighting continued through 1944 and into 1945. Soldiers of the 1st Canadian Corps fought their way up the Italian peninsula, along with the famous Eighth Army. More Canadians died in the fighting in northern Italy than in any other phase of the Italian campaign Canadians took part in the bitter fighting which led to the capture of the Rhineland. The Canadian Army, including the 1st Canadian Corps which had just arrived from Italy, pursued the Germans northeast across Germany and then into Holland, where they liberated the Dutch.

The Allies streamed across the Rhine and headed for Berlin. The Russians were also approaching the German capital from the east after taking Poland, Rumania and Hungary. Pushing on, they entered Germany and eventually made contact with the Allied forces in April, 1945.

On May 8, 1945, Germany surrendered and many of her leaders, Hitler among them, committed suicide.

**German surrender**

But, the war was not yet over, for the Japanese remained undefeated in the South Pacific. There were indications, however, that the tide was turning.

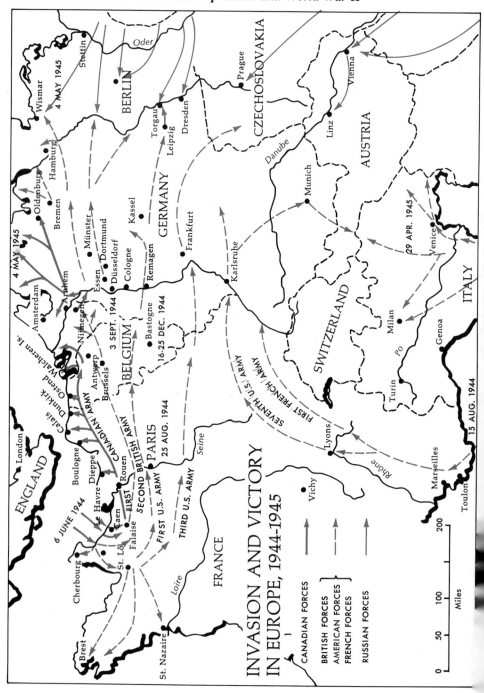

INVASION AND VICTORY
IN EUROPE, 1944-1945

CANADIAN FORCES

BRITISH FORCES
AMERICAN FORCES
FRENCH FORCES

RUSSIAN FORCES

Miles
0    50    100    200

By the summer of 1945 war in the Pacific had reached a most critical stage. The Japanese were driven out of Burma, the Philippines were retaken, and Japan was blockaded from the sea and bombed from the air.

The Pacific conflict came to a shocking end in August, 1945, when American bombers dropped atomic bombs on the Japanese cities of Hiroshima and Nagasaki.

The Japanese government sent an urgent appeal for peace. World War II was over.

After six years of conflict, the world faced a situation radically different from that of 1939. Germany, Italy and Japan were crushed; Britain and France were weakened by the losses of war. On the other hand, the United States emerged as the world's most powerful nation, with Russia following closely. The United States had greatly expanded her industrial strength, while Russia gained by conquest nearly 500,000 square miles of European territory.

One of the most appalling features of World War II was the staggering price paid by civilians living in areas of conflict. The world was horrified to discover the concentration camps where the Nazis carried out their "final solution" to the "Jewish Problem." Six million Jews had been brutally exterminated — never before in history had such a crime been committed against a people. Non-Jews too had suffered forced labour, torture and death in Nazi concentration camps.

Once more the victors of a world war tried to set up an organization to prevent the possibility of another war. The United Nations was established in San Francisco in June, 1945. The Canadian delegation under the leadership of Prime Minister Mackenzie King took an important part in the discussions.

The introduction to the Charter of the United Nations reveals the aims of the organization.

". . . to save succeeding generations from the scourge of war,

". . . to reaffirm faith in fundamental human rights.

". . . to establish conditions under which justice and respect for the obligations arising from treaties and other sources of international law can be maintained, and,

". . . to promote social progress and better standards of life in larger freedom."

The work of the United Nations is carried out by its principal bodies:

**General Assembly**

The General Assembly, the only branch on which all members have representatives, is a "parliament of nations" that controls, reviews, criticizes and approves the work of other branches, committees and commissions.

**Security Council**

The Security Council, with its permanent members, the United States, Russia, Britain, France and China and six non-permanent members who are elected by the General Assembly, is concerned with the settling of international squabbles which could result in war. The Council has the power to take more drastic action: breaking off diplomatic relations, restricting trade, coastal blockade, or even taking military action against transgressors.

**Economic and Social Council**

The Economic and Social council consists of eighteen members elected by the General Assembly. This branch is concerened with improving economic and social conditions throughout the world.

A number of special agencies work under the authority of the Economic and Social Council. One of the best known of these is the United Nations Educational, Scientific and Cultural Organization.

**International Court of Justice**

The International Court of Justice composed of fifteen elected judges, meets periodically in Holland to examine difficult situations, and issues decisions in terms of international law.

**Secretariat**

The Secretariat is made up of a Secretary-General and a large staff which take care of the details of running the UN.

## SUMMARY — SECTION 10

In 1931 the Statute of Westminster brought major changes to the structure of the British Empire. Great Britain gave up her long-held control over the self-governing Dominions of Canada, Australia, New Zealand, South Africa and the Irish Free State. These countries were admitted to the new **British Commonwealth of Nations** as equals with Britain.

The world was shocked in October, 1929, by the news of a "crash" on the stock market in New York City. This sudden, disastrous collapse introduced a dismal, world-wide period of unemployment, falling prices and economic disruption known as the Great Depression.

Mackenzie King's Liberal government lost the election of 1930 and the Conservative leader R. B. Bennett took over as Prime Minister.

In many countries economic conditions led to feelings of despair and desperation. Two unscrupulous dictators took advantage of the situation and rose to power — Benito Mussolini in Italy and Adolf Hitler in Germany. The two leaders formed a friendship pact which was later joined by a third partner, Japan. People around the world grew uneasy, since this powerful military combination had frightening potential.

A series of alarming events began with the invasion of Manchuria by Japan. Mussolini marched into Ethiopia and Hitler took the Rhineland, Austria and Czechoslovakia. The climax came when Germany invaded Poland in September, 1939. Britain and France immediately declared war and they were quickly followed by members of the Commonwealth of Nations.

In the beginning there was so little action in Europe that the conflict became known as the "Phoney War". But in 1940 German armoured forces rolled south from the Low Countries and eastward into France pushing the Allies to the English Channel. President Pétain of France signed a treaty with Germany, and France dropped out of the war, leaving Britain and the Commonwealth to fight on alone.

It was fortunate at this critical time that Winston Churchill became Prime Minister of Britain. He rallied the British people and held up the hope of eventual victory. Disappointed because the British would not give up, Adolf Hitler turned the full force of his power against England. He hoped that constant bombing might break the British will to carry on. This period was known as the Battle of Britain.

Even before Hitler's sweep through the Low Countries, Canadian troops were being given final training in Britain and a second force was being organized in Canada. During the four years of conflict the strength of the Canadian Army grew to more than 700,000 men and women. The Royal Canadian Navy, too, expanded rapidly from a small fleet into a navy with more than 600 ships. As in World War I, Canadian sailors accomplished outstanding work in protecting shipping lanes in the North Atlantic. Canadians also fought in sea battles in the Mediterranean, off the Aleutian Islands and in other places.

Benito Mussolini dreamed of adding to his Italian colonies in Africa by driving the British out of Egypt and the Sudan. His ambitions were set back in 1941 when his land forces were defeated by the British under General Wavell. A month later Adolf Hitler shocked the world by turning on his own ally, Russia. This was an unwise decision, since the Russians were determined soldiers and the German armies were trapped by the brutal Russian winter deep within this enormous land.

Another shocking event was the Japanese bombing of Pearl Harbour, an American naval base in Hawaii, in December. The Americans reacted by declaring war and entering the conflict on the side of the Allied powers. During December and on into 1942 the Japanese won victories in the South Pacific, overrunning Hong Kong, Thailand, Malaya, Singapore,

Burma, the Philippines, Dutch East Indies, New Guinea, New Britain and the Solomon Islands. In three months the Japanese had occupied a total area of some 1,000,000 square miles populated by more than 100,000,000 persons.

In order to test the German land defences in Europe, the Allied command in the summer of 1942 decided to launch an attack on the coast of France. A force of 5,000 Canadians and 1,000 British commandos conducted the raid on Dieppe. They were met by overwhelming fire from German defenders. This costly experiment showed that the coast could only be taken by overwhelming forces of Allied troops.

Meanwhile in North Africa the deadlock in desert warfare was broken when General Montgomery defeated the Afrika Korps at El Alamein. Then, as the Germans retreated they were caught between Montgomery's troops and another Allied force under the American commander General Eisenhower. There was no escape for the Afrika Korps. German power in North Africa was completely shattered.

The Allies were now able to cross the Mediterranean and proceed with the invasion of Sicily and the Italian mainland. Once in Italy, Allied advances were slowed down by rivers, mountains, bad weather and the stubborn resistance of the German troops who had taken over the defence of Italy.

The position of Adolf Hitler had changed greatly. He had been unable to invade Britain; the Allies controlled the Mediterranean and were moving northward into central Europe; the Russians were advancing from the east.

On June 6, 1944, the Allies invaded France, protected by an umbrella of bombers and fighting planes. The enemy grip on Europe was slowly loosened and the German retreat began. Hard fighting continued through 1944 and on into 1945. The Allies entered Germany and joined the Russians at Berlin. On May 8, 1945, the Germans surrendered and Adolf Hitler committed suicide.

But Word War II was not yet over, since the Japanese remained undefeated in the Pacific. But the situation was changing. As weeks went by, the Japanese were driven out of Burma, the Philippines and other regions. The final stages involved blockading Japan by sea and bombing the country from the air.

The Pacific conflict came to a shocking end in August, 1945, when the United States dropped atomic bombs on the Japanese cities of Hiroshima and Nagasaki. So devastating were the results that the government of Japan immediately made peace. World War II was over.

Even before the surrender of Japan, representatives of forty-five countries gathered in San Francisco to discuss the formation of a world-wide organization to replace the ineffective League of Nations. As a result of their discussions a new peacekeeping organization was founded — the **United Nations.**

# 11

## POSTWAR CANADA

Population growth ■ Immigration ■ Refugees ■ The Canadian mosaic ■ Growth of urban centres ■ Demand for new services ■ Cultural affairs ■ Canada Council ■ C.B.C. ■ Television ■ National Film Board ■ Economic expansion ■ New ways of earning a living ■ Oil, gas, iron, and uranium ■ Transportation ■ St. Lawrence Seaway ■ Retirement of Mackenzie King ■ Louis St. Laurent as Prime Minister ■ The Tenth Province ■ Cold War ■ John Diefenbaker ■ Election of 1957 ■ Diefenbaker as Prime Minister ■ Election of 1962 ■ Lester Pearson as Prime Minister ■ Canada's new flag ■ Canada Pension Plan, National Medicare Act and unification of the armed forces ■ Royal Commission on Bilingualism and Biculturalism ■ Canadian Centennial ■ Expo 67 ■ General de Gaulle ■ Robert Stanfield as Conservative leader ■ Retirement of Lester Pearson ■ Pierre Trudeau as Liberal leader and Prime Minister ■ Trudeaumania ■ Liberal victory in the election of 1968 ■ Legislation ■ Concern over Quebec ■ Kidnapping of James Cross and Pierre Laporte ■ War Measures Act ■ Death of Pierre Laporte ■ Release of James Cross ■ Results of the crisis ■ Scientific and technical advances ■ World-wide problems ■ American influence ■ Rising prices ■ Unemployment ■ Pollution ■ Danger to wild life ■ Plight of native peoples ■ Recognition of China ■ Stanfield on the attack ■ Election of 1972 ■ Liberal minority government ■ Canada looks to the future.

# 46   *Expansion and Growth*

AFTER WORLD WAR II, Canada entered a period of extraordinary expansion and prosperity. At the same time there was a rapid increase in population. From 1941 to 1947 the population rose from 11½ to 16½ million.

**Population growth**

Several factors contributed to the spurt in population growth. The Depression and war had held back marriages. After 1945 young Canadians began to marry at an earlier age, have children sooner and produce larger families. This trend continued for over a decade.

Furthermore, while the percentage of births was rising, advances in medicine and health services contributed to a decline in the percentage of deaths. The net result was that the percentage of population increase in Canada by 1957 was one of the highest in the world.

**Immigration**

Immigration contributed significantly to the population expansion. New citizens arrived from Britain, continental Europe, the United States and, to a lesser extent, from Asia and Africa. During the twelve years directly after the war, immigrants made up one-quarter of the population increase.

**Refugees**

In addition to persons admitted by the normal immigration process, many others, fleeing tragic circumstances in their homelands, were permitted entry. One hundred thousand refugees made homeless by World War II and thirty-six thousand refugees from Hungary, seeking a home after the Russians smashed a popular uprising in 1957, were allowed to settle in Canada.

During the early part of the century, immigrants had flocked to the Canadian West, drawn by the lure of free or inexpensive land for farming. But in the 1940's and 1950's, homesteading days were over, there were no great open spaces in the southern arable regions of the nation. In fact, many long-settled Canadian families were moving from farms into the cities. This was partly as a result of increased mechanization, since by using huge, motor-driven machines for ploughing, seeding and harvesting, fewer farmers were needed. Many farmers, too, felt that cities offered better economic opportunities.

While most of the earlier immigrants had been farmers in their native lands, many of the postwar immigrants were trained for work in a wide variety of city occupations. Thousands of professional men, skilled craftsmen and tradesmen were attracted to Canada's urban centres.

The arrival of new citizens from abroad brought new colour, variety and vitality to Canadian life, particularly in the larger cities, where foreign language newspapers, clothing styles, sports, music, radio programs, theatre, social clubs, food and festivals reflected the cultures of numerous nations. **Fresh variety in Canadian life**

The federal government has encouraged immigrants to keep alive elements of their own culture — their language, literature, history and arts — while at the same time assuming the rights and duties of Canadian citizens. We often refer to this arrangement as the "Canadian Mosaic" — a national pattern made up of all the separate ethnic groups. **The "Canadian Mosaic"**

The growth of Canadian cities, both in number and in size, was another outstanding feature of postwar Canada. By 1956, nearly one-half of all Canadians were living in cities with populations exceeding 40,000. **Growth of urban centres**

Villages grew to towns, towns expanded to become cities and cities spread their limits outward, as new suburbs took over land where cows had grazed and orchards bloomed.

The expanding population and growing cities demanded many new services: streets, highways, sewers, bridges, hydro lines, telephone lines, public transportation, schools, hospitals, municipal buildings, firehalls, police stations, libraries, parks, playgrounds, museums and theatres. Canada's economy adjusted itself to the seemingly endless needs of the growing nation. **Demand for new services**

Canadians began to show intense interest in cultural matters: books, **Cultural affairs**

# THE TREND TOWARDS URBAN LIFE
# IN CANADA 1871-1971

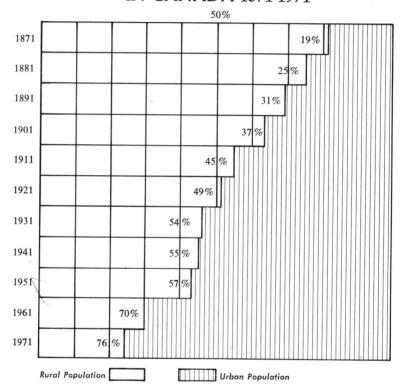

50%

| Year | Urban % |
|------|---------|
| 1871 | 19% |
| 1881 | 25% |
| 1891 | 31% |
| 1901 | 37% |
| 1911 | 45% |
| 1921 | 49% |
| 1931 | 54% |
| 1941 | 55% |
| 1951 | 57% |
| 1961 | 70% |
| 1971 | 76% |

Rural Population ☐    ▦ Urban Population

drama, music, dance and painting. The majority of Canadians lived in cities, which had cultural facilities to encourage and expand Canadian consciousness of the arts.

**Canada Council**

The report of the Royal Commission on National Development in the Arts, Letters and Sciences in 1951 set the pattern of government support for Canadian cultural development. It recommended that the government provide financial aid to universities, and that a Canada Council be created to encourage creativity on the part of all artists and scholars. In 1957, two multi-millionaires, Izaak Walton Killam of Nova Scotia and James Dunn of New Brunswick, died. They left almost $100 million to the government of Canada in the form of succession duties. Parliament voted to use the money for the newly founded Canada Council. Canada Council grants have helped creative people in areas ranging from dance to film-making. Orchestras, publishing houses, museums, theatre companies and many other groups have been able to explore new areas of artistic expression aided by money from the Council.

Before the founding of the Canada Council there had been some exciting cultural developments. The Dominion Drama Festival, founded

In the postwar years a booming economy and rapidly expanding population brought about a great demand for housing, and touched off a wave of new construction which is continuing to this day. In the suburbs of the major cities, entire new communities sprang up, as builders were forced to go further from the city to find suitable land. New roads and expressways then had to be built so that suburban residents could move about easily and have access to their work. The design and construction of the postwar house also underwent change. Larger lot sizes often allowed the suburban house to be built on a single level, and large gardens and front lawns were the rule. Window areas increased greatly and separate garages gave way to carports. Oil, gas or electric heating systems replaced coal furnaces, while in the kitchen a host of new gadgets such as electric dishwashers, stoves, refrigerators, mixers, blenders — the list is endless — lightened the housewife's work.

# POPULATION BY ETHNIC GROUPS 1871-1971

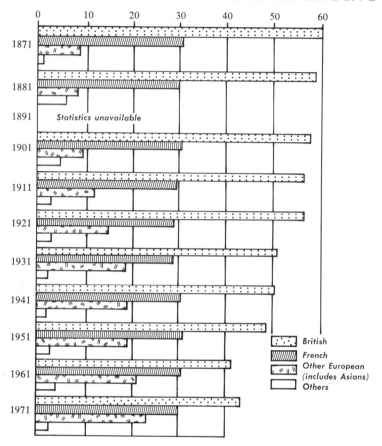

British

French

Other European
(includes Asians)

Others

in the 1930's, continued to encourage amateur actors and playwrights by means of its yearly drama contests. Two ballet companies of major importance were founded in the 1940's: The Royal Winnipeg Ballet and The National Ballet of Canada. A major achievement was the opening of the Shakespeare Festival at Stratford, Ontario. This festival has won an international reputation for artistic excellence.

As the government stepped in to provide financial assistance, new cultural facilities sprang up across Canada. The Fathers of Confederation Memorial Centre in Charlottetown, the Beaverbrook Art Gallery in Fredericton, Place des Arts in Montreal, Toronto's O'Keefe Centre, and the Queen Elizabeth Theatre in Vancouver are examples. Touring operatic, ballet and drama companies were founded from coast to coast, enriching communities which otherwise would not have the opportunity of experiencing these high quality performances.

The Canadian Broadcasting Corporation provided enormous scope **CBC** for creative Canadians. Producing daily programs required a large number of announcers, reporters, singers, musicians, writers, dramatists, producers, directors and technicians.

In the 1930's Great Britain had experimented with television as a medium for public broadcasting, but these efforts were given up when the war began. It was the Americans who, after the close of World War II, developed the "magicbox" for popular use. The enormous wealth and highly developed industry of the United States made it possible to mass-produce TV sets and establish broadcasting facilities.

American enthusiasm for television spilled across the border into **Television** Canada. In the beginning, Canadians living close to the border watched American programs sent out from American channels. The Canadian television era began in 1952 when the CBC broadcast its first programmes. Mass production brought down the cost of television sets

In the early days of television, many sets were designed in the same style as radios, with elaborate wood cabinets, and AM and FM radio receivers included. With relatively few television stations, and reception that was sometimes unpredictable, a built-in radio probably made the set more salable. By today's standards, picture areas were small. A typical large screen set had a picture of 116 square inches compared to the 315 square inches of a comparable set today. The popular small table model of 1949 seen here had a picture size of 72 square inches.

and thousands were purchased.

The coming of television strongly affected Canadian life. How Canadians arranged their daily schedules, especially on weekends, was often decided by what was on television. Worldwide events were broadcast into Canadian homes as they happened. The faces of famous persons became familiar by constant exposure on the TV screen. Distant peoples and places became better known and better understood by means of documentary and travel programs. And the flood of advertising influenced the buying habits of Canadian families.

Many people preferred to be entertained in the comfort of their own homes rather than going out to movies or sports events. "Hockey Night in Canada," broadcast on Saturday nights until very recently was the most popular Canadian show.

In the early stages of television many thought that Canadians would lose interest in books, records and radio, but as time passed, and the novelty of television wore off, this was not the case. Television has been adapted for numerous practical uses in manufacturing, national defence, transportation, health, medicine, science education, crime detection, space exploration, underwater photography and weather charts.

Provinces across Canada established television facilities to broadcast educational programs into school and homes. Although millions of dollars have been invested, as yet the number of television sets in the classrooms is small. In the future television could play a major role in education.

**National Film Board**

The National Film Board, founded in 1939, soon gained an international reputation for its superb documentary motion picture films. The success of the NFB encouraged film-makers throughout Canada.

**Economic expansion**

Canadian agriculture and industry expanded rapidly to meet the pressing needs of the war effort. As Canada was far from the battlefields, her industries, producing at peak efficiency, emerged undamaged from the war. The postwar demand for goods was enormous and, with slight modifications in the machinery, Canadian industry was able to fill the orders for cars, appliances, clothing and many other goods. Projects which had once been delayed by war now caused a boom in the building industry. New schools, homes, roads, factories and stores were quickly put up. Canada in 1947 experienced almost full employment, increasing production and a rising standard of living.

No longer were the majority of Canadians earning a living by farming, fishing, lumbering or running small businesses. By 1955 half of Canada's national income was earned by people working in jobs providing services. The modern, industrial country required large numbers of workers in the transportation, communication, education, government agencies, health services, recreation, repairs and so on. **New ways of earning a living**

One-third of the national income still came from the so-called primary industries — agriculture, lumbering, mining and fishing. Wheat had fallen from first to third on the list of Canada's exports and other agricultural products had fallen as well. The pulp and paper industry, however, continued to grow, and by the mid 1950's produced more than half the world's supply of newsprint. **Primary industries**

Canada's abundant supply of hydro-electric power made it possible to transform trees into paper rapidly and economically. Cheap, plentiful electricity also contributed to the booming aluminum industry which, by 1956, was second only to that of the United States. **Cheap electrical power**

A remarkable feature of this economic boom was the discovery and development of new natural resources. Industries grew up, based on iron ore, uranium, natural gas and oil. New settlements and towns developed in what had been empty stretches of land. **New resources**

In the late 1940's and early 1950's, oil strikes in Alberta revealed a vast supply of underground wealth. By the middle of the 1950's, oil was Canada's leading mineral export. During this period, the reserves of natural gas were tapped as well. **Oil and natural gas**

In the remote Ungava peninsula, along the Labrador-Quebec border, huge iron supplies were discovered. The area of the Labrador Trough was to prove rich in iron and other base metals. Mining towns sprang up in northern Ontario. **Iron**

Uranium, essential in producing atomic power, is another major Canadian natural resource. At the beginning, all uranium was refined in the United States. Canada, however, began to build immense nuclear reactors to provide the necessary power so that the refinement of uranium could be done here. **Uranium**

The expansion of mining and industry created new transportation problems. Mining products had to be moved from isolated regions, far from navigable waters and established transportation routes. **Transportation**

**Railways**  Railway lines were constructed to service newly opened nickel mines in northern Manitoba and copper mines in Ontario and Quebec. In order to carry iron ore from the Ungava region, 360 miles of railway were pushed through rock and forest to a new harbour constructed at Sept-Îsles on the St. Lawrence River. Sept-Îsles was equipped with facilities to receive load, and ship Ungava ore.

**Pipelines**  One of the major difficulties involved in the movement of oil and natural gas from western Canada was the great distances between the producing areas and the major markets in British Columbia, Ontario and Quebec. Although the price was high, it was agreed that the solution was an underground pipeline. Between 1950 and 1957 an oil pipeline was built from the fields of Alberta to Vancouver and a second pushed two thousand miles eastward to the city of Sarnia, Ontario, and on to Toronto.

Transportation of natural gas took on very much the same pattern as that of oil. A pipeline stretched from Alberta across the mountains to Vancouver and the American border; another eastward across the prairies and northern Ontario to Montreal in the province of Quebec.

**St. Lawrence Seaway**  One of the most dramatic transportation projects in this period was the construction of the St. Lawrence Seaway, a joint Canadian-American venture. The aims of the gigantic new seaway were to develop hydro-electric power and improve navigational routes so that ocean-going vessels might sail down the St. Lawrence to the Great Lakes.

Supporters of the seaway argued that it would make export of Canadian products and the import of foreign products easier, and provide a cheap means of transport for iron ore between Sept-Îsles and steel mills on the Great Lakes. It was pointed out, too, that in time of war an inland shipping route would be better protected than any along the sea coasts.

The project called for the construction of new canals and locks in the shallow portions of the St. Lawrence River between Montreal and Kingston, and major improvements in the existing Welland Canal joining Lakes Erie and Ontario.

Costing approximately one billion dollars, the immense project was finished by the spring of 1959. In a colourful ceremony the St. Lawrence seaway was officially opened by Queen Elizabeth II and President Dwight Eisenhower of the United States.

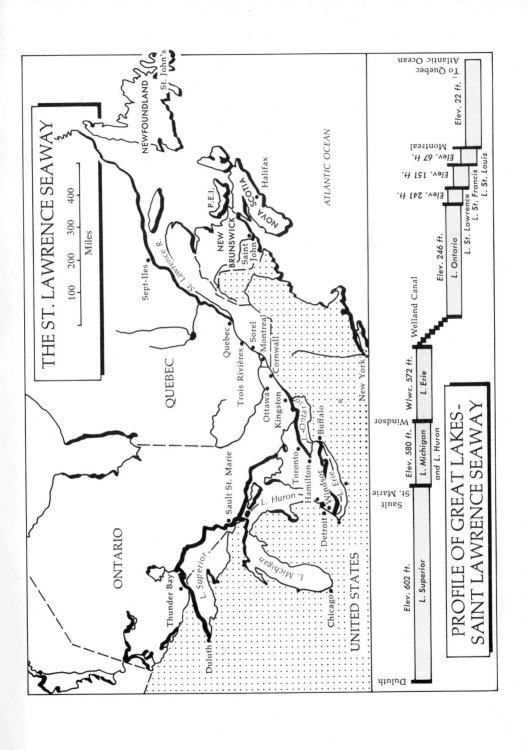

# THE ST. LAWRENCE SEAWAY

Miles
100 200 300 400

NEWFOUNDLAND
St. John's

P.E.I.

NOVA SCOTIA
Halifax

NEW BRUNSWICK
Saint John

ATLANTIC OCEAN

QUEBEC

Sept-Iles

St. Lawrence R.

Quebec
Sorel
Montreal
Trois Rivières
Cornwall
Ottawa
Kingston

ONTARIO

Sault St. Marie

L. Superior

Thunder Bay

L. Michigan

L. Huron

Toronto
Hamilton
Windsor
L. Erie
Detroit
Buffalo
L. Ontario

New York

UNITED STATES

Chicago

Duluth

## PROFILE OF GREAT LAKES – SAINT LAWRENCE SEAWAY

Duluth

Elev. 602 ft.
L. Superior

Sault St. Marie

Elev. 580 ft.
L. Michigan and L. Huron

Windsor

Wlwc. 572 ft.
L. Erie

Welland Canal

Elev. 246 ft.
L. Ontario

Elev. 241 ft.
L. St. Lawrence

Elev. 151 ft.
L. St. Francis

Elev. 67 ft.
Montreal

L. St. Louis

Elev. 22 ft.

To Quebec
Atlantic Ocean

A freighter approaches one of the locks on the St. Lawrence Seaway on its way to a port a thousand miles inland. In its first decade of service the Seaway was plied by vessels of 30 maritime nations, carrying 350 million tons of cargo. The Great Lakes are set into the eastern half of the continent like a string of ponds in the side of a hill, with the water pouring from the highest to the lowest in a series of steps. From Lake Superior at the top of the system, to the St. Lawrence River at the bottom, the water level drops a total of 602 feet. To raise a vessel through the system, as though on a giant staircase, a series of seventeen locks was constructed, each capable of accommodating vessels with a 25-foot draught. Through this giant waterway, which runs a distance of 2,300 miles, from the head of the lakes to the Atlantic Ocean, Canadian products such as wheat, pulp and paper, and iron ore can be shipped directly to the port of their destination. Carried in the opposite direction are such diverse things as automobiles from Japan, champagne from France and sugar from the West Indies which can be unloaded at the dockside of ports such as Toronto or Hamilton.

# 47. *Prime Ministers St. Laurent, Diefenbaker and Pearson*

IN THE ELECTION of 1945 the Liberal Party led by Prime Minister Mackenzie King was re-elected, although its majority was reduced. King had, in the previous year, skilfully handled the difficult problem of compulsory military service, avoiding a serious break between the province of Quebec which opposed conscription and the rest of Canada.

His health declining, the seventy-seven year-old Prime Minister resigned from office in 1948, after having spent twenty-one years as national leader.

Louis St. Laurent, a bilingual Quebec lawyer succeeded Mackenzie King as Prime Minister. St. Laurent was the first French-Canadian Prime Minister since Laurier, thirty-seven years before.

Louis St. Laurent, sixty-six years of age, had been Minister of Justice, and, as King's leading Quebec Minister, had helped convince Quebec to go along with the Conscription Act. In a very short time he had gained high respect and affection throughout Canada.

While leading the Canadian delegation to the United Nations, St. Laurent had been frustrated by the way the Russians used their veto to prevent the passage of motions they disliked. A growing awareness of the danger of an expanding, aggressive Soviet Union led St. Laurent and others to propose an alliance for mutual protection between Britain, Canada, the United States and friendly powers in Europe. In 1949 the North Atlantic Treaty Organization, commonly known as NATO,

393

was formed. The alliance grew to include Britain, the United States, Canada, Belgium, Denmark, France, Iceland, Italy, Luxembourg, Holland, Norway, Portugal, Greece and Turkey.

**The tenth province**

The idea of Newfoundland joining Canada as an additional province had been discussed by generations of Canadian citizens. The strategic position of Newfoundland, situated alongside north Atlantic shipping lanes, had been pointed out again during the war. But there was scant interest in Newfoundland in changing its political status from a self-governing member of the Commonwealth to a province of Canada.

The issue of union received little support until Joseph Smallwood became the Liberal Premier of Newfoundland. An energetic and popular leader, Smallwood was a leading spokesman for the advantages to be gained by joining the prosperous neighbour next door.

After first voting against union, the islanders, by a small majority, voted in favour of their Premier's proposal. On March 31, 1949, Canada gained its tenth province and 350,000 new citizens.

**Progress and prosperity**

The Liberal government under St. Laurent enjoyed a period of progress and prosperity during which the nation appeared relatively content and unified. In 1952, the Prime Minister recommended the appointment of Vincent Massey as the first native-born Canadian Governor-General of Canada. The following year Massey led the official Canadian delegation at the coronation of Queen Elizabeth II.

**The "Cold War"**

But if conditions were peaceful at home, they certainly were not abroad. Increasing tension between Communist and democratic nations had developed into an alarming situation known as the "Cold War." The Soviet Union stood as a threatening giant while the People's Republic of China was emerging as a new one. In Europe there were anxious moments when the Soviet Union and the Western nations seemed close to war over control of the city of Berlin, in Germany. In 1950 a war broke out in Korea when North Korean troops crossed into South Korea. A United Nations force, made up mainly of American and South Korean troops, faced the armies of North Korea and of the People's Republic of China, a Communist nation, which supported the North Koreans. Canada contributed an infantry brigade with artillery and a naval contingent to the UN force.

In 1956 Egypt seized control of the Suez Canal. The canal ran through Egyptian territory, but was, by treaty, an international waterway. The British Prime Minister, Anthony Eden, decided to occupy the Canal Zone, together with France, in order to uphold international rights to the canal and ensure the passage of oil from the Middle East. Israel, at the same time, attacked Egypt because of Egyptian raids over its borders and attempts by the Egyptians to block Israeli shipping. The Anglo-French attack was denounced as an aggressive act. Lester Pearson, Canadian Secretary of State for External Affairs, proposed the idea of a United Nations Expeditionary Force. This force would police the troubled area, on condition that the British, French and Israelis withdrew their troops and Egypt agreed to the intervention. The conditions were met and the UN force, which included Canadian military units, began to police the Suez Canal Zone. The UN soldiers were to remain for ten years.

**Peace-keeping** International peace-keeping forces under UN sponsorship were sent into the troubled Congo, and into Cyprus in 1964. Canada contributed military contingents to the forces in both countries. Tensions mounted in Asia and in the newly emerging nations of Africa.

**North American defence** The "Cold War" focused Canadian and American attention on the problem of defending North America in the event of a Russian attack from the north by bombers and/or inter-continental missiles, based in Siberia.

During World War II, Canada and the United States had cooperated closely on military matters. In 1955 the *Pinetree Warning Line*, stretching across the southerly portion of Canada was built in order to establish a radar alarm system against surprise attack. A second system, the *Mid-Canada Line*, was developed across the country in the latitude of southern Hudson Bay. This was followed by the *Distant Early Warning Line (DEW)*, stretching along the Arctic coastline. In 1958, both nations joined in a formal North American Air Defence system known as NORAD. The head of the organization was to be an American air force general, who would have a Canadian deputy. The system included Canadian interceptor planes, radar sites and anti-aircraft missiles.

**John Diefenbaker** The Conservative Party had been trying unsuccessfully to find a strong, appealing leader. In 1956, John Diefenbaker, a lawyer from

GREENLAND

ALASKA
(U.S.A.)

DISTANT EARLY WARNING LINE

PINETREE

NETWORK

Pacific Ocean

Headquarters,
Northern NORAD Region
NORTH BAY

UNITED STATES

Atlantic Ocean

COLORADO SPRINGS
(Headquarters NORAD)

### THE CANADIAN AIR DEFENCE SYSTEM

Prince Albert, Saskatchewan, was elected party chief. He was an agres-
sive speaker with a talent for rousing enthusiasm.

**Election of 1957**

During the political campaign leading up to the election of 1957,
Diefenbaker crossed the country from coast to coast thundering the
message that the Liberal Party had been in office too long. The Liber-

als, he said, had become so secure in power they treated Canadian citizens with arrogance.

The Liberals had, in fact, become complacent and their stifling of debate on the controversial gas pipeline from Alberta to central Canada had aroused public opposition. The Minister responsible, C. D. Howe, insisted on rushing through parliament the bill authorizing government assistance to the company building the pipeline. The government voted to end debate on the bill on its second reading in the Commons, in spite of strong opposition. The fact that the company chosen to build the pipeline was American added to the strong feeling against the Liberals.

Pipeline controversy

When the votes were counted in June 1957, the Conservatives had gained a majority — 112 seats to the Liberals' 105. John Diefenbaker had become the first Conservative Prime Minister in twenty-two years.

Diefenbaker as Prime Minister

The following year, confident that he had won the support of the people, Diefenbaker called another election. This time the Conservative Party won more seats than any other party since Confederation. They now had 208 members, the Liberals trailing poorly with 49. Prime Minister Louis St. Laurent had retired from office after the 1957 defeat and had been succeeded by Lester B. Pearson, the new leader of the opposition.

Although Prime Minister Diefenbaker enjoyed solid support in all provinces, including Quebec, he soon discovered that management of the nation was a very difficult process. The postwar period of prosperity was showing signs of decline, and the country was soon to enter a period of recession and increased unemployment. Diefenbaker encountered difficulties over the special problems of Quebec and its relationship to the federal government. It began to appear to some Canadians that the Prime Minister who had appeared so promising was lacking in decisiveness and initiative.

Diefenbaker's difficulties

Diefenbaker did achieve some significant accomplishments during his term of office. Western wheat growers were helped by substantial sales abroad and financial assistance at home. An impressive dam to provide irrigation and electric power was constructed on the south Saskatchewan River. A National Energy Board was established to study Canada's natural resources and make recommendations for their best

1    2    3    4

y. MOULD

In the period 1900-1960 male clothing remained surprisingly unchanged.   Minor
variations appeared in such items as vests and lapels and also in general cut or fit,
one year a loose fit setting the style, to be replaced by a closer fitting garment the
next season.   It is probably true to say there has been more change in accessories
—shirts, collars, ties, jewellery—than in the basic suit itself.   However, informal
male clothing had greatly changed by 1960, such clothing as (2), a tennis outfit,
being unthinkable in 1900.   The range and variety of mid-century evening or sports
wear probably reflect the diversity of modern man's interests.   (3) is an after-six
dress of the early sixties, a simple design in light silk organza with a black satin
sash.   Skirt length is once again high, though not as daringly so as the late
     1920's.    The range of women's costume by 1960 was incredibly varied.

usage. One of the most notable achievements of the Diefenbaker government was the enactment of the Canadian Bill of Rights in 1960,
which protected freedom of religion, speech and association.

The Prime Minister's difficulties increased. He quarrelled with some of his own cabinet members, disagreed with the American government over matters of defence, and dismissed the Governor of the Bank of Canada.

Canada's defence dilemma involved whether to arm the bombs carried by Canadian planes serving in NATO with nuclear warheads.

Canada was a strong supporter of the United Nations and its peacekeeping duties. Up to this date, Canada had chosen not to use nuclear arms, and at international conferences had urged other nations to limit their possession of these weapons. Yet, as a member of NATO and NORAD, Canada was committed to the military defence of western Europe and North America. Diefenbaker's cabinet was divided on the issue. When questioned in the Commons, Diefenbaker gave a long but unclear explanation of the government's policy towards nuclear arms. The United States State Department made a public statement correcting some of Diefenbaker's points and the whole area of an independent Canadian foreign policy and relations with the United States became key issues in the election campaign.

In the federal election of June, 1962, the political picture changed drastically, the Conservative Party was reduced to 116 members and the Liberals rose to 99. The New Democrats held 19 seats, Social Credit 30. The Conservatives were disheartened by their losses. During the following months quarrels shook the cabinet, ministers resigned in anger and the government was a shambles. **Re-election of the Conservatives**

In an election in the following spring the Liberals returned to power with Lester Pearson as the new Prime Minister. **Conservative defeat**

When the popular "Mike" Pearson took over the government he already had behind him a distinguished career. Unlike most Canadian Prime Ministers he had not been trained in law, but in history. In 1928 he had joined the Canadian Department of External Affairs, rising to the position of Minister in 1948. He had served as President of the United Nations, signed the North Atlantic Treaty on behalf of Canada, and represented the nation at NATO Council meetings. In 1957, Pearson was awarded the Nobel Peace Prize for his role in creating the United Nations peace-keeping force and for his contribution to world peace. Probably no previous Canadian leader had been so internationally well known. **Lester Pearson as Prime Minister**

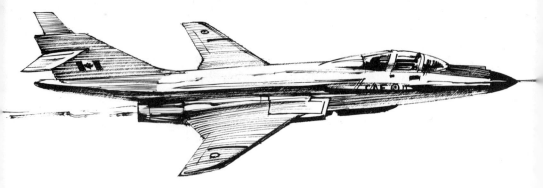

Since World War II aircraft developments have been spectacular. Highly sophisticated jet engines have revolutionized design and performance. The Canadian Air Defense Command has at its disposal a variety of aircraft, of which the CF-101 E Voodoo all-weather interceptor is one of the best. A twin-engine two-place airplane with speed in excess of 1,200 mph, its extreme combat radius, exceptional climbing ability and capacity to operate at great heights give it formidable striking power. Its armaments allow for considerable flexibility, as the plane is able to carry a variety of rockets and missiles.

During the political campaign leading up to the election, the Liberals had promised a vigorous, governmental program. After taking office, however, Pearson found he was handicapped by the lack of a solid majority in the House of Commons.

**Canada's new flag**

The selection of a new Canadian flag turned out to be a much more explosive question than had been expected. When the proposed maple leaf design was made public, there was a great outcry from those who wanted to keep the Union Jack, as well as from those who did not like the suggested design. The often bitter, often foolish, flag debate dragged on. In the end, Canada acquired its present flag, which was accepted by Canadians as the national symbol.

**Re-election of the Liberals**

In November, 1965, Pearson called for another election in the hope of increasing the number of Liberal seats in the House of Commons. The result was disappointing, since there was little actual change in the party standings. Nevertheless, the Pearson government, with some occasional help from the New Democratic and Social Credit parties, was able to govern. All parties became a bit cautious in their actions, as it was evident that Canadians wanted Parliament to get down to business.

New legislation

Several pieces of legislation having particular importance were proposed and passed. The Canada Pension Plan created a national old age pension plan to which all working people contributed. The National Medicare Act provided a medical insurance plan. The Canadian navy, army and air force were unified into a single service. This proposal created a storm of protest among Canadians who were or had been connected with the armed forces, and were proud of their own naval, army or air force traditions. Nevertheless, the act was passed and unification proceeded smoothly.

The French-English problem

In the meantime, the French-English question was proving a serious problem for the Pearson government. Quebec asked for "special status" in Canadian affairs and some radical leaders were urging a withdrawal from Confederation and the formation of a separate, French-speaking republic. In 1963 a small radical group was responsible for a number of bombings in Montreal and in 1964 unpleasant disruptions occurred during the visit of Queen Elizabeth to the city of Quebec.

The Royal Commission on Bilingualism and Biculturalism

In an effort to create real equality among Canadians, the government appointed The Royal Commission on Bilingualism and Biculturalism, which was to examine the total French-English problem and suggest practical solutions.

The Royal Commission proved most useful in bringing about open and frank discussion of viewpoints held by individuals and organizations. By 1967 the preliminary reports of the Commission had appeared and were being read with keen interest across Canada. In essence, the Commission suggested:

(1) full recognition of English and French as the official languages of Canada at the federal level as well as in Ontario, Quebec and New Brunswick.

(2) establishment of special bilingual districts wherever the minority comprised at least ten percent of the district population.

(3) agreement that English-speaking and French-speaking groups should co-exist as equals everywhere in Canada.

Canada's birthday party

The most exciting event in Prime Minister Pearson's last term of

office was the celebration of Canada's first one hundred years as a nation.

Expo 67

Among the many events organized for the Centennial was the spectacular Expo 67, an international exhibition in Montreal. Expo was praised widely for the beauty, flair and imagination of its island location, international pavilions, and overall design. The exhibition attracted 50,000,000 visitors.

Vive Quebec Libre!

Unfortunately, General Charles de Gaulle of France provided a jarring note in the Centennial celebrations. During his visit to the exhibition in Montreal the French leader concluded an emotional ad-

Canada's one hundredth anniversary was celebrated in towns and cities across the nation, but nowhere more spectacularly than at Expo '67, the great international World's Fair, held at Montreal. It was staged on two islands, Île Ste Helene and Île Notre Dame (the latter man-made), and on a peninsula, in the St. Lawrence River.

During the six months it was held Expo '67 attracted over fifty million visitors, both from Canada and every corner of the world. Adapting as the unifying theme "Man and His World," some sixty-two countries erected pavilions, many of extraordinary beauty and architectural ingenuity. Critics hailed the buildings as the "most exciting ever seen" and the design and landscaping of the island site as stunning. The fair provided a showcase for the country's best artists, designers, film makers and architects, giving them a chance to show the country and the world that their talents, given room to breathe, were second to none. To the average Canadian, Expo summarized in some brilliant, indefinable way, his affection for his country, and left him—for a while at least—with a sense of new national pride.

dress by shouting, *Vive Québec libre*! ("Long live free Quebec!") This wholly unexpected outburst, heard and viewed on television by millions, caused a great stir of anger and resentment, as the General's cry was interpreted as a direct appeal for Quebec's separation from Canada. Canadian leaders, both English and French, voiced their shock and anger that the French President would dare to attempt to meddle in Canadian affairs. Prime Minister Pearson rebuked the French visitor in a public statement and De Gaulle returned immediately to France, ignoring an official dinner to be given by the federal government in Ottawa.

# 48.
# Federal Election and National Crisis

BOTH THE CONSERVATIVE and Liberal parties elected new leaders within less than one year of each other, in the period of 1967-1968.

**Robert Stanfield**

Robert Stanfield, of Nova Scotia, whose father was a former member of the provincial legislature, was the new Conservative party chief. After studying at Dalhousie University he had attended Harvard Law School, specializing in law and economics. By 1940 he was a practising lawyer. During the following years his interest in politics grew. In 1947 he became president of the Nova Scotia Conservative Association and, the following year, leader of that party in the province. His new position, however, did not guarantee political success, as the Conservatives had not elected a single member to the provincial legislature. Stanfield reorganized his party and threw himself into vigorous political activity. By 1956 he was Premier of Nova Scotia, ending twenty-three years of Liberal control.

With his triumph in Nova Scotia, Stanfield won much favourable attention across Canada. At the National Conservative Party leadership convention, in September 1967, he was able to defeat other Conservatives and succeed John Diefenbaker. With new leadership, the party felt renewed courage and a surge of fighting spirit. One survey taken shortly afterward showed that the Conservatives stood nine per cent higher in national popularity than did the Liberals.

**Pierre Trudeau**

The Justice Minister in Lester Pearson's cabinet was Pierre Elliot Trudeau, a forty-seven-year-old lawyer of French and English descent from the Province of Quebec. His interests and enthusiasm ranged from skiing and scuba-diving to history and philosophy. Trudeau was an individualist, who often surprised the more traditional Members of Parliament with his casual clothes and frank statements. He had been educated at the University of Montreal, Harvard University and the University of London, and was both an intellectual and a romantic who enjoyed travel and adventure.

During the course of world-wide travels in 1948 this young man had hiked through Europe; spent a few days in a Yugoslavian jail for not having a visa; wandered through Palestine and hitched a ride on a truck to Jerusalem; visited the Khyber Pass; crossed Burma; travelled with a French convoy in Vietnam; arrived in Hong Kong and entered China in the closing stages of the civil war between the Communist and Nationalist forces.

When Lester Pearson retired from office in the spring of 1968, Trudeau defeated more experienced Liberal politicians and took over the party leadership.

As Prime Minister, Trudeau sensed that the nation was behind him, and called a federal election for June, 1968.

**Election of 1968**

During the campaign he promised that if his Liberal party were re-elected he would work to achieve a "Just Society" in Canada. This term was never completely defined by Trudeau or fully understood by the voters. It seemed to mean that the Liberals would provide opportunities for employment, satisfactory income, health care and personal freedom and gain a respected place for Canada in the international community. The "Just Society" suggested a higher quality of living for all Canadians.

Trudeau carefully made clear his own feelings regarding the position of Quebec within the structure of the nation. He rejected "Separatism" outright and was opposed, as well, to special powers for any province. Trudeau called instead for French and English Canadians to become equal partners within a united Canada.

Robert Stanfield's election campaign concentrated on several practical issues. Travelling about the nation, he stated that, if elected, his party would provide a minimum income for all Canadians suffering from poverty; take measures against all types of pollution; offer special help to Newfoundland and perhaps build a causeway between that island and Labrador. Although all these were useful proposals, critics pointed out that such programs would be very expensive, and wondered where the money would come from to pay for them. In general, both party leaders approached Canada's problems in a similar way and neither offered concrete solutions.

In an effort to secure much needed votes in Quebec, Stanfield announced his support for "the two nations policy" popular with some French Canadians. Unfortunately for the Conservatives, there was much confusion over what was really meant by "two nations." Did it mean "two cultures" or did it mean "two states"? Undoubtedly Stanfield wished to indicate support for "two cultures" but many Canadians had the uncomfortable feeling that perhaps he was in favour of the more radical solution. The misunderstanding caused by this issue proved embarrassing to the Conservative leader.

**"Trudeaumania"** Stanfield, conscientious and unhurried, often came across as dull on the television screen. He did not catch the imagination of the voters. As the election campaign proceeded, it became clear that Trudeau's personality was overshadowing all the policies, plans and issues put forward by both parties. An extraordinary condition, which the newspapers called "Trudeaumania," swept the country. Thousands and thousands turned out for public addresses. Young girls and women reached out to kiss the Liberal leader. The younger generation was attracted by Trudeau's youthful, modern life style; thoughtful people by his ideas, and his practical approach to political issues; idealists by his "Just Society" and many Canadians by the attractive, flamboyant image he presented. Before the campaign was finished, political commentators were forecasting a large majority for the Liberal party.

**Riot in Montreal** On the June evening before election day, 1968, Pierre Trudeau sat in a Montreal reviewing stand watching a colourful parade, concluding event of the St. Jean Baptiste Day festivities. St. Jean Baptiste is the patron saint of the Province of Quebec. What began as a lively, good-natured affair changed swiftly into an ugly riot, as several thousand "Separatists" began a violent demonstration. Howls and screams mingled with the wail of sirens and the thud of horses' hoofs. Fists swung and rocks flew. An upturned police car burst into flames. Women screamed. Injured persons with bleeding faces struggled to escape.

A pop bottle curving above the crowd crashed into the reviewing stand only six feet from Trudeau's position. Important officials and guests scattered and fled, but Trudeau remained where he was, two Mounties at his side. The crowd cheered his courage.

The following day the Liberals won the election with a very substantial majority, giving Canada's third French-Canadian Prime Minister a comfortable measure of control. It was the first time since 1958

Liberal victory

In the postwar years, the jet passenger plane took over from the propeller-driven types of earlier years, and dramatically shortened travelling times between the major cities of Canada as well as between Canada and other countries of the world. The 1970's brought into service jet aircraft with large passenger capacity, such as the Lockheed Tristar of Air Canada, a 585-m.p.h. plane capable of carrying 257 passengers and 23,000 pounds of freight. Powered by three Rolls Royce jet engines, it has a range of 3,260 miles and weighs 215 tons when fully loaded. From its beginnings in the bush and with the air mail flights of the 1920's, Canada's civil aviation has grown to a point where, in 1972, approximately 9.3 million passengers and 194,000 tons of freight were carried. It is estimated that we have over 1,600 airports, heliports and sea plane bases in present operation.

that any party had enjoyed a clear majority rule in the House of Commons.

**Legislation**

Early in his new term of office Prime Minister Trudeau and his party were involved with implementing changes in Canadian laws covering such matters as homosexuality, abortion, breathalizer tests, gun control, the parole system, penitentiaries, prisons and reformatories. Trudeau introduced the Official Languages Act, legalizing certain proposals made by the Royal Commission on Bilingualism and Biculturalism.

The Conservative leader, Robert Stanfield, felt that the Liberal government was not paying enough attention to such basic problems as unemployment, welfare and rising prices. During a public address delivered in Saskatchewan, Stanfield outlined his own ideas for improving what had become a serious situation: provide a suitable standard of living for all Canadians; withold welfare funds from persons who do not require them; arrange incentives so that people will want to work. At a later date he suggested changes in income tax laws to remove unfairness and hardship imposed on some groups of Canadian taxpayers. Not all members of the Conservative party agreed with their leader's proposals but his ideas were being discussed by Canadians across the country.

**Concern over Quebec**

During 1969 concern again grew over events taking place in Quebec. A minority among those supporting "Separatism" had turned to violent action, to disturbances, riots, looting and bombings. Arms were stolen and banks robbed to provide funds for further terrorist action. Bombs exploded in the Montreal City Hall, the federal Manpower Building, the Montreal Stock Exchange and in the Queen's Printer Book Store. Although Quebeckers, except for the radical terrorist minority, condemned the violence, fear and tension were now part of their everyday lives. Both the provincial government in Quebec and the federal government in Ottawa were alarmed by the threatening turn of events.

Not all of the violent actions were directed against English-speaking persons and institutions. There was reason to believe that there was a plot to kill Pierre Trudeau. A bomb was discovered in front of the home of Jean Drapeau, Mayor of Montreal.

Violence continued through the spring of 1970 as a militant group known as the Front de libération Québequoise (FLQ) pursued its reign of terror. This group was so arrogant and confident that it issued open threats and sometimes claimed responsibility for bombings.

On October 5, 1970, Canadians were jolted by the shocking announcement from Ottawa that a British diplomat, James Cross, had been kidnapped by armed men.

**Kidnapping of James Cross**

The following day a long, bold communiqué issued by the FLQ declared that James Cross was in their hands and would remain so until twenty-three recently arrested "political prisoners" were released from prison and allowed to fly to either Cuba or Algeria. These prisoners included seventeen convicted of criminal terrorist acts and six others charged with terrorist acts. Those charged were not free on bail. Under Canadian law there are no "political prisoners," that is, persons who have been imprisoned because of their political opinions. The terrorists also demanded a "voluntary tax" of half a million dollars in gold. If the government did not comply with these proposals, the communiqué said, the FLQ would have no hesitation in "liquidating" their captive.

Five days later, October 10, four disguised and armed men kidnapped Pierre Laporte, a Quebec cabinet minister.

**Kidnapping of Pierre Laporte**

It was apparent by this time that some strong counter-measures were necessary to smash the FLQ, which seemed to threaten the governments of Quebec and of Canada. The problem, was to gain control of the situation without sacrificing the lives of the British diplomat and the Quebec cabinet minister.

In the face of mass demonstrations and renewed bombings, the Premier of Quebec, Robert Bourassa, asked on October 15 for the assistance of the Canadian Armed Forces. Before the day was over, troops were being rushed into Quebec City and Montreal.

**Troops in Quebec and Montreal**

The federal government took immediate action to approve the War Measures Act, which outlawed the FLQ. Now the term "political prisoner" had legal meaning. The Act allowed the police to enter what they considered dangerous or suspicious buildings or other private places without a search warrant. The police now had the power to hold in jail, without bail, any person suspected of direct participation

**War Measures Act**

or complicity in recent violent events.

**Death of
Pierre Laporte**

The worst was still to come. On the night of October 17 another communiqué from the FLQ turned up. It was brief and grim:

"In face of the arrogance of the federal government and its lackey Bourassa, in the face of their obvious bad faith, the FLQ has therefore decided to act.

Pierre Laporte, minister of unemployment and assimilation, has been executed at 6:18 tonight by the Dieppe cell (Royal 22nd). You will find the body in the trunk of the green Chevrolet (J-2420) at St. Hubert base, entry No. 2.

We shall overcome.

FLQ

P.S. The exploiters of the Quebec people had better watch out."

In the beginning some believed that the communiqué was a hoax, but a short time later the body of Pierre Laporte was found in the trunk of a green Chevrolet.

A shudder of horror ran across Canada.

That evening Pierre Trudeau, spoke soberly to the nation:

"It is with shock and consternation I believe that all Canadians have learned of the death of Mr. Pierre Laporte, who was so cowardly assassinated by a band of murderers and I can't help feeling, as a Canadian, a deep sense of shame that this cruel and senseless act should have been conceived in cold blood and executed in a like manner."

Canadians were shocked and sickened by the brutal murder. With few exceptions the Canadian public and press gave strong support to the federal government and demanded harsh punishment for members of the FLQ.

**Release of
James Cross**

James Cross was still missing, and fear for his safety grew. Nearly seven weeks after the murder of Pierre Laporte the RCMP discovered the Montreal apartment in which Cross was being held by a few members of the FLQ.

The apartment was surrounded by heavily armed police and troops and desperate negotiations for the release of the British diplomat were started. It was eventually agreed that he would be set free if the kidnappers were guaranteed safe passage by airplane to Cuba. The demands were met and the eerie procession to the deserted grounds of Expo '67 began. At the former Canadian pavilion, an extension of the Cuban Embassy had been set up. The terrorists, driving an old, battered car, and armed with guns and dynamite, were surrounded on all sides by police cars and motorcycles. Within twenty-four hours they had been admitted to Cuba and James Cross was free.

The crisis in Quebec was over, but its effects lingered. Most of English-speaking Canada had supported the imposition of the War Measures Act. Some people called for strict new laws to control the activities of radical groups; for the use of identity cards for all citizens; for stronger measures against crime; supervision of radical newspapers and radio stations; and restoring the death penalty. Universities came under attack for allowing teachers to encourage revolutionary action. One Liberal Member of Parliament urged that restless young people with dangerous ideas should be conscripted into the Canadian Armed Services. On the other hand, many Canadians were shocked by the powers which the War Measures Act gave the federal government over the lives of citizens. They doubted that the situation had been as threatening as the government had indicated and felt that precious civic liberties should not have been suspended.

**Results of the crisis**

The crisis of 1970 forced Canadians to think very carefully not only about the situation in Quebec but about social and political conditions across the entire nation.

# 49.   *The Decline of Trudeaumania*

**Scientific and technical advance**

THE 1960's AND 1970's were times of exciting scientific and technical advance. Three-stage rockets took man into outer space and eventually to the surface of the moon. Computer systems were put to work in science, industry, transportation and government service. Jet passenger planes crossed from hemisphere to hemisphere in a matter of hours. Communication satellites, circling the planet, bounced television programs between Europe and America. Drilling rigs, like steel islands, brought crude oil up from the ocean's floor. The medical profession solved more secrets of the human body and created the miracle of heart transplantation.

**World problems**

It was also a world of sober problems. There were tense political situations and conflicts in countries in Africa, the Near-East, Asia, and along the borders of India, Pakistan and China. The long, tragic conflict in Vietnam devastated the small Southeast Asian country and created bitterness and tension in the United States, the country which fought on the side of South Vietnam.

The prosperity and industrial growth around the world increased competition among nations for markets for their resources, and manufactured goods. Populations were increasing so rapidly in certain regions of the world that some nations faced the problems of not having enough food, medical care or jobs.

**Conditions in Canada**

In Canada, the vigorous growth of the 1940's and 1950's continued but at a slower pace. The children of the postwar "baby boom" began looking for work and many found that there weren't enough jobs.

In 1900, when automobiles were cranky curiosities and the airplane had yet to fly beyond the drawing board, the main means of travel in Canada was by railroad. By 1945, however, air and road travel had caught up with "the iron horse" and as thousands of travellers switched over to buses, cars, and planes, railways were forced to cut their service or even close some lines completely. In the 1960's attempts were made to develop fast inter-city railroad services between some major population centres such as Toronto and Montreal, and, encouraged by the results, a completely new type of train was developed. The CN Turbotrain is as revolutionary in its mechanics as in its appearance. Powered by lightweight gas turbine engines such as those used in aircraft, the train travels easily at ninety-five miles per hour, making the Toronto to Montreal run in just over four hours. Due to a unique suspension system in which the cars are supported from above, the Turbo can take curves thirty per cent faster than ordinary trains. Airplane-like interiors provide passengers with air conditioning, reclining seating, indirect lighting, individual fold-down tables and, most interesting of all, an observation lounge directly behind the engines.

Many young Americans, opposed to serving in the war in Vietnam, were crossing the border into Canada. There was growing concern about the use of drugs, and increasing crime in Canadian cities.

THE DOMINION OF CANADA 1970

DAVIS STRAIT

FFIN ISLAND

UNGAVA
PENINSULA

NEWFOUNDLAND

Hudson Bay

Schefferville •

QUEBEC

Sept-Iles •

St. John's

P.E.I.

Sydney

NEW
BRUNSWICK

Charlottetown

NTARIO

Quebec City •

Fredericton •

Saint John

Halifax •

NOVA SCOTIA

Trois Rivières

Montreal

L. Superior

Sault St. Marie

Ottawa

ATLANTIC OCEAN

L. Huron

Toronto

L. Michigan

Hamilton

L. Ontario

London •

L. Erie

When the Liberal government of Pierre Trudeau took over power in 1968, the Canadian scene held a number of strange contradictions. Some citizens enjoyed high incomes, while others were looking for work. The standard of living had never been as high, yet some Canadians were living below the poverty level. National production was rising but much of it was controlled by foreign companies, chiefly American. As salaries went up so did the prices of food, clothing, farms and homes.

In an effort to ease conditions for the people who were out of work, the government revised the Unemployment Insurance Act, increasing benefits and admitting large numbers of persons to the plan who were previously ineligible. These changes brought an enormous increase in the cost of unemployment insurance, as thousands of people were added to the rolls. While many of these persons were genuinely in need of financial help, others deliberately abused their rights, and chose to draw weekly payments rather than work.

While the Conservative leader, Robert Stanfield, did not oppose proper unemployment payments, he protested loudly that the government was hiding the high cost of its new program and was allowing unscrupulous persons to take advantage of the Canadian people. As time went by, many Canadians were inclined to agree with him.

There were other sources of dissatisfaction. The Liberals put into effect laws which made it easier for people accused of various offences to get bail. Some prisoners were allowed weekend passes. Parole was granted much more freely than in previous years. The purpose of these measures was to protect innocent citizens and offer humane treatment to those convicted of crime. But some prisoners on leave disappeared, and some released on bail or parole returned to violence and robbery. Canadians questioned the wisdom of "coddling" dangerous thugs and criminals. There was some demand for the return of hanging as a penalty for murder and other serious crimes.

**American influence**

Many Canadians were concerned with the ever increasing influence of the United States on Canadian life. In addition to the impact of American culture through television, movies, radio and printed matter, there was the concrete factor of industrial ownership by American corporations and the use of American funds to promote new enterprises. Some Canadians felt that American participation was necessary to maintain a reasonable level of prosperity in Canada. Others feared that Canada was becoming no more than an "economic satellite" of its giant neighbour. This later group took up the cry of "let's buy Canada back."

Not the least of Canadian worries during the 1960's and early 70's **Rising prices** was the spiral of prices on everything from baby shoes to beef. Housewives wheeling shopping carts through supermarkets sighed in dismay as prices rose. Various groups and organizations were blamed for the shocking increase in prices. Industry blamed the unions and workers, and these in turn blamed high company profits. Primary goods producers blamed the "middlemen" and these blamed the retailers.

Food prices, of course, were only one part of the difficulty. The costs of other necessities were equally high. A suit priced at $75.00 in 1950 might easily sell for $175 in the early 1970's. And, in many areas of Canada, a house advertised at $19,000 in 1950 could bring $42,000 in the 1970's.

In the 1960's Canadians became conscious of the problem of pollu- **Pollution** tion. They reached the disturbing conclusion that their natural environment was threatened. The air of large cities was heavy with the smoke of factories and the exhaust fumes of jet planes, automobiles and trucks. Once clear lakes and streams were no longer safe for fishing and swimming. Oil spills from damaged tankers had on several occasions ruined miles of shoreline and killed hundreds of fish and birds.

The wide use of insecticides and pesticides; unregulated hunting **Wildlife** and fishing; and increased human activity in the once almost empty North were threatening the survival of much of the wildlife. The survival of the polar bear and the whale became matters of concern. Fishermen protested the heavy catches of fish taken off the Atlantic and Pacific coasts by fishing vessels from foreign countries. There was public outcry at home and abroad over the cruelty of Canadian trapping methods and the slaughter of baby seals on the springtime ice.

As Canadian interest in keeping a healthy, attractive environment grew, the government began to enforce and tighten up laws to protect our natural heritage. Penalties were imposed on individuals, groups and companies who deliberately polluted the environment. Local groups organized clean-up campaigns with the enthusiastic support of young Canadians.

**Plight of Native Peoples**

During the 1960's and on into the 1970's Canadians began to recognize the plight of the Native Peoples. In the far north Eskimos have largely shifted from a nomadic, hunting existence to life in villages where they shop in stores and send their children to modern schools. Dog teams have been replaced by roaring snowmobiles; caribou tents and igloos by wooden houses. Although this new way of life does provide the Eskimo with more comforts and healthier conditions, he must change his style of living, giving up customs and habits which had been part of his heritage for generations. This is not an easy adjustment to make. Also, the Eskimos are now more dependent upon government for work and income. As yet there is not sufficient industry in the North to employ large numbers.

Indian people are scattered across Canada, many of them living on reservations, where many suffer the indignities of inferior education, poor housing and inadequate health care. Outside the reservation, the Indian people are often the victims of discrimination. There is growing shame on the part of Canadians at the treatment of our "First People."

New leaders have risen among the Indian people in recent years, and demands for a better place in Canadian life are increasing. There have been protests regarding the breaking of old treaties, the lack of educational opportunities, the invasion of hunting grounds and discrimination in employment. At present the proposed creation of a huge hydro-electric project near James Bay in northern Quebec is of deep concern to Indians, because it could flood large areas, destroy wildlife and disturb the way of life of people living in the region.

**Recognition of Mainland China**

In late 1970 Canada gave diplomatic recognition to Mainland China. Since the time that the Chinese Communists took over that country in 1949 Britain, France, the United States, Canada and numerous other powers had refused to recognize the eastern giant. Instead, the regime of Chiang Kai-shek on the small island of Taiwan was accepted as the true Chinese government. By the late 1960's many Canadians felt that ignoring the mainland of China was an unrealistic policy. After several years of discussion between Canadian and Chinese

From the earliest days of our history, and even to the present time, the sheer size of the Canadian land mass has made communications one of the more serious obstacles to full national development.   Communities in the far north have been particularly isolated due to lack of road or rail links with other parts of the country and the often unreliable nature of short-wave radio communications.   In 1972, a communications satellite, Anik I, was launched, and with it a whole new approach to Northern communications began.   The world's first fully operational geostationary domestic satellite, Anik (meaning "brother" in the Inuit language) speeds around the earth 22,300 miles up, at exactly the same speed as the earth rotates on its axis, thus in effect always remaining at the same spot in the sky.   Signals from earth stations are transmitted to the satellite and reflected back to ground stations thousands of miles away, thereby bringing to these distant communities television and radio programmes as well as telephone communications.   Pictured here is a remote television station at Fort Nelson, B.C.   A nearby CBC transmitter picks up signals from this station and converts them into a form which can be received on television sets.   A second satellite Anik II was launched in April, 1973, as a back up to Anik I.

officials, the two countries agreed to establish embassies in each other's capitals and carry on normal diplomatic relations. This new agreement caused some dismay in the United States but soon afterward President

Richard Nixon himself was to visit China and begin to reestablish ties
with this vast land.

Robert Stanfield was, during these years, winning new friends across
Canada. Although he lacked the sparkle and fluency of the Prime
Minister, he had a straightforward quality, a keen sense of humour
and the ability to laugh at himself. He was, as Charles Lynch said,
"as comfortable as an old shoe." Stanfield did not project well on
television, but in small groups and on speaking platforms he was impressive. As a result, increasing numbers of Canadians turned up to
hear his public addresses.

Both inside and outside Parliament he kept hammering away at
Liberal policies, hitting particularly hard at economic issues. He protested the high unemployment rate of about six per cent of the
labour force and he lashed out at the wastefulness of rising costs in
unemployment insurance.

Stanfield's own remedy for the current ills included the following
proposals: reduction in personal and company income taxes; reduction
in the tax on building materials; reform of the entire tax system; and
fixing the dollar at a level permitting Canadian exports to compete
with those of other nations. He made it clear that a Canadian dollar
high in value-comparison with the currencies of other nations would
discourage foreign nations from buying our goods.

On September 1, 1972, Prime Minister Trudeau dissolved Parliament
and called a general election for October 30. All parties threw themselves into the flurry of electioneering.

Pierre Trudeau campaigned confidently on his own government's
past record and pointed out to the voters the advantages to be gained
by re-electing a party of integrity and action. His campaign slogan,
"The Land is Strong" expressed his feeling that most Canadians were
satisfied and optimistic about Canada.

Conservative leader, Robert Stanfield, on the other hand, concentrated on practical issues. "A Job for Canadians," was his slogan.

New Democratic leader, David Lewis, also stressed "bread and butter" affairs, sensing that Canadians were very concerned about the
high cost of living, about rising taxes, expensive housing, inadequate
old age pensions and high unemployment. He gained considerable
attention in the press, radio and television with charges that the gov-

In fashion, the period from the mid-sixties to the present day has been one of dizzying change.  By 1965 women's spike-heeled shoes and puffed up (bouffant) sprayed hair styles, and mens' clean-cut, college-boy clothes were on the wane. In their place came a new influence — from Carnaby Street in London, where long-haired girls in mini-skirts, and long-haired boys in lace and velvet Edwardian styles were the fashion world's pace-setters.  Pants now became part of every woman's wardrobe and could be found everywhere from the office to the opera.  Women's clothes became more masculine: tailored jackets, ties and boots, until at the peak of the "unisex" trend, it was difficult at times to tell men from women.  The early seventies saw an attempt to restore feminity in women's clothes with such things as the midi- and maxi-skirts.   These too have disappeared and the latest influence is a "thirties" revival — fluttery dresses, bare backs, and high heel platform sole shoes for women, and for men, sleeveless V-neck pullovers and baggy pants.   The woman in the picture is wearing a pant suit with vest, wide pants and platform shoes; the man a seersucker jacket with deep lapels and baggy pants.  His hair is collar length, in keeping with 1973 styles.

ernment was granting unnecessary help to large, prosperous companies. He named a number of corporations, which, he said, had become "corporate welfare bums."

The results of the voting were surprising to most Canadians. The Liberals had suffered severe losses while the Conservatives achieved major gains.

**Results of election**

The party standing, after several local recounts, stood as follows: Liberal 109, Conservative 107, New Democratic Party 30, Social Credit Party 15, Independents 2.

Because the Liberal losses were chiefly in Ontario and in western Canada some Canadians, notably in Quebec, believed that the election revealed an anti-French feeling across the nation. There seems to be little proof that this was so. Claude Ryan, distinguished editor of *Le Devoir*, Montreal, probably was close to the truth when he wrote:

> "They voted not against the man, not against Quebec, not against French power which Mr. Trudeau embodied with some of his colleagues, but rather against his general policies as applied to all Canada."

Pierre Trudeau was once again Prime Minister but this time he headed a minority government which might at any moment be toppled in the House of Commons. In the beginning, there was a widespread and uncomfortable feeling that another general election would be called shortly. Conditions, however, improved somewhat for the Prime Minister when the New Democratic Party agreed to support the government in Parliament so long as Liberal policies were what they considered reasonable. David Lewis was pleased to see that many NDP ideas, particularly in the areas of social welfare, were incorporated into the Liberals' program, as described in the Speech from the Throne in January, 1973.

Trudeau, realizing he had misjudged the mood of the Canadian people, changed certain features of his government's program. He made an effort to tighten regulations for Unemployment Insurance, which resulted in removing thousands of persons from the government's rolls. The Conservative leader, Robert Stanfield, understanding the sensitive political situation, refrained from causing the government to fall on at least two occasions, because he felt such action was not in the interests of Canada.

In the spring of 1973, Prime Minister Trudeau remained balanced on the tight-wire of national government, as his government tried to deal with the issues which troubled Canada in the 70's.

# 50.  *Canada Looks to the Future*

ON THE EVENING of January 14, 1952, Winston Churchill made an important speech at a dinner in Ottawa given by Prime Minister Louis St. Laurent. In closing his address Churchill made the following comments:

"When I first came here after the Boer War, these mighty lands had but 5,000,000 inhabitants. Now there are 14,000,000. When my grandchildren come here, there may be 30,000,000. Upon the surface of the globe there is no more spacious domain open to the activities and the genius of free men, with one hand clasped in enduring friendship with the United States and the other spread across the ocean to Great Britain and France. You have a sacred mission to discharge. That you will be worthy of it, I do not doubt."[1]

Churchill's words should remind us that as Canadians we have much to be thankful for.

Canadians have a stable, reliable system of government based on democratic practices refined over centuries of history. It is true that citizens at times may not be completely satisfied with the achievements of Parliament, but if so they have the right to change political conditions by means of the vote.

**Stable democracy**

Canadians enjoy the advantage of living in a vigorous, prosperous nation — a middle power on friendly terms with others around the globe. Canada is neither feared as an aggressive force nor suspected as a disruptive one. She has gained high respect through loyalty to friends, assistance to weaker nations, peace-keeping operations and membership in world organizations. As a result, Canadians travelling abroad will find themselves greeted with friendliness.

**Respected middle power**

[1]George Tait, *Famous Canadian Stories*, Toronto: McClelland & Stewart, 1953. Reprinted by permission of The Canadian Publishers, McClelland & Stewart Limited, Toronto.

**Social and cultural legislation**

Canada is a nation increasingly devoted to social justice for all citizens. Much legislation in recent years has concentrated on removing the hardships caused by poverty and unemployment; improving the condition of elderly people; providing a complete system of education; protecting the rights of individuals and minority groups. The government also takes an active role in encouraging the development of creative efforts and in promoting the growth of cultural activities.

**Open spaces**

Although Canada has its large, industrial cities, it is still a land of open spaces, patched by forests, plains, tundras and mountains; dotted with lakes and rivers. It is still possible to take long canoe trips, to fish in lonely lakes, to ski on mountain slopes, to see mountain goats and grizzly bears. These pleasures are unknown to many persons who live in over-populated and heavily industrialized nations.

**Natural resources**

Canada's vast territory is rich in natural resources. It used to be the proud boast of politicians and others that our resources were "inexhaustible." This is no longer true, as world consumption of raw materials has grown at a tremendous rate. Nevertheless, Canada does have a substantial supply of minerals, oil, wood, fish and water. Recent discoveries of oil sources at the mouth of the Mackenzie River and off the shores of the Maritimes have further increased potential reserves. These are welcome discoveries because the need for crude oil and its by-products will become even more urgent in the future. The total value of Canadian mineral production in 1970 reached the astonishing total of more than $5,000,000,000.

An abundant supply of natural resources provides a great economic advantage, since Canada gains income from export and also uses these raw materials for its own industry. Such industrialized nations as Britain and Japan are handicapped as they must import vast quantities of raw materials to run their mills and factories.

**Land of Opportunity**

For many years Canada has been referred to as "The Land of Opportunity." While the term has become a cliché, the idea to a large degree is still valid. Canada can offer great opportunities to those who are able to take advantage of them. Opportunities for education, travel, recreation, cultural activities and a large variety of occupations are available. Thousands of immigrants have come to Canada to build a better life, and the great majority have achieved their goal.

In the 1960's and 70's attention has focused on the northern reaches of Canada as a source of new wealth and energy. Vast sums of money have been spent charting, mapping and testing, in an attempt to tap the extensive reserves of oil which are believed to exist in these sparsely settled regions far beyond the great population centres. Modern equipment such as the helicopter makes it possible to explore and map with a speed and accuracy that would have astounded the surveyors of a few generations ago. The surveying device being used here is a tellurometer, a type of radar-operated distance finder of high accuracy. This instrument has taken the place of a ground measuring party and has made it possible to map and measure in areas and over terrain which would be inaccessible by foot.

In spite of this promise, we should not become self-satisfied and smug about our prospects. Important as our resources, discoveries and developments may be, they alone do not guarantee us a prosperous future and a respected place among the nations. The future of Canada does not lie so much in our forests, mines, factories, farms and fisheries as it does in the hands and minds of our people. As a nation we could become careless with the use of our resources, and waste them foolishly. We could become complacent, satisfied to rest on the achievements of the past. As a nation we could quarrel among ourselves over matters of race, religion and regional interest, sacrificing the unity of the country.

Prime Minister Pierre Trudeau undoubtedly was thinking of these dangers when, in an election speech, in 1968, he said:

There's beauty in this country, there's the tradition of history, of culture. But the future belongs to no one. What we get out of the country depends on what we put into it, on what we decide to share together.

## SUMMARY — SECTION 11

After World War II Canada entered a period of extraordinary prosperity and expansion. A rising birth rate plus increased immigration resulted in the population rising to more than 20,000,000. The arrival of new immigrants from abroad brought fresh variety and vitality into Canadian life.

By 1956 nearly one-half of all people in the nation were living in cities with populations of more than 40,000. Villages grew into towns, towns became cities and cities extended outwards into sprawling suburbs.

The pressing demands of the war led to expansion in agriculture, trade, manufacturing, business and mining. After the war new discoveries of oil, natural gas, iron and uranium contributed to economic prosperity. Transportation facilities increased — new railways were built, pipelines to carry ore and gas were laid and the St. Lawrence Seaway, a joint Canadian-American project, was opened.

Mackenzie King resigned in 1948 and was succeeded by Louis St. Laurent, Canada's second French-Canadian Prime Minister. During his term of office Canadian affairs remained relatively calm and prosperous.

The political situation changed suddenly in 1957 when the Conservative party won the general election and John Diefenbaker became the first Conservative Prime Minister in twenty-two years. His position in Parliament, however, was weak and he called another election the following year in which the Conservatives won more seats than any other party since the time of Confederation.

Diefenbaker's early promise, however, was not fulfilled. The Canadian people believed that the Conservative Prime Minister had not taken over strong control of government. In addition, postwar prosperity was beginning to fade.

In 1963 the Liberals were returned to power and Lester Pearson was Prime Minister. A new Canadian flag was chosen and the three armed services — navy, army and air force — were combined into a single, unified service. The French-English problem still simmered and a Royal Commission on Bilingualism and Biculturalism was created to investigate and make recommendations. One of the most exciting events of the period was Canada's celebration of her first one hundred years as a nation. Centennial celebrations included Expo 67 at Montreal, a colourful event that attracted 50,000,000 visitors from home and abroad.

A disturbing feature of Centennial Year was General Charles de Gaulle's visit to Expo 67. While in Montreal the French statesman concluded an address by shouting "Long live free Quebec!" This arrogant gesture on the part of a foreign visitor caused deep anger throughout the country.

Lester Pearson resigned in the spring of 1968 and was succeeded by Pierre Trudeau, a fluently bilingual Montrealer who had been Pearson's Minister of Justice.

In the general election of the following year Trudeau was opposed by Robert Stanfield, a Nova Scotian who had recently become leader of the Conservative party. In the election campaign Trudeau's personality overshadowed all the issues put forth by both parties. A remarkable condition "Trudeaumania" swept across the country. The younger generation was attracted by Trudeau's youthful life style; intelligent people by his ideas; idealists by his "Just Society" and many Canadians by the attractive, flamboyant image he presented.

Pierre Trudeau and the Liberal party won the election of 1968. It was a difficult period during which there were tensions in Quebec and a rising rate of unemployment.

As Prime Minister, Trudeau introduced bills to change laws dealing with homosexuality, abortion, breathalizer tests, gun control, the parole system, penitentiaries, prisons and reformatories. Alterations were made in the Unemployment Insurance Act allowing many more persons to receive weekly unemployment cheques.

Violent incidents in Quebec came to a climax in the autumn of 1970 when a British diplomat, James Cross, and a Quebec cabinet minister, Pierre Laporte, were kidnapped by members of the radical Front de libération du Québec (FLQ). In order to prevent additional violence, troops were rushed into the cities of Quebec and Montreal and the stern **War Measures Act** was passed by Parliament.

A shudder of horror ran across Canada on October 18 when it was announced that Pierre Laporte had been murdered by the FLQ.

There was still uncertainty about the safety of James Cross but six weeks later the Montreal apartment in which he was being held was discovered by the R.C.M.P. Desperate negotiations followed and it was agreed that the kidnappers would be allowed to fly to Cuba and that James Cross would be freed. Although the crisis in Quebec was over, its effects lingered long after the violence had passed.

Trudeau continued to face a number of serious economic and political problems. Prices of consumer goods continued to rise. The cost of unemployment payments went up as well. Indians and Eskimos demanded a more secure place in Canadian life. American influence on Canada was causing alarm. And there was increasing anxiety about environmental pollution and the threat to our wild life.

In the meantime, the Conservative leader, Robert Stanfield, was winning new friends across Canada. Both inside and outside Parliament he kept hammering away at Liberal policies, hitting hard at economic features. He protested the high employment rate and lashed out at hardships caused by rising prices. As a result an increasing number of Canadians turned out to hear his public addresses.

The election of 1972 resulted in almost an equal number of seats for the Liberal and Conservative parties. Prime Minister Trudeau once again took up the reins of office but this time he was in charge of a minority government that could be toppled at any moment in the House of Commons. His position improved when the New Democratic party agreed to support the government as long as liberal legislation was acceptable.

The Prime Minister, realizing he had misjudged the desires of the Canadian people, attempted to alter certain features of his own program. After the election, for example, efforts were made to tighten requirements for collecting unemployment insurance and thousands of persons were removed from the rolls.

In the spring of 1973, the Liberal government still clung to its position of rule in Parliament.

On May 22, 1979 Joe Clark, a Conservative, became Canada's prime minister.

| Cons. | Lib. | N.D.P | O.P. |
|-------|------|-------|------|
| 136.  | 114. | 26    | 6    |

By Sue Puruse

June 6 /

April 17, 1982, Constitution comes home.

Carol Maynard had this book so
consider yourself lucky however get it.

1983

# BRIEF BIOGRAPHIES

| | |
|---|---|
| JOHN STRACHAN | CHARLES TUPPER |
| EGERTON RYERSON | WILLIAM VAN HORNE |
| JOSEPH HOWE | WILFRID LAURIER |
| LOUIS PAPINEAU | PAULINE JOHNSON |
| ROBERT BALDWIN | ALEXANDER GRAHAM BELL |
| LOUIS LAFONTAINE | SIR ROBERT BORDEN |
| JOHN A. MACDONALD | SIR FREDERICK BANTING |
| GEORGES ÉTIENNE CARTIER | STEPHEN LEACOCK |
| GEORGE BROWN | EMILY CARR |
| LEONARD TILLEY | LOUIS ST LAURENT |

Many of the biographical sketches that follow are of persons whose careers and achievements have already been discussed in the text of ONE DOMINION. However, it is hoped that the sketches will interest and intrigue the reader by offering a more warmly human view of these persons.

Although it may sometimes seem that history is a long procession of battles, treaties, events and dates, it should never be forgotten that one of the most important features of history is the human element. History is essentially the story of people, a record of their joys and sorrows, successes and failures, hopes and fears.

THE 666 OZZY For President
CRUE WE Sold Our Souls For
SABBATH Rock And ROLL
civilized Derek Paré 1984, 85
evil Paul Brian Beneteau
Rousseau Ken Meloche

JOHN STRACHAN
*Educator and Bishop, 1778-1867*

EGERTON RYERSON
*Clergyman and Educator, 1803-1882*

Among that select group in Upper Canada known as the Family Compact, the recognized leader was a sturdy Scot, John Strachan. Strachan's huge receding brow, and deeply chiselled features gave notice that he was a man with a powerful will and a high intelligence, a sort of "spiritual drill sergeant."

Although he could be most gracious at times, Strachan was a forbidding person with a severe manner, the rough accent of his stone-mason father and a peculiar habit of whistling huskily to himself on almost any occasion.

Soon after arriving in Upper Canada in 1799, Strachan became deeply involved in the educational activities of the province. From his "academy" came many of the leaders of provincial life. He was also the guiding genius in the founding of King's College (later the University of Toronto) and Trinity College.

As a political leader, it was Strachan's ambition to create another England in the wilderness of Upper Canada, with the Church of England as its heart and soul. On many an evening, the Family Compact met in his well-appointed library to plan their strategy and tactics.

After the Rebellion of 1837, perhaps realizing that Upper Canada never would—or could—be like England, Strachan withdrew from politics.

At the age of 23, Egerton Ryerson sprang into the limelight of Upper Canada life with his stinging condemnation of Archdeacon Strachan and, more particularly, of the Church of England. Little did people realize that the plump, boyish-looking Methodist circuit rider was to devote his long life to attacking this citadel of privilege in his native province.

Ryerson was a strong, young man with tremendous determination and energy. His zeal for the Christian faith, coupled with a rich, deep voice and an amazing talent for public speaking, gained him early renown as "the boy preacher." One of his first charges was a small log church on the Mississauga flats, west of York. It is a measure of the young man's ability that he was only there one week before he had raised enough money to build a new church. However, it is to Ryerson the educator that Canada owes so much, for he was the founder of Ontario's educational system, which, in turn, has been the pattern used in several other provinces. He is also remembered as the founder of Upper Canada Academy (at Cobourg), which later became Victoria University, Toronto.

Following his death, the entire city of Toronto seemed in mourning, and his funeral was attended by school children as well as by many important leaders of Church and State.

### JOSEPH HOWE
*Writer and Reformer, 1804-1873*

### LOUIS PAPINEAU
*Rebel Reformer, 1786-1870*

There has perhaps never been as fiercely loyal a son of Nova Scotia as Joseph Howe. This sturdy, athletic man with fair hair and blunt, pugnacious features won the hearts of Nova Scotians with the warmth of his personality and his zeal for their welfare. Wherever he appeared on his numerous summer tours throughout the province, his grey suit and tall beaver hat were familiar to everyone. Throughout his career as a newspaperman and politician, he worked tirelessly to improve the lives of his fellow Nova Scotians. Government, education, agriculture, railways, mail services, fisheries and many other matters were of concern to Howe. His views of government were based on British institutions and traditions. "All we ask for," he said, "is what exists at home [Great Britain]."

Howe's most outstanding characteristic was his mastery of the English language (except when he tried to write poetry). With his silver-tongued oratory, no less than with his pen, he could persuade the most sceptical and reluctant of persons.

When he died, Nova Scotians were deeply shocked and saddened by their loss. The Halifax *Morning Chronicle* commented: *From 1827 until the day of his untimely death, 'Joe Howe' has been the head and front of all great political changes in Nova Scotia.*

The life of Louis Joseph Papineau was a tragedy. He was a man who possessed rare qualities and yet, by failing to control his arrogance and quick temper, he set the seal of defeat on his career.

From the time of his youth, Papineau was recognized as a warm, friendly man with a grace and charm that were particularly attractive to women. However, he was also able to attract and inspire men. The lines of his face were an outward expression of the energy and determination that marked his life, and his eyes, perhaps even more indicative of his personality, seemed to offer defiance to all comers.

Papineau's greatest gift—and the one he abused most often—was his ability to sway audiences. It has been said of him: "He had a fine presence and eloquence so marked that 'to speak like a Papineau' is still in Quebec high praise for an orator." His fiery, passionate speeches captivated his listeners; however, his eloquence often betrayed him into making rash and irresponsible statements. Although an admirer of British institutions, Papineau spoke more and more harshly of British rule in Lower Canada—yet he never proposed effective remedies for the abuses he so roundly condemned. Papineau proved himself incapable of giving leadership to the reform movement in Lower Canada.

**ROBERT BALDWIN**
*Moderate Reformer, 1804-1858*

**LOUIS LAFONTAINE**
*Canadien and Canadian, 1807-1864*

Robert Baldwin has never been an appealing figure. He was a shy, reserved man with "a solemn, slightly self-righteous air." Physically, he was tall, but a slight stoop and a tendency to overweight gave him the appearance of a shorter man. His face seldom reflected any signs of feeling or emotion.

In many ways, Baldwin was completely unsuited to political life. Although a man of great integrity, he was not a natural orator; he did not possess a magnetic personality; he had little desire for personal fame or fortune.

Baldwin's reputation lies in his selfless devotion to the high ideals that governed his life. While he was a member of the Legislature, he was present at every sitting, as well as attending to the details of his many official duties. As a result, his health was seriously impaired, a condition that he refused to regard as important.

In spite of his shortcomings, Baldwin's contributions to the Province of Canada cannot be overlooked. As well as being a leader in the movement for responsible government, he was instrumental in revising the system of law courts and in laying the foundations of the modern system of municipal government in the Province of Ontario.

The career of Louis Hippolyte Lafontaine marks an important milestone in the political development of Canada, for he became the first French Canadian to hold important political office outside Canada East.

Born on the outskirts of Montreal, the young Lafontaine bore a remarkable facial resemblance to Napoleon Bonaparte. It seems that Lafontaine was proud of this and even went so far as to train a lock of hair to droop on his forehead in characteristic Napoleonic manner.

In his youth, Lafontaine was an ardent supporter of Papineau; however, he stubbornly opposed the call to arms by the *Patriotes* in 1837. With Papineau in exile, Lafontaine became l e a d e r of the French-Canadian Reformers.

Lafontaine had to pay a high price for his political beliefs. In 1841, rejected by the electors of his old constituency of Terrebonne in Canada East, he was ultimately forced to seek election to the Provincial Assembly in an exclusively English-speaking riding in Canada West; in 1849, after he and Baldwin had introduced "The Rebellion Losses Bill," Lafontaine's home in Montreal was attacked, and his library was burned by an angry English mob.

Lafontaine retired from political life in 1851 and later became Chief Justice of Canada East.

## JOHN A. MACDONALD
*Nation-Builder, 1815-1891*

## GEORGES ÉTIENNNE CARTIER
*Patriote and Patriot, 1814-1873*

In appearance, John Alexander Macdonald was, to say the least, homely— a tall, lanky, loose-limbed man with a large, bulbous red nose. To his opponents he was a buffoon, an impression that seemed to be confirmed by his gaudy clothes, jaunty manner and bawdy jokes. It is recorded that: "his pranks were the street-corner gossip and family joke of the nation." And yet, if anyone looked closer, it was impossible to miss a touch of sadness in his eyes or fail to see the prematurely lined face of the husband who spent many an evening at the bedside of an invalid wife; and those who were his closest friends knew that, to his dying day, he mourned the loss of his first son, dead at thirteen months of age.

As a politician, Macdonald had few equals. On the platform, he could control an audience as no other man of his day, while in the more informal setting of the political picnic he would amble amidst laden tables, greeting voters by their first names, recalling and inquiring after their wives and children.

Sir John A. Macdonald is one of the most important figures in North American history, for it was he, more than any other person, who bisected the continent and shaped a nation out of a few scattered British colonies.

From the time of the conquest of New France, one of the great political problems in British North America has been the discovery of an acceptable basis for co-operation between the French- and English-speaking inhabitants. It was to this problem that Georges Étienne Cartier devoted much of his career.

Cartier has been described as "a little man in a hurry." Even his bristly head of hair seemed incapable of repose. As a youth, Cartier was a follower of the rebel Papineau, composing poetry that was sung by the *Fils de la Liberté* as they paraded through the streets of Montreal. Later, disappointed by Papineau's irresponsible behaviour, Cartier became a follower of Lafontaine.

In his contribution to the Confederation movement, Cartier combined the virtues of Papineau and Lafontaine, but excelled them in vision and accomplishment.

Cartier believed that Confederation was the only alternative to annexation to the United States. When arguing in favour of Confederation, his theme, reiterated time and time again, was: "We French Canadians are British subjects like the others, but British subjects speaking French." His alliance with Macdonald marked the most important step then made toward active co-operation between the two races.

### GEORGE BROWN
*Publisher and Politician, 1818-1880*

### LEONARD TILLEY
*Father of Confederation, 1818-1896*

A notable figure on Toronto's King Street, where he was so often seen striding along, was George Brown, owner and editor of *The Globe*.

Impressively large (over six feet tall) with a ruddy complexion, red hair to match his fiery temper and bushy sideburns, Brown was very much a man of action. To every task he brought tireless mental energy and physical vigour. He once wrote his election campaign manager: "Put plenty of work on me; I can speak *six* or *eight* hours a day *easily*."

Despite his dislike of Macdonald, Brown was willing to bury his personal feelings in the interests of Confederation. He played a leading part at the Charlottetown and Quebec Conferences, in the long and bitter Confederation debates in the Province of Canada, and in the negotiations with the British government. He even went so far as to relax his u s u a l l y stiff, personal manner. For example, during the London Conference of 1865, he and Macdonald went together to the races at Derby for an afternoon of relaxation. There, no doubt egged on by the mischievous Macdonald, Brown joined in pelting the crowd surrounding their carriage with pea-shooters and little bags of flour.

Even after his retirement from active politics in 1865, Brown continued to exert considerable political influence through the columns of *The Globe*.

Samuel Leonard Tilley, born at Gagetown, New Brunswick, of Loyalist stock, was a short, dapper man with small, sharp features and bright eyes. He was a deeply religious person and it was his habit before delivering an important address to spend some time in prayer and meditation.

Tilley was an ardent supporter of Confederation and contributed greatly to the success of the Charlottetown and Quebec Conferences. After the defeat of his pro-Confederation ministry in New Brunswick in 1865, he made an exhausting provincial tour, during which he sought to rally support for the proposed union. In almost every county, his clear, ringing voice, dignified manner and obvious sincerity convinced many people of the logic and necessity of Confederation. It was a great achievement of statesmanship and one for which he is justly famous.

After Confederation, Tilley served in Macdonald's cabinet. It was his duty, as Minister of Finance, to pilot the National Policy programme through Parliament and put it into effect. He retired from federal politics in 1885 to serve as Lieutenant-Governor of his native province.

## CHARLES TUPPER
*Father of Confederation, 1821-1915*

## WILLIAM VAN HORNE
*Bon Vivant and Railway-Builder, 1843-1915*

Charles Hibbert Tupper is a fine example of the men, now known as the Fathers of Confederation, whose determination and effort created the Dominion of Canada. Tupper was small and dapper with a quick step and a clear, sharp voice. He impressed his fellow Nova Scotians as a man with no time to waste. The low, broad forehead, heavy brows, square jaw and clenched lips, all bespoke a will of rare intensity and driving force. One can admire Tupper for his character and achievements, but it is difficult to feel affection for this cold, blunt-spoken man.

Although he was very successful in the practice of medicine, it was not long before he entered politics and soon became premier of Nova Scotia. Undoubtedly, his greatest single achievement was in browbeating his province into Confederation in the face of great opposition from Joseph Howe and a large segment of the population.

Tupper served Canada for many years in various cabinet posts, in particular, as the first Minister of Railways and Canals (1879-1884). As Minister, Tupper organized the Department and introduced the bill giving the C.P.R. its charter in 1881.

The American-born William Cornelius Van Horne was a man of seemingly boundless energy and tremendous enthusiasm for living. Even on his death-bed, he was overheard to say: "When I think of all I could do, I should like to live five hundred years."

As a boy, Van Horne's interests varied from a delight in drawing moustaches on the magazine portraits of famous men to Sunday fossil-collecting excursions (a hobby which lasted his entire life, and one for which he gained renown). A plump little man with a large, hairy nose and a bull-like head, Van Horne was a true bon vivant, eating richly and heartily and drinking his liquor neat.

In 1881, Van Horne took charge of the construction of the C.P.R. After touring the Lake Superior shore, he remarked typically: "It's two hundred miles of engineering impossibility. But we'll bridge it." On the prairies, when the Blackfoot Indians tore up tracks, Van Horne quickly presented a lifetime C.P.R. pass to Crowfoot, their chief, with a reminder not to remove any more rails if he wanted to live to ride on them. Despite the incredible geographical and financial problems involved, he brought the project to completion.

**WILFRID LAURIER**
*Nation-Builder, 1841-1919*

**PAULINE JOHNSON**
*Poet, 1861-1913*

Among Canadian statesmen Wilfrid Laurier ranks with the greatest.

He was a tall, slight figure of a man, always elegantly dressed. A member of an old French-Canadian family, he had an old-fashioned courtesy and a warmth of manner that never failed to impress; and yet there was also a quality of dignified reserve. It took his colleagues and acquaintances a long time to realize that behind this façade were the will-power and shrewdness that made Laurier a great political leader.

Like Macdonald, Laurier was more interested in broad general questions than in details; like Sir John, he realized that it was of fundamental importance that French and English Canadians co-operate if Canadian nationhood were to survive. A lifelong admirer of English history and politics, he spent much of his political life persuading his fellow French Canadians to support moderate policies based on English liberal principles. He was, in fact, utterly devoted to Canada and her interests. In a speech to the House of Commons during the Riel affair in 1885, Laurier stated his political belief: *Canada has been the inspiration of my life. I have had before me, as a pillar of fire by night, and a pillar of cloud by day, a policy of true Canadianism, of moderation, of conciliation.*

As a young girl, Pauline Johnson was instilled with deep pride in her Indian heritage, a love of nature and an intense loyalty to her native land. Her father was the Chief of the Six Nations, her mother was an English-woman. The name "Johnson" had been given to Pauline's great grandfather when he became an Anglican. She chose to use her tribal name — Tekahionawake.

Tekahionawake began to write poetry based on Indian legends and traditions when she was very young. An invitation to take part in an evening of Canadian literature in Toronto was to change the course of her life. Tekahionawake read her poem "A Cry from an Indian Wife," which described the Indian side of the Northwest Rebellion. For fifteen years Tekahionawake toured Canada, reading her poems. Her travels took her to the United States and Britain, and her books of verse, *White Wampum* and *Canadian Born*, sold well. Finally, Tekahionawake settled in Vancouver, where she wrote one of her best known books, *Legends of Vancouver*.

A simple, eloquent memorial to this gifted Indian poet stands in the burial ground of His Majesty's Chapel of the Mohawks at Brantford, Ontario.

## ALEXANDER GRAHAM BELL
*Scientist and Inventor, 1847-1922*

## SIR ROBERT BORDEN
*Wartime Statesman, 1854-1937*

Alexander Graham Bell once remarked that he would rather be remembered as a teacher of the deaf than as the inventor of the telephone.

The Bell family immigrated from Scotland to Brantford, Ontario. Later, Bell moved to Boston, where he helped open a school for the deaf and taught at Boston University.

In the course of scientific experiments, Bell often worked on the process of telegraphy. While trying to perfect his multiple telegraph, he stumbled on the principle of telephony. At first, he and his assistant were only able to transmit voice sounds but not words. Then, on March 10, 1876, in a makeshift laboratory in a Boston rooming house, the first telephone call in history took place.

"Mr. Watson, come here, I want you!" Bell exclaimed, after accidentally pouring the acid of a battery over his clothes. These words travelled over the telephone to Bell's assistant in another part of the house.

Following the invention of the telephone, Bell continued to live a creative life. He established the Volta Laboratory for research, invention and work for the deaf, where he and his associates discovered a way of making phonograph records on wax discs.

Sir Robert Borden, a Nova Scotian, was a modest, hardworking Prime Minister whose enormous contribution to the development of Canadian autonomy is often overlooked.

While practising law in Halifax, he was persuaded to run for office. The reluctant candidate became leader of the Conservative party, and, in 1911, Prime Minister.

Borden was a devoted, courageous Prime Minister. Like Sir John A. Macdonald, he believed that one of Canada's most important and difficult objectives was to keep a separate existence in North America. To Borden, the British Empire was an association of states which could help promote world peace and security.

During the war Borden insisted that Canada be given a voice in shaping policy. At the Imperial War Conference under Lloyd George, Borden's concept of recognition of the Dominions as autonomous nations with an adequate voice in foreign policy was recognized. He participated actively in the Imperial War Cabinet in 1918. Borden headed the Canadian delegation to the Paris Peace Conference where public recognition of Canada's independent status was achieved. Canada signed the treaty separately from Britain and became a member of the League of Nations.

### SIR FREDERICK BANTING
*Medical Discoverer, 1891-1941*

### STEPHEN LEACOCK
*Political Economist and Humorist,
1869-1944*

For thousands of years there was no remedy for a human blood condition known as diabetes. In 1922 a young Canadian doctor discovered a treatment that has saved the lives of countless people around the world.

For eight weeks during the summer of 1921 Banting and an assistant, Charles Best, worked in a borrowed laboratory at the University of Toronto where they conducted a series of experiments involving dogs, which proved that fluid from a small gland located behind a dog's stomach was the magic factor required to control diabetes. Insulin was first tried on a young boy dying of diabetes. For the first time in history a diabetic's life was saved.

News of insulin spread across the world, making Banting famous. He was granted honorary degrees by great universities, and awarded the Nobel Prize which, with characteristic modesty, he shared with Dr. Best. Perhaps the most satisfying tribute, was the creation of the Banting and Best Department of Medical Research at the University of Toronto, and the Banting Foundation. The Banting Institute is another tribute to him. To the end of his life, Banting worked to understand the mysteries of the human body. He was killed in Newfoundland, in an air crash.

After returning from an imperial tour in 1908, Stephen Leacock explained the significance of his journey as follows: "When I state that these lectures were followed almost immediately by the Union of South Africa, the Banana Riots in Trinidad, and the Turco-Anglican War. I think you can form some idea of their importance."

This tall, angular, usually dishevelled professor, with a constant twinkle in his eye, a unique "campus character," brought international fame to Canada and helped Canadians laugh at themselves. By using ordinary incidents and ordinary language he could create hilarious situations. Leacock was first known as a pioneer political economist, and headed the Department of Economics and Political Science at McGill University. Yet it is as a humorist that Leacock is remembered and loved all over the world.

Leacock published his first book *Literary Lapses* himself, then took it to London where an English publisher brought it out. In one of Leacock's best known collections of humorous stories—*Sunshine Sketches of a Little Town*—he takes characters who are typical of a small town and treats us to the humour of everyday living.

### EMILY CARR
*Painter and Author, 1871-1945*

### LOUIS ST LAURENT
*Dignified Leader, 1882-1973*

Some of the most striking canvases ever painted in Canada were executed by a robust, dynamic woman from British Columbia who at various times studied art in San Francisco, London and Paris; operated a kennel for sheep dogs; created pottery; kept boarders in her home; taught art; lived among West Coast Indians; and wrote books. She had an undying love for nature and for animals both wild and tame.

After studying in Europe, Emily Carr adopted a bold, daring style of painting that focused on broad patterns rather than on small details.

After years of discouragement, the situation changed in 1927 when the National Gallery of Ottawa organized an important exhibition of paintings including fifty by Emily Carr.

Appreciation of her talent followed swiftly; in consequence, her paintings appeared in many exhibitions and sold readily to galleries and private collectors. Also encouraging was the admiration she received from members of the famous Group of Seven who at the time were making a vital impact on Canadian art.

Among the delightful books for which Emily Carr is remembered are: *The House of All Sorts, Klee Wyck,* for which she won the Governor-General's Award for non-fiction in 1941, *The House of Small,* and *Growing Pains.*

Louis St. Laurent entered politics reluctantly. He was a successful middle-aged Quebec lawyer, but when Prime Minister Mackenzie King called on him to serve as Minister of Justice in 1941, St. Laurent agreed, providing he would return to private life after the war was over. However this talented Canadian was to serve his country for sixteen years, as Minister of External Affairs and then as Prime Minister.

In many ways, St. Laurent was the most Canadian of all previous Prime Ministers. He had neither nostalgia for Europe nor a sense of isolation from the rest of Canada. Some have said that the fluently bilingual St. Laurent lived as a French Canadian with true joie de vivre, and thought as an Anglo-Saxon, approaching problems logically and solving them methodically.

St. Laurent won the deep affection of the country, and was known as "Uncle Louis." In him Canada found a dignified, lovable symbol, and he won the highest respect throughout the nation. As he said, "I am convinced that Montcalm and Wolfe were merely the instruments of an all-powerful Providence . . . sent to create a situation where the descendants of the two great races would find themselves together on the northern part of the American continent."

# INDEX OF ILLUSTRATIONS

Collective index entries have been made as follows:

# INDEX

Collective index entries have been made as follows:

Painted by ROBERT HARRIS, 1883